Origins and Challenges of Psychological Assessment in Ibero-American Countries

Silvia Viviana Pugliese
José Livia Segovia • Solange Muglia Wechsler
Editors

Origins and Challenges of Psychological Assessment in Ibero-American Countries

Springer

Editors
Silvia Viviana Pugliese
National University of Rosario
Rosario, Santa Fe, Argentina

José Livia Segovia
Federico Villarreal National University
Lima, Peru

Solange Muglia Wechsler
Pontificia Universidade Catolica de Campinas
Campinas, São Paulo, Brazil

ISBN 978-3-032-21379-2   ISBN 978-3-032-21380-8 (eBook)
https://doi.org/10.1007/978-3-032-21380-8

English translation of the 1st original Spanish edition published by Editorial Universitaria Universidad Ricardo Palma, Lima, 2025

The original submitted manuscript has been translated into English. The translation was done using artificial intelligence. A subsequent revision was performed by the author(s) to further refine the work and to ensure that the translation is appropriate concerning content and scientific correctness. It may, however, read stylistically different from a conventional translation.

This Springer imprint is published by the registered company Springer Nature Switzerland AG
The registered company address is: Gewerbestrasse 11, 6330 Cham, Switzerland

Foreword

Psychology is the science that seeks to understand the origins and functioning of human behavior. This understanding enables psychologists to make accurate predictions about how people will behave in specific situations. Psychological variables are complex and interactive in nature; on one hand, they are rooted in the neurobiological domain, and on the other, they are strongly influenced by the sociocultural context. The drive to simplify this complexity sometimes leads to two classic forms of reductionism: biological and social. Biological reductionism mistakenly assumes that human behavior is solely determined by our neurobiological system; however, the brain is not a gland that secretes human behavior, although, of course, it plays a fundamental role that must be considered in each case. Sociological determinism, in contrast, posits that behavior is determined by the sociocultural context and that, therefore, human conduct can be explained by contextual contingencies. This is the insidious idea underlying all attempts at social engineering.

The human condition is neither a mere product of neurobiological processes nor an automatic reflection of contextual parameters. Psychology recognizes the active role of each person, of each individual, with freedom of choice as the foundation of dignity and responsibility. The individual exists, and psychology is the science that seeks to understand them. This special nature of the psychological straddling—the biological and the cultural, yet not reducible to either—is precisely what makes the measurement and assessment of psychological variables so distinctive. Measuring psychological constructs follows the general laws of measurement found in other scientific fields, as it must, but it also has unique features that make it particularly interesting from an epistemological perspective. Measuring the distance between Lima and Madrid, a task for physicists, is not the same as measuring the distance between people from Lima and those from Madrid, which is the domain of psychologists.

This book addresses all these issues, tracing and analyzing how psychological assessment has emerged and developed in the various Ibero-American countries studied: Argentina, Bolivia, Brazil, Chile, Costa Rica, Ecuador, El Salvador, Spain, Guatemala, Mexico, Paraguay, Peru, Uruguay, and Venezuela. It is a unique and original work; never before has such a comprehensive and systematic treatment been undertaken. It will therefore serve as the cornerstone for future developments in psychological assessment in Ibero-America. As the authors of the various chapters masterfully demonstrate, assessment has arisen and evolved in a distinctive manner in each country, yet within this diversity a common factor is evident: the commitment to developing objective and equitable psychological assessment, grounded in empirical evidence. The phrase *what cannot be measured cannot be improved* is often attributed to Lord Kelvin, and this idea—the need to base our evaluative arguments on solid, empirical foundations—runs throughout the book. Rigorous assessment is an essential prerequisite for accurate diagnosis, which in turn leads to effective psychological intervention. If we fail at the first step, in assessment, the subsequent processes of diagnosis and intervention will be compromised.

In the assessment process, professionals rely on various types of data: some derived from their direct interaction with the individuals being assessed, others provided by people close to them, such as parents, friends, colleagues, or teachers, and, thirdly, data obtained through measurement instruments such as tests, questionnaires, or scales. Measurement instruments do not make decisions on their own; it is the professionals who, drawing on test results, their experience, and other data, make the decisions. When using data from tests, it is essential to ensure that the scores obtained meet appropriate psychometric standards. They must be reliable, free from error, and, in addition, sufficient evidence of validity must be provided to ensure that the test accurately measures the construct for which it was designed. Not only must tests demonstrate adequate psychometric properties, but professionals must also use them correctly, avoiding undesirable consequences and ensuring consequential validity.

Professional organizations, such as the Official Colleges of Psychologists (COP), have always been deeply concerned with the proper use of tests, establishing *Test Commissions* to promote their appropriate use. International organizations, such as the International Test Commission (ITC), the European Federation of Psychologists' Associations (EFPA), and the American Psychological Association (APA), among many others, have also developed programs in this regard. Every effort must be made to ensure that individuals are assessed objectively and fairly, as stipulated in the ethical codes of the psychology profession.

The activities undertaken by national and international organizations to improve test use are varied, but they can generally be grouped into two main strategies, known as the *restrictive* and *informative* approaches. The restrictive approach refers to all actions aimed at ensuring that only qualified individuals are permitted to use tests. This can be achieved through legal requirements, which are rare, or by introducing restrictions on the acquisition and use of tests. The informative strategy focuses on disseminating information about test quality and making it available to professionals, so they have all the necessary data when selecting and using an instrument. A good example of this is the expert evaluations of test quality conducted by some Test Commissions of the Official Colleges of Psychologists; see, for example, these evaluations for Spain on the COP website:

This very book can rightly be considered part of the activities within the informational strategy, as it provides professionals with information from each country regarding psychological assessment. It is a highly necessary and timely work, since, although we previously had data for some countries, this comprehensive perspective is extremely enriching and will undoubtedly be fundamental in continuing to promote high-quality assessment in Ibero-America. Sincere congratulations are due to the authors of the various chapters, to the editors who conceived and made this publication possible—Professors Silvia Viviana Pugliese, Solange Muglia Wechsler, and José Livia—and to the distinguished institutions that supported its publication: Universidad Federico Villareal, Colegio de Psicólogos del Perú, and the Interamerican Society of Psychology (SIP).

With great discernment, the book is aimed at a broad audience interested in psychological assessment, including students, professionals, faculty, and researchers. All of them will find up-to-date and highly relevant information on psychological assessment in the respective countries. Moreover, the book will foster collaboration and mutual understanding between academics and practitioners—a necessary symbiosis, as research and practice are two sides of the same coin; one cannot exist without the other.

We stand on the shoulders of giants; to continue building our psychological science, it is essential to understand the work of those who came before us, and in this regard, this book will be an invaluable resource. It will also enable us to comprehend and be prepared for the significant advances currently taking place in the field of psychological assessment, such as tele-assessment, computerized adaptive approaches, ecological momentary assessment, and new psychometric models, to name just a few.

Finally, I would like to reiterate my gratitude and congratulations to all those who made the publication of this book possible, as it will mark a turning point in the study of psychological assessment in Ibero-America.

Nebrija University
Madrid, Spain
Member of the Academy of Psychology of Spain
Madrid, Spain
Member of the European Academy
Salzburg, Austria

José Muñiz
jmuniz@nebrija.es

Preface

According to the Economic Commission for Latin America and the Caribbean (ECLAC, 2022), the region's population in 2022 reached just over 660 million people. The increasingly slower population growth is mainly due to declining fertility rates, with projections indicating that the region's population will reach approximately 751.9 million by 2056. Currently, Brazil (215,313) and Mexico (127,504) are the most populous countries, while Uruguay (3423) and Panama (4489) have the smallest populations. The region as a whole is considered to be experiencing a relatively rapid aging process, and it is projected that by 2047, the number of people aged 60 and over will surpass those under 15 years of age. Life expectancy has also increased due to improvements in population nutrition and urban infrastructure, the expansion of basic sanitation services and access to drinking water, as well as the importation of medical and health technologies, the adoption of modern healthcare methods, such as the use of antibiotics, and vaccination programs. The average life expectancy is now 72.2 years.

Within this context, psychology is currently developing in this part of the world, as Ardila (1969) states: "Psychology, like other sciences and professions, is intimately related to the cultural conditions of the environment in which it arises…" p.63. Historically, it is worth noting that the first legal recognition of the psychology profession occurred in Brazil in 1962. Psychology also emerged as a practical discipline that sought to collaborate with other fields, especially medicine and education, and as a branch of philosophy. Scientific psychology in Latin America is considered to have begun in 1891, when Víctor Mercante founded the first experimental psychology laboratory in San Juan, Argentina (Pantano, 1997). This process continued in Chile (1920), followed by Brazil (1923) with the arrival of Waclaw Radecki from Poland, and in 1934 with the arrival of Walter Blumenfeld from Germany to Peru. Regarding psychology associations, the first was the Argentine Society of Psychology (1908) (Alonso, 1999), followed by the Society for Psychological, Psychiatric, and Related Studies (1942), the Brazilian Association of Applied Psychology (1949), the Mexican Society of Psychology and the Uruguayan Society of Psychology in 1953, the Peruvian Society of Psychology (1954), the Colombian Federation of Psychology (1955), among other organizations (Ardila, 1969).

With respect to psychology degree programs, it is noted that the first was established in 1947 at the National University of Colombia, in 1948 at the University of Chile, in 1950 at the University of Santo Tomas de Villanueva (Cuba), in 1953 at the Pontifical Catholic University of Rio de Janeiro (Brazil), in Argentina at the National University of the Littoral—Rosario campus (1956), in Peru at the National University of San Marcos (1955), in 1956 at the Central University of Venezuela, and in 1958 at the National Autonomous University of Mexico (Klappenbach & Pavesi, 1994; Gallegos, 2005).

One of the most important institutions is the Interamerican Society of Psychology (SIP), founded in 1951 in Mexico. On this subject, Maluf (2012) notes: "…the SIP continues to fulfill its objectives, representing psychology as a science and as a profession in North America, Central America, South America, and the Caribbean. Thus, it is today the oldest and most active psychology society in Latin America, bringing together Spanish- and Portuguese-speaking psychologists." p. 215. The SIP organizes Interamerican Congresses, the first of which was held in 1953 in Santo Domingo; it also publishes the Interamerican Journal of Psychology.

Psychological assessment is a subdiscipline of psychology concerned with analyzing the personality of an individual or group of individuals, with the aim of diagnosis, guidance, selection, or recommending psychotherapy. This is achieved through a complex process that, using specific instruments, gathers information on which hypotheses are formulated and statements are deduced, which are then tested to reach diagnostic conclusions. At times, it has been considered equivalent to psychometrics, that is, the construction, training, and application of instruments. The teaching of psychological assessment and the scientific development of psychological instruments have varied across countries.

One of the critical issues identified by Alarcón (1997) concerns the lack of originality, particularly in the development of psychological tests. There is a greater tendency to adapt foreign tests rather than develop original instruments. Several tests have been developed in Latin America, including the Mira y López Myokinetic Test, the Lourenço Filho ABC Test, the Olmo Barranquilla Rapid Test, the Arrigo Angelini Vocational Interests Inventory, and the A-51 Test, which was constructed by Blumenfeld.

A review of the chronology of events in Argentina, where psychological methods and techniques played a leading role, is presented, providing insight into the history of psychological assessment in this country. An overview dating back to the late nineteenth century helps explain why some techniques achieved greater development and dissemination, while others failed at the outset of their adoption. Several autobiographical accounts from pioneers in Psychological Assessment and interviews are highlighted, as well as the role played by key institutions in the field, such as ADEIP (Argentine Association for the Study and Research in Psychodiagnosis) and AIDEP (Ibero-American Association for Psychological Diagnosis and Assessment). The current situation is discussed, noting how various psychology programs at Argentine universities emphasize psychological diagnosis, while recognizing that undergraduate training is insufficient for professional practice.

The chapter on Bolivia traces the late introduction of psychology programs in universities, due to political, economic, and geographic factors, and then analyzes how content related to Psychological Assessment is incorporated into the curriculum. The use of and attitudes toward psychometric and projective tests are analyzed based on data obtained from questionnaires and interviews with psychologists from different regions of the country. The difficulty in accessing test materials is highlighted as a factor affecting both teaching and practice, resulting in a low number of psychologists who administer projective and/or psychometric techniques. Consequently, one of the main challenges is to encourage the development of local tests, the adaptation and validation of instruments, and their publication in indexed journals. Academic centers place greater emphasis on undergraduate training and promote research and practice in psychological assessment.

The chapter on Brazil reviews its history of struggles and achievements in gaining recognition for the importance of Psychological Assessment. Each stage has marked a significant milestone, beginning in the nineteenth century with the importation and translation of tests produced in Europe and the United States. In the 1970s, the use of psychological tests was strongly questioned, and the ensuing debates led to the founding of what is now known as the Brazilian Institute of Psychological Assessment (IBAP), marking a turning point in policies for the growth of the field. Significant support was provided by the Federal Council of Psychology, with resolutions based on the standards of international organizations such as the *International Testing Commission* (ITC). This joint and sustained policy has resulted in a fourfold increase in approved tests in recent years and the establishment of multiple research laboratories at major universities, focusing on the development and/or adaptation of tests.

The origins of Psychological Assessment in Chile are closely linked to the development of Psychology and the national historical context, both of which negatively impacted the creation or adaptation of psychological techniques and regulatory controls. Nevertheless, it is noteworthy that since 1962, ongoing research on intelligence tests, such as the WISC, and projective tests, especially the Rorschach test, has also become widespread. At national conferences, research on methodology, measurement, and assessment has gained prominence, leading to the establishment of the Chilean Association of Methodology, Measurement, and Assessment [ACMME]. In light of the current situation, there is a recognized need to strengthen academic training, establish research teams for the development or adaptation of tests, and implement regulatory mechanisms to monitor the validity of techniques in use, in line with international guidelines, to ensure fair and ethical assessment.

A general overview of psychological assessment in Costa Rica is presented, particularly in clinical and forensic settings, beginning with the path toward the consolidation of Psychology in the country and the introduction of the first psychological tests. In recent years, the accelerated integration of psychologists into public institutions, where psychological assessment is a key practice that requires specific training, has been highlighted, as emphasized in the country's Code of Ethics and Professional Conduct. Not only is the importance of evidence for the validity and reliability of psychological tests underscored, but also the impact of the examiner, the conditions of administration, and those responsible for scoring. The development of high-impact tests as predictors of academic achievement is also noted, emphasizing the contribution of psychometrics to the development of instruments for this specific area. However, many of these are developed by other professionals.

In Ecuador, psychological assessment historically developed from the fields of psychiatry and education before becoming established within psychology, under a positivist framework. The first tests were used in the 1930s, primarily to assess intelligence in relation to academic performance. The establishment of the Institute of Psychology at the Central University of Ecuador in 1950 significantly contributed to the development of psychological assessment in various specializations, including educational psychology, vocational guidance, clinical psychology, and organizational psychology. A notable characteristic is that tests created in other countries are taught and used in psychological practice; there are very few instruments adapted and validated locally, and no tests have been developed in Ecuador that reflect the country's reality and cultural diversity.

Regarding El Salvador, the historical development of psychology is systematized, highlighting the cultural differences of Salvadoran reality, as well as the psychosocial issues related to civil war, natural disasters, violence, poverty, and social marginalization. The role of the Salvadoran university is highlighted in consolidating national and international research efforts aimed at standardizing tests and other professional technological resources for assessment, diagnosis, and psychological intervention across various areas of psychological practice. Notably, the first school of psychology was established in 1956, with implementation primarily in the social and clinical fields, adopting an integrated, interdisciplinary, and ethical approach in accordance with international standards. This has occurred while overcoming deeply rooted myths and misconceptions about psychology, particularly concerns regarding the lack of standardized tests and the need to consider the cultural differences reflected in the Salvadoran context.

In Spain, psychological assessment and psychometrics are regarded as disciplines with a strong professional and academic tradition, with their origins dating back to the creation of the National Institute of Psychotechnics in 1928 and the establishment of the School of Psychology and Psychotechnics in 1958. Since then, their evolution and progress have been continuous, with the beginning of university-level psychology degrees marked in 1968. In the field of psychological assessment, the differentiated areas have followed their own developmental paths, converging in the recognition of the importance of proper use of assessment instruments and their impact on professional practice. Psychological assessment is highly valued by psychologists and psychology students, with significant contributions from Spanish psychology to the European Association of Psychological Assessment and the European Journal of Psychological Assessment. Methodologically, Spain's contribution to the European Association of Methodology and the journal Methodology is also noteworthy. The scientific productivity of Spanish authors further supports these aspects.

In Guatemala, the development of psychological assessment is established in three areas: research, teaching, and professional practice. The earliest research focused on psychometrics, with the translation and adaptation of tests of general abilities, differential aptitudes, and reading to the Guatemalan context. The pioneers in teaching and training psychologists were at the University of San Carlos of Guatemala (USAC) through the Faculty of Humanities, later followed by the School of Psychological Sciences and the Universidad del Valle de Guatemala, with initial contributions observed in the field of education, which requires neuropsychological, psychoeducational, and neurological assessments. The incorporation of psychometric tests into professional practice was gradual due to several limitations in access to measurement instruments. With the introduction of reproduction rights and the sale of psychometric tests over the past five decades, a new phase of psychometrics and assessment began in the country, enabling the norming and adaptation of instruments with multicultural relevance.

In Mexico, psychological assessment is considered a central activity in the professional practice of psychologists, with its development closely linked to academia and the strengthening of psychology as a university discipline. Psychometrics is integrated into practice as an area that has contributed to this development. The historical development of psychological assessment is reflected in the curricula of undergraduate psychology programs. In the 1960s, psychology began a significant period of expansion and consolidation as an academic discipline. This growth included the founding of the Faculty of Psychology at the Universidad Veracruzana in the Xalapa region (1963) and, a decade later, the establishment of the Faculty of Psychology at UNAM as an independent entity from the Faculty of Philosophy in 1973. Additionally, the National Council for the Teaching and Research of Psychology (CNEIP) began operations in 1971. It is recommended that teaching should promote the creation of research projects that support the development or adaptation of assessment instruments and encourage the generation of norms and standardization processes for Mexico, given the diverse conditions of its context.

This chapter presents a review of the historical milestones, current status, and future challenges of psychological assessment in Paraguay within the discipline, science, and profession of Paraguayan psychology. The review covers the history of psychological assessment in academic training, professional practice, and current research, based on interviews with psychology faculty and professionals, as well as articles published in recent years. The results reflect more than 60 years of training: the current professional profile and the challenges to be addressed in a globalized context of national accreditation and certification processes. Key challenges include strengthening research on assessment and the development of psychological instruments for professional use, as well as undergraduate and postgraduate thesis research, and establishing research groups involved in these areas. The need for general regulation of the profession and accreditation of academic programs is also emphasized.

The origins and development of psychological assessment in Peru are presented, from the first intelligence assessments conducted in 1909 to current research on the construction, validation, and standardization of instruments in different regions of the country. The training efforts led by the College of Psychologists of Peru, as well as the educational and outreach work carried out by universities, are also emphasized. Various lines of psychometric research exist in the country, including developmental assessment, family, occupational health, addictions, and positive psychology. The limitations of psychological assessment in Peru are analyzed, as well as prospects for joint efforts between the College of Psychologists and universities to develop instruments that consider the sociocultural characteristics of the Peruvian population, catalog tests, and raise awareness of their use.

An overview and historical account of psychological assessment in Uruguay is provided, highlighting key historical milestones in its development. It is noted that this evaluative work, now characteristic of psychologists, was not so in its early stages. The first precedents date back to the 1930s, specifically to the Laboratory of Experimental Psychopedagogy within the framework of the National Council of Primary and Secondary Education. In the 1950s, the University of the Republic established the Course in Applied Psychology for Children, as part of the Medical Assistant Courses (Faculty of Medicine), and the Bachelor's Degree in Psychology at the Faculty of Humanities. The strong presence of psychoanalysis facilitated the introduction of projective techniques and the concept of psychodiagnosis. It is concluded that psychological assessment predates psychology as a discipline in Uruguay, contributing to its establishment and being closely linked to the development of professional identity and its conflicts with discrimination from other professions.

Psychological assessment began in Venezuela in 1936 with training courses that preceded the formal establishment of the academic discipline. The development of psychological assessment in Venezuela is divided into three periods: origin, expansion, and restriction/reinvention. An overview of its current situation is presented, based on data obtained from an online survey completed by undergraduate and graduate program directors, as well as practicing psychologists. The contributions of Venezuelan psychologists to the field are highlighted, as well as the legal, social, political, and ethical challenges impacting professionalism, emphasizing the resilience of psychologists in remaining active and productive in academia, organizations, and professional associations. It is proposed to broaden the perspective to incorporate new conceptualizations and technologies in assessment, to work more collaboratively and flexibly, and to share goals that enhance psychological assessment in each region of the country and throughout Latin America.

The selection of countries represented in this book is based solely on the presence of SIP members who are part of the Psychological Assessment Working Group and who conduct their professional and academic activities in their respective countries.

This book aims to help psychologists in Ibero-America become familiar with the history and evolution of Psychological Assessment, tracing its development from its origins to the present landscape and its future challenges.

For the authors, it is an honor that this book features a Foreword by the distinguished ITC member and Rector of Nebrija University (Madrid), Dr. José Muñiz.

As editors and on behalf of the Psychological Assessment Working Group, we thank Ricardo Palma University (Peru), the College of Psychologists of Peru, and the Interamerican Society of Psychology; without their support, this work would not have been possible.

Rosario, Argentina — Silvia Viviana Pugliese
Lima, Peru — José Livia Segovia
Campinas, Brazil — Solange Muglia Wechsler

References

Alarcón, R. (1999). Psychology in Latin America in the 20th century: an analysis of its characteristics, Revista de Psicología de la PUCP, 17(2).

Alonso, M. (1999). "Psychology in the Americas." Buenos Aires: SIP.

Ardila. (2003). Latin American psychology: What are the main achievements and contributions of half a century of scientific and professional activity? Perspectivas Psicológicas, 3, 7–16.

Ardila, R. (1968). Development of Latin American psychology. Revista Latinoamericana de Psicología, 1, 63–71.

Economic Commission for Latin America and the Caribbean (ECLAC), Demographic Observatory, 2022 (LC/PUB.2022/13-P), Santiago, https://repositorio.cepal.org/bitstream/handle/11362/48488/1/S2200706_es.pdf

Gallegos, M. (2005). Fifty years of the history of psychology as a university institution in Argentina. Rev. Latinoamericana de Psicología, 37(3), 641–652. Retrieved October 8, 2022, from http://pepsic.bvsalud.org/scielo.php?script=sci_arttext&pid=S0120-05342005000300021&lng=pt&tlng=es

Klappenbach, H.; Pavesi, P. (1994). A history of psychology in Latin America. Revista Latinoamericana de Psicología, 26(3), 445–481.

Maluf, M. (2012). Interamerican Society of Psychology: history, trajectory, and projects. *Revista de Psicología (PUCP)*, *30* (1), 215–220. Retrieved May 3, 2023, from http://www.scielo.org.pe/scielo.php?script=sci_arttext&pid=S0254-92472012000100009&lng=es&tlng=es

Pantano, D. (1997). The beginnings of psychology in Argentina. San Juan: Secretariat of Culture of San Juan.

Acknowledgments

For the authors of this book, it is an honor to have the foreword written by the distinguished member of the *International Testing Commission* and Rector of the *Universidad Nebrija* (Madrid), Dr. José Muñiz. As editors, and on behalf of the Psychological Assessment Working Group of the *Interamerican Society of Psychology*, we would like to thank the Editorial Committee, composed of Drs. Andrés Pérez Acosta and Miguel Gallegos, as well as the *Interamerican Society of Psychology*, without whose support this work would not have been possible.

Contents

1 **Introduction** 1
Silvia Viviana Pugliese, José Livia Segovia, and
Solange Muglia Wechsler

2 **Odyssey of Psychological Assessment in Argentina** 13
Silvia Viviana Pugliese

3 **Reality and Challenges of Training, Publications, and Practice in Psychological Assessment in Bolivia** 33
Marion K. Schulmeyer

4 **The Development of Psychological Assessment in Brazil: Actions, Perspectives, and Challenges** 47
Solange Muglia Wechsler, Ana Paula Porto Noronha, and
Makilim Nunes Baptista

5 **Origins and Challenges of Psychological Assessment in Chile** 61
Eugenia V. Vinet and Marcela Alejandra Rodríguez-Cancino

6 **Psychological and Educational Assessment in Costa Rica: Origins, Current Status, and Future Perspectives** 77
Vanessa Smith-Castro, Eiliana Montero-Rojas, and
Carlos Saborío-Valverde

7 **Psychological Assessment in Ecuador: Past, Present, and Future Challenges** 99
Claudio López-Calle, Manuel Capella, and Andrea Freire Pesántez

8 **Development and Challenges of Psychological Assessment in El Salvador** 115
Carlos Marcel Weil Cruz

9 **Psychological Assessment and Psychometrics in Spain** 123
Paula Elosua and Juan Carlos Sierra

10 Development and Paradigms of Psychological Assessment: A Perspective from Guatemala 139
Sandra Luna-Sánchez, Claudia García de la Cadena, and Patricia Rodas

11 Advances and Challenges in Psychological Assessment in Mexico 161
Rosa Angélica Torres Marmolejo

12 An Overview of the Past, Present, and Future of Psychological Assessment in Paraguay: Current Reality and Challenges 179
Norma Coppari

13 Psychological Assessment in Peru: History, Psychometric Research, and Perspectives 193
Walter Lizandro Arias Gallegos, Carlos Renzo Rivera Calcina, Miguel Ángel Vallejos Flores, and José Livia Segovia

14 Psychological Evaluation in Uruguay 211
Evelina Kahan Kruchik and María Susana Martínez Ferreira

15 Psychological Assessment in Venezuela: Origins, Expansion, Restriction/Reinvention, and Challenges 231
Carmen Chilina-León, Eleonora Vivas Peñalver, Luisa T. Angelucci Bastidas, Janet Guerra Rendón, Aysbel González Álvarez, and María Carolina Berrios

Index 255

About the Contributors

Aysbel González Álvarez Specialist in Data Analysis in Social Sciences, B.A. in Clinical Psychology—Dynamic Clinical emphasis. Director of the School of Psychology and Professor of Psychometrics at the Central University of Venezuela. Areas: psychometrics, psychological assessment, measurement and research of psychological and social variables, clinical psychology.

Luisa T. Angelucci Bastidas PhD in Psychology, Master's in Psychology, Bachelor's in Psychology. Dean of the Faculty of Humanities and Education at Andrés Bello Catholic University. Professor at Simón Bolívar University and Andrés Bello Catholic University. Retired professor from Universidad Simón Bolívar. Area: Psychology and health, psychometrics, research methodology.

Makilim Nunes Baptista Master's in Clinical Psychology, PhD in Sciences from the Department of Psychiatry and Medical Psychology at UNIFESP, Postdoctoral fellow at the University of Algarve (Portugal), professor in the Stricto Sensu Graduate Program at the Pontifical Catholic University of Campinas. Author of several scales related to depression, suicide, burnout, social support, and emotional self-regulation.

María Carolina Berrios Specialist in Organizational Development, Bachelor's in Psychology. Coordinator of virtual training and methodological consultant at Asesores de Desarrollo Integral, s.c. Area: organizational development, human development assessment, teaching in virtual learning environments.

Carlos Renzo Rivera Calcina Psychologist and Master of Science in Public Health from the National University of San Agustín. He also holds a specialization in sampling and probabilities, descriptive and inferential statistics from the University of California, Berkeley (online), and another specialization in Gender Statistics from the Economic Commission for Latin America and the Caribbean (ECLAC). His research areas include: psychometrics, antisocial behaviors in adolescents, family and gender-based violence. International affiliate member of the

American Psychological Association (APA) and member of the violence and assessment working groups of the Interamerican Society of Psychology (SIP).

Manuel Capella Doctora en Psicología Crítica (University College London), Máster en Psicología Social (Universidad Complutense de Madrid) y Psicóloga Clínica (Universidad de Guayaquil). Profesora asociada del Departamento de Psicología de la Pontificia Universidad Católica del Uruguay. Docente de pregrado y posgrado. Ponente en eventos académicos nacionales e internacionales. Autora de diversas publicaciones sobre salud mental, violencia, historia, colonialidad, pedagogía, identidad profesional, interculturalidad, acción colectiva y temas afines.

Carmen Chilina-León PhD in Psychology, MSc in Child Development, B.A. in Psychology. Founding Director of Asesores de Desarrollo Integral s.c. and academic coordinator of MOIDI e-Learning. Postgraduate professor and researcher at Universidad Católica Andrés Bello. Psycho-educational consultant. Areas: processes in comprehensive human development, psychological assessment and intervention, school psychology.

Norma Coppari PhD in Psychology. Master's in Behavioral Science from UNAM-IZTACALA. Master's in Education from Universidad Americana. Former Coordinator of the Department of Psychology Research/UNINORTE. Postgraduate tutor in Psychology at UNAM. *Level II Researcher*, *(Pronii)* CONACYT. Director of CDID and Editor of the EUREKA-CDID Scientific Psychology Journal http://www.psicoeureka.com.py. Former National Representative of SIP-Paraguay, Behavioral Scientist-Therapist. Director and Founder of CEFEC "Center for Training in the Behavioral Approach." Author of over 100 published scientific articles, books, and book chapters. International speaker. Rubén Ardila Award for Scientific Research in Psychology (2023).

Carlos Marcel Weil Cruz MSc in Clinical Neuropsychology. Professor and Research Coordinator, School of Psychology, and Professor in the Master's Program in Clinical Psychology, Dr. José Matías Delgado University, El Salvador, Central America. Author of articles in specialized journals.

Paula Elosua Professor of Psychometrics at the University of the Basque Country (Spain). Principal investigator of the psychometric research group; has served as Secretary General of the International Test Commission, and is currently President-Elect of Division 2 (Psychological Assessment and Evaluation) of the *International Association of Applied Psychology*. Author of numerous articles, books, and research studies related to psychometrics, she collaborates through associations such as SIP, COP, IAAP, and ITC in the development and dissemination of guidelines and standards to improve the construction/adaptation and use of tests.

Miguel Ángel Vallejos Flores Psychologist, PhD in Education and Psychology. He also holds a Master's in University Teaching and another in Drug Dependence and Violence. He is National Dean of the College of Psychologists of Peru (CPsP), Secretary General of the National Council of Deans of Peru 2022–2023, and Board Member at SUNEDU. RENACYT-certified researcher, associate professor at the National University Federico Villarreal, Vice President of the Peruvian Association of Psychotherapy Cognitive Behavioral, Past President of the Peruvian Association of Addiction Psychologists. National Award in the field of Addictions 2015—CPsP and Past President of the CPsP Addictions Commission. Has worked as a consultant on addiction issues with both international and national organizations, served as a resident advisor on addiction treatment, and Director of Addiction Treatment Centers. He has also been a speaker at national and international academic events and is the author of articles published in high-impact journals.

Andrea Freire Pesántez She holds a degree in Economics and a Master's in Business Administration (Universidad del Azuay), as well as a Master's in Applied Statistics (Escuela Superior Politécnica del Litoral). She is a Statistics professor and researcher at Universidad del Azuay. Her research areas include Statistical and Econometric Analysis, Market Research, and Psychometrics.

Walter Lizandro Arias Gallegos Psychologist and PhD in Psychology from UNSA. Master of Science in Education with a specialization in Cognitive Psychopedagogy. Full-time Associate Professor at Universidad Católica San Pablo. Certified research professor by Concytec. Author of eight books and several publications in indexed journals in Peru and abroad. Member of the Ibero-American Network of Work and Organizational Psychology, the Ibero-American Network of Researchers in the History of Psychology, the Peruvian History Society, the Interamerican Society of Psychology, the International Association of Applied Psychology. Founding member and past president of the Peruvian Society for the History of Psychology. Editor of the UCSP Psychology Journal and the Peruvian Journal of the History of Psychology. Member of the Psyché Research Group at UCSP. Recipient of the UCSP Award for Excellence in Scientific Research (2017, 2019, 2022), Bicentennial Psychologist Award by CPP-CDR-III (2021), National Psychology Award by CPP (2023), Early Career Scientific Contribution Award "Maritza Montero" by SIP (2023), and National Psychological Research Award by CPP (2024).

Claudia Garcia de la Cadena PhD in Cognitive Neuroscience from Universidad de la Laguna, Spain and a Master's in Psychobiology with emphasis in Neuropsychology from de National Autonomous University of Mexico (UNAM). Dr. García de la Cadena was Director of the Psychology Department at the University of the Valley of Guatemala and for the past 10 years has been Director of the Master's Program in Applied Neuropsychology. She has been a professor and researcher for 26 years. She has a clinical practice working with children, adolescents, adults, and older adults, conducting neuropsychological assessments and providing individual and family interventions. Author of scientific articles national and international speaker. Member of Interamerican Psychological Society (SIP), Latin American Association of Neuropsychology (ALAN) and International Group on Metacognition.

Janet Guerra Rendón Specialist in Child Development and its Deviations, B.A. in Psychology. Professor at Universidad Católica Andrés Bello. Coordinator of Social Outreach Programs, Internships, and Undergraduate Thesis for the School of Psychology. Virtual tutor at MOIDI eLearning. Areas: school psychology, clinical psychology of children and adolescents, psychological assessment and intervention.

Evelina Kahan Kruchik Master's in Gerontology. Diploma in Psychotherapy in Health Services. Adjunct Professor, Institute of Clinical Psychology, Faculty of Psychology (University of the Republic, Uruguay). Coordinator of the Core Curriculum Unit: Clinical Psychology Tools. Author of books, book chapters, and articles in specialized journals. Speaker at national and international scientific events. Member of AUDEPP.

Claudio López-Calle Doctor en Pedagogía (Universidad Nacional Autónoma de México), Máster en Educación y Desarrollo del Pensamiento y Licenciado en Ciencias de la Educación con especialización en Psicología Educativa (Universidad de Cuenca). Profesor de la Facultad de Psicología e investigador del Departamento de Educación de la Universidad de Cuenca. Miembro de la Sociedad Interamericana de Psicología (SIP) y de la Red Ecuatoriana de Investigación en Psicología (REIPsi). Sus áreas de investigación incluyen la psicometría, la política educativa y la historia de la psicología.

Sandra Luna-Sánchez PhD in Psychology. Dr. Luna has experience in clinical practice, teaching, counseling, rural community work, forensic psychology, and providing support to women victims of violence, as well as to children and adolescents at risk. She is the Coordinator of the Master's Program in Advanced Psychotherapy at Universidad Francisco Marroquín. She holds a specialization in Integrative Cognitive Psychotherapy from Fundación Aiglé in Argentina. Author of book chapters and articles in specialized journals. Founding member of the Guatemalan College of Psychologists, and member of APA and ALAPJ. Former President of the Interamerican Society of Psychology (2017–2019).

María Susana Martínez Ferreira PhD in Psychology and Master's in Psychoanalysis. Full Professor, Institute of Clinical Psychology, Faculty of Psychology (University of the Republic, Uruguay). Coordinator of the Psychological Diagnosis and Assessment Program. Member of the Admissions Committee for the PhD in Psychology. Member of APU, FEPAL, and IPA. Author of books, book chapters, and articles in specialized journals. Speaker at national and international scientific events.

Eiliana Montero-Rojas PhD in Educational Measurement and Evaluation from Florida State University, and Bachelor's in Statistics from the University of Costa Rica. Full professor since 1993 and currently retired from that institution, she taught at the School of Statistics and was a researcher at the Institute of Psychological Research. The American Statistical Association (ASA) awarded her the distinction of "Educational Ambassador 2010–2011."

Ana Paula Porto Noronha Psychologist, Master's in School Psychology, and PhD in Psychology: Science and Profession from the Pontifical Catholic University of Campinas. Postdoctoral fellow at the University of Minho, Portugal. Professor in the Stricto Sensu Graduate Program in Psychology at the University of São Francisco. Author of several psychological tests and 300 scientific publications on psychological assessment.

Eleonora Vivas Peñalver PhD in Psychology, M.Phil, Lic. in Psychology. Coordinator of the Master's Program in Psychology and the Doctorate in Social Sciences and Humanities at Simón Bolívar University. Professor at Simón Bolívar University. Areas: psychological and program evaluation, psychology and health.

Silvia Viviana Pugliese Bachelor's and PhD in Psychology. Postgraduate professor in the Specialty of Psychodiagnosis (National University of Rosario), in Diploma Programs on Psychodiagnosis (UDA), and in Intervention and Approaches to Violence (RAICES). President of the Latin American Association of Rorschach and Other Projective Techniques (ALAR). Author of books, book chapters, and articles in specialized journals. Speaker at national and international scientific events. Member of ADEIP, SIP, APA, ALAR, International Society of the Rorschach, APOP (Madrid).

Patricia Rodas PhD in Psychology. Dr. Rodas has experience in teaching psychological assessment and human development at both undergraduate and graduate levels at Universidad del Valle de Guatemala. She holds a specialization in Integrative Cognitive Psychotherapy from Fundación Aiglé in Argentina. Dr. Rodas is the author of several book chapters and peer-reviewed journal articles, and she has presented her work at national and international conferences. She is an active member of the Society of Interamerican Psychology (SIP), the American Counseling Association (ACA), and the American Psychological Association (APA).

Marcela Alejandra Rodríguez-Cancino PhD in Psychology from the Universidad de La Frontera. For 23 years, she has taught in the area of Psychological Assessment. She has professional experience in psychodiagnosis and psychotherapy with children and adolescents. Her research focuses on psychometrics, assessment of cognitive functioning, test use, and cultural relevance of psychological assessment instruments. She is currently the principal investigator of two projects on cognitive assessment, Co-Investigator of the International Project on psychologists' attitudes toward the use of tests in Ibero-American countries, and member of the Ibero-American Association of Psychological Diagnosis and Assessment (AIDAP/AIDEP), the International Test Commission (ITC), the Interamerican Society of Psychology (SIP), and the Scientific Society of Psychology of Chile (SCP).

Carlos Saborío-Valverde Master's in Forensic Psychology from John Jay College of Criminal Justice in New York, Master's in Clinical Psychology from UNIBE, and Advanced Doctoral Studies Diploma in Clinical Neuropsychology from the University of Salamanca. Retired from the Judiciary, where he served as a Forensic Expert and Coordinator of the Forensic Psychology Unit in the Department of Legal Medicine. Associate Professor at the School of Psychology, UCR. Coordinator of the Master's in Forensic Psychology at UNIBE and consultant/trainer for the Professional Association of Psychologists of Costa Rica.

Marion K. Schulmeyer Bachelor's and PhD in Psychology from the Universidad Pontificia de Comillas-Madrid. Dean of the Faculty of Humanities, Communication, and Arts, Director of the Psychology Program at the Universidad Privada de Santa Cruz de la Sierra, UPSA. Professor of Statistics and Thesis workshops at the undergraduate level, and in various graduate programs. International peer reviewer for psychology program certification and accreditation processes. Editor-in-Chief of the Ibero-American Journal of Diagnosis and Psychological Assessment. Author of books, book chapters, and articles in specialized journals. Interested in research, supporting the development of Psychology in Bolivia, and documenting its evolution in various fields.

José Livia Segovia Full professor and researcher at the Faculty of Psychology, Universidad Nacional Federico Villarreal, Peru. PhD in Psychology, Master's in Clinical Psychology, and B.A. in Psychology. Postgraduate studies: Learning Disabilities, Statistics and Research, Mental Health in Populations, Teaching and Research, University Teaching in Health, University Accreditation, and Management in Higher Education. Member of the Interamerican Society of Psychology, Psychometric Society (USA), General Council of Psychology of Spain, Brazilian Institute of Psychological Assessment, International Test Commission, European Association of Methodology, and the American Psychological Association (APA). Vice Dean of the College of Psychologists of Peru (2010–2012), National Research Award (2013—College of Psychologists of Peru), National Psychology Award 2018 (College of Psychologists of Peru), Past Dean of the Faculty of Psychology at Universidad Nacional Federico Villarreal (2015–2019), certified researcher by CONCYTEC, Research Director at the Office of the Vice Rector for Research at Universidad Nacional Federico Villarreal.

Juan Carlos Sierra Full Professor of Psychological Assessment and Human Sexuality at the University of Granada (Spain). Director of the Clinical Psychophysiology and Health Promotion Research Group and Principal Investigator of the Human Sexuality Laboratory at the Mind, Brain, and Behavior Research

Center. Bachelor's in Psychology from the University of Santiago de Compostela (Spain) and PhD in Psychology from the University of Granada. Specialist in Clinical Psychology.

Vanessa Smith-Castro Bachelor's in Psychology from the University of Costa Rica (UCR) and PhD in Social Psychology from Philipps University of Marburg, Germany. Currently, she is a Full Professor at UCR, where she teaches research methods and psychometrics. Between 2013 and 2019, Vanessa directed the Institute for Psychological Research at this institution. She currently leads several research projects in this academic unit in the areas of social psychology and psychometrics. Associate editor of the journals Actualidades en Psicología, Revista Costarricense de Psicología, Avances en Psicología Latinoamericana, Apuntes de Psicología, and Revista Española de Pedagogía (REP).

Rosa Angélica Torres Marmolejo PhD in Education and Human Development (ULSA, Bajío), **research focus on Education and Socioemotional Development.** Postdoctoral **Candidate** in contemporary relational and intersubjective psychoanalysis (UIC). Master's in Psychoanalytic Psychotherapy for Children and Adolescents (UVQ). Specialization in Mental Health (APAB). Bachelor's in Psychology from the University of Guanajuato. Faculty member (ENOL). Diploma in Systemic Family Therapy, Cognitive Behavioral Psychotherapy, Pediatric Clinical Neuropsychology, Parenting, Autism Therapy, Developmental Disorders, Academic Counseling, Inclusive Education, and Historical-Cultural Approach. Published articles: "Assessment of Socioemotional Competencies in Preschool" and "Indicator System for Assessing Socioemotional Competencies in Preschool," Revista de Investigación de la Salle, Bajío. Graduate and undergraduate professor. Counselor, psychologist, and psychotherapist. **Member** of the SIP working group on assessment and measurement and the study group on School Coexistence (Ibero, León).

Eugenia V. Vinet PhD in Psychology from the University of Barcelona. For 38 years, she has taught in the area of Psychological Assessment. She has worked professionally in the field of Clinical Psychological Assessment of adolescents, young adults, and adults. Her research focuses on the development of culturally relevant, psychometrically sound, and fair instruments to reflect the Chilean and Latin American context. She is currently Associate Professor at the University of La Frontera, Principal Investigator of the International Project on Psychologists' Attitudes Toward Test Use in Ibero-American Countries, founding member of the Ibero-American Association for Psychological Diagnosis and Assessment (AIDAP/AIDEP) and the Chilean Scientific Society of Psychology (SCP), and a member of the International Test Commission (ITC).

Solange Muglia Wechsler Professor, Graduate Psychology Department of Pontificia Universidade Catolica de Campinas (SP-Brazil) Executive board of the Brazilian Association for Creativity and Innovation (CRIABRASILIS). Leader of research group on Psychology Assessment of Human Potential.

Chapter 1
Introduction

Silvia Viviana Pugliese, José Livia Segovia, and Solange Muglia Wechsler

Beginnings of Psychology and Psychological Assessment in Latin America and Spain

The various chapters of this book address the development of Psychology and focus on the challenges of Psychological Assessment in Ibero-America. The text reflects on its key figures, institutions, ideological shifts, and the consequences of adherence to prevailing theories in professional practice, which initially centered on educational and occupational contexts and later expanded to clinical and other applied areas. Throughout this trajectory, similar developments can be observed in some cases, while in others, growth has been uneven.

The origins of Psychological Assessment date back to 1800 in Paraguay, where basic courses in Psychology were taught in seminaries and secondary schools, especially in religious training centers. At that time, there was a particular interest in psychological assessment applied to educational settings: intelligence tests, maturity assessments, vocational guidance, and personality tests. This approach would later be replicated in other regions.

In 1891, the first Psychophysical Laboratory was established in San Juan, Argentina, with the aim of determining the abilities and individual differences of students. This orientation led to a specialization in statistical techniques. Víctor

S. V. Pugliese (✉)
National University of Rosario, Rosario, Santa Fe, Argentina
e-mail: silviavpugliese@gmail.com

J. L. Segovia
Federico Villarreal National University, Lima, Peru
e-mail: jlivia@unfv.edu.pe

S. M. Wechsler
Pontificia Universidade Catolica de Campinas, Campinas, São Paulo, Brazil
e-mail: wechsler@puc-campinas.edu.br

S. V. Pugliese et al. (eds.), *Origins and Challenges of Psychological Assessment in Ibero-American Countries*, https://doi.org/10.1007/978-3-032-21380-8_1

Mercante, founder of the Psychophysical Laboratory, maintained that "behind school law and the art of teaching, there is a science, or there should be." The main objective was to provide a scientific foundation for future public sector educators.

In 1893, the first course in Moral Psychology was offered in Mexico as part of the curriculum at the National Preparatory School.

In 1905, a laboratory linked to education was established at the Normal School of Copiapó in Chile.

In 1909, the first intelligence assessments were conducted with schoolchildren in Lima, Arequipa, Cuzco, and Puno, Peru.

In 1916, Mexico established its first Experimental Psychology Laboratory at the National Autonomous University of Mexico.

In 1923, Brazil also adopted this orientation with the arrival of W. Radecki from Poland.

In Argentina, psychotechnical studies became increasingly focused on occupational and educational domains. Thus, in 1922, the Central Psychophysical Aeronautics Office was created, the first institutional model of Applied Psychology. At the same time, Psychotechnical Institutes were established to conduct psychotechnical studies aimed at optimizing human resources and the educational system.

In the 1920s, Uruguay established its first Psychophysical Laboratory, reflecting a concern for the educational field. In 1925, Sebastián Morey Otero taught the first course in Experimental Psychology, and in 1926, he introduced the subject of Experimental Psychology into the professional curriculum at the Normal Institute for Young Women.

Meanwhile, in 1928, Spain established the National Institute of Psychotechnics, which would later become the Professional Guidance Institutes of Madrid and Barcelona. That same year, the application of psychometric techniques in education reached the normal schools of El Salvador.

In 1934, with the arrival of W. Blumenfeld from Germany to Peru, the first attempts began to measure intelligence, physical endurance, and intellectual vigor, following the guidelines of Wundt's Structuralism. In 1935, systematic research in psychometrics began, with several studies conducted at the Institute of Psychology and Psychotechnics and the National Psychopedagogical Institute.

In 1936, in Venezuela, through training courses, psychological assessment was initiated in institutions such as the Venezuelan Child Council, the Mental Hygiene League, and the Mental Hygiene Division of the Ministry of Health and Social Welfare. These institutions began to use psychological tests for diagnostic purposes.

In Ecuador, by the late 1930s, studies using the Rorschach Psychodiagnostic were conducted with prison and indigenous populations.

Continuing in the educational field, in 1943, Venezuela established the Psychometrics Section of the School Hygiene Directorate of the Ministry of Health, and that same year the "Paidological Office" was opened.

Likewise, in Uruguay (1944), psychological studies emerged alongside the Educational Reform. This period was characterized by an Experimental and Psychometric Psychology, and later, a fundamentalist approach oriented toward the fields of Education and Medicine. Emphasis was placed on the functional interpretation of tests, particularly regarding the refinement of selection, adaptation, application, and evaluation criteria for techniques. During that decade, psychology entered the clinical field with the creation of the Psychology Laboratory at the Psychiatric Clinic of the Faculty of Medicine for the study of adult mental pathology, and the Medical-Psychological Clinic at the Pedro Visca Hospital, focused on child psychology. At that time, psychodiagnosis was the essential and almost exclusive task of the psychologist. Psychology, psychodiagnosis, and test administration were nearly synonymous.

In 1949, the Institute of Psychology and Psychotechnics was established at the Central University of Venezuela, dedicated to Vocational Guidance for new students.

In 1955, in Peru, the first locally developed psychological test was recorded: the Noetic Perceptual Integration Test, designed to assess schizophrenic patients through language from a humanistic-existential perspective.

The adaptation of foreign tests began in Chile in 1962, marking the start of studies on the adaptation and standardization of the Wechsler intelligence tests, which established a research tradition that continues to this day.

In 1975, in Uruguay, due to political circumstances, the University School of Psychology (EUP) was created, beginning its courses in 1978, with the authority to grant the title of Psychologist. The university organizational chart shows that it was given the status of School rather than Faculty; furthermore, it awarded the title of Psychologist after 4 years of higher education, in contrast to the Licentiate in Psychology, which required 5 years of study. This academic reduction is evident in the conception and professional objectives, limiting the role to diagnostic tasks.

In Venezuela, in 1978, the Psychology Laboratory was established at the University of the Andes, attached to the Faculty of Medicine, with the aim of conducting research and teaching in Social Health Psychology. In 1988, it became the Center for Psychological Research. Part of its research and thesis advisory work resulted in assessment instruments that were later published and shared with other educational institutions.

In 1979, in Uruguay, the Catholic University of Uruguay established the first private Faculty of Psychology authorized to grant the title of Licentiate in Psychology. In 1987, the Institute of Psychology of the University of the Republic (IPUR) was created, unifying previous curricula and becoming the only training center at the University of the Republic, a public institution; and only on March 15, 1994, was the Faculty of Psychology of the University of the Republic established.

In Europe, in 1995, Spain established the Test Commission within the General Council of Psychology with the aim of organizing activities and projects to improve the quality and use of tests in the country.

Legal Recognition of the Profession

Brazil was the first Latin American country to enact, on August 27, 1962, Law 4119, concerning the scope of professional practice. This law established that the administration and evaluation of psychological tests were exclusive activities of psychologists. At the same time, the National Traffic Board (COTRAN) of that country mandated a psychotechnical examination for drivers. Despite these measures, it was not until 1974 that official recognition of the Psychology degree was granted and the right to obtain a professional license in Psychology was conferred.

In 1964, the Salvadoran Society of Psychology established the legal and ethical foundations regulating the profession.

In 1968, in Chile, the College of Psychologists was created, an institution responsible for overseeing the profession and mandating membership. These functions were revoked by the military government in 1981.

In 1977, Costa Rica enacted the law establishing the College of Professional Psychologists.

In 1978, Venezuela enacted the Psychologists' Law. In 1981, the Code of Ethics of the Federation of Psychologists was approved, which remains in force, regulating the management and use of Resources and Instruments in Psychological Work, emphasizing that tests are for "psychological use."

In 1985, Argentina passed the Law on Professional Practice of Psychologists. The scope of the title "Psychologist/Licentiate in Psychology" was defined through Ministerial Resolution 2447 dated 9/20/85. Although psychological assessment was never in question as part of the professional scope, prior to that date, assessments could only be conducted upon the request of a psychiatrist. With the enactment of this law, autonomous professional practice was recognized, and by Ministerial Resolution 136/2004, the Psychology degree was included as a "field of public interest."

In 1987, El Salvador also recognized the professionalization of the field by creating the Board of Oversight of the Psychology Profession, which in 2003 became part of the Superior Council of Public Health.

In 1997, during the XVII Annual Meeting of the Brazilian Society of Psychology, the Brazilian Institute for Assessment and Research in Psychology was founded; later, it was known as the Brazilian Institute of Psychological Assessment (IBAP), marking a milestone in the development of the field of psychological assessment.

In 1999, in Uruguay, Law No. 17154 was enacted, establishing the profession of Psychologist and approving the Professional Code of Ethics for Psychologists, which was endorsed by the Coordinating Committee of Psychologists of Uruguay (CPU), the Uruguayan Society of Psychology (SPU), the Faculty of Psychology of the University of the Republic (UdelaR), and the Faculty of Psychology of the Catholic University of Uruguay (UCU). It is worth noting that Chapter III of this Code specifically addresses psychological assessment.

In 2001, another significant milestone occurred in Brazil, when the Federal Council of Psychologists developed a document (approved by Resolution 025/2001) defining the minimum criteria that psychological tests must meet to be approved for professional use. Subsequently, in 2003, these standards were compiled in the Psychological Test Assessment System (SATEPSI); these standards were made public, and information was provided on which techniques were approved.

In 2019, in Paraguay, the Law on the Professional Practice of Psychology was enacted.

Psychological Societies, Especially Related to Psychological Assessment

The early developments in Psychology motivated its pioneers to establish scientific societies; thus, in 1908, the Argentine Society of Psychology was founded, being the first in Latin America.

Later, in Uruguay, in 1929, the Alfred Binet Association was created, focusing on psychological research for educational purposes. Its creation marked "the beginning of the evolutionary process of Psychology and indirectly and incipiently shows the emergence of Psychology as a profession." This laboratory enabled the training of the first psychotechnicians.

Also in the educational field, in 1930, in Ecuador, the first test related to reading and writing acquisition was administered. It was a test by the German H. Winkler, published in 1925 and brought from Germany. Professors César Sylva and Ernesto Guevara Wolf used it and published the results in a text entitled: "Diagnosis of Psychobiological Dispositions for Learning to Read and Write."

Professional societies were subsequently established in other countries: in 1942, in Ecuador, the Society for Psychological and Psychiatric Studies and Related Disciplines was founded. In 1949, the Brazilian Association of Applied Psychology was created. In 1951, the Interamerican Society of Psychology (SIP) was founded. In 1952, in Argentina, the Medical Society of Rorschach Psychodiagnosis was established. In 1953, in Uruguay, the Society of Psychology was founded. In 1954, the Peruvian Society of Psychology was established.

Other scientific societies related to psychological assessment include the founding of the Psychoanalytic Association of Uruguay (APU) in 1955. This development allowed the psychoanalytic theoretical framework to influence psychological assessment and highlighted the value of diagnostic interviews.

In 1957, in Guatemala, the Department of School and Vocational Guidance was created.

In the 1960s, in Costa Rica, within the university setting, the first Assessment Committee was formed, with the objective of establishing an admissions system for students wishing to enter the university. This committee would later become the Center for Psychological Research (CIP) and, subsequently, the Institute for Psychological Research (IIP), which focused on the development, validation, and application of tests for the university admissions process.

In 1986, the Spanish Society of Psychological Assessment (SEEP) was founded in Madrid, which, in 1990, joined the European Association of Psychological Assessment.

Around the same time, other organizations interested in psychological assessment emerged in Latin America. Thus, in 1971, in Mexico, the National Council for the Teaching and Research of Psychology (CNEIP) was created, focusing on information processing at the cognitive level and its role in knowledge acquisition, the identification of components of thought, and intelligent behavior. In 1988, in Argentina, the Association for Studies and Research in Psychodiagnosis (ADEIP) was established, aiming to bring together all psychologists in the country interested in psychodiagnosis.

In 1997, the Instituto Brasileiro de Avaliação e Pesquisa em Psicologia (IBAPP) was created, which, in 2001, began to analyze the quality of tests for technical advice, a task carried out with the collaboration of professionals in the field. In 2010, in El Salvador, the Pro Education Foundation implemented its own Center for Psychological Assessment and Care (CEAP).

In 2015, the Network of Psychology Schools of the Consortium of State Universities of Chile [Red Psi-CUECh] created the Chilean Association of Methodology, Measurement, and Assessment [ACMME]. In 2015, in Costa Rica, the Interinstitutional Commission on High-Impact Tests was established, with the aim of providing a set of minimum quality standards for the development, validation, application, and interpretation of high-impact tests.

Creation of Psychology Degree Courses

In 1920, in Mexico, the first School of Psychology was founded within the Faculty of Philosophy and Letters at the National Autonomous University of Mexico (UNAM). It was not until 1949 that the first curriculum for the Psychology degree program incorporated a greater number of courses focused on research, methodology, and psychometrics. In 1959, the first cohort of the Bachelor's in Psychology graduated from the aforementioned university, which would grant the title of Psychologist. In 1974, the Psychology degree received official recognition, allowing access to the professional license in Psychology.

In 1936, in Venezuela, the first Chair of Psychology was established at the Pedagogical Institute of Caracas, which, a year later, became the Chair of Psychology and Psychometrics.

In 1940, the University of Costa Rica was founded, becoming the first higher education institution in the country to offer Psychology. In 1946, the University of Chile promoted the training of psychologists. That same year, in Guatemala, the Psychology degree was created in the Faculty of Humanities at the University of San Carlos. In 1949, in Venezuela, the Central University established the Institute of Psychology and Psychotechnics, focused on Vocational Guidance.

In the 1950s, in Uruguay, the Course in Applied Child Psychology was incorporated into the Medical Assistant career, taught at the Faculty of Medicine of the University of the Republic.

In 1951, the School of Psychology was established in the Faculty of Humanities at the University of El Salvador. The implementation of psychology studies also took place in other countries. This was followed by other establishments at the Pontifical Catholic University of Rio de Janeiro (Brazil) in 1953; and in 1954, the School of Psychology and Psychotechnics within the University of Madrid for the 1954/55 academic year.

In 1955, it was implemented at the Universidad Mayor de San Marcos (Lima, Peru).

In 1956, the Psychology degree was created at the Rosario campus (Santa Fe) of the Universidad del Litoral (Argentina). That same year, the School of Psychology was founded in the Faculty of Humanities at the Central University of Venezuela, later becoming the School of Psychology. In Uruguay, Psychology was placed within the field of Social Sciences, and the Bachelor's in Psychology was offered at the Institute of Psychology of the Faculty of Humanities and Sciences at the University of the Republic.

In Ecuador, the Institute of Psychology was transformed into the School of Psychology at the Central University.

In 1957, the Psychometry Assistant career was offered at the Institute of Biotypology of the Faculty of Medicine at the National University of Cuyo (Mendoza, Argentina).

In the 1960s, the Academic Aptitude Test (PAA) was implemented for the University of Costa Rica, to be administered to incoming students of that academic unit. The total number of correct answers determined the score obtained; in addition, the indicator called "Admission Average" was added to determine the ranking of applicants.

In 1963, in Paraguay, the first Psychology degree was created at the Catholic University of Asunción. Regarding the approach to teaching assessment, there is consensus that the Classical Test Theory and its principles were strongly emphasized, with some introduction to Item Response Theory. In 1966, the University Baccalaureate in Psychology was established, and in 1972, the Bachelor's degree began to be offered as an undergraduate qualification.

In 1968, in Spain, Psychology acquired the status of a university degree, and its teaching began in the Faculties of Philosophy and Letters at the Universities of Madrid and Barcelona. In the 1980s, a profound curricular transformation took place, including: Methodology of Behavioral Sciences; Personality, Psychological Assessment and Treatment, among other subjects. In current Psychology curricula, courses in psychological assessment/diagnosis and psychometrics are mandatory components of the curriculum structure.

In 1970, Schools of Psychology were established at two Catholic universities: the Pontifical Catholic University of Ecuador and the Catholic University of Santiago de Guayaquil. From their inception, these universities were oriented toward psychoanalysis, and thus psychological assessment followed that trend. The first director of the School of Psychology at the Pontifical Catholic University of Ecuador was also a professor of Rorschach Psychodiagnosis. In Quito, in the clinical area, there was widespread use and strong application of tests such as: the Rorschach Test, Karl Koch's Tree Test, Karen Machover's Human Figure Test, Louis Corman's Family Drawing Test, and intelligence tests such as the Ken E-G-Y test, the Otis test, the Bender Visual-Motor Gestalt Test, Raven's Progressive Matrices, and the Goodenough test.

In 1972, the first laboratory for Behavior Analysis was established at the National Autonomous University of Mexico (UNAM).

In 1974, the Higher Technician in Psychometrics career was created at the Bolivian Catholic University.

In 2012, in Uruguay, the Specialization in Psychological Assessment was created, granting the title of Specialist Oriented to the Clinical, Occupational, Judicial, or Forensic Field.

Currently, there are four test publishers operating in Spain: CEPE, GiuntiEOS Psychometrics, Pearson, and TEA Ediciones. These companies offer training for the use of the tests they market. Additionally, the General Council of Psychology provides its members with a Continuing Distance Education Program (FOCAD) that includes topics on test construction and use.

Conferences

The implementation of formal meetings such as Workshops, Forums, Congresses spurred numerous research initiatives.

These gatherings enabled researchers, academics, and psychologists to come together to discuss the latest advances and reflect on their professional practices. In these scientific meetings, Psychological Assessment was a central topic.

In 1919, in Montevideo, the Second American Congress of the Child was held, where the "Mercante compass" was presented. This instrument allowed for the comparison of tactile sensitivity between blind and sighted individuals. It also made it possible to determine the relationships between intelligence and tactile acuity, as well as between physical and intellectual fatigue and tactile sensitivity.

In 1938, in Rosario, Argentina, the First National Conference on Psychotechnics was held, driven mainly by teachers and professionals from various disciplines, with the aim of disseminating advances in scientific Psychology.

In 1947, in Rio de Janeiro (Brazil), the First Latin American Course in Psychology was organized by Emilio Mira y López.

In 1950, in Montevideo, the First Latin American Congress of Psychology was organized, highlighting the value of various psychological techniques, particularly regarding the Rorschach Psychodiagnostic and its contribution to the diagnosis of Schizophrenia.

In 1953, the First Inter-American Congress of Psychology was held in the Dominican Republic.

In 1954, the First Argentine Congress of Psychology took place. Of the presentations, 11.59% focused on psychological assessment techniques. One of the proposals was the creation of Psychology degree programs at various universities.

In 1964, the First University Seminar on Psychology was held, organized by students at the University of El Salvador.

In 1969, in Peru, the Seminar on the Construction of Psychological Tests was held at the National University of San Marcos. That same year in Brazil, the First Latin American Rorschach Congress was formalized.

In 1985, in Spain, the Congress on Psychological Assessment was organized.

In 1996, in Argentina, the Association for the Study and Research in Psychodiagnostics (ADEIP) organized the First National Congress of Psychodiagnostics, which has since been held annually. In 1997, the First Ibero-American Congress of Psychological Assessment was held, organized by the Ibero-American Association of Psychological Assessment (AIDEP), which is held biennially in different Ibero-American countries.

In 2021, in Peru, the First International Symposium on Tests was organized, which led to the creation of the National Commission of Psychological Tests.

Publications

Psychological information and scientific publications have been available since the last century. Their development and continuity have varied across Ibero-America. Below is a list of these publications, which is not intended to be exhaustive.

In 1910, the Annals of the Institute of Psychology of Argentina became the first specialized journal in Latin America.

In 1937, in Ecuador, Carlota Félix de Garcés published the "Manual of Intelligence." In 1938, Velasco and Carbo published "Mental Tests: with locally obtained norms," in which they presented the B.D. Test, the Concordia Collective Test, and the Piéron Collective Test; for the latter, they reported the results of its application in schools in Quito.

In 1944, the Institute of Psychology at the University of Chile created the "Archives of Psychology," which provided a platform for publications related to test adaptation.

In 1945, in Argentina, Jaime Bernstein, together with Enrique Butelman, founded the publishing house Paidós, which would play an important role in disseminating specialized texts on Psychological Assessment and test materials.

In 1946, in Argentina, Kapelusz published "The Tests" by Bela Székely and in 1947 the "Manual of Professional Guidance" by Mira y López.

Between 1947 and 1948, in Uruguay, a biannual publication "La Hoja de Psicología" was issued, supported by the Center for Psychological Studies of Montevideo, which emphasized psychotechnical studies.

In 1949, in Brazil, the journal "Arquivos Brasileiros de Psicotécnica" was published.

In 1950, the book "School Psychometrics" by Jacinto Bastidas was published, which is a compendium of mental tests. It became widely known in Ecuador.

In 1951, in Guatemala, the book "Considerations on the Szondi Test" by Barrios Peña was published.

Between 1952 and 1961, in Argentina, the "Treatise on Applied Psychology" was published, compiled by Henri Piéron. Volume II addressed Psychotechnical Methodology.

In 1969, the first Latin American Journal of Rorschach was published, with its initial issues printed in Brazil. It continues to be published currently still circulating from Argentina but virtually and is open access.

In 1972, in Spain, Álvarez Villar published "Clinical Psychodiagnosis."

In 1974, the first Argentine text dedicated to Psychodiagnostics was published: "Projective Techniques and the Psychodiagnostic Process" by M. Siquier Ocampo, M. García Arzeno, and collaborators.

In the 1980s, the journal "Current Issues in Psychology" of the Institute of Psychological Research (IIP) and the "Costa Rican Journal of Psychology" of the Professional College of Psychology were published.

In 1985, in Spain, the journal "Evaluación Psicológica/Psychological Assessment" was published. It was later renamed the "European Journal of Psychological Assessment."

In 1991, in Argentina, ADEIP launched the journal Psicodiagnosticar. The aim was to publish research and experiences in the field of psychodiagnostics and psychological assessment. This publication was included in PSICODOC and incorporated into the Basic Core of Argentine Scientific Journals of Conicet (Res. 2982/09).

In 1994, in La Paz (Bolivia), the first book on assessment was published: "Ch'iki: Conception and Development of Intelligence in Quechua Preschool Children from the Titikachi Community."

In 1995, the Ibero-American Association of Psychological Assessment (AIDEP) began publishing the Ibero-American Journal of Psychological Diagnosis and Assessment (RIDEP), with the first issues edited in Argentina.

In 2001, in Argentina, ADEIP published the translation and adaptation of the "International Guidelines for Test Use: Argentine Version" with authorization from the International Test Commission (ITC).

In 2001, in Brazil, the Instituto Brasileiro de Avaliação e Pesquisa em Psicologia (IBAPP) launched the journal "Avaliação Psicológica," the first specialized publication on the subject, which continues to be published and is open access.

In 2006, in Peru, the book "Measurement in Psychology and Education: Theory and Applications" was published.

In 2010, in Brazil, the book "Psychological Assessment: Guidelines for the Regulation of the Profession" was published.

Current Obstacles

This book addresses the topic of Psychological Assessment as it is developed and implemented in Ibero-American countries. In the course of this discussion, it becomes evident that countries such as Argentina, Bolivia, Ecuador, Paraguay, Peru, and Venezuela face common obstacles, the most prominent being related to the use of foreign tests and the limited opportunities to develop local techniques, mainly due to economic constraints. In some countries (such as Bolivia and Venezuela), there is also the inability to acquire test materials. The lack of financial resources limits the adaptation and/or standardization of tests; moreover, in some countries (for example, Argentina), the transfer of rights to adapt materials to the national context has been denied.

In countries such as Chile, the deregulation of undergraduate training has resulted in deficits in the application of assessment techniques. In other countries, such as Mexico, academic training is highly diverse, with a practical distinction between a psychometric approach and a dynamic or clinical approach.

Current Challenges

One of the major barriers lies in access to the development of local tests that are responsive to context, cultural diversity, socioeconomic disparities, neurodiversity, and gender diversity.

The adaptation and/or standardization of foreign techniques ensures the reliability and validity of the results obtained, in order to formulate psychological diagnoses that incorporate psychometric, descriptive, and psychodynamic criteria. The goal is to integrate the assessment of the individual across all domains, weaknesses, and strengths. Only in this way can we avoid stereotyping individuals based on deficiencies or pathology.

Except for Brazil, there is a notable need in other countries for an institution to certify the scientific validity of current techniques and to identify those that have become obsolete.

In the post-pandemic period, the virtual publication and distribution of materials have increased, often without preserving fidelity to the original. Therefore, it is necessary to establish regulations governing the use of test materials.

It is essential to promote research, especially in light of the growing influence of digital technology in assessment. Contributions from fields such as Engineering, Computational Linguistics, Computer Science, and Artificial Intelligence are opening new areas of exploration, where "data," as a unit of analysis derived from applications, mobile devices, and social networks, enables the analysis, classification, and prediction of behavior.

There is a need to develop undergraduate and graduate training programs in Psychological Assessment to address new demands and emerging areas, with the aim of understanding human subjectivity for prevention, intervention, and research.

Chapter 2
Odyssey of Psychological Assessment in Argentina

Silvia Viviana Pugliese

Historical Context of Psychological Assessment in Argentina

A tour through the chronology of the events that had psychological methods and techniques as protagonists allows us to tie knots and understand the vicissitudes through which they passed through the history of Psychology in Argentina. This helps us to understand why some techniques achieved greater development and diffusion and why others were shipwrecked at the beginning of their incorporation. It also helps us to understand the ups and downs in the recognition and hierarchization of this area of Psychology. History takes us to 1891, when Victor Mercante founded the first Psychophysical Laboratory in Latin America at the Escuela Normal de Varones, in San Juan (Pantano, 1997). This was only 12 years after the creation of the first laboratory of this type in the world, founded in Leipzig (1879), by Wundt, considered the father of experimental psychology. Mercante's objective for the creation of the laboratory was to determine individual capacities and differences. Mercante maintained that behind the school law and the art of teaching there is a science or there should be one. Therefore, he specialized in statistical techniques applied to the psychology of the learner. The predominant idea was to provide future educators in the public sector with a scientific level. In 1898 Horacio Piñero created the Laboratory of Experimental Psychology at the National School of Buenos Aires and in 1901 at the University of Buenos Aires (UBA).

The latter soon became a real melting pot where both French clinical (Janet, Charcot, Dumas) and experimental measurements were present, both coinciding in their physiological basis. The laboratory had three sections; one of them was "Psychometry." In 1906 the Pedagogical section of the Faculty of Legal Sciences of the National University of La Plata (UNLP) was created, whose first director was Victor Mercante. It should be noted that Experimental Psychology there was applied

S. V. Pugliese (✉)
National University of Rosario, Rosario, Santa Fe, Argentina

S. V. Pugliese et al. (eds.), *Origins and Challenges of Psychological Assessment in Ibero-American Countries*, https://doi.org/10.1007/978-3-032-21380-8_2

to education, where they combined laboratory experiments with statistical methods, seeking collective standards that would account for the school population. This orientation of the UNLP would later differentiate it from the UBA, the latter more influenced by the French psychopathological model. In 1908 Horacio Piñero, José Ingenieros, and Victor Mercante founded the Argentine Society of Psychology, becoming the first society of Psychology in Latin America. This society published the Annals of the Institute of Psychology (1910, 1911, and 1914), which was the first specific journal in Latin America (Alonso, 1999). On the other hand, Josepha Joteyko, a Polish researcher linked to positivism, considered that Paidopsychology was part of Applied Psychology and adhered to the experimental methodology of Psychology, through the use of instruments (stesiometer, ergograph, dynamometer). Joteyko and Mercante shared the idea of elaborating a pedagogy based on the science of childhood and adolescence, which allowed for closer ties between European and Argentine researchers, but this relationship was abruptly interrupted by the outbreak of World War I (Dussel, 2014). A disciple of Mercante, Alfredo Calcagno, was training in Belgium, and at the beginning of the World War I he had to return to the country in 1914. His return coincided with the creation of the Faculty of Educational Sciences at the UNLP, where Mercante was Dean and Calcagno joined as a professor (Lores Arnais, 2001). Calcagno argued that basic and applied research were "two sides of the same coin," and showed his ability and interest in psychological research. In May 1919, the Second American Congress of the Child was held in Montevideo, where Calcagno presented his micro-hafi-esthesiometric compass, later called "Mercante's compass," manufactured by Zimmermann of Leipzig. This compass measured tactile acuity to compare the tactile sensitivity of blind and sighted people. It also made it possible to determine relationships between intelligence and tactile acuity, as well as physical and intellectual fatigue and tactile sensitivity. The complete work on this compass was published in 1925 (Lores Arnais, 2001). Calcagno invented several devices destined to the research carried out at the Laboratory of Experimental Psychology and Psychopedagogy of the UNLP. In addition to the one mentioned above, in 1924 he presented two models of osmiostimeters, instruments to measure olfactory sensitivity. This "positivist" stage of Argentine psychology was followed by another of "anti-positivist reaction," where experiment and objective observation had fallen into disrepute while idealism, which neither complements nor opposes psychoanalysis, was emerging (Klappenbach, 1995). It should be noted that from 1915 to 1930 there was a shift, as in Europe, from the biological and social model of positivism to the philosophical and psychological one, taking intuition as a method. In 1922, the Gabinete Psicofísico Central de Aeronáutica was created, the first institutional design of Applied Psychology inspired by the European model. With a view to accident prevention, its objective was the selection of aeronautical, civilian, and military personnel. The psychic examination evaluated psychomotor activity, attention, and resistance to emotional stimuli, which, together with other tests, made it possible to determine the subject's profile (Rossi et al., 2001). In the 1920s, institutes appeared such as: the Instituto de Psicotecnia y Orientación Profesional (1925) proposed by Jessinghaus, in Buenos Aires, aimed at carrying out psychotechnical studies to optimize human resources; and later the Instituto de Psicología del Consejo Nacional de Educación (1929) was created with the objective of studying the school population in order to optimize the educational system. The latter worked closely with the Argentine Psychological Society and had a Psychometry section headed by José Alberti, which produced works such as: "Electrical activity of the brain" and "Biological foundations of thinking" (Dagfal, 1997). It is worth noting that, in this period, Educational Psychology was exercised and conceived from Medicine. Argentina went through a military coup, in 1930, when the universities were intervened and the laboratories were eradicated and, until 1945, the idea that "the mind is an earthly matter and can be approached from science" was discouraged (Vilanova, 1995: 93). In 1934, the Mental Hygiene Clinic was created at the Hospital de Clínicas under the direction of Telma Reca. Given the activity that began to unfold in this clinic, the need for more agents arose, which led to the organization, in 1937, of a course for visitors for the administration of the social survey and probably their task was limited to taking tests (Rossi et al., 2001), a course that was later transferred to the UBA. In 1936, the 2nd Argentine Medical Congress was held, with a clear concern for the rise and "successes" of "quackery and quackery" (Klappenbach, 1995). One of the proposals that emerged from the Congress was to integrate psychological education into medical training, aiming at the unity of the patient and attending to the doctor–patient relationship. Psychology is conceived there as: a) a basic explanatory science of mental processes and b) a capacity for diagnostic perception and for influencing psychic life. The subject included a special chapter on "Methods of psychological exploration." In 1938 Mira y López arrived from Spain and Bela Székely from Hungary. In the same year, the First National Conference on Psychotechnology, held in Rosario, was promoted mainly by teachers and professionals from different disciplines with the aim of disseminating the advances of scientific psychology, its different areas of application and the social usefulness of its knowledge (Gentile, 1997). Dr. María Cristina Richaud de Minzi (personal communication, April 2022), former director of the Centro Interdisciplinario de Investigaciones en Psicología Matemática y Experimental (CIIPME) recalls that Horacio Rimoldi, although a medical doctor, was very interested in psychology. This interest led him, in 1939, to apply for a British Council (England) scholarship to learn psychometry at Spearman's school. It was there that Rimoldi was initiated in the study of psychometrics applied to behavior and the mathematical approach to test development and factor analysis. When he returned to Argentina, he created the Institute of Experimental Psychology of the National University of Cuyo, in 1942. The following year Rimoldi produced his first work: "Essay of typification of a mental test." The accent was on the experimental and the use of psychometric formulations. He had the collaboration of Nuria Cortada de Kohan and carried out the massive taking of the Raven's Progressive Matrices Test (RAVEN) to schoolchildren and workers. In the 1940s, Psychology presented a growing philosophical predominance, which, added to the productive and social changes of the postwar period, led to the criterion of training professional and psychotechnical counselors. In this period, commercial and manufacturing institutions commissioned psychological research on employees and workers (Moreno, personal communication,

May 2003). In 1942, Osvaldo Loudet presented a project for the creation of the Specialization in Psychiatry in the Faculty of Medical Sciences at the UBA, with special emphasis on the studies of medical psychology, with a Kretschmerian orientation, which included: Psychotherapy, Technique of Expertise and Evaluation and Psychoanalytic Methods. That same year, the Argentine Psychoanalytic Association was founded by Enrique Pichon-Rivière, Arnaldo Rascosvky, Angel Garma, Celes Ernesto Cárcamo, and Marie Langer (Graciela Echaire, personal communication, October 2022).

In 1943, H. Rimoldi, who had studied with Spearman in England, founded in Mendoza "the first laboratory with psychometric material" (Rossi et al., 2001: 95). In 1946, Juan Domingo Perón was elected president, thus initiating the period known as the first Peronism. It followed the same line of the previous government, in terms of direct interference of the political power in universities, maintained an anti-positivist position and introduced scholasticism and Thomism; with an active participation of Catholic nationalist sectors, and, therefore, also opposed to psychoanalytic ideas. During this period, the Society of Psychologists of Buenos Aires and the Federation of University Students of Argentina disappeared. Many university professors resigned and others were exonerated, among them Bernardo Houssay (Nobel Prize in Medicine) and Alfredo Calcagno and Horacio Rimoldi. Subsequently, in 1949, Perón "formally prohibited psychological experimentation on humans" (Vilanova, 1995: 94). Given the need to manage collective subjects, tests became the form of psychological intervention in the two strategic areas in government plans: education and work. Therefore, they left aside not only experimental laboratory psychology, but also French psychopathology, as it was more focused on individuals (Dagfal, 1997). In 1945, Jaime Bernstein together with Enrique Butelman founded the Paidós publishing house, which would play an important role in the dissemination of specialized texts and test material. The following year, Editorial Kapelusz published "Los Tests" by Bela Székely, a work that was reedited and expanded on several occasions. In 1947, the same publishing house published the "Manual de Orientación Profesional" by Mira y López, a true treatise on psychotechnics and professional orientation. With this book, the publishing house launched the "Biblioteca de Ciencias de la Educación" under the direction of Alfredo Calcagno. It was followed by the "Tratado de Psicología Aplicada" compiled by Henri Piéron (1952, 1961), the second volume of which is dedicated to psychotechnical methodology (Klappenbach, 2002). In 1948, the course for Psychiatric Assistants was created under the Ministry of Social Assistance and Public Health, and in the same year it was taught at the Institute of Applied Psychopathology (today the Ameghino Health Center). The objective of this course was training in psychodiagnosis and psychotherapy, aimed at training specialized technicians. These assistants, in fact, were dedicated to the practice of psychodiagnosis and psychotherapy. Psychodiagnosis was performed at the request of physicians and included mental tests of intellectual and characterological level. In 1948, the School of Psychology Technicians and courses for Teachers was created in La Plata. There, Educational Assistants graduated, basically their training was on: "Educational Psychology," in charge of Jaime Bernstein; and "Techniques of

Psychological Exploration," in charge of Bernardo Serebrinsky (Moreno, 1997). At the same time, from the Department of Psychology of the Province of Buenos Aires, Bernardo Serebrinsky and Ricardo Moreno applied the psychodiagnostic criteria based on projective material, observing its usefulness for the approach to educational problems. On the other hand, Nuria Cortada, as director of the School Health Psychometry Department in Buenos Aires, focused vocational orientation on personality factors. In 1949, the Institute of Educational Psychology and Vocational Guidance was created in La Plata. This later became the Directorate of Educational Psychology and Vocational Guidance. Its first director was Ricardo Moreno, who changed the then-prevailing style (biotypological) to psychodiagnostic, with the Rorschach, RAVEN, and Thematic Apperception Test (TAT) as its axes. Jaime Bernstein and Bernardo Serebrinsky worked there (Moreno, personal communication, May 2003). From this period, we can still highlight the institutions that preceded the training of psychologists: the Institute of Experimental Psychology, founded in Mendoza by Horacio Rimoldi in 1942; the Institute of Psychopedagogical Research, founded in San Luis by Plácido Horas in 1948; three institutions in Tucumán (the Institute of Psychotechnics and Professional Guidance directed by Aybar, the Institute of Educational Sciences, and the Institute of Philosophy) and the Bachelor's Degree in Psychotechnics and Professional Guidance, which began in 1950 and lasted 5 years; the Psychotechnics Office, created in Paraná in 1951; the Institute of Educational Psychology and Professional Guidance, created in La Plata in 1948; and the Institute of Psychology, founded in Rosario by Erminda Benítez de Lambruschini in 1954. (Courel & Talak, 2001, cited in Gallegos, 2005: 644). Ricardo Moreno founded the Psychology Institute of the General Education Council in Tucumán, and later a similar one in Santiago del Estero in the early 1950s. Later, similar institutes were replicated in La Plata and Salta with Oscar Oñativia (Moreno, 1997). In Córdoba, Alberto Chattás conducted research on the administration of the Gesell and Rorschach tests for children. His disciple, Bernardo Serebrinsky, also from Córdoba, followed the same line of work at the Organization, Health and Education (OSE), a dispensary for the Jewish community, established in 1951 in Buenos Aires (Rossi et al., 2001). During the 1950s, under the influence of Rimoldi's teachings, psychometrics gained a foothold and expanded institutionally. A student, Nuria Cortada, achieved an early and significant academic foundation as head of the "Psychometric Seminars" in the "Psychology II" department at the University of Buenos Aires (UBA), with García de Onrubia as the chair. Thus began the university teaching of psychometry (Minzi, personal communication, April 2022).

This overview reveals the shifts that took place in the first half of the twentieth century. Initially, there was the influence of German psychology with the creation of experimental psychology laboratories, dedicated to "sensory measurements." In the 1920s, psychotechnics primarily oriented toward the educational field began to gain ground. Meanwhile, in another movement, the "clinical observation" method of psychopathology, strongly influenced by France, gained prominence and was highly valued by the Argentine intellectual community of the time, without abandoning experimental research. This line of thought is clearly reflected by Piñero when he criticizes the North American laboratories, influenced by Wundt, because "they do too much psychometry, and psychometry is only a small chapter of psychology" (quoted by Klappembach in Pantano, 1997, p. 118). In the 1930s, statistical and biotypological approaches were introduced with the aim of optimizing the educational system by systematizing the study of the school population. In the early 1940s, occupational and educational psychology institutes with a psychotechnical focus expanded, with the use of intelligence tests at both the workplace and educational levels becoming more prominent. In the 1950s, the psychodiagnostic approach displaced biotypologies, and projective techniques began to be strongly considered, neutralizing the exclusive use of psychometric criteria. Thus, it can be inferred that those with an Anglo-Saxon background promoted psychometry and psychostatistics, while those influenced by French clinical studies placed greater emphasis on clinical observation and projective techniques, more in line with the growing psychoanalytic movement of the time. As Norma Contini puts it, there was a shift toward a psychodiagnostic approach to include projective techniques, due to "the widespread development, acceptance, and prestige" of these techniques (Wechsler, 2014). In 1951, the Psychotechnical Office was created under the Education Sciences section in Paraná, focused on determining physical and intellectual aptitudes and vocational guidance. From then until 1957, the Psychometric Assistant program was offered at the Biotypology Institute of the Mendoza School of Medicine, which only required secondary education (Dagfal, 1997). In 1952, Nuria Cortada de Kohan standardized the RAVEN for the city of Buenos Aires, using a sample of 800 cases (Personal communication, May 2003). Oscar Oñativia later repeated it in La Plata and Salta. In 1952, the Rorschach Psychodiagnostic Medical Society was created, bringing together interested professionals, creating a space for the exchange and dissemination of the test. Its founders included Antonio Duarte, Juan Carlos García Badaraco, Jorge Antonio Insúa, Raúl Usandivaras, and Juan Carlos Pizarro Crespo. The fledgling society was recognized by the International Rorschach Society in 1953. Graciela Echaire adds: "Years later, with the incorporation of psychologists into the institution, it was renamed the Argentine Association of Rorschach Psychodiagnosis (personal communication, October 2022). That same year, the program for Psychotechnical Assistants was created, with Jaime Bernstein as its director, at the Faculty of Philosophy, Letters, and Educational Sciences, affiliated with the National University of Litoral in Rosario. Dr. Richaud de Minzi mentions that "between 1952 and 1955, Dr. Rimoldi was invited to join the Educational Testing Service at Princeton University, New Jersey." Guided by his curiosity about cognitive processes, he made his first discoveries in cognitive psychology: the diagnostic skills test and the problem-solving technique. This method of assessing problem-solving is unique in that it focuses on the process, not the result, and proposes, as an innovative technique, a series of questions to follow the cognitive strategy process. This entailed developing a methodology that would facilitate the assessment of cognitive processes, considering not only the information items requested, but also the temporal sequence in which they occur (personal communication, April 2022). Between 1945 and 1955, it was argued that psychology did not meet society's need for practical knowledge. Individual differences were only relevant in contrast to the normality proposed by statistical methods.

Norms were constructed by administering tests and questionnaires to thousands of subjects. Standardization would allow the transition from an academic discipline to a psychotechnical one. Psychology discovered a new statistical mathematical model, freeing it from Psychiatry and Philosophy. "Mental tests" became the intervention par excellence. In 1953, the Peronist government launched the Second Five-Year Plan, establishing a relationship between psychology and work in terms of productivity and efficiency. Its instrument was psychological techniques for professional training and guidance. At that time, psychotechnical institutes had proliferated, issuing "psychophysical certificates" requested by companies and institutions (Dagfal, 1997). Since a "psychophysical" evaluation was required, the physician was considered more authorized to assess both the physical and psychological aspects. Training in psychodiagnosis had achieved autonomy and recognition, but Bernardo Serebrinsky, unlike Telma Reca, felt it necessary to extend it to psychotherapy. In this sense, and with the aim of providing systematic training, he founded the School of Cultural Psychotherapy in 1953 (Rossi et al., 2001). In 1954, the First Argentine Congress of Psychology was held. Ricardo Moreno, a member of the Organizing Committee, reported that of the ten topics offered, one was on "Psychological Screening Techniques: Psychostatistics and Projective and Psychometric Tests." Mariano Yela (Spain) participated with his paper on "The Psychological Significance of Factor Analysis." Nuria Cortada presented papers on "Typification of a Projective Test" and "Gestalt Principles in Projective Techniques." A total of 11.59% of the presentations were on Psychological Screening Techniques, distributed as follows: eight papers on the Rorschach; two on the TAT; three on the Myokinetic Test; one on Factor Analysis; and the rest on psychological theory and screening techniques. Of all the presentations listed, he emphasized their strong "dynamic" orientation and the fact that no experimental work or quantitative research on basic psychological functions was presented (Moreno, personal communication, May 2003). One of the proposals of the first congress was the creation of a Psychology program, which was established in 1956 at the National University of Litoral, based in Rosario, and the following year in Buenos Aires (Moreno, personal communication, May 2003). Also in 1956, a Psychology program was established at the National University of Córdoba, in Córdoba, and at the University of Salvador, in Buenos Aires. Curiously, in 1954, after the congress, the Ministry of Public Health issued Resolution 2282, better known as the "Carrillo Law," which regulates psychotherapy and psychoanalysis, establishing "that technical assistants may collaborate with physicians [...] but are prohibited from practicing psychotherapy and psychoanalysis." Future psychologists would be included among the "medical assistants." In fact, the curriculum for the Psychology study plan at the University of Buenos Aires (UBA), developed in 1956 and clearly oriented toward clinical training and psychotherapy, was never implemented. The Psychology program at the University of Buenos Aires (UBA) began with a different program in 1957, this time focused on Clinical Psychodiagnosis, given that Marcos Victoria, its first director, believed that only a physician could cure through physical or psychological means. Consequently, in 1959, he included Psychodiagnosis and eliminated Psychotherapy and the possibility of obtaining a doctorate from the curriculum.

Thus, graduates of the program were defined as physician's assistants, specializing in Psychodiagnosis (Carrillo Law, 1954). This meant that psychologists could only perform psychodiagnosis under the prescription of a psychiatrist and were prohibited from psychotherapy. This situation continued until 1985, when laws governing the professional practice of psychologists were passed, recognizing the independent practice of the profession in various areas, including psychotherapy. The curriculum for the program at the University of Buenos Aires (UBA) included Statistical Methodology, taught by Nuria Cortada de Kohan; Theory and Interpretation of Mental Tests, taught by Nicolás Tavella; and Projective Techniques, taught by Jaime Bernstein. The techniques taught included Terman Merrill, Weschler, RAVEN, Differential Ability Test (DAT), Rorschach, TAT, Child Apperception Test (CAT), Goodenough, Bender, and Interview. Jaime Bernstein, along with Plácido Horas (San Luis), Oscar Oñativia (Salta), Nuria Cortada de Kohan (Buenos Aires), and Nicolás Tavella (Buenos Aires, Tucumán, La Plata), expanded the use of these instruments to include school populations, professional orientation, and clinical psychodiagnosis. All of this was communicated to future psychologists through their respective departments (Cortada de Kohan, personal communication, May 2003). Along these lines, the creation of the National Institute of Mental Health in 1957 stands out. Its objective was to address mental health and early diagnosis, with Mauricio Goldemberg, as its first head.

Nicolás Tavella, recognized for his influence on the study and application of psychological assessment techniques, especially psychometric ones, from his position as Advisor to the Technical and Research Coordination of the Ministry of Education of the Province of Buenos Aires (1956–1958), directed: The factor analysis of Bernardo Serebrinsky's "Verbal Intelligence" and "Logical Intelligence" and the standardization of the Jhonta Vocabulary Test. Jaime Bernstein deserves a separate paragraph for having played a triple role: teacher, adapter, and creator of techniques, and, later, editor. Bernstein standardized the RAVEN, Goodenough, and Bellak Child Apperception Inventories nationwide. He adapted Personality and Interest Inventories by Allport, Bell, Kuder, and Rogers and translated texts from Psychometry (Castillo, n.d.). Bernstein was also director of the Department of Vocational Guidance at the University of Buenos Aires (UBA), created in 1958. He was joined by Nicolás Tavella and Nuria Cortada de Kohan as deputy directors. Vocational Guidance tests were standardized there: the DAT, the Thurstone Primary Aptitude Test, among others (Kohan, 1997). Another important event in 1958 was the withdrawal of Bleger, Pichón Rivière, and Liberman from the Argentine Psychoanalytic Association and their inclusion in the academic life of the recently created Psychology program. Bleger, who served as a professor of Psychoanalysis in both the Buenos Aires and Rosario programs, defined the role of the psychologist, directing it toward Psychohygiene and Psychoprophylaxis. The hegemony of medical discourse shifted the professional profile of the psychologist, excluding them from the field of illness and placing them in the care of everyday life; although the aspirations of the students were influenced by the medical model, and consequently directed toward psychotherapeutic care. Since the country had its first psychology graduates, the Argentine Rorschach Society, in 1959, decided to accept psychologists and other higher education graduates with demonstrated Rorschach proficiency as full members. As a result, Guida Kagel, Vera Campo, Cristina Melgar, Antonio Duarte, Juan Escarrá, Juan García Baradaco, Nélida de García Badaraco, Jorge Insúa, Leonardo Magran, Osvaldo Silva, Raúl Usandivaras, Irene Orlando, and Andrés Cabo y André became members (Passalacqua, 1994). For this reason, in 1958, it was renamed the Argentine Society of Rorschach Psychodiagnosis (SAR). Among the contributions generated by this society, it is worth highlighting those of Pizarro Crespo and the connection that Vera Campo established between Kleinian psychoanalysis (dominant at that time) and Rorschach. They contributed to the recognition of the usefulness of the test by the members of the Argentine Psychoanalytic Association.

Since 1963, the SAR trained Rorschachists in 3-year courses. In 1968, the SAR created the Research and Consulting Center. Graciela Echaire adds: "I personally knew three of the SAR's first Rorschach teachers, Dr. María Melgar, Dr. Vera Campo, and Professor Guida Kagel, with whom I studied the Rorschach and conducted research" (personal communication, 2022). In 1969, the SAR published a scientific journal featuring Argentine and international works on the Rorschach. Beginning in 1982, the journal was renamed "Rorschach Psychodiagnosis and Other Projective Techniques." For its part, the SAR brought together the Rorschachists who formed the so-called Argentine School. In 1967, Sofía Slullitel and Elizabeth Sorribas, among other full members of the SAR, founded the Rorschach and Other Projective Techniques School in Rosario, which in 1980 became known as the Rosario Rorschach Association. Both associations have organized national and international scientific events on projective techniques. Among their original contributions is the creation of the tactile Rorschach, the first projective test for the blind (Oñativia, 1972). In 1960, at the Fourth Argentine Conference on Psychiatric Care, a modification to the course on Psychiatric Assistants was proposed. Among other specialties, the following are proposed: Psychometry; Vocational Counseling and Career Guidance; and Psychopedagogy, all under the supervision of a physician. That same year, Paidós Publishing House translated and published Pichot's "Mental Tests." It was a guide to some 140 psychological examination instruments. It followed suit with Palmade's "Psychotechnics." With these works, Paidós inaugurated a series of publications of translations and adaptations, especially of projective techniques. Surprisingly, it intended to replace "Piéron's Treatise," or rather, deny its existence by presenting Pichot's work as "the first comprehensive exposition and the first guide in French to systematically present some 140 psychological examination instruments" (Bernstein, 1960).

During the 1960s, the controversy raged between the so-called actuarial psychology (statistical analysis, prediction, and validity) and clinical psychology (projective techniques and methods). This controversy was masterfully addressed by Jaime Berenstein, who was part of the creative and integrative thinking movement, in his article "Two Psychologies" (Bernstein, 1993), where he raises the differences in criteria for the validation of psychometric and projective techniques. He emphasizes:

> Psychometric tests measure anonymous individuals, unidentified except by age and, occasionally, sex, and they are measured in relation to individuals in an equally anonymous group to establish their quantitative placement within that group: therefore, their validity and reliability must be verified. Projective tests, on the other hand, operate on an identified individual personality [...] the projective method is validated by the concurrence and recurrence of the data obtained from the examinee's Gestalt. (p. 67)

Bernstein (1993) ends his article by stating the need to integrate both methods, but not at any price: "Our censure should be reserved for those who would like to close all doors but one: Dogmatism determines scientific anemia" (p. 81). Nicolás Tavella was the promoter of "factor analysis" for the construction and validation of tests in the country. It is worth noting that, in 1960, being director of the Department of Psychology at the UBA, and at the request of Enrique Butelman, he presented two projects: "Factor Analysis and Psychology" and "Construction of an Intelligence Test for Lower First Grade" (Luque, 2001). During this period and following the experimental and statistical method, Nicolás Tavella began his prolific bibliographic production with his first book: "Applied Statistics" (1960), to continue with the "Manual for the construction of objective tests of school performance" (1968), "The teacher and Vocational Guidance" (1977), "Statistical Design" (1994), "Psychometric theories and test construction" (1999) and "Psychological techniques of evaluation and exploration" (2000). The training of psychologists varied across the country. At the National University of Rosario, the carrier lasted 4 years and awarded a degree in Psychology; at the National University of La Plata, it also lasted 4 years, but the degree was Clinical Psychologist, Occupational Psychologist, or Educational Psychologist; and at the University of Buenos Aires, the duration was measured by subject (not by year) and the degree was Bachelor of Psychology. Program profiles also varied, and some universities modified their carrier. For example, the private University of Salvador (created in 1959) in Buenos Aires offered a 7-year program, offering training in Psychometric Techniques, Projective Techniques, Rorschach, and Psychoanalysis with supervised practice (Graciela Echaire, personal communication, October 2022). Among the universities that have been modifying their curricula and profile, we can mention the Psychology program at the UNL in Rosario, implemented in 1984, where it went from psychotechnical to psychological by adding a psychoanalytic theoretical basis that forged the professional identity as non-medical psychoanalysts. Psychodiagnosis evolved from a psychiatrist's assistant tester, a technician without autonomous training in interpreting data, to a psychoanalyst who used Clinical Psychology tests within a framework characterized by limited psychoanalysis, with closure and return with the prospect of treatment, which was often undertaken by the psychologist himself. According to Fernando Silberstein (personal communication, April 2022), this model was forged "on a hypothetical-deductive epistemology and a Kantian paradigm, in part because Philosophy programs in the country followed German philosophical currents." He adds that "it is easy to distinguish this German philosophical imprint in the body of programs and writings from the first 30 years of the program."

Influence of Political Changes on the Profession

In 1967, the country's political changes once again impacted the profession: Law 17.132 strengthened the Carrillo Law. It prohibited psychologists from practicing psychotherapy and psychoanalysis, limiting them to psychodiagnosis and research only. In the private sector, psychodiagnosis could be performed under the prescription of a psychiatrist. However, in public hospitals, the reality was that Mental Health was sustained by psychologists. Thus, there was a university that trained clinical psychologists with a marked psychoanalytic influence (Kleinian first and Lacanian later), but with an illegal professional status. Consequently, the model to imitate was that of the psychoanalyst, although they were denied access to official training that would legitimize them as such, as they could not aspire to admission to the psychoanalytic program within the Argentine Psychoanalytic Association. However, the efforts made by many psychologists to establish a bridge between psychoanalysis (primarily Kleinian) and projective techniques facilitated the incorporation of psychologists into the field of mental health, with a growing demand for psychodiagnostics and consultations. Course syllabi, which gradually adopted various names, included various techniques from the beginning of the degree program, including graphics such as: Human Figure Drawing, Bender, Tree, Myokinetic Psychodiagnostic Test (PMK), Wartegg, Rorschach, TAT, CAT, Desiderative, and Rosenzweig. Later, the following were also taught: Free Drawing, House-Tree-Person Test (HTP), Two People, Couple, Family, Educational Couple, Person in the Rain, Phillipson's Object Relations, Rotter and Sacks Sentence Completion, and the Z Test. Also, the Myokinetic Psychodiagnosis of Emilio Mira y Lopez, included in the Techniques Program in the 1960s at the Faculty of Psychology of the University of Salvador, is noted for its accurate personality diagnoses. Graciela Echaire points out that "in the first Faculties of Psychology, there was important research. For example: in the Rorschach I and Rorschach II Chairs at the University of Salvador, whose Chair was María Melgar, in the 1960s and 1970s, we professors conducted research, as it was held that teaching should be accompanied by research and teaching." In 1968, these Chairs, together with the universities of Buenos Aires and La Plata, organized the Clinical Rorschach Conference, attended by prominent Rorschachists such as Juan Pizarro Crespo of the National University of La Plata; Oscar Oñativia of Salta; Héctor Pellegrina of Mendoza; and Maria Cristina Melgar and Ester García Arzeno of Buenos Aires. Research focused on clinical, educational, occupational, and forensic areas" (personal communication, October 2022).

Due to the Argentine School's contributions to the Rorschach test and its institutional participation, in 1969, Buenos Aires hosted the First Latin American Rorschach Congress, convened by the Latin American Rorschach Association (ALAR). In 1980, the 4th Latin American Rorschach Congress was held in Rosario, and in 2019, the 17th Latin American Rorschach Congress was held in Buenos Aires. In 1970, Horacio Rimoldi returned to Argentina and organized the CIIPME (Center for the Study of Psychology), through which psychology entered the Argentine scientific system. As Cristina Richaud de Minzi recalls, "this Center prioritizes an interdisciplinary approach to research, at the intersection of psychology, medicine, and the exact sciences. It highlights new topics to address: the problem of psychological measurement, stimulus scaling, the study of cognitive processes, and problem-solving" (Personal communication, April 2022). At the same time, the 1970s were marked by questioning psychodiagnosis from different theoretical perspectives (Lacanianism, systemic, Gestalt), arguing that it serves to label or discriminate. Psychodiagnosis was disqualified in relation to psychotherapy, giving the latter a higher priority (Verthelyi, 1989). Fortunately, from another sector, concern for materials and the need for population norms and patterns that take into account sociocultural background grew. Likewise, guidelines were expanded, and administration and interpretation techniques were modified. Jaime Bernstein creates the Two-Person Test, based on the Machover; the interpretation criteria of the Object Relations Test (ORT) and the CAT are adapted, and the ORT replaces the TAT.

In 1974, the first national text dedicated to psychodiagnosis was published: "Projective Techniques and the Psychodiagnostic Process" by María Siquier de Ocampo and María García Arzeno (Siquier de Ocampo, 1974). The authors, with a clear Kleinian influence, delimited the role of the psychodiagnostician, differentiating them from the testist and the psychotherapist. After the last military trial (1976–1983), programs at private and public universities diverged notably with respect to psychodiagnosis and the theories taught, as highlighted by Fernando Silberstein (personal communication, April 2022). From the 1980s onward, psychological currents influenced by Anglo-Saxon empiricism and an international rise of nominalism influenced the discrediting of theoretical coherence as a validation model, which became increasingly visible. Fernando Silberstein emphasizes: "We can delve into the reasons why Argentine intellectual elites were attracted to European philosophical currents, especially German ones, and also, depending on the context, to some French currents, whose local reception generated a kind of theoretical tension between the two." He added that, as in some European countries, empirical-statistical currents did not have sufficient recognition in universities. That model ended with the millennium, due to external political causes (personal communication, April 2022).

One of the first doctoral theses dealing with psychological assessment topics was by Dr. Nora Leibovich de Figueroa, on the topic: "Construction of an Anxiety Scale" (1983), at the University of Buenos Aires (Figueroa, personal communication, March 2022). Over the years, other aspects and methods were incorporated until an "Eco-evaluative" vision was reached, both in the construction and interpretation of the data obtained, as a response to the complexity of human behavior in its context. The theoretical framework proposed by Nora Leibovich is interactionist–transactionist in nature. Upon the return of democracy, there was a sustained increase in the number of Psychology students and graduates in the university environment, without responding to realistic expectations of the labor market. Psychology programs multiplied, especially in the private sector. From the beginning, academic training was more oriented toward a professional profile, and more specifically toward clinical practice, rather than the development of the discipline itself. However, it was not until 1985 that the independent practice of the profession was recognized. Following a call from the Ministry of Education and Culture of the Nation and with the participation of representatives from public and private universities and the Federation of Psychologists of the Argentine Republic (FePRA), which the author of this chapter had the honor of representing along with other colleagues, the responsibilities of the title of "Psychologist/Psychologist Graduate" were defined. These were embodied in Ministerial Resolution 2447 of September 20, 1985. Among these responsibilities, the following stand out, related to Evaluation: 1. Study and explore psychological facts at different stages of the individual's development, covering both normal and abnormal aspects. 3. Perform psychological diagnosis, prognosis, and follow-up tasks. 6. Construct and develop psychological methods, techniques, and instruments. (n.d.) This resolution was the basis for the enactment of national and provincial laws on the professional practice of psychologists, thus providing legal coherence between training and professional practice.

In 1987, at the First Psychodiagnostic Conference held in Rosario, which brought together psychologists from across the country, Fernando Silberstein proposed founding a scientific institution. This proposal bore fruit, and on September 18, 1988, the Argentine Association for the Study and Research in Psychodiagnosis (ADEIP) was founded. The association's clear objective was to build a forum that would encompass all techniques and engage participation from across the country, with federal representation. Elizabeth Sorribas was its first president. Given the devaluation of psychodiagnostic practice, the aim was to promote development, research, and publications on psychological techniques. With this objective, regional and national scientific activities were organized, and the publication of the "Informative Bulletin" (quarterly and for internal circulation) was published since 1989, and the annual "Psicodiagnosticar" journal since 1990. The latter is included in PSICO DOC and, since 2009, has been incorporated into the Basic Core of Argentine Scientific Journals of the National Council for Scientific and Technical Research (CONICET) through Resolution 2982/09. In keeping with its objectives, she wrote and edited the "Code of Ethics for Psychodiagnostics" (2000), and also translated, adapted, and edited the "International Guidelines for the Use of Tests: Argentine Version" (2000), with the approval of the International Test Commission (ITC), of which she is also a member. Subsequently, "Considerations on the Use of Tests in the Forensic Field" was published (2015). ADEIP has a specialized library named "Jaime Bernstein," in his honor and because his family gave him his entire library on Psychodiagnosis. ADEIP, AAPRO, and the Rorschach Association of Rosario are active members of the International Rorschach Society (IRS), whose current president is Fernando Silberstein. At the same time, psychological assessment was gaining popularity and acceptance of psychometric standards, which encouraged the adaptation of some test versions into Spanish and others from English-speaking countries, as highlighted by Norma Contini (Wechsler, 2014). In 1995, the Ibero-American Association of Psychological Diagnosis and Evaluation (AIDEP) was founded, with María Martina Casullo as a founding member and first president. AIDEP fostered an increase in the use of these techniques in both clinical and research settings. This association promoted scientific meetings with national and international experts. Argentina hosted the 3rd, 5th, and 7th Ibero-American Congresses on Psychological Assessment, and since its founding, it has published the "Revista Iberoamericana de Evaluación Psicológica" (RIDEP), (https://www.aidep.org/ridep) indexed in Redalyc, Psicodoc, PsycINFO, Latidex, Cengage, EBSCO, Scopus, and Thomson Reuters Web of Science. RIDEP, from issues 1 to 15, was published in Argentina and includes articles by Argentine researchers. Regarding research, in 1999 there were approximately 16,000 researchers in public institutions (Alonso, 1999). The growing interest and dedication to research began in 1995 due to changes in the National Education Law and a more balanced relationship between quantitative and qualitative research.

Current Status of the Evaluation

The various psychology programs offered at Argentine universities generally emphasize psychological assessment and diagnosis. However, it is acknowledged that undergraduate training is insufficient for professional practice. Norma Contini highlights that postgraduate specialization courses in Psychodiagnosis and Psychological Assessment began to be created in the 1990s (Wechsler, 2014). Based on a document prepared by FePRA and the Association of Academic Units of Psychology (AUAPSI), the Ministry of Education, Science, and Technology declared the Psychology program a "degree of public interest" through Ministerial Resolution 136/2004. This resolution requires students to participate in pre-professional internships, which include the application of psychodiagnostic techniques. The impetus given to the study and research of assessment techniques by ADEIP and AIDEP can be observed in Table 2.1, a list that, without claiming to be exhaustive, reflects the movement generated. Many of the works have been doctoral theses. It should be noted that some of the works presented in Table 2.1, along with other psychometric tests, are available in PsicometriAr5, a database of psychometric instruments developed or adapted for use with the Argentine population. It has registered 108 tests conducted since 2014. This database is promoted by Guadalupe de la Iglesia.

Beginning in 2000, there was a shift in the expectation of validation in the techniques used. Scientific journals began to accept only papers in this area, using the empiricist model. There was a boom in research careers, previously almost forbidden to psychologists, especially due to the limited number of positions available for the profession. Thus, expectations in the field began to change (Silberstein, personal communication, April 2022). Also worth noting in this regard is the activity developed by the CIIPME. Courses were offered on classical psychometrics and new psychometrics, introductory statistics, state-of-the-art statistical techniques, and the administration and interpretation of new techniques. Numerous psychological tests have been developed and adapted in very different areas. Dr. Richaud de Minzi

Table 2.1 Some research on evaluation techniques promoted by ADEIP and AIDEP

Noceti, E., & Sorribas, E. (1982). Rorschach. Psychoanalytic Reading of Hysteria. Paidós.
Leibovich de Figueroa, N. (1988). The Spielberger State-Trait Anxiety Scale. The Study Conducted in Argentina. In Psychometric Techniques and Psychological Assessment (pp. 200–223). Tekné Publishing.
Burde, L., & Sorribas, E. (1993). Rorschach. Psychoanalytic Reading of Psychosomatic Disorders. Laborde editor.
Martín, M. I., Allemand, S. & Martín R. (1998). The Little Balls Test. Diagnosis of the Bond Between Donor and Recipient in a Kidney Transplant. Medicina (Buenos Aires), 58, 13–21. Casullo, M. M. (1998). Adolescents at Risk. Paidós. 5 https://psicometriar.com.ar/
Taborda, A. (2000). WIPPSI, Human Figure and Bender. Regional Scales. Lumen.
Passalacqua A. (1997). ESPA. Suicidal Potential Scale with the Rorschach (Argentine school). Journal of the Research Institute of the Faculty of Psychology (UBA), 2(1), pp. 73–87
Zdunic, A. (2002). Zulliger-SC Test – Job Evaluation. Paidós.
Leibovich de Figueroa, N. (2000). ISRA Self-Assessment Questionnaire. Argentine adaptation. In A. Cano-Vindel & J. J. Miguel-Tobal (Eds.). ISRA Inventory of Anxiety Situations and Responses (pp. 97–120). TEA Ed.
Passalacqua, A. (2003). EFYR. Ego Functioning Reality Scale with the Rorschach (Argentine school). Available at: https://www.aacademica.org/000029/224.pdf
Querol, S., & Chaves Paz, M. (2004). Person in the Rain. Argentine adaptation. Editorial site.
Sneiderman, S. (2012). Desiderative Questionnaire. Reading from the David Liberman Algorithm (DL). Paidós.
Brenlla, M., Barbenza C. & Taborda, A. (2013). WISC IV Argentine Adaptation. Paidós.
Lunazzi, H. (2006). Rorschach SC. Normative tables for Argentina. Psimática. Agosta, C., Barilari, Z. & Colombo, R. (2013). Revised Sentence Inventory (for the assessment of child abuse). CAUQUEN.
Kacero, E. (2013). Bender Visuomotor Gestalt Test. Psychodynamic Reading. Torres, S. & Russo S. (2003 and 2011). TAT. Psychoanalytic Reading. Biblos.
Díaz de Dragotta, M. (2016). Person with a Weapon. Regional Scales. Mendoza, University of Aconcagua.
Veccia T. (2017). Fairy Tale Test. Cross-cultural Study. Subjectivity and Cognitive Processes, 21(1), 219–239.
Contini N. (2022). Bender. Updated Norms. EDUNT.
Pugliese, S. (2022). Pfister's Colorful Pyramids Test. Suicide Risk Diagnosis in Adolescents. Psimática.
Silberstein, F. (1998). Rorschach. Complementary Technique for Interpretation. UNR Editora.

(personal communication, April 2022) highlights some of them, which can be seen in Table 2.2.

In the configuration of the area of Psychological Evaluation, María Casullo (2008), professor and researcher at the UBA, from an integrative perspective, highlights: Every evaluation supposes a process through which, based on a certain model or theory—implicit or explicit—an attempt is made to understand and analyze a concrete phenomenon, real or symbolic, in its manifest or latent aspects [...] through the administration of diverse techniques: interviews, observations, drawings, questionnaires, scales, narratives, inventories [...] There is no unique model of psychological evaluation, even though some lines of work usually propose their own as the legitimate one. And he reaffirms it by adding: "evaluating is a comprehensive

Table 2.2 Some of the tests constructed or adapted

Perinatal Psychology
Oiberman, A., Orellana, L. & Mansilla, M. (2006). Intelligence assessment in Argentine infants: Argentine Sensorimotor Intelligence Scale. Archivos Argentinos de Pediatría Journal, 104(4), 316–325.
Oiberman, A. (2008). Observing infants: mother-infant and father-infant bonding techniques.
Oiberman, A.J., Santos, M.S., Mansilla, M., Dehollainz, I., Trucco, M.A., Menghi, M.S. et al. (2010). Preliminary results from 7 Argentine provinces within the framework of a proposed national assessment of sensorimotor intelligence in infants aged 6 to 30 months. Research Yearbook, 17, 213–227.
Positive Psychology
Mesurado, B. (2008). Factorial Validity and Reliability of the Optimal Experience Questionnaire (Flow) for Children and Adolescents. Ibero-American Journal of Psychological Diagnosis and Evaluation, 25(1), 159–178.
Oros, L. B., Cuello, M. & Richaud, M. C. (2021). Assessing Children's Serenity: Alternatives to Self-Report and Observer Report. Interdisciplinaria, 38(2). https://doi.org/10.16888/interd.2021.38.2.3
Richaud de Minzi, M. C. (2002). Empathy and Attachment as Precursor Variables of Affective-Cognitive Development. Argentine Inventory of Children's Perception of Their Relationship with Their Parents. Version for 4–6 year olds. Inter-American Journal of Psychology, 36(1 and 2), 149–165.
Richaud de Minzi, M. C. (2005). Short version of the Inventory of Children's Perceptions of Relationships with Their Parents for adolescents. Psicodiagnosticar, 15, 99–106.
Richaud de Minzi, M. C. (2007). Argentine Inventory of Children's Perceptions of Their Relationships with Their Parents. Version for 8–12 year olds. Ibero-American Journal of Evaluation, Ibero-American Journal of Psychological Diagnosis and Evaluation, 23(1), 63–81.
Richaud de Minzi, M. C. & Bei, E. (2013). Construction of a scale to assess the family context from the parents' perspective. Interdisciplinaria, 30(2), 283–296.
Moral Development, Forgiveness
Moreno, J. E. & Pereyra, J. M. (2004). CASA Questionnaire of Attitudes toward Situations of Grievance: manual, theoretical framework, validation, administration, and research. Universidad Peruana Unión. Faculty of Education and Human Sciences.
Developmental Psychology
Richaud de Minzi, M. C. (1991). Multidimensional Locus of Control Scale for 6-Year-Old Children. The Journal of Psychology, 125(1), 5–25.
Richaud de Minzi, M. C. (1991). Multidimensional Locus of Control Scale for Children Aged 9 to 12 Years. The Journal of Psychology, 125(1), 5–25.
Richaud de Minzi, M. C. (2003). Coping Questionnaire for Adolescents. Adolescence, 38(150), 321–330.
Richaud de Minzi (2003). Multidimensional Locus of Control Scale for Adolescents. Factorial and Construct Validity of the Argentine Multidimensional Locus of Control Scale for Adolescents. 4th Ibero-American Congress on Psychological Assessment, Lima, Peru, July 2003.
Richaud de Minzi, M. C. (2006). Argentine Coping Questionnaire for children aged 8 to 12. Mexican Journal of Psychology, 23(2), 196–201.
Richaud de Minzi, M. C. & Sacchi, C. (2006). Loneliness Scale for adolescents. Adolescence, 39(156), 701–710.

(continued)

Table 2.2 (continued)

Ghiglione, M. E., Richaud de Minzi, C. (2009). Short version of the Argentine Coping Questionnaire for Children. Acta Psiquiátrica y Psicológica de América Latina, 55(4), 239–248.
Pragmatic Language Assessment
Abraham, M. V., de Minzi Richaud, M. C., Bogliotti, E., Rohde, M. & Romero, B. (2019).
Pragmatic Neurolinguistic Assessment for Severe Aphasic Patients with Sequelae or Degenerative Causes: ICRA-R Battery. Cuadernos de Neuropsicología/Panamerican Journal of Neuropsychology, 13(2), 134–144. DOI: 10.7714/CNPS/13.2.210

concept that contains, as a subcategory, psychodiagnosis, which is understood as a form of evaluation that is fundamentally carried out in the clinical field, in relation to the health-disease process… It is always necessary to ensure the theoretical and ecological-cultural validity of each of the techniques, as well as the reliability of the results or scores obtained (230, 231, 233). From another theoretical perspective, however, in agreement with Casullo, Graciela Echaire endorses Rappaport's words: "the use of techniques must derive from the needs of each case, in order to apply the tests required for the understanding of each subject" (personal communication, October 2022).

Current Perception and Obstacles Regarding Evaluation

In 2021, the chapter's author conducted an online survey with psychologists, specifically psychodiagnostics. From this convenience sample, to which 109 psychologists responded, it is possible to highlight the following: 59.5% of the sample has more than 20 years of practice; 50.74% use projective tests, 29.25% psychometric tests, and 20.01% both; and 55.6% do not use scales. Those who use scales were asked whether they opt for outdated local scales or updated foreign scales; 90.6% preferred the former. Of those who responded, only a group of 34 psychologists have adapted or are adapting a test, and only 24 have standardized or are doing so. Analyzing the main obstacles to carrying out the task of adapting and/or standardizing foreign tests, we can highlight: a) Economic problems; b) Lack of professionals for administration, analysis, and complementary studies; c) Problems with publication, and d) Refusal to transfer rights "to Argentina" (explicit in Bender II and WAIS IV). In some cases, it is not accepted as a doctoral thesis. These difficulties are exacerbated when considering the development of local techniques. In cases where they have been able to adapt and/or standardize a foreign test, funding came from: 65.5% universities, 20.70% CONICET; 13.8% foundations; 20.7% mixed (public and national); and 24.1% national funds. Here we can see that numerous variables come into play, since, as Fernando Silberstein maintains, "scientific communities do not act alone ex nihilo" (personal communication, April 2022); several processes intervene. Among them, it is possible to highlight: paradigms of those who make up the competition juries, those who grant subsidies, as well as publication policies, favoring some theoretical lines to the detriment of others, among others. To conclude, it can be said that in Argentina the development of psychological techniques was more marked by sociopolitical reasons, both national and global, including: health policies, university policies and intra-university power structures, rather than by scientific reasons. The presence of representatives of theoretical approaches that discredit psychological assessment in universities cannot be ignored. Likewise, some multinational companies require their psychologists to administer "canned tests" to their staff using techniques developed and standardized in other countries. Recently, online sales of test materials, where a file is sent to the buyer to print, have multiplied, as has the use of photocopied materials. Both behaviors are completely at odds with the Code of Ethics for Psychodiagnostics and the International Guidelines for the Use of Tests—Argentine version.

Challenges Looking to the Future

Psychodiagnostics professionals are aware of the need for instruments created and/or adapted, as well as updated scales for Argentina, but the survey reveals the obstacles to achieving these goals. Along with these, other challenges that remain include: a) the passage of a law regulating the use of psychological assessment instruments, promoting their exclusive sale to psychologists and dissemination only in scientific media; and b) the creation of a specialized body to rule on authorized and updated instruments. Regarding the first point, the author of this chapter has presented bills on several occasions (2003, 2012, 2015, and 2018); however, she has not been able to obtain their approval by legislators. Given this reality, the antinomy of realism/ethics and ethics/utopia gains strength, as real-life conditions become unethical due to working with foreign, outdated techniques and/or non-original materials. Ethical constraints become utopian, given the obstacles to creating and maintaining local techniques and adapting and updating foreign techniques.

Acknowledgments The author thanks Lic. Graciela Echaire and Dr. Norma Contini, who generously reviewed the manuscript and whose comments enriched this chapter.

References

Alonso, M. (1999). *Psicología en las Américas*. SIP.
Bernstein, J. (1960). Las guías de tests en la bibliografía castellana. In P. Pichot (Ed.), *Los tests mentales* (pp. 7–10). Paidós.
Bernstein, J. (1993). Dos Psicologías. *Psicodiagnosticar*, 52–85.
Castillo, C. (n.d.). J. Bernstein. In *Diccionario Biográfico*. Biblioteca Virtual de Salud-Psicología Argentina. http://www.bvs-psi.mdp.edu.ar/
Casullo, M. M. (2008). La evaluación psicológica. In A. L. Duarte (Ed.), *Ayer y hoy. 50 años de enseñanza de la Psicología* (pp. 230–240). EUDEBA.

Dagfal, A. (1997). Discursos, instituciones y prácticas en la etapa previa a la profesionalización de la psicología en Argentina (1945-1955). *5. Cuadernos Argentinos de la Historia de la Psicología Año 3, N° 1-2. Universidad Nacional de San Luis* (pp. 173–195).

Dussel, I. (2014). Victor Mercante y la producción de un discurso científico sobre la educación. *Archivos de Ciencias de la Educación*. http://www.archivosdeciencias.fahce.unlp.edu.ar/article/view/Archivos08a03

Gallegos, M. (2005). Cincuenta años de historia de la psicología como institución universitaria en Argentina. *Rev. Latinoamericana de Psicología, 37*(3), 641–652. Obtenido de Recuperado em 08 de outubro de 2022, de http://pepsic.bvsalud.org/scielo.php?script=sci_arttext&pid=S0120-05342005000300021&lng=pt&tlng=es

Gentile, A. (1997). Primer Congreso Argentino de Psicología. *Cuadernos Argentinos de Historia de la Psicología, 3*, 159–172.

Klappembach, H. (1995). Psicología y campo médico en Argentina: años '30. *Cuadernos argentinos de Historia de la Psicología*, 159–226.

Klappembach, H. (2002). Dos editoriales en los comienzos de la profesionalización de la Psicología en Argentina. (ADEIP, Ed.) *Boletin Informativo de ADEIP N° 44*, 26–32.

Kohan, N. C. (1997). Autobiografía. *Cuadernos Argentinos de Historia de la Psicología, 3*(1/2), 199–206.

Kohan, N. C. (mayo de 2003). Comunicación personal.

Lores Arnais, M. (2001). Características de la Investigación Psicológica en los estudios estesiométricos de Alfredo Calcagno. *IX Anuario de Investigaciones. Universidad de Buenos Aires, Facultad de Psicología, UBA*.

Luque, E. (2001). Nicolás Tavela: la Investigación Psicoestadística. In L. Rossi (Ed.), *Psicología: su inscripción universitaria como profesión*. Buenos Aires.

Moreno, R. (1997). Algunos recuerdos personales sobre 50 años de Psicología. *Cuadernos Argentinos de Historia de la Psicología*, 207–214.

Moreno, R. (mayo de 2003). Comunicación personal.

Oñativia, O. (1972). *Rorschach tactil*. Paidós.

Pantano, D. (1997). *Inicio de la Psicología en Argentina*. Secretaria de Cultura- de San Juan.

Passalacqua, A. (1994). *El Psicodiagnóstico de Rorschach. Sistematización y nuevos aportes*. Klex.

Richaud de Minzi (abril, 2022). Comunicación personal.

Rossi, L., et al. (2001). *Psicología: su inscripción universitaria como profesión. Una historia de discursos y prácticas*. EUDEBA.

Siquier de Ocampo, G. A. (1974). *Técnicas Proyectivas y el proceso psicodiagnóstico I y II*. Nueva Visión.

Wechsler, S. M. (2014). Test develoment and use in five Iberian Latin American countries. *International Journal of Psychology, 49*(4), 233–239. https://doi.org/10.1002/ijop.12068

Verthelyi, R. F. (1989). *Temas de Evaluación Psicológica*. Lugar.

Vilanova, A. (1995). El dilema olvidado de la Psicología Latinoamericana. *Cuadernos Argentinos de Historia de la Psicología, 1*(1/2), 83–99.

Chapter 3
Reality and Challenges of Training, Publications, and Practice in Psychological Assessment in Bolivia

Marion K. Schulmeyer

Country Context

To understand the situation and challenges faced by psychological assessment in Bolivia, it is necessary to contextualize the country in which it takes place. On one hand, in the 1970s, the beginnings of the Psychology program were affected by political instability that caused the closure of universities, a situation that was not fully normalized until the arrival of democracy during an extreme economic crisis in the mid-1980s (Mesa et al., 2007; Schulmeyer, 2014b). On the other hand, the country's economic and geographic realities have also influenced and continue to affect the development of the profession. Economically, Bolivia typically has the lowest development indicators in all of Latin America (United Nations Development Programme, 2022), which hinders access to education, increases dropout rates, and limits access to continuing education and graduate courses, among other issues. This reality, along with its landlocked status, isolates the country, making the importation of books and other sources of knowledge difficult and expensive. Until the arrival of the Internet in 1989 and its nationwide availability (achieved between 1995 and 2001), access to knowledge was limited (Gómez Tellez, 2016). Currently, the use of ICTs in education finally provides access to information that was unavailable just a few years ago, but the lack of awareness of its existence persists in many universities.[1]

[1] This comment is based on information received every year from my graduate students, who come from various professions and universities across the country and confirm that the information collected by Sainz (2009) has not changed.

M. K. Schulmeyer (✉)
Universidad Privada de Santa Cruz de la Sierra, Santa Cruz de la Sierra, Bolivia
e-mail: marionschulmeyer@upsa.edu.bo

S. V. Pugliese et al. (eds.), *Origins and Challenges of Psychological Assessment in Ibero-American Countries*, https://doi.org/10.1007/978-3-032-21380-8_3

Bolivia was the last country on the continent to establish a Psychology program, and many years passed between the opening of the first program in La Paz and the establishment of programs in other departments of the country. As a result, the development of the profession is quite uneven from one department to another, with a history of more than 50 years in the capital, but in most departments, the trajectory is approximately 25 years. In the 1990s, with the arrival of private universities, academic offerings increased (Aguilar, 1983; Alonso & Eagly, 1997; Calderón, 1999; Schulmeyer, 2014a, 2014b). Currently, around 54 universities are operating in Bolivia, of which at least 24 offer Psychology programs in one or more of their branches.

Eight years ago, in Bolivia, the Psychology program was offered at five autonomous public universities (Schulmeyer, 2014a, 2014b). Since then, the program at the Public University of El Alto in La Paz has been added. The Bolivian Catholic University, a private university under a special regime, offered the program in two cities and now offers it in three. Additionally, around 12 private universities were offering Psychology, which, considering that some offered it at multiple branches, resulted in a total of 22 programs. Today, about 17 private universities are offering the program, with an estimated total of 27 programs. In total, there are currently 36 Psychology programs offered in Bolivia.

Assessment Training

Beginning in 2006, with the change in government, private universities were unable to open new programs or reformulate existing ones because the Private Universities Regulation was under review. This process ended in 2012, and 2 years later, the Regulation for curricular redesigns was approved. As a result, all private universities in Bolivia were required to submit updated programs, which were implemented starting in 2017. The requirements of the new Private Universities Regulation significantly increased the number of hours in the programs (to 4800). This mandate to redesign curricula allowed most private universities to remove two semesters from their programs, while increasing the number of courses offered per semester. Previously (Schulmeyer, 2013a, 2013b, 2014a, 2014b), programs lasted eight to ten semesters (M = 9.42; Mode = 10), and now they last seven to ten semesters (M = 8.4; Mode = 8). Most private universities operate under a modular system, meaning students take one course at a time, each lasting 19 working days. These programs plan for 14 courses per year, but in practice, the academic year allows for a maximum of 11 courses. The ten-semester duration and the semester system are maintained mainly at the Private University of Santa Cruz de la Sierra (Universidad Privada de Santa Cruz de la Sierra) and at public universities.

An analysis of Psychology programs shows that they include between one and nine courses dedicated to the area of assessment (M = 3.82; Mode = 2). Previously, the mean, median, and mode of assessment-related courses per degree program were four, and there was no significant difference in the proportion of courses in this area between private and public universities (Schulmeyer, 2016). However, there is now a significant difference, with a greater proportion of courses dedicated to assessment in public universities (χ^2 (16, N=23) = 32.15; p = 0.010).

On the other hand, in the curricula prior to the redesign at private universities, there were 66 courses dedicated to this area, referred to by 20 different names (Schulmeyer, 2016). Currently, there are approximately 90 courses with 25 different names, as shown in Table 3.1. Consensus is neither a possibility nor under discussion. However, there have been notable changes in course titles. Courses mentioning "psychometrics" in their name have decreased (from 24% to 14%), as have those mentioning "projective techniques" (from 31% to 19%). The proportion of "psychodiagnosis" courses has remained virtually unchanged (from 21% to 22%). In contrast, there has been an increase in courses with more generic titles related to "psychological assessment" (from 15% to 25%). This latter trend aligns with a recommendation we made in 2016, as many "Psychometrics" courses appeared to focus on "psychological assessment," combining objective and projective tests without differentiating the theoretical foundations of each type.

In 2016, we observed that in more than half of the "Psychometrics" courses, content on objective and projective tests was mixed. We also found a strong presence of psychoanalytic content and references in all syllabi, along with limited knowledge of psychometric theory. It is necessary to analyze current course content to determine how these issues are addressed today, but the absence of courses focused on measurement theory persists. Of the three courses that existed before the curricular redesign, two remain: one at the Bolivian Catholic University and another at the Private University of Santa Cruz de la Sierra.[2]

Table 3.1 List of courses offered in Psychology Programs (2022)

Assessment	Psychodiagnostics	Projective techniques	Psychometrics
Neuropsychological Assessment	Psychodiagnostic Models	Psychological Assessment and Projective Techniques	Construction and Psychological Test Validation
Psychological Assessment	Clinical Psychodiagnostics	Projective Techniques	Psychometric Assessment
Seminar on Psychological Assessment	Educational Psychodiagnostics	Other	Applied Psychometrics
Psychological Assessment Techniques	Psychodiagnostics and Intervention	Interview	Psychometric Techniques
Human Resource Assessment		Psychological Interview	Test Theory
		Vocational Guidance	Psychometric Tests

[2] One of the private universities offers the course "Construction and Validation of Psychometric Tests" in the second and third semesters, which are the two assessment courses in its curriculum; however, the content of these courses corresponds to Psychological Assessment.

The lack of knowledge regarding test construction and validation leads psychologists to believe they can assemble a collage of items from various tests, modify the wording, and remove items at will. They then use the "Frankenstein" instruments they have created for research without verifying their psychometric properties, as well as for making clinical, educational, forensic, and other decisions. This situation is even more common in organizational settings, where tests are adapted to the preferences of management, and business administrators engage in assessment as much as psychologists do. In all these cases, practitioners remain convinced they are measuring what they believe they are measuring, simply because, based on their intuition, it seems so.

We do not have updated data on the psychological tests taught in the various programs. In the analysis conducted prior to the redesign (Schulmeyer, 2016), it was found that the syllabi mentioned eight intelligence or cognitive aptitude tests (*WAIS, WISC, WIPPSI, RAVEN, Domino, Cards, DAT*, and *EFAI;* ten instruments for assessing child development, among which the *Bender*, the Psychomotor Development Test *(TEPSI*), and the Denver Developmental Screening Test (DENVER) were notable; two vocational interest tests (*Kuder Preference Record* and *Professional Interests and Preferences*) and only one program mentioned seven objective personality assessment instruments (*MMPI, 16PF, MCMI, Big Five, MIPS, DISC, and CPS*). The syllabi also referenced 17 different projective tests, the most frequently mentioned being the *Desiderative Test* and the *Sentence Completion Test* among the verbal tests; *DAP, Koppitz,* or *Goodenough, DAF, HTP, Tree Test, Person in the Rain* and the *Kinetic Family Drawing* among the graphic tests; and the two most frequently taught thematic tests were the *TAT* and the *CAT*.

We believe it is unlikely that there have been major changes in this content, as it was observed that, to a large extent, the free availability of tests determines what is taught, and the possibility of accessing online tests remains prohibitive, given the country's economic reality. This holds true even when considering the offerings of some assessment companies that provide their tests at more affordable prices for educational programs. Nevertheless, there are individual initiatives by psychologists who produce high-quality, unlicensed replicas of some tests and sell them at more affordable prices, allowing for their physical administration rather than on digital platforms.

Research and Publication

Ten years ago, when analyzing psychometric research conducted in Bolivia, we reviewed undergraduate theses and the publications we were able to access. This resulted in a limited bibliographic sample, as accessing these sources was not easy then, nor is it now.

At that time, we accessed undergraduate theses from 2 out of 5 public universities and 4 out of 13 private universities and found only 20 theses in the psychometric field. All these works were supervised by a small group of psychologists (Schulmeyer et al., 2013).

We also reviewed the production of articles focusing on the study of psychological tests in scientific journals. This effort led us to find six articles and one book. Three articles on test adaptation and validation were authored by faculty from the Catholic University of Bolivia and published in its psychology journal, *Ajayu* (Guaygua & Roth, 2008; Roth & Exeni, 2010; Sologuren & Gómez, 2008), and one evaluation proposal was published in another of its indexed journals (Peredo, 2000). The other two articles presenting evaluation proposals were written by faculty from Universidad La Salle (Velasco, 2008; Wile & Vargas, 2010), published in their journal *Fides et Ratio* (Schulmeyer et al., 2013). In all cases, the researchers published in journals managed by their respective universities.

This situation led us to believe that it was necessary to begin forming research groups and to improve the dissemination and visibility of ongoing research (Schulmeyer, 2013a, 2013b). Indeed, this has been happening, and publications have increased. There are still few indexed psychology journals, and it remains difficult to convince senior academics of the need for journals to be digital, the value of indexation, or the problems associated with print-only formats, which results in much information being lost and good research appearing in all types of publications. However, it is now possible to access a greater number of Bolivian studies online, as some universities have digitized their print publications, making available work that until recently remained inaccessible to most readers.

For this review, publications were searched using Google Scholar, the list of Bolivian journals registered in Scielo, Bolivian journals in the field of education, journals associated with various academic programs, and the Google Scholar profiles of leading researchers. Articles related to psychological assessment and test validation conducted by Bolivian psychologists with national teams were sought. In this way, 32 articles were found, which, given the aforementioned difficulties, are certainly an underrepresentation of the research being conducted in the country.

This search identified 11 articles related to assessment, but only 8 were authored by psychologists (Guzmán de Rojas, 2013; Guarachi Ramos, 2016; Peredo, 2000; Rodrigo Mendizábal et al., 2021; Salgado Sandoval, 2022; Soraide Castedo, 2022; Taboada & Pinto, 2018; Wile & Vargas, 2010). Four articles addressed aspects related to training and practice in psychological assessment (Schulmeyer et al., 2013; Schulmeyer, 2016; Schulmeyer & Piotrowski, 2017; Velasco, 2008). Finally, we found 22 articles on test construction or validation, of which 17 were written by psychologists (Alfaro Urquiola, 2020; Aponte Daza et al., 2022; Carrillo Mamani & Hidalgo Maynasa, 2021; Franco Jiménez, 2017; Guaygua & Roth, 2008; Huarachi Ortega, 2021; Joffre, 2020; Limachi Alcon, 2020; López Moreno & Schulmeyer, 2018; Martínez Raya & Alfaro Urquiola, 2019; Pelliza de Trigo, 1989; Roth, 2020; Roth & Exeni, 2010; Roth & Gonzáles, 2019, 2021; Sologuren & Gómez, 2008; Videa, 2017). We do not have information on the use of the few tests developed in the country or whether psychologists take these publications into account beyond the handful of professionals directly involved with them in the academic field.

Finally, through searches in virtual libraries and online, we identified three books related to assessment, two published in La Paz: *Ch'iki: Conception and Development of Intelligence in Quechua Preschool Children from the Titikachi Community*

(Romero, 1994) and *School Maturity Assessment Battery for Children Aged 5 to 7 Years* (Paniagua, 2011)*; and* one published in Santa Cruz, *Kinetic Family Drawing: Its Usefulness in Identifying High-Conflict Families* (Schulmeyer, 2013a, 2013b).

Use of Psychological Tests and Attitudes Toward Psychometric Testing

To gather information on the use of tests, assessment practices, and the attitudes of Bolivian psychologists toward psychometric tests, data were collected through a questionnaire administered to 238 psychologists and interviews with 44 psychologists in various departments of the country. Research on the professional activities of psychologists is uncommon, and obtaining participation from colleagues was very difficult, even with the support of the presidents of the departmental professional associations and psychologist friends from different regions. However, this is not unique to our profession. In general, in the country, people are reluctant to complete online instruments.[3] On this occasion, in order to obtain responses from 238 psychologists ($e = 0.06$), after months of distributing the questionnaire virtually, it was necessary to collect data in written form across seven departments of the country. Despite all efforts, a representative sample was not achieved, and 43% of the responses came from psychologists in the department of Santa Cruz, 13% from Chuquisaca, 12% from La Paz, 6% from Cochabamba, 5% from Tarija, 3% from Potosí, and 1% from Beni (we couldn't get information from Pando and Oruro). As this is a small, incidental sample that does not represent the entire population of psychologists in Bolivia, the data obtained should be considered a preliminary approximation to a reality that requires further investigation.

This sample consisted of psychologists with a mean age of 36.46 years ($SD = 9.59$), 62% ($n = 144$) were women, 25% ($n = 60$) were men, and the remainder did not respond. Of the total, 49.2% ($n = 125$) were all-but-thesis (ABT) graduates and 50.8% ($n = 121$) held a licentiate degree. In Bolivia, students must complete and defend a thesis to be awarded a licentiate degree; therefore, there is a low graduation rate. Since there has been no law regulating the professional practice of psychologists, ABTs have been allowed to work in the field. For this reason, they were included in the sample. Among those with a licentiate degree, the mean number of years since graduation was 9.3 years (SD = 6.67), 24.8% ($n = 59$) held a specialization, 63.0% ($n = 26.5$) a master's degree, and 1.7% ($n = 4$) a doctorate.[4]

[3] To collect data in a previous study, more than 100,000 emails were sent and 285 participants from the general population were obtained. This situation only improved during the COVID quarantine; in the post-COVID period, the usual resistance returned.

[4] This proportion of people with Master's and Doctoral degrees does not reflect the reality of the country, but it is to be expected that individuals with higher levels of education are more open to supporting research efforts.

The main areas of practice among the psychologists who completed the questionnaire were Clinical and Health Psychology, School Psychology, Work and Organizational Psychology, and Legal Psychology, listed in order of prevalence. Many also work in Higher Education, as university teaching is often a complementary activity. It should be noted that psychologists were first included in the National Health System in 2014 (Schulmeyer, 2015), and even now, relatively few work within it. Since then, efforts have been made to make the presence of psychologists mandatory in the national education system. To date, however, only private schools employ one or more full-time psychologists on staff. Notably, the psychologists' areas of training align closely with their areas of professional practice: clinical training is primarily provided at the undergraduate level, while the other areas are typically covered through postgraduate courses.

Most Commonly Used Instruments

Sixty-seven percent of psychologists reported using assessment instruments in their professional practice. The list of instruments mentioned is extensive (>50), but the two most frequently cited instruments were the *Person in the Rain* and the *Bender Visual-Motor Gestalt Test*. Among the projective tests mentioned at least three times were: the *Human Figure Drawing* test (HFD), the *House-Tree-Person* test (HTP), the Draw-a-*Family* test (DAF), and the *Lüscher Color Test*. Among the objective tests, those available in paper-and-pencil format or free online were most prominent: the *Situational Personality Questionnaire* (SPQ), the 16 Personality Factor Questionnaire (16PF), the *DISC,* Raven's *Progressive Matrices*, and the *Myers-Briggs Type Indicator* (MBTI). Table 3.2 presents a sample of the most commonly used instruments, listing those that psychologists report using most frequently.

In the interviews, psychologists mentioned 16 projective tests, with the *Person in the Rain* test cited most frequently, along with other graphic tests. However, they gave greater prominence to the *Thematic Apperception Test* (TAT) and the *Rorschach* than the respondents to the questionnaire did. Among objective tests, they highlighted the *Minnesota Multiphasic Personality Inventory (*MMPI), *Millon Index of Personality Styles* (MIPS), and the *16PF*, although their use in practice is limited (Schulmeyer & Piotrowski, 2017). The interviews also revealed that psychologists in clinical and health practice rely primarily or exclusively on the interview.

Attitudes Toward Tests

When evaluating psychologists' attitudes toward the use of psychometric tests ($n = 138$), 73% were in complete agreement that testing should be restricted to qualified psychologists. Sixty-nine percent indicated that, if used correctly, tests are very helpful. Sixty-three percent strongly agreed that the use of testing must be legislated

Table 3.2 List of tests ranked first in frequency of use

Personality
16PF (Sixteen Personality Factor Questionnaire)
SPQ (Situational Personality Questionnaire)
IPDE (International Personality Disorder Examination)
DISC Personality Profile
MBTI (Myers-Briggs Type Indicator)
MMPI (Minnesota Multiphasic Personality Inventory)
Intelligence and Development
Battelle Developmental Inventory
DAT-5 (Differential Aptitude Tests)
EDM (Differential Memory Assessment)
Raven's Progressive Matrices
Bender-Gestalt Visual-Motor Test
WAIS-III (Wechsler Adult Intelligence Scale, 3rd Ed.)
WPPSI (Wechsler Preschool and Primary Scale of Intelligence)
WISC (Wechsler Intelligence Scale for Children)
Clinical Aspects and Others
CSI (Coping Strategy Inventory/Coping Questionnaire)
Piers-Harris Self-Concept Scale
MCMI (Millon Clinical Multiaxial Inventory)
BAI (Beck Anxiety Inventory)
IPDE (DSM-IV Module)
PAEE (Critical Thinking Assessment)
CHASIDE Vocational Guidance Test

and regulated. Fifty-nine percent considered tests useful only if complemented with other sources of information, and 57% believed that training should include courses on the construction of psychological tests.

When presented with a series of issues related to the use of psychometric tests, we identified four aspects considered problematic by at least half of the psychologists. Sixty-two percent view ignoring contextual, cultural, and other factors that affect test validity as a frequent or very frequent problem. Fifty-three percent of psychologists consider the inability to consult with other psychologists about their assessments a frequent or very frequent problem, and 50% see the use of photocopies and the administration of tests by unqualified individuals as problematic.

On the other hand, a study based on interviews with 44 psychologists in the health sector from La Paz, Chuquisaca, Cochabamba, and Santa Cruz (Schulmeyer & Piotrowski, 2017) found that their understanding of the psychometric properties of the tests they use is limited. One of the main issues highlighted was the lack of information about the quality of tests published in the country, as well as a general unawareness of their existence. Overall, the psychologists reported that their knowledge of assessment was not acquired during their academic training. Although the use of tests is influenced by university curricula and test availability, they often rely on many instruments that are not taught in the classroom.

These limitations help explain why many psychologists do not use psychometric tests in their practice. The main reasons include: a) lack of time to administer tests given their patient load (health sector), b) working with rural populations who do not speak Spanish (health and education sectors), c) not having access to preferred tests due to the cost of online instruments (organizational and educational sectors), d) lack of appropriate (adapted and validated) tests for the populations they serve, leading to distrust in the results, and e) working with children with very low reading and numeracy skills. (Bolivia has the lowest reading comprehension level in Latin America according to UNESCO, 2022.)

In the interviews, when asked whether they believed the use of projective tests would increase or decrease in the future, 48% thought it would increase because these tests help with differential diagnoses, allow for the identification of anxiety, depression, and personality states, and help complement the interview. Thirty percent of psychologists believed their use would decrease, mainly due to a lack of validity, a lack of clinical utility, and because patients already know what is expected of them in order to give socially desirable responses (Schulmeyer & Piotrowski, 2017).

When asked about the future of objective tests, 48% believed their use would increase, citing that these instruments assess all types of mental disorders, are standardized, and are usually reviewed. Fourteen percent thought their use would decrease because the tests are not suitable for the populations they serve (Schulmeyer & Piotrowski, 2017). This view is largely due to the limited schooling of some populations, particularly in rural areas, and the difficulties many people have in understanding written language or completing drawing tasks.

Challenges of Psychological Assessment in Bolivia

This book, entitled *Origins and Challenges of Psychological Assessment in Ibero-American Countries,* presents the history of psychological assessment in various Ibero-American countries. Until now, the Bolivian case has not been extensively addressed due to the scarcity of available information. Some condensed information can be found in the chapter *Psychological Assessment in South America: Perspectives from Brazil, Bolivia, Chile, and Peru* by Solange Muglia Wechsler, Marion K. Schulmeyer, Eugenia V. Vinet, and José Livia, published recently.

In Bolivia, however, there is only a single reference to the origins of psychological assessment. Via (2000) notes that in 1974, when psychometrics was still prominent in Latin America, the Bolivian Catholic University launched a Higher Technician in Psychometrics program aimed at training school counselors. This program was short-lived, closing after the graduation of its first cohort, and there are no further references to its development. Apart from this brief initiative, there is little documentation on the evolution of the field.

According to senior psychologists trained at that institution, psychometrics was seen as something largely foreign to professional psychology practice. This raises the question of whether the absence of psychometrics in current psychology training programs reflects the initial separation established at the outset of psychological education in Bolivia—a situation not observed in other countries, where psychometric content initially occupied a significant part of the psychology curriculum.

Despite the concerns outlined above, our review of new psychology program curricula revealed some efforts to strengthen assessment training. We believe that current educational processes may also benefit from expanded access to online resources, which could help reduce the knowledge gaps acknowledged by psychologists in earlier interviews (Schulmeyer & Piotrowski, 2017). However, the need for information on test construction and validation, as indicated by psychologists in our surveys, remains unmet.

A major challenge is achieving a cultural shift that enables professionals to learn how to access information through digital technology in order to stay up to date in a globalized context. In fact, in our interviews, we observed that psychologists who had received training abroad were more likely to seek ongoing professional development and demonstrated a positive attitude toward evidence-based assessment (Schulmeyer & Piotrowski, 2017).

Moreover, we believe that improvements made to the training process will have a positive impact on both research and assessment practice. Bolivia is one of the countries with the fewest publications in Latin America (Scimago, 2022), and the challenge for universities is to create the conditions for faculty and students to acquire the necessary training to increase these indicators. As we have seen, publications on assessment experiences and instrument validation have been on the rise. As the presence of indexed journals is promoted and academics become aware of the importance of generating and disseminating knowledge, they will seek to publish their research in these outlets, and this trend will continue to grow.

On the other hand, psychologists report a lack of tests adapted to the characteristics of the populations with whom they work. In this regard, as programs truly teach the theoretical and statistical foundations underlying assessment instruments, it will be possible to take on the challenge of creating tools tailored to population groups who face difficulties with written language, have low levels of schooling, and come from diverse cultural and linguistic backgrounds, thereby contributing to improved outcomes in professional practice.

The problems affecting assessment, at least in the health sector, are not limited to the lack of appropriate instruments; they are more structural in nature. The lack of financial resources allocated to public health makes it impossible to have the time and space required to conduct assessment processes with the necessary level of detail (Schulmeyer & Piotrowski, 2017). As a result, most professionals rely more on the clinical interview than on the use of any type of instrument.

However, the impact of economic constraints is present in all areas of professional practice, not just in the health sector. For instance, entrepreneurs who acquired distribution rights from international test publishers were eventually forced to close due to insufficient sales. Furthermore, Bolivian psychologists cannot afford to pay 20–40 dollars for each article they may need for research, nor to purchase access to online assessments, because, except in particular cases—such as multinational companies or private clinical practice—these costs cannot be recovered. As a result, it is common to rely on photocopied tests, restrict oneself to open-access sources, or resort to illegal means to obtain online materials. In everyday practice, many psychologists use projective techniques, which require only paper and pencil and do not depend on the examinee's reading ability. Photocopied objective tests, which can also be administered with paper and pencil, are likewise frequently used because of their minimal cost.

After reviewing the development of psychology programs and publications, we can conclude that the country is making progress in training, research publications, and assessment practice. These advances, however, coexist with significant limitations in access to resources and appropriate tools, as described above. Precisely for this reason, we consider it important to continue strengthening the training process to achieve a positive medium- and long-term impact in all areas of assessment. To this end, it is necessary to include specific courses that teach test design as well as the analysis and understanding of psychometric properties.

However, we also believe that there are aspects related to the economic inequality of our country, both in comparison to others and within its own borders, that limit training, research, publication, and professional practice opportunities in general. This makes it necessary to invest more effort and creativity to continue advancing and to accelerate progress by taking advantage of the opportunities offered by new technologies.

This brief overview of training, research, assessment practice, and the attitudes of psychologists in the country toward projective and psychometric tests likely shows that we have made less progress compared to other countries, but we face similar challenges in the field of psychological assessment.

Some issues that may surprise readers unfamiliar with the Bolivian context include: the use of instruments without information on their reliability and validity when making decisions about individuals; the use of tests and materials without respecting copyright (through photocopying, for example); or the possibility of practicing psychology without being formally licensed. These situations arise both from gaps in professional knowledge and the extreme economic limitations faced by many families, as well as from the health, education, and labor systems in general. These issues raise profound ethical questions that go beyond the scope of this chapter but represent significant challenges. Among them is the need for a legal framework for professional practice that sensibly regulates these aspects.

References

Aguilar, G. (1983). Historia de la Psicología en Bolivia. *Revista Latinoamericana de Psicología, 15*(3), 311–325.

Alfaro Urquiola, A. L. (2020). Validación del Cuestionario de Violencia en el Noviazgo (CUVINO-R) en una muestra de jóvenes paceños. *Ajayu, 18*(1), 102–120. https://doi.org/10.35319/ajayu.181230

Alonso, M., & Eagly, A. (1997). *Psicología en las Américas*. Sociedad Interamericana de Psicología.

Aponte Daza, V., Ponce, F. A., Aráoz Cutipa, R., & Pinto, B. (2022). Validez interna y externa del Cuestionario Breve de Afrontamiento al Estrés (COPE-28) en cuidadores informales. *Ajayu, 20*(1), 1–21.

Calderón, R. (1999). La psicología en Bolivia. In M. Alonso (Ed.), *Psicología en las Américas* (pp. 47–65). Sociedad Interamericana de Psicología.
Carrillo Mamani, H. D., & Hidalgo Maynaza, V. (2021). Validación de escala de predicción del riesgo de feminicio con base en la identificación de violencia grave en la pareja. *Compás Empresarial, 11* , 5–39. https://doi.org/10.52428/20758960.v11i33.152
Franco Jiménez, G. (2017). Análisis psicométrico de la Escala GFranco Eutanasia. *Revista de Estudiantes de Psicología*, 36–44.
Gómez Tellez, N. (2016). Historia del Internet en Bolivia. In E. Quiroz (Ed.), *Bolivia Digital. 15 miradas acerca de Internet y sociedad en Bolivia* (pp. 31–59). Vicepresidencia del Estado, PNUD.
Guarachi Ramos, R. (2016). Diferencias en los valores percentilares de las pruebas de verificación diagnóstica. *Revista de Investigación Sicentia, 5*(1), 3–13.
Guaygua, M., & Roth, E. (2008). Desarrollo y Adaptación del Inventario de Situaciones Sociales (ISS): Validación Factorial, de Criterio y Cálculo de Confiabilidad. *Ajayu, 6*, 207–230.
Guzmán de Rojas, C. (2013). Evaluación neuropsicológica de los procesos cognitivos en la epilepsia. *Ajayu, 11*(2), 193–227.
Huarachi Ortega, V. (2021). Validez del test de matrices progresivas escala coloreada de Raven en estudiantes de 6 a 11 años. *Warisata. Revista de Educación, 3*(7), 10–27.
Joffre, B. (2020). Manual de la escala de actitudes hacia el consumo de tabaco (EACT). *Revista de Estudiantes de Psicología, 8*, 47–57.
Limachi Alcón, M. (2020). Evaluación del desarrollo madurativo en niños de 4-5 años en etapa preescolar. *Investigación Psicológica, 24*, 109–119.
López Moreno, A., & Schulmeyer, M. (2018). Validación de la Escala de Satisfacción con la Vida de Diener en población boliviana. *Boletín Tesape Arandu, 34*, 7–12.
Martínez Raya, G. D., & Alfaro Urquiola, A. L. (2019). Validación de la escala de autoestima de Rosenberg en estudiantes paceños. *Fides et Ratio, 17*, 83–99.
Mesa, J., Gisbert, T., & Mesa, C. (2007). *Historia de Bolivia* (6th ed.). Editorial Gisbert.
Paniagua, M. (2011). *Batería de evaluación de la madurez escolar para niños de 5 a 7 años*. Universidad La Salle de La Paz.
Pelliza de Trigo, M. (1989). Standarización del Test de Matrices Progresivas Escala General – J.C. Raven. *Runayay, 2*, 53–67. https://iifhce.hum.umss.edu.bo/publicaciones/revistas?page=2.
Peredo, R. (2000). Reflexiones y criterios sobre el diagnóstico psicológico en niños. *Revista de Ciencia y Cultura, 8*, 141–151.
Rodrigo Mendizábal, N., Cordero Altamirano, A., Fernández Reyes, C., Antezana Cavero, M., Pérez Arce, J., & Hidalgo Maynaza, V. (2021). Medición del Desarrollo Moral en los estudiantes de primer, quinto y séptimo semestre de 5 carreras de la Univalle, Sede La Paz – Bolivia, en la Gestión 1 – 2019:Una aplicación de la prueba Defining Issues Test (DIT), de Kohlberg y Test de Reacción Valorat. *Compás Empresarial, 11*(32), 120–142. https://doi.org/10.52428/20758960.v11i32.65
Romero, R. (1994). *Ch'iki concepción y desarrollo de la inteligencia en niños quechua preescolares de la comunidad de Titikachi*. Editorial Garza Azul.
Roth, E. (2020). Spanish adaptation and validation of the Zoll & Enz's Empathy Questionnaire in Bolivian children. *Ajayu, 18*(1), 52–77.
Roth, E., & Exeni, S. B. (2010). Exploración de la validez y la confiabilidad del instrumento de la Medición de la Disposición de CAmbio en Fumadores Habituales. *Ajayu, 8*(2).
Roth, E., & Gonzáles, F. (2019). *Adaptación boliviana de la escala sentir y pensar de Garton y Gringart para la medición de la empatía en niños*. Working Papers. Unidad de Investigación Experimental, 3.
Roth, E., & Gonzáles, F. O. (2021). Medición de la empatía en niños bolivianos: Adaptación y validación de la Escala "Sentir y Pensar" de Garton y Gringart. *Ajayu, 20*(2), 222–241. https://doi.org/10.35319/ajayu.202107
Sainz, P. (2009). *Actitudes del profesorado con respecto al uso de Tecnología de la información Comunicación en la Enseñanza Superior*. Tesis de Maestría del Master TIC en Educación. Análisis y diseño de procesos, recursos y prácticas formativas. Universidad de Salamanca.

Salgado Sandoval, R. (2022). Experiencia de evaluación de las habilidades socioemocionales para alumnos de primaria desde un enfoque socioformativo. *Revista Boliviana de Educación, 4*(7), 20–30.
Schulmeyer, M. K. (2013a). 20 años de Psicología en las Universidades Privadas de Bolivia. *Ajayu, 11*(2), 118–137.
Schulmeyer, M. K. (2013b). *Dibujo Kinético de la Familia. Su utilidad en la identificación de familias conflictivas*. Universidad Privada de Santa Cruz de la Sierra.
Schulmeyer, M. K. (2014a). Carreras de Psicología y formación profesional en Bolivia. In T. Caycho (Ed.), *Ensayos sobre Historias de la Psicología en Latinoamérica*. Fondo Editorial Universidad Inca Garsilaso de la Vega.
Schulmeyer, M. K. (2014b). Desarrollo de la psicología en Bolivia: Formación, investigación y asociación. In G. Salas (Ed.), *Historia de la Psicología en América del Sur. Diálogos y perspectivas* (pp. 41–64). Nueva Miranda Ediciones.
Schulmeyer, M. K. (2015). La Psicología en Bolivia: formación y situación laboral. *informaciópsicológica, 109*, 3–18. https://doi.org/10.14635/IPSIC.2015.109.3
Schulmeyer, M. K. (2016). La formación en evaluación psicologica en Carreras de Psicología de Bolivia. *Interamerican Journal of Psychology, 50*(2), 288–300.
Schulmeyer, M. K., & Piotrowski, C. (2017). Assesment practices of psychologists in the Mental Health System in Bolivia. *Journal of Projective Psychology & Mental Health, 24*, 116–132.
Schulmeyer, M. K., López, G., & Ortuño, A. (2013). Formación e investigación psicométrica en Bolivia. *PSICENCIA. Revista Latinoamericana de Investigación Psicológica, 5*(2), 123–129.
Scimago. (2022). *SCImago Journal & Country Rank*. https://www.scimagojr.com/countryrank.php
Sologuren, L., & Gómez, J. (2008). Adaptación del Cuestionario de Interacción Social (Ciso-A). *Ajayu, 6*(1), 96–122.
Soraide Castedo, L. (2022). Intrumento de valoración de la pertinencia de la planificación y ejecución de proyectos formativos que utilizan el método Kolb. *Revista Ciencia & Sociedad, 2*(1), 1–17.
Taboada, R., & Pinto, B. (2018). Evaluación neuropsicológica en dos niños con trastorno por déficit de atención e hiperactividad. Estudios de caso. *Ajayu, 16*(1), 81–121.
UNESCO. (21 de abril de 2022). *La UNESCO publica diagnóstico de aprendizajes de estudiantes bolivianos y llama a abordar las desigualdades en el sistema educativo*. UNESCO. https://www.unesco.org/es/articles/la-unesco-publica-diagnostico-de-aprendizajes-de-estudiantes-bolivianos-y-llama-abordar-las
United Nations Development Programme. (2022). *Human Development Report 2021/2022. Uncertain times, unsettled lives: Shaping our future in a transforming world*. UNDP.
Velasco, C. (2008). El psicodiagnostico en la formación del psicólogo clínico cognitivo comportamental. *Fides et Ratio, 2*, 79–85.
Via Orellana, F. (2000). Historia y formación del psicólogo en Bolivia. *Revista Ciencia y Cultura, 8*, 51–62.
Videa, P. (2017). Propiedades psicométricas del test de madurez mental de California. *Investigación Psicológica, 17*, 11–28.
Wile, M., & Vargas, B. (2010). Escala de comportamiento para madres y padres con niños pequeños. *Fides et Ratio, 4*, 69–86.

Chapter 4
The Development of Psychological Assessment in Brazil: Actions, Perspectives, and Challenges

Solange Muglia Wechsler, Ana Paula Porto Noronha, and Makilim Nunes Baptista

Historical Perspective on the Use of Tests in Brazil

Psychological tests began in Brazil at the end of the nineteenth century, influenced by the European movement in the field of individual assessment, particularly by the Wundt Laboratory in Leipzig, Germany (Angelini, 1995). The late 1940s saw the widespread recognition of the importance of tests in educational, clinical, and personal assessment, when various institutions were organized (Pasquali, 2010). Examples include the creation of the *Institute of Selection and Professional Guidance* [(ISOP]—Instituto de Seleção e Orientação Profissional) and the scientific journal Brazilian Psychotechnic Archives (Arquivos Brasileiros de Psicotécnica*)*, which featured publications on psychological tests, later renamed Brazilian Psychology Archives (Arquivos Brasileiros de Psicologia, Pessoti, 1988).

The period between 1950 and 1960 was highly productive for psychological testing in the country, especially in the areas of vocational guidance and professional selection (Pfromm Netto, 1996). Funding from state agencies, such as *the National Service for Commercial Learning* ([SENAC]—Serviço Nacional de Aprendizagem Comercial) *and the Industrial Social Service* ([SESI]—Serviço Social Industrial), was crucial in supporting the development of specific intelligence and personality tests, which continued to be used for many years (e.g., the G-36 and the PMK). In

S. Muglia Wechsler (✉)
Pontificia Universidade Catolica de Campinas, Campinas, São Paulo, Brazil
e-mail: wechsler@puc-campinas.edu.br

M. N. Baptista
Pontifical Catholic University of Campinas, São Paulo, Brazil
e-mail: makilim.nunes@puc-campinas.edu.br

A. P. P. Noronha
São Francisco University, Campinas, São Paulo, Brazil
e-mail: ana.noronha@usf.edu.br

S. V. Pugliese et al. (eds.), *Origins and Challenges of Psychological Assessment in Ibero-American Countries*, https://doi.org/10.1007/978-3-032-21380-8_4

1962, the legal regulation of the psychology profession was established (Law No. 4.119/62), which declared the use of psychological tests to be the exclusive domain of psychologists. At this time, the *National Traffic Board* ([COTRAN—Conselho Nacional de Transito) also began to require the mandatory "psychotechnical examination," which greatly expanded the use of psychological tests in the field of traffic, a requirement that persists to this day despite ongoing criticism of this process (Wechsler et al., 2014, 2019).

Beginning in the 1970s, a second period of approximately 20 years began, during which tests were not considered sufficiently important to warrant financial and professional investment, and the study and application of psychological tests became trivialized (Alchieri & Cruz, 2003). Significant criticism arose from both scientists and society at large, as it became apparent that the tests had not been developed or adapted for Brazilian culture, leading to the view that they could not effectively measure Brazilians' cognitive and personality traits (Alves, 2009). As a result, Brazilian tests, or their adaptations to national standards, were unavailable for a long time (Hutz, 2009). The effort to address this situation came from researchers in the field of psychological assessment, as well as support from the representative professional body, Federal Council of Psychology ([CFP]—Conselho Federal de Psicologia), thus initiating a third period marked by significant development in the field, as will be detailed in the following section.

The Development of the Field of Psychological Assessment

Concerns about the quality of psychological assessment in the country were also present among the boards of the Regional and Federal Psychology Councils. In 1980–1981, the Regional Psychology Council-01, in Brasília, organized meetings to define a policy aimed at developing the field of testing through the involvement of renowned researchers (Pasquali, 2010). This topic also gained prominence at Psychology congresses, reflecting ethical concerns about the quality of results from psychological tests that were inadequate for the country's context.

Thus, on October 25, 1997, during the XVII Annual Meeting of the Brazilian Society of Psychology, a proposal was made by researchers in the field to establish *the Brazilian Institute for Assessment and Research in Psychology* ([IBAPP]—Instituto Brasileiro de Avaliação e Pesquisa em Psicologia), later renamed the *Brazilian Institute of Psychological Assessment* ([IBAP]—Instituto Brasileiro de Avaliação Psicológica], 2022a). The purpose of founding IBAP was therefore to promote the development of the field of psychological assessment and to represent it in organizations and institutions related to professional practice in Psychology. This interest encompasses a range of areas, including the development and validation of techniques and procedures, training, postgraduate education, research, and publication. The first president of IBAP was Dr. Luiz Pasquali, and the vice president was Dr. Solange Wechsler. The other two authors of this chapter also served as presidents of IBAP in subsequent administrations.

The founding of IBAP was a milestone in the growth of the field of psychological assessment from both scientific and professional perspectives, as contributions had been scarce and had negligible impact on professional training prior to this (Wechsler et al., 2022). In 2022, IBAP celebrates its 25th anniversary, with an extensive history of initiatives that have shaped psychological assessment in Brazil. It is also noteworthy that IBAP has organized 11 national congresses to date, in different locations across the country, with more than 1000 participants, and these events have featured a growing number of studies on the adaptation and/or validation of psychological tests for our context (Instituto Brasileiro de Avaliação Psicológica, 2022b).

In 2001, IBAP launched the journal *Avaliação Psicológica* (Psychological Assessment), the first specialized journal on the subject in Brazil, with free access. This journal continues to this day with its twentieth volume and quarterly publication index. It is indexed in national, Latin American, and international reference databases, including electronic journals in Psychology (PEPSIC), the Regional Online Information System for Scientific Journals from Latin America, the Caribbean, Spain, and Portugal (LATINDEX), and SCOPUS. Since its inception, the journal Psychological *Assessment* (Avaliação Psicológica) became a vital source for disseminating scientific publications in the field, with its quality recognized at the highest level of scientific classification in the country, as A1 in QUALIS-CAPES. At this time, IBAP also joined the *International Testing Commission* (ITC) and produced its first newsletter in the field.

The Leading Role of the Advisory Committee on Psychological Assessment (CCAP) and the System for the Assessment of Psychological Tests (SATEPSI)

A significant boost for the field of psychological assessment came from the support of the professional body, the Federal Council of Psychology ([CFP], Conselho Federal de Psicologia). Concerned about the number of complaints regarding the misuse of practices involving tests, the CFP established an expert committee called the *Advisory Committee on Psychological Assessment* ([CCAP]—Comissão Consultiva em Avaliação Psicológica). The establishment of the CCAP was a decisive factor in the country's field development (see Baptista et al., 2011; Bueno & Peixoto, 2018; Noronha & Reppold, 2010; Primi, 2010; Wechsler et al., 2019; Zanini et al., 2021, among others).

The first CCAP was established in 2001 to evaluate test quality and provide technical guidance to address societal concerns. Initially, the CCAP was composed of invited psychologists, that is, those who were not part of the Council system and who had recognized expertise in psychological tests. Currently, due to increased demand for testing evaluations, the CCAP comprises eight psychologists, all of whom hold doctoral degrees.

However, it was not until 2017 that the CFP issued regulations defining the criteria for joining the CCAP and the tasks assigned to its members. In addition, the CCAP's functions included to elaborate drafting documents and regulations, to prepare technical reports on testing, and to advise the CFP on advancing the field. Approximately 30 members have served on the CCAP. Considering that all of them were professors in the field of Psychological Assessment, it is possible to infer the historical significance of the area over a period of less than 20 years.

According to Noronha et al. (2004), the CFP has contributed, over the last decades, with initiatives to create spaces for dialogue with the scientific community to resolve impasses in the field. For example, in 1980, it appointed a *National Commission on Psychological Tests* (Comissão Nacional de Testes Psicológicos), which was reestablished in 1986. In 1997, the CFP appointed the *Interinstitutional Chamber of Psychological Assessment*—CCAP (Câmara Interinstitucional de Avaliação Psicológica) to propose actions in response to the veto by the then President of the Republic, which prohibited the psychological assessment of drivers. The presidential veto was later overturned.

Recalling other relevant historical achievements, specifically those of the CCAP, can be verified at the website (https://satepsi.cfp.org.br/docs/LinhadotempoWeb.pdf). After defining the criteria for test evaluation and the systematic process of submission and analysis, which took place from 2001 to 2003, the CCAP began to evaluate tests, with the support of external reviewers, and to disseminate information about their quality through the SATEPSI online portal (Conselho Federal de Psicologia, 2022). Thus, the test evaluation process began to be conducted by anonymous peers, similar to the process for scientific articles (Primi & Nunes, 2010).

In this context, in light of the recommendations from the First National Forum on Psychological Assessment in 2000, the CFP drafted a document (Resolution 025/2001) defining the minimum criteria that tests must meet to be approved for professional use. This Resolution was based on the standards of international organizations, including the *International Test Commission (2001),* the *American Educational Research Association, the American Psychological Association,* and the *National Council on Measurement* (1999). CCAP revised this Resolution and established five criteria as minimum and mandatory requirements for psychological instruments (Conselho Federal de Psicologia, 2018), which should be included in psychological test manuals:

1. Presentation of theoretical foundations, with special emphasis on the definition of the constructs assessed by the test.
2. Definition of the objectives of the testing context and application, detailing the target population.
3. Presentation of empirical evidence regarding the technical characteristics of test items in a Brazilian sample, except for projective/expressive methods.
4. Presentation of empirical evidence of validity and estimates of the accuracy of interpretations for test results, specifying the procedures adopted with Brazilian samples.
5. Presentation of the scoring and interpretation system, explaining the underlying logic of the procedure, which may be:
   (a) For objectively scored tests, it must be referenced to Brazilian norms.

(b) For projective tests, as opposed to norm-referenced interpretation, the authors must present the theoretical background as well as the logic of the interpretation.

This Resolution also specified that studies on the validity, accuracy, and norms of psychological tests would have a maximum period of 15 years, counted from the date of approval of the psychological test by the CFP plenary.

The significant impact of the CCAP was the creation of a list of approved tests, published online by the CFP starting in 2003, called the *System for the Assessment of Psychological Tests* ([SATEPSI], Sistema de Avaliação de Testes Psicológicos, 2022). Thus, the purpose of SATEPSI is to indicate whether the test submitted for CCAP evaluation meets the scientific standards required of a psychological instrument, as described in the test manual, that is, whether it was approved according to the criteria already presented (Nunes & Primi, 2010; Primi, 2010; Reppold & Noronha, 2018). Due to the scientific rigor and accuracy of SATEPSI, this system attracted international attention and was described in a special section of the *International Journal of Testing* dedicated to the evaluation of international test review systems (Bartram, 2012; Evers, 2012), highlighting our model for South American countries (Rojas & Grisales, 2022).

An important contribution of SATEPSI to improving psychological practice is the public *online* dissemination of tests approved or disapproved by the Psychological Assessment Committee. Information on tests approved by CCAP is published on the SATEPSI website (Sistema de Avaliação dos Testes Psicológicos, 2022). In this way, psychologists became familiar with the scientific requirements for administering psychological tests. Although, in principle, the related criteria may seem obvious, it is essential to note that, in the years preceding the publication of the *Resolution*, a significant portion of test manuals lacked the necessary information on the construction process, psychometric studies, and construct definitions. The significant impact of SATEPSI on the training of psychologists should be emphasized, as stated by Noronha et al. (2010, 2013), also the improvement of psychological manuals over all these years, thus demonstrating that there was a shift in the perception of tests among psychologists and within society, contrasting with the strong critical opposition that existed previously (Reppold et al., 2017; Reppold & Noronha, 2018). In the past 15 years, the number of approved tests available to professionals has nearly quadrupled, reflecting a steady output from Brazilian researchers, according to Cardoso & Silva-Filho (2018).

Guidelines for the use of psychological tests, as well as the organization of both online and in-person meetings on psychological assessment, also originated from CCAP, thus demonstrating the progress in the field thanks to the support of the Federal Council of Psychology. The first psychological assessment guide was published in 2007 and republished in 2013, followed by a revision, with most of the material prepared by the CCAP. It compiles answers to the main questions received by the CFP through SATEPSI regarding psychological assessment and became an important reference not only for the Regional Psychology Councils but also for students in training and professionals in practice (Conselho Federal de Psicologia, 2022).

In 2010, the book *Psychological Assessment: Guidelines for the Regulation of the Profession* (Avaliação Psicológica, Diretrizes na Regulamentação da Profissão, Conselho Federal de Psicologia, 2010) was published. The work involved several professors and researchers with significant contributions to the field. The chapters addressed topics still in need of discussion, such as ethical principles, the process of test evaluation and the methods used, mandatory psychological assessments, among others. CCAP members served as editors and authored several chapters.

The year 2011 was designated the *Year of Psychological Assessment* by the CFP, marking a significant achievement in the professional, scientific, and political spheres. In this regard, psychological assessment, although recognized as professional practice, has not always been highly valued by a significant portion of psychologists. When it is established as the theme for a dedicated year, it gains the visibility necessary for its expansion. The initiative encompassed a comprehensive set of actions, including the publication of a book, the promotion of a professional award, and numerous events across all regions of the country, among other initiatives. Regarding the book, more than 20 articles were prepared, organized into three main areas: psychological assessment in institutional contexts, training in psychological assessment, and validation criteria (Conselho Federal de Psicologia, 2011).

Psychological Assessment Laboratories and Working Groups of the National Association of Graduate Studies and Research in Psychology (ANPEPP)

Researchers in Psychology have been concerned with providing scientifically sound instruments to address criticisms of psychological tests, which was the main objective behind the creation of *Psychological Assessment Research Laboratories*. Unlike the early centers of applied psychology in the country, also called "Laboratories" in the eighteenth and nineteenth centuries, which were mainly dedicated to the application of educational and psychological tests as previously mentioned, the primary focus of these research laboratories was to conduct systematic studies aimed at the development and/or adaptation of psychological tests for the country, meeting psychometric scientific criteria of validity, reliability, and population norms (Wechsler et al., 2019).

By the mid-1990s, there were four pioneering research laboratories in psychological assessment, located at major Brazilian universities: the Laboratory for Research in Assessment and Measurement ([LABPAM]—Laboratorio de Pesquisa e Avaliação) at the University of Brasília, founded in 1988 by Prof. Dr. Luiz Pasquali; the Center for Research in Psychodiagnosis ([CPP]—Centro de Investigação em Psicodiagnóstico) at the Ribeirão Preto campus of the University of São Paulo, founded in 1975 by Prof. Dr. André Jacquemin; the Laboratory of Psychological Assessment and Measurement ([LAMP], Laboratório de Avaliação e Medidas Psicológicas) at the Pontifical Catholic University in Campinas, founded in 1994 and coordinated by Prof. Dr. Solange Wechsler; and the Measurement Laboratory [(LM]—Laboratório de Medidas) at the Federal University of Rio Grande do Sul, founded in 1988 by Prof. Dr. Cláudio Hutz (Bueno & Peixoto, 2018). These laboratories and professors provided significant impetus to research and specialized training in psychological assessment in Brazil, established research lines, and played prominent roles in organizing the events and associations. By 2020, there were 69 Psychological Assessment Laboratories in universities across different regions of the country (Silva-Filho et al., 2021).

Indeed, the significant contribution to improving psychological instruments stems from the considerable increase in researchers interested in psychological assessment. There was considerable growth in the number of working groups on psychological assessment within the National Association of Graduate Studies and Research in Psychology (ANPEPP) over nearly three decades since its establishment (Cunha, 2003). The first ANPEPP working group (GT) in psychological assessment was organized by psychology researchers in 1989. It was named *Perspectives in Assessment and Diagnosis in Psychology* (Perspectivas em Avaliação e Diagnóstico em Psicologia). This group met at consecutive ANPEPP congresses under the same name until 2008, when the number of researchers required a division into two groups. In 2014, due to the number of participants, there was a need to subdivide into five working groups (GTs): Research in Psychological Assessment, Projective Methods in Psychological Assessment Contexts, Cognitive and Neuropsychological Assessment, Assessment in Positive Psychology and Creativity, and Psychological Assessment, Personality and Psychopathology (Nascimento & Vasconcelos, 2016).

Undoubtedly, the expansion of the Working Groups (GTs) exemplifies the field of psychological assessment's growth in the country. The organization of these groups has provided a scientific and even political space for the field. From a scientific and academic perspective, these groups have been organized to produce articles and books, making a significant contribution to the improvement of training and performance in the area of psychological assessment (Amaral & Verlang, 2008; Boruchovitch et al., 2012; Hutz, 2009, 2010, 2014; Noronha et al., 2006; Nunes & Primi, 2010; Vázquez & Hutz, 2018; Nakano, 2018). In turn, these groups have debated policy issues in the field and have drafted position papers on specific topics, which are subsequently submitted to the CFP.

Brazilian Institute of Psychological Assessment (IBAP) and Its Contributions

The Forum of National Entities of Brazilian Psychology ([FENPB]—Forum de Entidades Nacionais da Psicologia Brasileira) brings together several scientific associations in Psychology, among which is the Brazilian Institute of Psychological Assessment (IBAP—Instituto Brasileiro de Avaliação Psicológica), whose mission is to propose joint actions that consolidate Brazilian Psychology. IBAP has played a prominent role, being considered one of the most active and representative organizations in the field of Psychological Assessment among the 27 entities that make up the FENPB, and is frequently consulted by other entities to take a position on controversies regarding important issues such as the assessment of firefighters, pilots, firearm licensing, and others. IBAP's contributions in various aspects of training, professional practice, and research have been consolidated over the course of each administration, as evident in the timeline of its achievements (Instituto Brasileiro de Avaliação Psicológica, 2022a). Below, we highlight some of IBAP's main accomplishments during this period.

During the 2005–2007 administration, IBAP advised the Federal Council of Psychology (CFP) on the draft resolution to create the first *Specialization Course in Psychological Assessment*, which was later implemented at the University of Castelo Branco (Rio de Janeiro). This course is aimed at training professionals with greater expertise and practical knowledge. Subsequently, these courses were extended to various regions of the country, strengthening the proposal for the title of *Specialist in Psychological Assessment*, which was officially recognized only in 2019 (Conselho Federal de Psicologia, 2019). This specialty is considered one of the 13 others already recognized by the CFP.

Between 2009 and 2011, IBAP initiated the CFP-proposed *Thematic Year on Psychological Assessment* (PA), with several activities designed to advance PA in Brazil. To this end, IBAP organized cycles of debates and promoted texts written by leading authors in the field of psychological assessment in the country. A professional award was also established to recognize new talents in writing and reflection on emerging topics. IBAP also played an active role in developing the new *National Curriculum Guidelines* (DCN), with proposed actions to increase the inclusion of Psychology in Primary and Secondary Education.

During this period, IBAP launched the *Compendium of Psychological Assessment*, the first of its kind in Latin America (Baptista et al., 2019), which included 60 chapters divided into three sections covering the foundations of Psychological Assessment, practices in specific contexts, cognitive and hybrid constructs, as well as personality assessment, among other equally relevant topics in PA. Other books were published under the IBAP imprint, a mark of quality for reference books in PA in Brazil, including: P*sychological Assessment: A Guide for Professional Practice (Avaliação Psicológica, um guia para a prática professional*, Oliveira et al., 2020); *Psychological Assessment in Childhood and Adolescence* (Avaliação Psicológica na infância e na adolescência, Mansur-Alves et al., 2021); *Training and Teaching Strategies in Psychological Assessment* (Estratégias de formação e Ensino em avaliação psicológica, Oliveira et al., 2021); and *Tutorials in Data Analysis Applied to Psychometrics* (Tutoriais em análise de dados aplicados à psicometria, Faiad et al., 2021). Three additional books under this imprint are being prepared for publication during the current administration (2022–2023), focusing on Psychological Assessment in older adults, Positive Psychology, and a sequence to the book on Tutorials in Data Analysis Applied to Psychometrics.

IBAP has organized courses on assessment techniques and strategies for the professional community, always aiming to expand professionals' theoretical and technical training. Additionally, IBAP has hosted webinars for the same purpose. In recent years, a historical series of interviews has also been initiated with some of the most prominent IBAP members and professionals who have influenced IBAP policy and history, thereby contributing to the preservation of IBAP's history in Brazil (Instituto Brasileiro de Avaliação Psicológica, 2022a).

A bold and important initiative was proposed in the field to provide qualified instruments with evidence of validity for students, faculty, and researchers associated with IBAP. This initiative is the *IBAP Institutional Testing Repository* (RIT-IBAP), which aims to collect and disseminate a database of open-access instruments for unrestricted use, thereby fostering collaboration among researchers. Thus, the RIT can disseminate research instruments or items among its members. Currently, the RIT contains 16 scales from various areas and constructs, such as tests of abstract reasoning, socioemotional skills, anxiety, professional interests, character strengths, emotional regulation, satisfaction with romantic relationships, among others (Instituto Brasileiro de Avaliação Psicológica, 2022b).

Perspectives and Challenges for IBAP

It is noteworthy, both globally and in Brazil, that psychological assessment, in relation to achievement and education, had to confront the challenges posed by the COVID-19 pandemic to professional practice and training (Baptista et al., 2021). In addition, legal issues regarding the release of psychological test sales to anyone, as approved by the Supreme Court in 2021, have posed an immense challenge in defending the arguments for psychological assessment. During the pandemic, IBAP developed brochures (some in collaboration with the CFP) and specific guidelines for faculty and higher education psychologists, guiding online psychological assessment and generating handy documents in times of significant change and uncertainty (IBAP, 2022c). Indeed, various policy and advocacy initiatives in the field have been carried out throughout IBAP's existence and can be consulted in the online timeline (Instituto Brasileiro de Avaliação Psicológica, 2022a).

Even so, there are several future challenges for IBAP in the next 2 years and, perhaps, in the coming decade. Some have already been implemented but require further discussion, maturation, reformulation, and new implementations. After a difficult period of coping with the consequences of social isolation during the COVID-19 pandemic, the world will never be the same, and Psychology—more specifically, the field of psychological assessment—has faced and continues to face significant challenges.

One of the initiatives already underway in *Resolution* 09/2018 relates to justice and human rights, the non-prejudice of individual differences, color, race, sexual orientation, disabilities—in other words, the rules and processes of psychological assessment must be based on evaluating specific differences and the consequences of differentiated processes, along with specific norms. Obviously, this is a broad and controversial topic; however, it must be debated in all spheres. Even regarding territories, which are vast in Brazil both geographically and culturally, issues concerning specific norms must be widely discussed to assess the need for scales developed/modified for specific groups with proper standardization characteristics.

Another challenge will be the use and mediation of new technologies (ICT), including equivalence studies, in the development of techniques, the collection of appropriate evidence for online tests, the quality of norms, and the assessment process. Such considerations aim to ensure equity and access to these technologies for the population, as many regions of Brazil still lack private internet access, and many Brazilians lack the economic means or digital literacy to utilize these resources.

In addition to these challenges, another equally fundamental issue concerns the training of Brazilian psychologists, particularly in psychological assessment, from both the perspective of educational institutions and of student- and/or professional-initiated actions for our educational system. Therefore, concern for the technical training of these professionals must always be a constant objective for IBAP. The approval of the specialization area in psychological assessment has already been a significant step; however, there are other initiatives to consider, such as the offering of courses and certifications that IBAP could provide for basic, intermediate, and advanced training in psychological assessment, as well as for specific approved instruments.

There is also a lack of specific tests for individuals with special educational needs (Wechsler & Nakano, 2016). Many available tests are administered to children in classrooms, adolescents, or "regular" adults. To date, few tools are available to assess individuals with visual, hearing, or giftedness-related disabilities. Among the cognitive tests approved by SATEPSI, those assessing intelligence and attention predominate, highlighting the need for research in other areas of mental functioning and personality (Reppold et al., 2017).

Another possibility would be for IBAP to assist and/or complement the assessments conducted by the Advisory Commission on Psychological Assessment (CCAP), as the CCAP's work depends on the current policies of the political group that won the election, and each term lasts 3 years. Thus, there would be less dependence on policies that can be costly to achieve goals that have already been attained. Furthermore, the shared use of psychological instruments also presents a future challenge, as various professional groups may use the same scales. For example, depression scales could be used by psychologists and psychiatrists, benefiting both fields. This discussion has also begun, and a scale has already been shared between psychologists and speech therapists; other scales could also benefit from such decisions.

In general, IBAP continues to hold its biennial meetings in pursuit of improvements in the field of Psychological Assessment, always aiming to disseminate scientific information, contribute to the professional training process, and represent the field in federal, state, and professional bodies of interest to psychologists. Over the past 25 years, IBAP has been a key player in shaping important decisions in Brazilian psychology, consistently prioritizing training, ethics, and the advancement of psychological assessment in Brazil.

In summary, IBAP is a driving force, as stated by Noronha and Santos (2021) and Cardoso and Silva-Filho (2018). The establishment of SATEPSI, along with various other initiatives already thoroughly highlighted (Mansur-Alves et al., 2016), can be recognized as a significant step in the process of scientific maturation and social recognition of Psychology in Brazil. After two decades, it is readily apparent that professional practices have been vigilant regarding quality, and psychologists have sought frequent professional development. The creation of the *Specialist Title in Psychological Assessment* improved the practice of psychologists engaged in psychological assessment.

Finally, the developmental trajectory of the field of psychological assessment in the country has shown that we have faced significant challenges as well as many achievements. As we have presented, these challenges must continue to be addressed on multiple fronts, encompassing a wide range of areas such as educational policy and its effects on the training of psychologists, the publishing market and its impact on test sales, professional and ethical issues in psychological practice, the training of psychologists, and the development of national tests, among others. The history of IBAP over these 25 years has demonstrated possible pathways that may serve as a model for the development of psychological assessment in other Ibero-American countries.

References

Alchieri, J. C., & Cruz, R. M. (2003). *Avaliação psicológica: Conceito, métodos e instrumentos*. Casa do Psicólogo.

Alves, I. C. B. (2009). Reflexões sobre o ensino da avaliação psicológica na formação do psicólogo. In C. S. Hutz (Ed.), *Avanços e polêmicas em avaliação psicológica* (pp. 217–246). Casa do Psicólogo.

Amaral, A. E. V., & Werlang, B. S. (2008). *Atualizações em Métodos Projetivos para Avaliação Psicológica*. Casa do Psicólogo.

American Educational Research Association, American Psychological Association, & National Council on Measurement in Education. (1999). *Standards for Educational and Psychological Testing*. American Psychological Association.

Angelini, A. L. (1995). Abertura do I Encontro de Técnicas de Exame Psicológico: Ensino, pesquisa e aplicações. *Boletim de Psicologia, 45*(102), 9–18.

Baptista, M. N., Nunes, M. L., Reppold, C. T., Nunes, C. H. S. S., Carvalho, L. F., Primi, R., Noronha, A. P., Seabra, A. G., Wechsler, S. M., Hutz, C. S., & Pasquali, L. (2019). *Compêndio de Avaliação Psicológica*. Editora Vozes.

Baptista, M. N., Rueda, F. J. M., Castro, N. R., Gomes, J. O., & Silva, M. A. (2011). Análise de Artigos sobre Avaliação Psicológica no Contexto do Trabalho: Revisão Sistemática. *Psicologia em Pesquisa, 5*(2), 156–167.

Baptista, M. N., Scaduto, A. A., & Pinheiro, N. N. B. (2021). Avaliação Psicológica em Tempos Atuais [editorial]. *Interação em Psicologia, 25*(3). https://doi.org/10.5380/riep.v25i3.84129

Bartram, D. (2012). Concluding thoughts on the internationalization of test reviews. *International Journal of Testing, 12*(2), 195–201. https://doi.org/10.1080/15305058.2011.649869

Boruchovitch, E., Santos, A. A. A., & Nascimento, E. (2012). *Avaliação psicológica nos contextos educativos e psicossociais*. Casa do Psicólogo.

Bueno, J. M. H., & Peixoto, E. M. (2018). Avaliação Psicológica no Brasil e no mundo. *Psicologia: Ciência e Profissão, 30*(número especial), 108–121. https://doi.org/10.1590/1982-3703000208878
Cardoso, L. M., & Silva-Filho, J. H. (2018). SATEPSI e a qualidade técnica dos testes psicológicos no Brasil. *Psicologia: Ciência e Profissão, 38*(2), 40–49. https://doi.org/10.1590/1982-3703000209112
Conselho Federal de Psicologia – CFP. (2010). *Avaliação Psicológica: Diretrizes na regulamentação da profissão.* https://site.cfp.org.br/publicacao/avaliacao-psicologica-diretrizes-na-regulamentacao-da-profissao/
Conselho Federal de Psicologia – CFP. (2011). *Ano da Avaliação Psicológica.* https://anotematico.cfp.org.br/
Conselho Federal de Psicologia. (2018). *Resolução 9. Estabelece diretrizes para a avaliação psicológica.* https://www.studocu.com/pt-br/document/centro-universitario-uniateneu/aconselhamento-psicologico-e-psicoterapia-breve/resolucao-cfp-no-09-2018/23887041
Conselho Federal de Psicologia. (2019). *CFP publica resolução que torna a avaliação psicológica uma especialidade da Psicologia.* https://site.cfp.org.br/cfp-publica-resolucao-que-torna-a-avaliacao-psicologica-especialidade-da-psicologia/
Conselho Federal de Psicologia. (2022). *Cartilha de Avaliação Psicológica.* https://site.cfp.org.br/publicacao/cartilha-avaliacao-psicologica-2022/
Cunha, J. A. (2003). *Psicodiagnóstico-V.* ArtMed.
Evers, A. (2012). The internationalization of test reviewing: Trends, differences, and results. *International Journal of Testing, 12*(2), 136–156. https://doi.org/10.1080/15305058.2012.658932
Faiad, C., Baptista, M. N., & Primi, R. (2021). *Tutoriais em Análise de Dados aplicados à Psicometria.* Vozes.
Hutz, C. S. (Ed.). (2009). *Avanços em polêmicas em avaliação psicológica.* Casa Psicólogo.
Hutz, C. S. (2010). *Avanços em avaliação psicológica e neuropsicológica com crianças* (Vol. II). Casa do Psicólogo.
Hutz, C. S. (2014). *Avaliação em Psicologia Positiva.* Hogrefe.
IBAP – Instituto Brasileiro de Avaliação Psicológica. (2022a). *Linha do tempo: Ações do IBAP de 1997 a 2021.* https://www.ibapnet.org.br/o-ibap/sobre-o-ibap
IBAP – Instituto Brasileiro de Avaliação Psicológica. (2022b). *Congressos.* https://www.ibapnet.org.br/congressos-do-ibap
IBAP – Instituto Brasileiro de Avaliação Psicológica. (2022c). *Série Histórica de Entrevistas do IBAP.* https://www.ibapnet.org.br/serie-historica-de-entrevistas-do-ibap
International Test Commission. (2001). *International Guidelines for Test Use, International Journal of Testing, 1*(2), 93–114. http://dx.doi.org/10.1207/S15327574IJT0102_1
Mansur-Alves, M., Silva, R. S., & Fernandes, S. C. A. (2016). Impact of the Psychological Testing Assessment System (SATEPSI) on scientific publications in psychological assessment. *Psico-USF, 21*(1), 179–188. https://doi.org/10.1590/1413-82712016210311
Mansur-Alves, M., Muniz, M., Zanini, D. S., & Baptista, M. N. (2021). *Avaliação Psicológica na Infância e Adolescência.* Vozes.
Nakano, T. C. (2018). *Psicologia positiva aplicada à educação.* Vetor.
Nascimento, E., & Vasconcelos, A. G. (2016). O percurso da avaliação psicológica nos simpósios da ANPEPP. *Avaliação Psicológica, 15*(1), 125–128.
Noronha, A. P. P., Alchieri, J. C., & Primi, R. (2004). Parâmetros Psicométricos: uma Análise de Testes Psicológicos Comercializados no Brasil. *Psicologia Ciência e Profissão, 24*(4), 88–99. https://doi.org/10.1590/s1414-98932004000400011
Noronha, A. P., Santos, A. A. A., & Sisto, F. F. (2006). *Facetas do fazer em avaliação psicológica.* Vetor.
Noronha, A. P. P., Carvalho, L. F., Miguel, F. K., Souza, M., & Santos, A. A. (2010). Sobre o ensino de avaliação psicológica. *Avaliação Psicológica, 9*(1), 139–146.

Noronha, A. P. P., & Reppold, C. T. (2010). Considerações sobre a avaliação psicológica no Brasil. *Psicologia: Ciência e Profissão, 30*(número especial). https://doi.org/10.1590/S1414-98932010000500009

Noronha, A. P. P., Castro, N. R., Ottati, F., Barros, M. V. C., & Santana, P. R. (2013). Conteúdos e metodologias de ensino de avaliação psicológica: um estudo com professores. *Paideia, 23*(54), 129–139. https://doi.org/10.1590/1982-43272354201315

Noronha, A. P. P., & Santos, A. A. A. (2021). Histórico da formação em Avaliação Psicológica no Brasil. In K. L. Oliveira, M. Muniz, T. H. Lima, D. S. Zanini, & A. A. A. Santos (Eds.), *Formação e estratégias de ensino em Avaliação Psicológica* (pp. 13–20). Vozes.

Nunes, C. H., & Primi, R. (2010). Aspectos técnicos e conceituais da ficha de avaliação dos testes psicológicos. In A. D. Santos, A. A. Anache, A. D. Villemor-Amaral, B. S. G. Werlang, C. T. Reppold, C. H. S. S. Nunes, & R. Primi (Eds.), *Avaliação Psicológica: Diretrizes na regulamentação da profissão* (pp. 101–128). Conselho Federal de Psicologia.

Oliveira, K. L., Schelini, P. W., & Barroso, S. M. (2020). *Avaliação Psicológica: guia para a prática profissional*. Editora Vozes.

Oliveira, K. L., Muniz, M., Lima, T. H., Zanini, D. S., & Santos, A. (2021). *Formação e Estratégias de Ensino em Avaliação Psicológica*. Editora Vozes.

Pasquali, L. (2010). Histórico dos instrumentos psicológicos. In L. Pasquali (Ed.), *Instrumentação psicológica: Fundamentos e Práticas* (pp. 11–47). Artes Médicas.

Pessoti, I. (1988). Notas para uma história da psicologia brasileira. In Conselho Federal de Psicologia (Ed.), *Quem é o psicólogo brasileiro* (pp. 17–31). Edicon.

Pfromm Netto, S. (1996). Pioneiros da Psicologia Escolar: Mira y López. *Psicologia Escolar e Educacional, 1*(1), 87–88. https://doi.org/10.1590/S1413-85571996000100015

Primi, R. (2010). Avaliação Psicológica no Brasil: Fundamentos, Situação Atual e Direções para o Futuro. *Psicologia: Teoria e Pesquisa, 26*(número especial), 25–35. https://doi.org/10.1590/S0102-37722010000500003

Primi, R., & Nunes, C. H. S. S. (2010). O SATEPSI: propostas de aprimoramento. In Conselho Federal de Psicologia (CFP) (Ed.), *Avaliação Psicológica: Diretrizes na regulamentação da profissão* (pp. 129–148). Conselho Federal de Psicologia.

Reppold, C. T., Serafini, A. J., Ramires, D. A., & Gurgel, L. G. (2017). Análise dos manuais psicológicos aprovados pelo SATEPSI para avaliação de crianças e adolescentes no Brasil. *Avaliação Psicológica, 16*(1), 19–28. https://doi.org/10.15689/ap.2017.1601.03

Reppold, C. T., & Noronha, A. P. (2018). Impacto dos 15 anos do SATEPSI na avaliação psicológica brasileira. *Psicologia, Ciência e Profissão, 38*(número especial), 6–15. https://doi.org/10.1590/1982-3703000208638

Rojas, A. N. H., & Grisales, F. A. L. (2022). Desarrollo del instrumento para evaluar la calidad técnica de pruebas psicológicas. *Revista Colombiana de Psicología, 31*(2), 65–76. https://doi.org/10.15446/rcp.v31n2.93018

Silva-Filho, J. H., Martins, H. A., & Silva, A. G. B. (2021). *Catálogo dos laboratórios de avaliação psicológica no Laboratório de Avaliação Psicológica*. UFAM, Editora Nila Press.

Sistema de Avaliação dos Testes Psicológicos-SATEPSI. (2022). *Testes favoráveis*. https://satepsi.cfp.org.br/testesFavoraveis.cfm

Vazquez, A. C., & Hutz, C. S. (Eds.). (2018). *Aplicações da psicologia positiva: Trabalho e organizações*. Hogrefe.

Wechsler, S. M., Oakland, T., Leon, C., Vivas, E., Almeida, L., Franco, A., Pérez-Solis, M., & Contini, N. (2014). Test development and use in five Iberian Latin American countries. *International Journal of Psychology, 49*(4). https://doi.org/10.1002/ijop.12068

Wechsler, S. M., & Nakano, T. C. (2016). Cognitive assessment of Brazilian children: Past, present perspectives and challenges. *International Journal of School and Educational Psychology, 4*(4), 215–224. https://doi.org/10.1080/21683603.2016.1163654

Wechsler, S. M., Hutz, C. S., & Primi, R. (2019). O desenvolvimento da avaliação psicológica no Brasil: Avanços históricos e desafios. *Avaliação Psicológica, 18*(2), 121–128. https://doi.org/10.15689/ap.2019.1802.15466.02

Wechsler, S. M., Schulmeyer, M. K., Vinet, E. V., & Livia, J. (2022). Psychological assessment in South America: Perspectives from Brazil, Bolivia, Chile, and Peru. In S. Layer (Ed.), *International histories of psychological assessment* (pp. 295–323). Cambridge University Press. https://doi.org/10.1017/9781108755078

Zanini, D. S., Reppold, C. T., Muniz, M., Noronha, A. P. P., & Rueda, F. J. M. (2021). Por que regulamentar o uso e acesso aos testes psicológicos? *Avaliação Psicológica, 20*(3), 390–399. https://doi.org/10.15689/ap.2021.2003.22437.13

Chapter 5
Origins and Challenges of Psychological Assessment in Chile

Eugenia V. Vinet and Marcela Alejandra Rodríguez-Cancino

Historical Context of Psychological Assessment in Chile

In a concise historical synthesis, Salas and Lizama (2009) and Urzúa et al. (2015) place the beginnings of psychology in Chile in 1889, with the establishment of the Pedagogical Institute at the University of Chile, which forged a close link between psychology and educational improvement. The origins of psychology in Chile are also associated with the works "Origins of Sensations" and "Applied Psychology" by Schneider and Villalobos in 1890 (Calderón, 2000).

The following events are highlighted in the accounts of Salas and Lizama (2009) and Urzúa et al. (2015): 1) the creation of the country's first experimental psychology laboratory at the Normal School of Copiapó in 1905; 2) the establishment of the Psychology Laboratory at the University of Chile in 1908; 3) the founding of the Institute of Psychology at the University of Chile in 1941; 4) the introduction of formal psychology training in the country (Decree 1023) in 1946; 5) the launch of the first Special Psychology Course at the University of Chile in 1947, which, according to Ligüeño and Parra (2007), was the first undergraduate psychology program in Latin America; and 6) the creation of the School of Psychology at the Pontificia Universidad Católica de Chile in 1954.

In its early period, Chilean psychology was marked by the measurement and assessment of intellectual processes. In 1905, at the experimental psychology laboratory of the Normal School of Copiapó, the first attempts were made to measure intelligence, physical endurance, and intellectual vigor, following the structuralist guidelines of Wundt (Urzúa et al., 2015).

Between 1925 and 1928, the Ministry of Public Instruction, now the Ministry of Education, commissioned Professor Luis Tirapegui to develop the

E. V. Vinet · M. A. Rodríguez-Cancino (✉)
Department of Psychology, Universidad de La Frontera, Temuco, Chile
e-mail: eugenia.vinet@ufrontera.cl; marcela.rodriguez@ufrontera.cl

S. V. Pugliese et al. (eds.), *Origins and Challenges of Psychological Assessment in Ibero-American Countries*, https://doi.org/10.1007/978-3-032-21380-8_5

Binet-Simon method for the mass measurement of intelligence in Chilean children (Moretti, 2018). In 1944, the Institute of Psychology at the University of Chile created the "Psychology Archives," which served as a platform for publications related to test adaptation (Calderón, 2000). Among the earliest studies were Grassau's work on the Binet Test and Bernales' research on the Terman intelligence test. Additionally, the first Special Psychology Course at the University of Chile included a course on test construction and application (Salas, 2014). In the 1950s, in the city of Concepción, "Mental Measurements" was a required subject in teacher training, alongside courses such as "Educational Psychology" and "Adolescent Psychology" (Urzúa et al., 2015). All of this, as Bravo (2004) notes, reflects the importance of psychometrics in the early days of Chilean psychology, when new professionals needed valid instruments for their work. On the other hand, Bravo (2004, 2013) also highlights that for approximately 25 years, the country's two psychology schools had distinct orientations. At the University of Chile, the experimental and positivist perspective predominated, while at the Pontificia Universidad Católica, the phenomenological and psychoanalytic, and later the behaviorist, approaches prevailed, creating a balance in the initial training of psychologists.

In the early 1960s, the Pontificia Universidad Católica developed several studies focused on the Piagetian model of development. In 1962, studies also began on adaptation and standardization of the Wechsler intelligence tests, establishing a research tradition that continues to this day. This was complemented, in the field of personality assessment, by the first studies of the Minnesota Multiphasic Personality Inventory (MMPI) (Bravo, 2004; Villegas & Rodríguez, 2007). At the same time, the University of Chile resumed publication of its journal under the name "Archives of the Central Institute of Psychology," where psychological tests became one of the main topics for submitted works (Ligüeño & Parra, 2007). By 1969, approximately 42% of undergraduate psychology theses were focused on the adaptation and validation of tests, following the Latin American trend of concentrating psychological research in the area of psychometrics (Urzúa, 2008).

In the 1970s, the University of Chile became notable for its work with projective tests, with particular emphasis on developments related to the Rorschach Test (Villegas & Rodríguez, 2007). By this time, psychology in Chile had become a "mature" and diverse discipline, officially recognized as a profession in 1968 with the creation of the Chilean College of Psychologists, which was granted legal authority to oversee professional practice. The breakdown of Chile's institutional framework in 1973, followed by the period of military dictatorship (1973–1981), had a significant impact on Chilean psychology and on Psychological Assessment in particular.

At the end of the dictatorship, in 1981, the General Law of Chilean Universities was enacted, restructuring the few existing universities in the country and allowing for the creation of new university institutions. These new institutions were primarily private, multifunctional, and polyvalent, aiming to offer as many degree programs as possible, often with little formalization (Didier, 2014) and/or without mechanisms to certify that they met minimum quality assurance standards (Urzúa et al., 2015). In parallel, Chilean professional associations lost their legal authority to regulate professions and the requirement for mandatory membership (Urzúa et al., 2015).

For professional psychologists, including the use of tests, this meant that certification and regulation of professional practice have not been in place since 1981. Although the College of Psychologists has ethical guidelines and standards for professional conduct, including specific regulations for the use of tests (Colegio de Psicólogos, 1999), it currently lacks legal authority for oversight (Winkler et al., 2007).

Current Context of Psychological Assessment in Chile

There is no systematic and direct evidence regarding developments in psychological assessment and the proper use of tests since the 1980s. However, Vinet and González (2013), based mainly on a review of the literature, identified three events that have contributed to the decline in the quality of Psychological Assessment in the country: 1) the proliferation of undergraduate programs; 2) the deregulation of professional practice; and 3) stagnation in the creation or adaptation of psychological tests.

The proliferation of undergraduate psychology programs in various regions of the country has led to great diversity in training (Calderón, 2000; Ligüeño & Parra, 2007). According to data from Vinet and González (2013), the number of universities offering psychology degrees increased from two in 1980 to 46 in 2013. In the year 2023, according to the Ministry of Education (2022), there were 41 universities offering psychology degrees through 107 programs leading to the professional title of psychologist. These programs were distributed across different regions of the country and offered in various formats: daytime (72 programs), evening (29 programs), and others (6 programs).

The unregulated growth in the supply of professional training has become problematic due to the low quality of some programs and the difficulties new psychologists face in entering the workforce (Villegas et al., 2003). Specifically, in the field of Psychological Assessment and Psychometrics, there is no consensus on the most relevant training content, and each program or university is free to determine its own curriculum. As a control mechanism, the State proposed the creation of accrediting bodies for universities, degree programs, and curricula (Moyano & Ramos, 2013), with the aim of analyzing whether the profile proposed by each university's program actually corresponds to the service provided to its students. However, this does not truly constitute a quality certification system in terms of evaluating content important to the profession.

The regulation of professional practice was undermined by the loss of oversight functions previously exercised by the College of Psychologists. Currently, the College has just under 6000 registered members out of nearly 60,000 practicing psychologists in the country (Superintendencia de Salud, 2019), suggesting that its influence over professional practice is very limited. In the field of Psychological Assessment, there is a lack of adherence to theoretical, methodological, and ethical requirements for tests. This has allowed psychologists to use numerous projective techniques in their professional activities that do not meet psychometric standards (Vinet & González, 2013). According to Didier (2014), one factor that contributed to the widespread use of projective techniques was the demands of the job market, which required psychologists to have knowledge of and proficiency in these techniques as a prerequisite for personnel selection. Furthermore, as the authors of this chapter note, at the national level, unlike in other countries, there is no registry of tests authorized for professional use nor explicit adherence to standards international regulations governing the use of tests and their procedures for adaptation and standardization. In summary, the loss of regulatory functions over the profession by the College of Psychologists has prevented, among other things, the establishment of mechanisms to safeguard the minimum knowledge required for professional practice. Similarly, measures to sanction malpractice have been lacking, which has particularly affected the proper use of tests in Psychological Assessment contexts.

The stagnation in the creation or adaptation of psychological tests, as a consequence of poor training quality and the decline in initiatives to develop psychological tests, has reduced the availability of psychometrically supported tests (Didier, 2014; Vinet & González, 2013). Furthermore, the dissemination of research in Psychological Assessment and Psychometrics has been limited, as evidenced by a 10-year review (2002–2012) of the three most prestigious psychology journals in the country, which identified only 41 articles on psychological tests (Vinet & González, 2013). In contrast to this deficient situation, the increase in the number of psychology postgraduates in the country, from both foreign and national programs, especially over the past two decades, appears to have fostered greater awareness of the need to create indigenous instruments or to examine the relevance of foreign tests in accordance with international standards (Vinet et al., 2023).

Current initiatives in the field of Psychological Assessment and Psychometrics have been synergistically strengthened by three events since the turn of the millennium. The first is the notable creation of the Network of Psychology Schools of the Consortium of State Universities of Chile (Red Psi-CUECh). Currently, Red Psi-CUECh includes 16 state universities, 13 of which have psychology programs accredited by the National Accreditation Commission. These programs share a common framework of fundamental and mandatory requirements that define a graduate profile of transversal and professional competencies for Chilean psychologists (Calderón et al., 2007; Moyano & Ramos, 2013).

Although training in psychological assessment and diagnosis has historically been considered one of the core elements of the psychology degree (Bravo, 2004, 2013; Calderón, 2000; Villegas & Rodríguez, 2007), it is only since 2011 that this training has been systematized into a specific macro-competency agreed upon by Red Psi-CUECh. This macro-competency includes the specific skills and competencies in psychological assessment and psychometrics required for the various professional fields of psychology (Moyano & Ramos, 2013). In addition, Red Psi-CUECh has strengthened psychological research by organizing an annual national disciplinary congress since 2006, hosted by one of the member universities. A specific area included in these congresses is methodology, measurement, and assessment. Notably, at the 2015 congress, Red Psi-CUECh supported the creation of the Chilean Association of Methodology, Measurement, and Assessment (ACMME), a group of national researchers focused on the exchange and promotion of scientific knowledge in the subdisciplines of research methodology, data analysis, psychometrics, and applied assessment procedures.

The second event that has strengthened Psychological Assessment and Psychometrics is the establishment, at the Pontificia Universidad Católica de Chile, of two research and development centers that have prioritized the creation of psychological assessment tools. These are: 1) the Measurement Center (MIDE-UC; https://mideuc.cl/), focused on measurement and assessment applied to education, organizations, and society; and 2) the Center for the Development of Inclusion Technologies (CEDETi-UC; www.cedeti.cl), dedicated to the development and promotion of technological tools that contribute to improving the quality of life for people with disabilities and in educational settings. In addition to developing multiple tests for cognitive assessment and personnel selection, this center is currently responsible for the national adaptation of the Wechsler Intelligence Scales, a task carried out in collaboration with other institutions and regional universities to ensure greater national representativeness of normative data.

Finally, the third significant event is the current initiative of the Interamerican Society of Psychology (SIP), developed by the Working Group on Measurement and Assessment (GT-ME), to conduct a diagnostic study on attitudes and practices regarding test use in various Ibero-American countries. This work aims to subsequently propose joint development plans in accordance with international regulations led by the International Test Commission (ITC). This initiative to improve test use has been promoted by the European Federation of Psychologists' Associations (EFPA) in Europe, and is also supported by the Ibero-American Federation of Psychology Associations (FIAP), the ITC, the General Council of Psychology of Spain, and the professional associations of the participating countries (Muñiz Fernández et al., 2021). The most relevant aspects of this project, and especially the findings from Chile, are described by Vinet et al. (2023) and will be summarized below.

Empirical Study on Attitudes and Test Use in Chile

The project Use of Psychological Tests in Ibero-American Countries, developed by the GT-ME of the SIP, began informally in 2013, following the XXXIV Interamerican Congress of Psychology held in Brasilia. The symposium "Use of Tests in Latin America: Current Situation and Improvement Projects" was presented there, organized by Paula Elosua (Spain) and with contributions from Spain, Portugal, Argentina, Brazil, and TEA Ediciones (see Alchieri & Barreiros Porto, 2025). It included representatives from Argentina, Bolivia, Brazil, Chile, Colombia, Spain,

Guatemala, Paraguay, Peru, Portugal, the Dominican Republic, and Venezuela, who formed a group with shared interests in the field of tests and Psychological Assessment. Between 2014 and 2015, under the leadership of Paula Elosua, they developed a project and an online survey to investigate the characteristics of test use in different countries.

In Chile, based on the Ibero-American proposal, a specific project (DFP18-0033) was developed and approved by the Research Directorate of the Universidad de La Frontera, which is available upon explicit request from interested parties. This project and its results are described below in the following three sections.

Survey and Procedure of the Empirical Study

The online survey for the project Use of Psychological Tests in Ibero-American Countries was based on European studies developed for the same purpose (e.g., Muñiz & Fernández Hermida, 2000; Muñiz Fernández et al., 2021). It included three sections: The first section collected personal data, academic background, and professional practice information from psychologists; this information was requested through closed-ended response options. The second section addressed test use and began with the question: "In your professional practice, do you regularly use psychological tests and/or questionnaires?" requiring a dichotomous response (Yes/No). If the answer was negative, respondents were asked to indicate the reasons for nonuse through four closed options and two open-ended options. Subsequently, through closed-ended questions, further details were gathered about regular use, including the objectives for test use and the age groups in which the tests were applied. At the end of this section, information was collected on the instruments most frequently used in professional practice. Participants could list up to ten tests, starting with the one used most frequently and continuing in decreasing order of use.

The third section included two parts, both answered using graded responses (1 to 5 points). The first part asked about the frequency of various problems encountered in the use of psychological tests in the country; the second part assessed the degree of agreement or disagreement with 20 attitudinal statements regarding the use of tests. Further details on the specific content of this survey can be found in the report by Vinet et al. (2023).

In Chile, the survey was distributed through the College of Psychologists, the Chilean Society of Clinical Psychology, the Scientific Society of Psychology of Chile, and undergraduate psychology programs at various Chilean universities. According to Vinet et al. (2023), these institutions "invited their members or graduates to participate, providing them with the link to access the online survey" (p. 6). It should be noted that participation was voluntary, anonymous, unpaid, and without time restrictions. The survey was available for completion on the website of the Official College of Psychologists (COP) of Spain from October 17, 2017, to June 5, 2018, and interested individuals accessed it through a specific link for Chile, completing it in approximately 15 min. The responses were initially compiled in an Excel data file, which was made available to researchers for analysis.

Characterization of Chilean Participants in the Empirical Study

Vinet et al. (2023) report that 381 psychologists participated in this study, meeting the following inclusion criteria: 1) currently practicing psychology professionally, 2) being Chilean, 3) signing an informed consent document, and 4) responding to at least two of the three sections of the survey. It is noteworthy that, of these 381 participants, 353 completed all three sections of the instrument.

Among their sociodemographic data, 71.7% of participants reported being female. Their average age was 41.35 years (SD = 11.36), with a mean of 14.17 years (SD = 9.98) of professional experience. Although psychologists from various geographic regions responded to the survey, the majority (50.7%) were concentrated in the Metropolitan Region, where the country's capital is located.

Regarding their professional and/or academic training, most participants (77.4%) had some form of postgraduate education (Specialization: 29.1%; Master's: 39.4%; and Doctorate: 8.9%). When asked about their main field of professional practice, the majority indicated Clinical and Health Psychology (46.5%), followed by other areas such as Higher Education and Research (14.2%), School Psychology (13.4%), and Work and Organizational Psychology (12.3%), among others. It is noteworthy that 72.7% of participants reported having a second field of professional practice, and 27.8% a third field. According to the authors of this chapter, this phenomenon may be consistent with a generalist initial training, with the multipurpose training described by Didier (2014), or with the broad diversification and limited regulation of professional psychology practice in Chile—issues that should be empirically investigated.

Results of the Empirical Study

The most relevant results of the study conducted in Chile are presented below, grouped into three areas. Two are based on information provided by the psychologists who participated in the survey, while the other derives from a systematic review of Chilean studies on the psychometric quality of the 20 tests most frequently mentioned by participants. For further details on these results, it is recommended to consult Vinet et al. (2023).

Characteristics of Test Use in Chile

The descriptive analyses of the data reported by the participants indicate a habitual use of tests among Chilean psychologists (79.3%), with the area of assessment/diagnosis showing the highest average frequency (48.7%). Recruitment or personnel selection (12.7%), screening (10.6%), and research (9.6%) were the other areas of test use most frequently mentioned. To a lesser extent, areas such as counseling or guidance, program and intervention evaluation, and teaching were also reported. When describing test use according to the life stage of those assessed, participants reported their use across all stages, with a notable emphasis on adolescents and young adults aged 13 to 25 years (30.3%) and adults aged 26 to 64 years (35.4%). Test use in children aged 3 to 12 years was lower (28.8%), while use in the extreme stages of the life cycle (under 3 years and older adults) was infrequent.

Among the reasons for not routinely using tests in professional practice, reported by 20.7% of participants, the main factors were: 1) distrust regarding their use as support for professional practice (39.2%), 2) lack of validation studies for the instruments at the national level (19.0%), 3) the belief that tests are unnecessary (16.5%), and 4) insufficient training for the use of psychological tests (13.9%).

The 20 Most Frequently Used Tests in Chile and Their Psychometric Quality Evidence

The information collected on the tests most frequently used by participants identified 267 different tests. From these, the frequency with which each test was reported was extracted, and a list was compiled of the 20 tests with the highest percentages in the sum of the first three mentions (Vinet et al., 2023). This calculation is detailed below in Table 5.1.

In accordance with the guidelines of international organizations responsible for safeguarding the ethical use of psychological tests, such as the Standards for Educational and Psychological Testing (American Educational Research Association [AERA], American Psychological Association [APA], and National Council on Measurement in Education [NCME], 2014/2018), the instruments to be used must have evidence supporting their reliability, validity, and fairness, as well as normative data that allow for appropriate interpretation of their results. In objective or psychometric tests, reliability refers to the precision or consistency of scores across test replications; validity relates to the theoretical and empirical support for the interpretations drawn from test results; and fairness refers to the absence of bias toward specific population groups. Normative data provide indicators of the typical behavior of a known reference group to which the assessed individual may belong. Meeting these requirements ensures the ability to make useful inferences about an individual's performance.

The information presented in Table 5.1 shows that only seven of the most frequently used tests in Chile can be classified as psychometric or objective. According to the work of Vinet et al. (2023), the majority (13 out of 20) of these tests are categorized as "projective" instruments. Authors such as Lilienfeld et al. (2000), Sabogal (2004) and Sneiderman (2011) argue that the psychometric quality of projective tests is subject to criticism; since based on the psychometric model they lack reliability and validity estimates and, generally, do not have adequate normative data. However, if it is acknowledged that the psychological processes assessed by these tests occur and deepen within the subjectivity and psyche of the individual and are not addressed by the psychometric model, it becomes necessary to investigate these processes and response forms. Thus, to provide useful information,

Table 5.1 The 20 most frequently used tests in Chile

Test	Sum of mentions in the top three spots	%
Psicodiagnóstico de Rorschach	111	29,13
Escala Wechsler de Inteligencia para niños (WISC)*	87	22,84
Dibujo de la Persona Bajo la Lluvia	78	20,47
Test de Apercepción Temática para niños (CAT)	54	14,17
Test de Colores de Luscher	54	14,17
Escala Wechsler de Inteligencia para Adultos (WAIS)*	50	13,12
Test de Zulliger	42	11,02
Test de Relaciones Objetales (TRO)	38	9,97
Dibujo Casa-Árbol-Persona	36	9,45
Dibujo de una Familia	30	7,87
Dibujo de la Figura Humana	22	5,77
Test Gestáltico Visomotor de Bender	21	5,51
Cuestionario de 16 Factores de Personalidad de Cattell*	18	4,72
Test Desiderativo	14	3,68
Inventario Multifásico de Personalidad de Minnesota (MMPI)*	13	3,41
Inventario de Depresión de Beck (BDI)*	13	3,41
Inventario de Preferencia Personales de Edwards*	11	2,89
Test de Apercepción Temática (TAT)	10	2,63
Inventario Clínico para Adolescentes de Millon (MACI)*	10	2,63
Dibujo de un Árbol	8	2,10

Note: The seven tests marked with an asterisk (*) correspond to Psychometric Tests, the remaining 13 are Projective Techniques

these techniques should also have systematic evidence regarding their psychometric quality, even if such quality is defined in their own epistemic terms (Vinet et al., 2023).

In order to explore the status of the 20 most frequently used tests in Chile with respect to evidence of their psychometric quality, Vinet et al. (2023) conducted, between October 2019 and April 2020, a systematic review of the literature available in the electronic databases WoS, Scopus, and SciELO, supplemented by Google Scholar and non-indexed Chilean journals belonging to the Chilean Association of Scientific Psychology Journals (ACRCP), covering a 20-year period (1999–2019). Studies exploring reliability, validity, and/or the presence of normative data in these 20 tests were sought. The results of this inquiry are quite concerning, as only 11 articles corresponding to research in the Chilean population were found. These refer to only 5 of the 20 tests: WISC, WAIS, MMPI, BDI, and MACI. As can be seen, these five tests are psychometric in nature, which thus reflects a high use in Chile of instruments that lack support for their psychometric properties and are predominantly projective in nature.

Problems in Test Use and Attitudes Toward Their Use Among Chilean Psychologists

Regarding the problems in test use, this group of psychologists perceives that the set of surveyed problems occurs only with moderate frequency in Chile. Thus, according to Vinet et al. (2023), the following are not frequent problems:

> "Conducting assessments using inappropriate tests; Making interpretations that go beyond the limits of the test used; Ignoring local conditions that may affect the validity of the tests; Using tests by unqualified individuals; Failing to consider the standard error of measurement in test scores; Not being sufficiently up to date regarding the tests used; Lacking opportunities to compare one's own assessments with those of other psychologists; and Photocopying tests" (pp. 11-12).

According to Vinet et al. (2023), these findings would reflect a kind of paradox, since, although there is an appreciation for the correct use of tests, psychologists still widely use instruments that lack psychometric foundation or violate basic standards for test use, while perceiving that such erroneous practices are not common.

On the other hand, the EFA results of the 20 attitudinal items show that, consistent with analyses conducted in Spain (e.g., Muñiz & Fernández-Hermida, 2000; Muñiz et al., 2020), participants' attitudes toward test use cluster around five relevant dimensions. On one hand, participants indicate that the use of tests (their administration, scoring, and report writing) should be exclusive competencies of professional psychologists (F1, Exclusivity), and that the proper use of tests provides reliable, useful, and high-quality information (F3, Confidence). On the other hand, participants' responses suggest a conviction that it is necessary to control the development and commercialization of tests (F2, Restriction), and that professional organizations, supported by official legislation, should exercise greater regulation and oversight in Chile regarding test use practices and the minimum competencies required of users, in accordance with international standards and guidelines (F5, Institutional Regulatory Control). Finally, there is a clear perception that the knowledge acquired during undergraduate training regarding the use of psychological tests has not been sufficient to meet the demands of professional psychological practice (F4, Limited Initial Training).

The identified dimensions may reflect that, at the attitudinal level, there is some internalization of desirable behaviors in test use. However, the results regarding the identification of problems and tolerance of these suggest that this internalization is not fully reflected in professional practice with tests.

Challenges for Psychological Assessment in Chile: What Is Necessary and Urgent?

The current landscape of Psychological Assessment in Chile and the findings of the recent empirical study invite reflection on the needs and challenges that must be addressed. The aim is to improve this important area of psychologists' professional performance and to strengthen best practices in the use of assessment instruments. In this regard, at least three key areas can be identified, which are detailed below.

Test Use Based on Specialized Training

As previously mentioned, the decisions a psychologist makes through a psychological assessment process impact the life trajectory of individuals. This underscores the high level of responsibility that this professional activity entails and the need for it to be conducted within strict ethical and regulatory frameworks.

Considering the current lack of regulation in undergraduate training in Psychological Assessment and the reports from surveyed psychologists indicating deficits in their initial training for test use (Vinet et al., 2023), the authors of this chapter consider it highly necessary to begin recognizing this area as a specialized field that therefore requires ad hoc training. This includes, in addition to improving undergraduate education, the creation of new postgraduate and post-degree training programs, which, through high quality standards, facilitate the development of the necessary competencies to ensure appropriate, ethical, and evidence-based test use that safeguards the rights of those being assessed.

Test Use Within a Clear Professional Regulatory Framework

As evidenced in the empirical study by Vinet et al. (2023), there is consensus among Chilean psychologists on the need to establish mechanisms to regulate malpractice in test use. One of the organizations that could carry out this regulation is the Chilean College of Psychologists. However, as previously mentioned, it has lost legal oversight of the profession and therefore currently lacks the necessary tools to do so.

Vinet et al. (2023) suggest that adopting a restrictive strategy that limits test use only to psychologists qualified for their use (Muñiz et al., 2015) would allow progress in regulation. This strategy could be implemented through the establishment of a "test use accreditation system" that ensures psychologists who use tests possess the necessary competencies and knowledge to use them effectively and ethically.

Another strategy worth replicating is that developed by the Conselho Federal de Psicologia (Federal Council of Psychology-CFP) of Brazil, through the Sistema de Avaliação de Testes Psicológicos (Psychological Test Assessment System—SATEPSI) (Moraes Cardoso & da Silva-Filho, 2018). Since 2001, SATEPSI has evaluated and certified the technical and scientific quality of tests and, on this basis, determines whether they are "approved" as instruments for professional use by psychologists. Vinet et al. (2023) point out that the CFP considers the use of "non-approved" tests to be a violation of professional ethics, and therefore in Chile this could become a clear regulatory tool for tests, allowing the use only of those that are psychometrically and scientifically most appropriate for the Chilean population.

Implementing such mechanisms involves various efforts and organization at the professional level in the country, and is currently perceived as not very feasible. However, it is expected that the sociopolitical and legislative changes Chile is undergoing will allow for their implementation in the not-too-distant future.

Use of Tests Based on Scientific Evidence

Tests are one of the core tools in the psychological assessment process. However, for them to be truly useful, it is necessary that they are supported by evidence regarding their accuracy, the quality of the inferences that can be drawn from their application, their impartiality, and the presence of culturally relevant normative data to guide their interpretation. All these requirements can only be met after psychometric and/or scientific examination of their properties, so that, according to Prieto and Muñiz (2000), they may be considered "efficient tests."

In Chile, as discussed in this chapter, there is a drive to develop initiatives that meet these requirements in test use; however, it is necessary to strengthen them and ensure their continuity. As Vinet et al. (2023) mention, it is essential to establish in Chile the need for research teams responsible for constructing, translating, and/or adapting tests, explicitly adhering to international guidelines in this regard (ITC, 2001; AERA, APA & NCME, 2014/2018), and for periodically examining the psychometric quality and normative references of these instruments, as such evidence can guarantee fair and ethical assessment when instruments are used. Additionally, it is necessary to ensure the cultural relevance of the tests used in psychodiagnostic processes. This can be achieved through research that includes minority groups in the population who are regularly excluded from the development of normative data, thereby taking into account the cultural diversity present in the country. The projective tests widely used in Chile (Vinet et al., 2023) are not exempt from these requirements, making it necessary to promote the creation of specialized research teams capable of conducting studies or research consistent with the nature of these tests, focusing on the quality of their measures, their use, and their adaptation to the Chilean population.

Since conducting research alone does not guarantee a concrete impact on practices related to test use, it is also necessary to establish mechanisms that allow psychologists easy access to objective, expert, up-to-date, and periodic information on the quality of tests evaluated in research. This would contribute to the selection of instruments for assessment processes and ensure that this task is carried out on a sound basis. From another perspective, this is also essential to safeguard the rights of individuals undergoing assessment, since decisions that impact their life trajectory emerge from the application of these instruments; for this reason, such decisions should be made using tools that meet high quality standards.

An effective and already proven strategy is the one developed by the Test Commission, created by the COP of Spain, which since 2010 has systematically reviewed tests published in Spain by evaluating them with the Revised Test

Evaluation Questionnaire (CET-R) (Hernández et al., 2016). This evaluation is presented in a "test report" available free online, which all psychologists can access to make informed decisions about the suitability, advantages, and limitations of the instrument they wish to use (Fonseca-Pedrero & Muñiz, 2017). Undoubtedly, establishing a similar mechanism in Chile would enhance best practices in test use.

Final Remarks

The authors of this chapter consider it necessary and urgent to coordinate: 1) training in Psychological Assessment and Psychometrics, 2) best practices in the professional use of tests, and 3) essential research on the psychological tests most frequently used in Chile. These actions would directly benefit those being assessed by ensuring fair evaluation processes supported by ethical and scientific standards. The historical review shows that since the beginnings of psychology in Chile, there has been an interest in conducting psychological assessments based on empirical evidence; however, this motivation has diminished in recent decades. Today, changes are needed in the culture of Psychological Assessment in the country to recover the initial drive that motivated the founders of the discipline and to overcome some of the shortcomings highlighted in this work.

References

Alchieri, J. C., & Barreiros Porto, J. (2025). Memorias del XXXIV Congresso Interamericano de Psicologia. https://sipsych.org/books/memorias-del-xxxiv-congresso-interamericano-de-psicologia/.

American Education Research Association, American Psychological Association & National Council on measurement in education. (2014/2018). *Estándares para pruebas educativas y psicológicas* (M. Lieve, Trans.). American Educational Research Association.

Bravo, L. (2004). Cincuenta años de psicología en la Universidad Católica. *Psykhe, 13*(1), 197–204. https://doi.org/10.4067/S0718-22282004000100016

Bravo, L. (2013). Cincuenta años de la psicología en Chile: Una perspectiva personal. *Psykhe, 22*(1), 125–137. https://doi.org/10.7764/psykhe.22.1.631

Calderón, R. (2000). Antecedentes sobre el rol del psicólogo y su formación. En: G. Miranda, R. Calderón & X. Bugueño (Eds.), Psicología contemporánea: Disciplina, profesión, formación (pp. 51–106). Universidad Católica Cardenal Raúl Silva Henríquez.

Calderón, C., Cuadra, A., Denegri, M., González, S., Juliá, M. T., Moyano Díaz, E., & Redondo, J. (2007). Mejoramiento de la formación general y específica de los profesionales psicólogos del Consorcio de Universidades del Estado mediante el diseño e implementación de un marco curricular común basado en competencias. In *Proyecto Fondos Innovación Académica, Programa MECESUP 2, Ministerio de Educación.*

Colegio de Psicólogos. (1999). Código de Ética Profesional. https://www.colpsi.cl/1-normativa-vigente/.

Didier, N. (2014). Selección de personal en Chile. *Revista Iberoamericana de Psicología, 7*(1), 103–114. https://reviberopsicologia.ibero.edu.co/article/view/rip.7109

Fonseca-Pedrero, E., & Muñiz, J. (2017). Quinta evaluación de tests editados en España: mirando hacia atrás, construyendo el futuro. *Papeles del Psicólogo, 38*(3), 161–168. https://doi.org/10.23923/pap.psicol2017.2844

Hernández, A., Ponsoda, V., Muñiz, J., Prieto, G., & Elosua, P. (2016). Revisión del modelo para evaluar la calidad de los tests utilizados en España. *Papeles del Psicólogo, 37*(3), 192–197. http://www.papelesdelpsicologo.es/pdf/2775.pdf

International Test Commission. [ITC]. (2001). International guidelines for test use. *International Journal of Testing, 1*(2), 93–114. https://doi.org/10.1207/S15327574IJT0102_1

Ligüeño, S., & Parra, D. (2007). La psicología en la Universidad de Chile: Una propuesta de estudio para comprender la historia de la psicología en Chile. *Cuadernos de neuropsicología, 1*(3), 223–235. http://pepsic.bvsalud.org/scielo.php?script=sci_arttext&pid=S0718-41232007000300005&lng=pt&tlng=es

Lilienfeld, S., Word, J., & Garb, H. (2000). The scientific status of projective techniques. *Psychological Science in the Public Interest, 1*(2), 27–66. https://doi.org/10.1111/1529-1006.002

Ministerio de Educación, Subsecretaría de Educación Superior. (2022). Buscador de carreras universitarias. Disponible en. https://acceso-sup.mineduc.cl/acceso-buscador/buscador-cu.

Moraes Cardoso, L., & da Silva-Filho, J. H. (2018). Satepsi e a qualidade técnica dos testes psicológicos no Brasi. *Psicologia: Ciência e Profissão, 38*(Numero spe), 40–49. https://doi.org/10.1590/1982-3703000209112

Moretti, R. (2018). Una tecnología para ayudar a construir naciones: La adaptación chilena de la Escala Stanford-Binet por Luis A. Tirapegui. *Revista De Psicología, 27*(2), 1–6. https://doi.org/10.5354/0719-0581.2018.52306

Moyano, E. & Ramos, N. (2013). Transformaciones en la formación de psicólogos en universidades del Estado de Chile. *Integración Académica en Psicología, 1*(2), 29–37. https://integracion-academica.org/vol1numero2-2013/21-transformaciones-en-la-formacion-de-psicologos-en-universidades-del-estado-de-chile.

Muñiz, J., & Fernández Hermida, J. R. (2000). La utilización de los tests en España. *Papeles del Psicólogo, 76*, 41–49. http://www.papelesdelpsicologo.es/resumen?pii=838

Muñiz, J., Hernández, A., & Ponsoda, V. (2015). Nuevas directrices sobre el uso de los tests: investigación, control de calidad y seguridad. *Papeles del Psicólogo, 36*(3), 161–173. http://www.papelesdelpsicologo.es/pdf/2609.pdf

Muñiz, J., Hernández, A., & Fernández-Hermida, J. R. (2020). Utilización de los test en España: el punto de vista de los psicólogos. *Papeles del Psicólogo, 41*(1), 1–15. https://doi.org/10.23923/pap.psicol2020.2921

Muñiz Fernández, J., Hernández, A., Elosua, P., & Wechsler, S. (2021). El uso de los test en España y Latinoamérica: Perspectivas actuales y retos futuros. *Anuario Internacional De Revisiones En Psicología, 1*, 67–94. https://www.uv.es/uvweb/idocal/es/instituto-investigacion-psicologia-rrhh-del-desarrollo-organizacional-calidad-vida-laboral-idocal/publication-uso-test-espana-latinoamerica-perspectivas-actuales-retos-futuros-1285952314908/Novetat.html?id=1286185809831.

Prieto, G., & Muñiz, J. (2000). Un modelo para evaluar la calidad de los test utilizados en España. *Papeles del Psicólogo, 77*, 65–71. http://www.papelesdelpsicologo.es/resumen?pii=1102

Sabogal, T. L. F. (2004). Pruebas proyectivas: Acerca de su validez y confiabilidad. *Duazary, 1*(2), 134–137. https://dialnet.unirioja.es/servlet/articulo?codigo=4788105

Salas, G. (2014). El Informe Nassar (1955) sobre la formación de psicólogos en Chile. *Revista de Psicología, 23*(1), 109–112. https://doi.org/10.5354/0719-0581.2014.32879

Salas, G., & Lizama, E. (2009). *Historia de la psicología en Chile. 1889–1981*. Editorial Universidad de La Serena.

Sneiderman, S. (2011). Consideraciones acerca de la confiabilidad y validez en las técnicas proyectivas. *Subjetividad y Procesos Cognitivos, 15*(2), 93–110. http://www.redalyc.org/articulo.oa?id=339630258005

Superintendencia de Salud. (2019). Estadísticas de Prestadores Individuales de Salud a Marzo de 2019. Disponible en: http://www.supersalud.gob.cl/documentacion/666/articles-18219_recurso_1.pdf.

Urzúa, A. (2008). Elementos contextuales a la investigación en psicología en Chile. *Revista Interamericana de Psicología, 42*(3), 446–461. https://pepsic.bvsalud.org/scielo.php?script=sci_arttext&pid=S0034-96902008000300004

Urzúa, A., Vera-Villarroel, P., Zúñiga, C., & Salas, G. (2015). Psicología en Chile: análisis de su historia, presente y futuro. *Universitas Psychologica, 14*(3), 15–32. https://doi.org/10.11144/Javeriana.upsy14-3.pcah

Villegas, J., Marassi, P., & Toro, J. P. (2003). Problemas centrales para la formación y el entrenamiento profesional del psicólogo en las Américas. Sociedad Interamericana de Psicología.

Villegas, J., & Rodríguez, M. (2007). *Historia de la Investigación Científica de la Psicología en Chile*. Publicaciones Facultad de Ciencias Sociales, Universidad Central.

Vinet, E., & González, N. (2013). Desarrollos actuales y desafíos futuros en la evaluación psicológica en Chile. *Psiencia. Revista Latinoamericana de Ciencia Psicológica*, 134–138. .

Vinet, E., Rodríguez-Cancino, M., Sandoval Domínguez, A., Rojas-Mora, P., & Saiz, J. L. (2023). El Empleo de test por psicólogos(as) chilenos(as): Un inquietante panorama. *Psykhe*. https://doi.org/10.7764/psykhe.2020.25293

Winkler, M., Pasmanik, D., Alvear, K., & Reyes, M. (2007). Cuando el bienestar psicológico está en juego: La dimensión ética en la formación profesional de psicólogo. *Terapia Psicológica, 25*(1), 5–24. https://doi.org/10.4067/S0718-48082007000100001

Chapter 6
Psychological and Educational Assessment in Costa Rica: Origins, Current Status, and Future Perspectives

Vanessa Smith-Castro, Eiliana Montero-Rojas, and Carlos Saborío-Valverde

Introduction

Unlike other countries where educational and psychological assessment have followed clearly distinct paths, in Costa Rica psychologists have developed significant expertise in both fields, specifically a) in professional practice, particularly through the use of psychological tests in clinical and forensic settings, and b) in educational contexts through the development and application of standardized tests for admission to higher education institutions (Adis, 1975, 1991; Román & Pavlosky, 2019; Thomas, 1975).

This chapter provides an overview of the current state of assessment in these fields and offers reflections on the major challenges the country faces in measurement and psychometrics. The text is organized into four main sections. It begins with a brief review of the consolidation of psychology as an academic and professional discipline in Costa Rica. The second section focuses on the use of instruments in clinical and forensic fields. The third section describes the development and validation of high-stakes standardized tests for university admission. The chapter concludes with a critical appraisal and an outline of future perspectives.

We hope that this brief overview of the current state of our work in assessment will serve as a historical record to guide the necessary actions in the training and professional development of psychologists, thereby strengthening a culture of high-quality psychological and educational assessment grounded in the highest and most rigorous ethical and scientific standards.

V. Smith-Castro (✉) · E. Montero-Rojas · C. Saborío-Valverde
University of Costa Rica, San José, Costa Rica
e-mail: vanessa.smith@ucr.ac.cr; eiliana.montero@ucr.ac.cr; carlos.saboriovalverde@ucr.ac.cr

S. V. Pugliese et al. (eds.), *Origins and Challenges of Psychological Assessment in Ibero-American Countries*, https://doi.org/10.1007/978-3-032-21380-8_6

Brief Historical Overview of Psychology in Costa Rica

Psychological and educational assessment in Costa Rica is closely linked to the development of psychology as an academic and professional discipline, the history of which is relatively recent (See Fig. 6.1). Although there are records of psychological thought in Costa Rica dating back to the early nineteenth century, it was not until after the Second World War that psychology began to develop as a scientific discipline in the country, a process closely associated with two key institutions: the University of Costa Rica (UCR) and the Costa Rican Social Security Fund (abbreviated in Spanish as CCSS) (Adis, 1975, 1991; López-Core, 2013; Thomas, 1970, 1975).

The UCR was founded in 1940 and was the first higher education institution in the country to teach psychology, initially as a subject within various social science and health programs, and later as a specific degree (Adis, 1975, 1991). The CCSS, also established in 1940, is the public health care system, which offered outpatient psychiatric and neurological services and provided open training courses in psychology and psychopedagogy from its inception (López-Core, 2013; Thomas, 1975).

By the late 1950s, the first professionals in psychology and education trained at universities in the United States and Europe began to arrive in the country, most of them specializing in clinical and applied psychology and becoming part of both the UCR and the CCSS. One of these professionals was Gonzalo Adis Castro, regarded as one of the leading advocates of psychology as a scientific discipline in the country. Upon his arrival, Adis joined the UCR as a lecturer and simultaneously joined the National Psychiatric Hospital of the CCSS.

At the university, Adis established the first Evaluation Committee, charged with setting up an admissions system. This committee would later become the Centre for Psychological Research (CIP in Spanish) and subsequently the Institute for Psychological Research (IIP in Spanish), which initially focused on the development, validation, and application of tests for the university admissions process (IIP, 2022). At the CCSS, Adis founded the Psychology Service, which conducted the

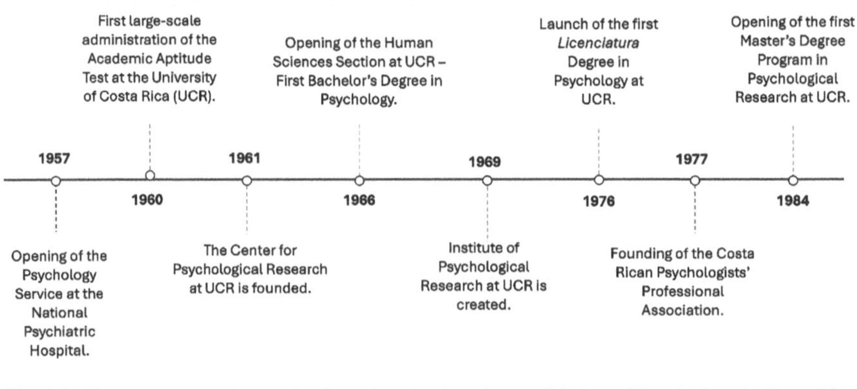

Fig. 6.1 Key moments in the academic and professional consolidation of Psychology in Costa Rica

first psychodiagnostic assessments, translated and adapted tests such as the Minnesota Multiphasic Personality Inventory, the Wechsler-Bellevue Intelligence Test, and the Incomplete Sentences Test, among others (Adis, 1991; López-Core, 2013). These two settings are foundational milestones for psychology in Costa Rica and, as will be seen, are also defining for the type of psychological and educational assessment carried out in the country.

By the 1960s and 1970s, academic and professional psychology had firmly developed. In 1966, undergraduate training in psychology began at the UCR, with the creation of the "Human Sciences" Section of the Faculty of Science and Letters. Initially, the department provided complementary training for various disciplines. Later, in 1966, the department began to offer the first degree in Psychology. By 1972, the Licenciatura degree was introduced, giving the discipline an even more professional character (School of Psychology [Escuela de Psicología, EPS in Spanish], 2022).

The consolidation of psychology training during the 1980s was accompanied by a rapid increase in employment opportunities for professionals, with the creation of posts in public institutions such as the National Children's Hospital, the Ministry of Health, the Institute on Alcoholism and Drug Dependence, the Costa Rican Prison System, and the Judiciary, among others, where psychological assessment became an essential part of professional practice (Campos et al., 1990).

The 1980s, marked by a profound economic and geopolitical crisis, also coincided with the founding of the College of Psychology Professionals (CPPCR in Spanish)[1] and the creation of the first postgraduate program in psychology at the UCR in 1984, focused on psychological research. In the same year, the hospital's Clinical Psychology residency program at the CCSS was opened. This program, in collaboration with the UCR, trained the first clinical psychologists. Also, in the mid-1980s, the first national and international psychology congresses were held in the country, and leading academic journals began publishing (the IIP's *Revista Actualidades en Psicología* and the CPPCR's *Revista Costarricense de Psicología*) (Campos et al., 1990).

In the 1990s, one of the most notable developments in psychology was the establishment of multiple psychology training programs at private universities. For example, the Catholic University of Costa Rica offered the Psychology degree in 1997, and the Ibero-American University opened the Faculty of Psychology in 1998, offering the country's first master's program in Clinical Psychology (Román & Pawlowski, 2019).

The 2000s, in turn, were characterized by the introduction of quality assurance systems for professional training to distinguish the quality of education amid the proliferation (with little oversight) of training programs (National System of Accreditation of Higher Education [SINAES in Spanish], 2022). At the same time,

[1] Professional associations in Costa Rica are public law entities of a non-state nature, which have been legally assigned functions, powers, and authorities under public law for the protection of the public interest and the rights of their members. Any person practicing psychology in Costa Rica must be registered in this organization.

the 2000s saw an increase in the specialization of academic offerings in psychology (a greater diversity of postgraduate programs) and greater internationalization of faculty members (Román & Pawlowski, 2019).

Currently, the country has 2 public higher education institutions offering degrees in Psychology and more than 18 private universities providing the program (National Council of Rectors [Consejo Nacional de Rectores, CONARE in Spanish], 2022; National Council for Private University Higher Education [Consejo Nacional de Educación Privada, CONESUP in Spanish], 2022). Interestingly, psychological assessment and psychometrics are mainly absent from the curricula of these universities. For example, of the 15 programs listed on the websites of public and private universities in the country reviewed as of July 2022, only half include courses entitled "Techniques for Psychological Assessment," "Psychological Testing," or "Psychometrics." In the remaining programs, these subjects are not clearly identifiable. Likewise, clinical and forensic assessment, as specific subjects, are rarely included in curricula (see https://universidades.cr/universidades).

In terms of professional labor market dynamics, the CPPCR currently has more than 11,000 registered members (of whom more than 8000 are active), adding 400–500 new members per year (CPPCR, 2022). The saturation of employment opportunities has been a constant concern in our field, given the indiscriminate growth of academic offerings described above. According to the most recent graduate follow-up studies, psychology professionals typically take an average of 3 years to find employment. Currently, 9% are unemployed, 11% are underemployed, and nearly 19% work in roles only loosely related to their psychology training (CONARE, 2019). Professionals primarily work in the private sector, with the highest demand in Organizational Psychology, Clinical and Health Psychology, and Educational Psychology (Baltodano-Chacón et al., 2021; CONARE, 2019; Sibaja-Molina et al., 2016).

Regarding psychological assessment specifically, more than 800 professionals are currently authorized to conduct mental examinations for firearm licensing, adoption, or employment in childcare centers (CPPCR, 2022). This group of professionals has specialized training in this type of psychological assessment, including the administration of psychological tests. In this regard, the CPPCR has a Code of Ethics and Professional Conduct that defines and regulates best practices in psychological assessment, clearly stating the requirement of using scientifically and professionally validated instruments and techniques, with robust theoretical and empirical foundations, as well as appropriate psychometric evidence for the development of various professional practices, particularly for the use of tests in clinical practice (CPPCR, 2022).

In summary, within the context of the recent development of psychology as a discipline and profession in Costa Rica, assessment and measurement have been present since its inception in two main fields: psychological assessment in clinical contexts and the development of standardized entrance examinations for higher education. Both fields witnessed significant progress, but important limitations and challenges have also been identified. In the following sections, we present an overview of the current state of these two major areas of work.

Assessment in Clinical and Forensic Contexts: Conceptual Considerations

A universally agreed-upon concept of psychological assessment within the field of professional psychological practice is perhaps unlikely, given the vast diversity of approaches and traditions that characterize our discipline. Nevertheless, it is important to begin this section with conceptual considerations that support a systematic approach to the development of psychological assessment in our country.

Psychological assessment can be understood as a process involving the collection, analysis, integration, and communication of results in response to a specific referral question about an individual's psychological functioning (Saborío & Miranda, 2021). In this sense, it is necessary to distinguish it from other brief, superficial explorations that offer broad generalizations about individuals and their functioning across various applied fields of psychology.

Psychological assessment is a complex process characterized by a detailed evaluation of psychological functioning, which involves gathering, evaluating, and integrating results from psychometric instruments and collateral information, as well as evidence obtained directly from observation of the individual, aimed at elucidating more specific and definitive traits, processes, and abilities. Psychological assessment requires high-level integrative processes involving specialized knowledge, clinical judgment, and a significant degree of expertise in a particular area of professional practice or psychological application, similar to any problem-solving process to develop a clear, cohesive, and comprehensive case formulation/conceptualization. Therefore, assessment should follow an iterative hypothesis-testing approach to collect and evaluate data to inform the decision-making process, including the systematic drawing of inferences to weigh data and assess discontinuities (American Psychological Association [APA], 2020a; APA, 2020b; American Educational Research Association [AERA] et al., 2014).

In this sense, it is necessary to distinguish between the process of psychological assessment and psychometric assessment or psychodiagnosis. According to Wright et al. (2022), while psychometric assessment involves the use of tests and inventories to evaluate an individual's characteristics, psychological assessment uses the data arising from these tests and many other sources in a convergent and integrative manner (addressing any discrepancies) to inform clinical conclusions and decisions. These authors argue that only psychological assessment integrates data in an integrative way, drawing on critical thinking skills and knowledge of psychological constructs, literature, and theories to inform conclusions and decisions.

Although psychodiagnosis may be one of the purposes of the psychological assessment process (AERA et al., 2014), it should be distinguished from psychological assessment in terms of the broader scope and explanatory power of the latter. The very notion of psychodiagnosis is directly related to some system of psychopathology classification. Here, it is essential to consider that the process of psychodiagnosis, as defined in classification manuals such as the DSM or ICD, has been the subject of intense criticism in the psychological literature, which has questioned whether their categorical diagnoses are valid operationalizations of how psychopathology occurs in human nature. These classification systems have been criticized on grounds of reliability and validity, with arguments that these traditional taxonomies are of limited utility because they propose arbitrary boundaries between psychopathology and normality (Carragher et al., 2015; Kotov et al., 2017, 2021; Rodríguez-Seijas et al., 2015).

High levels of comorbidity between disorders, the considerable heterogeneity among individuals diagnosed with the same disorder, and the existence of high diagnostic instability are among the principal criticisms. Thus, some authors have noted that although classification is the cornerstone of clinical diagnostic practice and research, existing psychiatric classification systems are not adequately supported by scientific evidence (Carragher et al., 2015; Kotov et al., 2017, 2021; Rodríguez-Seijas et al., 2015).

In light of this controversy, psychology must move beyond the traditional approach based on categorical psychodiagnosis and adopt evidence-based models and best-practice principles of psychological assessment, particularly in high-stakes professional fields such as clinical and forensic settings.

Contributing to this discussion on the need for empirically supported psychological assessment, Arbisi and Beck (2016) emphasize that, in forensic and health contexts, psychological assessment involves making high-risk decisions, for which the use of assessment techniques can have a profound impact on individuals' lives and well-being. It is therefore essential to identify standards and principles that provide a framework for establishing evidence-based assessment. Thus, in forensic and health settings, it is highly recommended to apply guidelines, models, standards, and best-practice principles to guide the psychological assessment process and professional conduct.

Regarding psychological assessment in general, the APA has recently published two guidelines: one outlining the competencies required of psychologists conducting psychological assessments, and another outlining recommended practices for quality education and training in psychological assessment (APA, 2020a, 2020b). Both documents offer a series of guiding principles for best assessment procedures to promote higher-quality professional practice in this field. Recently, Krishnamurthy et al. (2022) proposed guidelines for the scope of personality assessment, presented as "best practices" based on established professional ethics and contemporary research evidence. Another highly relevant document is the Standards for Educational and Psychological Testing (AERA et al., 2014), which sets forth principles to promote the reliability, validity, and fairness of psychometric assessment tools.

In the forensic field specifically, the guidelines for forensic psychology (APA, 2013) are noteworthy, as well as the contributions of Heilbrun (2001) and Heilbrun et al. (2009), which outline the principles of forensic assessment that have served to develop models of best practice in this professional domain, aligning with what has been termed evidence-based psychological assessment (see also Arbisi & Beck, 2016; Bornstein, 2017; Krishnamurthy et al., 2022; Melton et al., 2018; Otto et al., 2014; Sellbom & Hopwood, 2016; Wright et al., 2022).

These authors highlight the use of multi-method assessment to obtain a comprehensive picture of the persons across multiple levels or domains of functioning, and the implementation of strategies to address how heuristics and biases inadvertently contaminate the generation of clinical hypotheses. The authors also point out the need to integrate nomothetic and idiographic approaches into the assessment process, as well as the importance of understanding the person's psychological functioning in light of the salient features of their particular social context and culture. Finally, these scholars highlight the value of incorporating dimensional aspects of psychological functioning, moving beyond categorical diagnostic approaches, and using a theory- and science-based framework to integrate information and reconcile apparently incongruent findings through case conceptualization or formulation.

Clinical and Forensic Psychological Assessment in Costa Rica: Current State

In light of the guiding principles described above, it should be noted that in recent years Costa Rica has promoted assessment practices that align with these best practices, as reflected in the Code of Ethics and Professional Conduct of our professional association, which requires the use of instruments and techniques with scientific and professional support, with solid theoretical and empirical foundations, and appropriate psychometric evidence. It also involves integrating different sources, considering the individual's particular context and assessment environment, and accounting for limitations encountered during the evaluation process (CPPCR, 2022).

To analyze in greater detail the professional practices in the field of psychological assessment in Costa Rica, the following analysis presents the strategies and instruments currently used in our country. This analysis is part of a larger study measuring several variables associated with the use of psychological assessment instruments among psychologists working in clinical and forensic settings, who were surveyed online in 2022 (Saborío, personal communication, 18 July 2022).

Of the 135 individuals who responded to the survey, approximately 78% were public-sector employees, and only these individuals are included in the following analyses to characterize a more homogeneous group. In addition, those who do not engage in psychological assessment as part of their professional duties were excluded, resulting in a final sample of 91 individuals.

On average, this group of professionals has 14.9 years of professional experience, is predominantly female (79%), and holds a specialization in clinical psychology or a master's degree in psychology (72%). They work for the country's Judiciary (49.5%), CCSS (26.4%), and Prison System (20.9%). This is a group of professionals employed in the public sector, with sufficient experience and professional training, so these results cannot be generalized to all psychologists in the country.

However, they represent a group whose clinical or forensic professional environment requires adherence to standards and best practices that meet the ethical and scientific requirements for providing evidence for decision-making.

Table 6.1 shows the most frequent types of assessment in these areas. In the forensic field, there is considerable variability in the psycholegal matters that must be addressed by psychology specialists, reflecting the importance the justice system places on the evidence these professionals provide to support legal decision-making. The assessment covers various populations (minors and adults, both alleged victims and offenders) and types of cases (family, domestic violence, criminal, civil, and sentence enforcement).

Table 6.1 Psychological evaluations by type and context

Type of assessment	Clinical context	Forensic context
Family law forensic assessment		12.5%
Criminal forensic assessment of alleged adult victims		11.9%
Domestic violence forensic assessment of alleged victims		11.6%
Criminal forensic assessment of alleged child victims		11.6%
Juvenile criminal forensic assessment of alleged offenders		10.7%
Adult violence risk assessment		10.4%
Domestic violence forensic assessment of alleged offenders		8.6%
Civil law forensic assessment		8.6%
Juvenile offender violence risk assessment		6.7%
Criminal forensic assessment of alleged adult offenders		4.0%
Standard penitentiary assessment		3.4%
Psychodiagnostics of apparent affective disorder (depression, anxiety, bipolar disorder)	13.0%	
Psychodiagnostics of personality-related characteristics	11.4%	
Psychodiagnostics of apparent thought disorder (psychosis, schizophrenia)	10.3%	
Psychodiagnostics of apparent reactive condition to life events (adjustment disorder or post-traumatic stress disorder)	9.2%	
Cognitive/neuropsychological assessment in older adults	8.1%	
Psychodiagnostics of common mental conditions in childhood and adolescence	8.1%	
Assessment of hospitalized patients with mental disorders (per protocol, for intervention or management)	8.1%	
Cognitive/neuropsychological assessment in minors	7.0%	
Suicide risk assessment in adults	7.0%	
Assessment of hospitalized patients with medical conditions (per protocol, for intervention or management)	5.4%	
Follow-up assessment (reevaluation)	5.4%	
Suicide risk assessment in minors	3.8%	
Adaptive capacity and functioning assessment (for procedures, intervention, or management)	3.2%	

In the clinical setting, psychological assessment is primarily used to address referral questions in psychodiagnostic evaluation across various clinical conditions, which is understandable, given that the clinical professionals in this study work within the health system, in hospital or clinic settings that serve both inpatients and outpatients. Overall, the data clearly show that the psychological assessments conducted by the professionals in this sample are used in contexts where high-impact decisions must be made, both legally and in terms of health.

Regarding assessment practices, the surveyed professionals assigned medium or high importance to the use of psychological tests relevant to the referral question (98%), to the need of corroborating the examinee's self-report with other sources (97%), to consider the margin of error of psychological tests when interpreting them (92%), to using norms representative of the assessed individuals (97%), to taking measures to ensure appropriate environmental conditions for assessment (95%), to applying standardized technical criteria in the administration and interpretation of tests (98%), to considering indicators of reliability and validity in the tests they use (100%), as well as their theoretical foundations (97%) and their applicability to the target population (98%).

These results indicate awareness of the importance of a series of good assessment practices, which contrasts with previous surveys in which, in the clinical field, brief and projective instruments predominated (Miranda & Prado, 2014). Furthermore, in this study, none of the professionals working in the forensic setting reported using instruments traditionally categorized as psychodynamic or projective (e.g., the Human Figure, Incomplete Sentences Test, Family Drawing). In contrast, only a few in the clinical field did. This is a highly satisfactory result, reflecting a higher standard of rigor in the selection of psychometric assessment instruments by psychologists conducting high-impact assessments, such as those in clinical and forensic contexts.

These findings are consistent with previous data from other contexts, showing that multi-scale inventories and instruments measuring constructs relevant to the forensic field are most frequently used. At the same time, projective techniques are the least used across all types of assessment (McLaughlin & Kan, 2014). Indeed, according to Archer et al. (2016), a key requirement for empirically supported forensic tests is adequate standardization. Taking this criterion into account, it is possible to rule out the use of a range of techniques, such as Incomplete Sentences Tests and projective drawing tests. In contrast, instruments such as the Minnesota Multiphasic Personality Inventory (MMPI-2, MMPI-2-RF, MMPI-A) or the Personality Assessment Inventory (PAI) are examples of tools that fully meet this criterion.

In this regard, Table 6.2 shows that the most widely used psychological tests are the MMPI and the PAI, which are commonly used instruments in various forensic surveys. In particular, different versions of the MMPI have emerged as the most widely used multi-scale instrument in a variety of forensic assessment contexts (Archer et al., 2006; Boccaccini & Brodsky, 1999; Lally, 2003; Viljoen et al., 2010). However, it should be noted that, for instruments measuring cognitive and neuropsychological constructs, the data reveal frequent use of brief, exploratory tools and limited use of robust neuropsychological batteries.

Table 6.2 Most commonly used tests in clinical and forensic settings by instrument type

Instrument type	Test	Index of use
Multiscale personality and psychopathology	Minnesota multiphasic personality inventory (MMPI-2, MMPI-RF)	2.07
	Personality assessment inventory (PAI)	1.74
	Symptom Checklist-90-revised (SCL-90-R)	1.45
	Brief symptom inventory (BSI-50)	1.19
	NEO personality inventory (NEO PI-R)	0.91
	Rorschach inkblot test (Exner/R-PAS models)	0.76
Cognitive and/or neuropsychological	Neuropsychological screening battery in Spanish (NEUROPSI)	1.49
	Test of nonverbal intelligence (TONI-3, TONI-4)	1.27
	Neuropsi attention and memory (NAM)	1.19
	Mini-mental state examination (MMSE, MMSE-2)	1.14
	Behavior rating inventory of executive function: Adult (BRIEF-A)	0.98
	Kaufman intelligence test (K-BIT, K-ABC)	0.95
Instruments for children and adolescents	Minnesota multiphasic personality inventory: Adolescent (MMPI-A)	1.21
	Trauma symptom checklist for children/youth (TSCC, TSCYC): Briere	1.05
	Behavior rating inventory of executive function: Second edition (BRIEF-2, BRIEF-P)	0.62
	Personality assessment inventory: Adolescent (PAI-A)	0.55
	Wechsler intelligence scale for children (WISC-IV, WISC-V)	0.40
	Attention deficit hyperactivity disorder rating scale (EDAH)	0.37
Self-report scales of specific constructs	Trauma symptom inventory (TSI, TSI-2): Briere	1.05
	Beck depression inventory (BDI, BDI-II)	0.65
	State-trait anger expression inventory (STAXI, STAXI-2)	0.57
	Cambridge examination for mental disorders of the elderly: Revised (CAMDEX-R)	0.53
	State-trait anxiety inventory (STAI)	0.51
	Suicide probability scale (SPS/EPS)	0.50

Note. The index corresponds to the average response to the question *"How frequently have you used this test in the last 12 months?"* on a response scale of 0 = never, 1 = low, 2 = medium, and 3 = high

Regrettably, a notable issue is the frequent use of instruments that lack psychometric evidence for the Costa Rican population. Except for the MMPI-2, MMPI-A, and BDI-II, which have accumulated some empirical evidence of reliability and validity through UCR graduation theses, the other instruments lack such evidence in our country. This represents a vulnerability in professional practice in these fields, considering the minimum standards required today for good assessment practice.

High-Impact Standardized Tests in Educational Contexts: Conceptual Clarifications

Unlike the clinical and individually administered tests described above, standardized tests are administered to large groups of examinees (large-scale application) in a standardized manner. But, as those used in clinical and forensic contexts, these tests must be developed according to a rigorous process of construction and empirical validation, using psychometric methods. Given their particular characteristics, it is essential to provide conceptual clarifications before describing their development in Costa Rica. These tests are also considered high-stakes, especially when their results have significant consequences for individuals' life projects. Therefore, the process of constructing and validating these tests should be scientifically grounded, drawing on accumulated knowledge from theory and research on measurement, assessment, and psychometrics (AERA et al., 2014; Downing & Haladyna, 2006).

Every standardized high-stakes test should be developed according to specification tables that describe the indicators of the constructs to be assessed, the types of items required to measure them, and the weighting of each item. Based on the specification table, items are constructed and validated. Once these items have been administered in pilot studies, they are subjected to psychometric analyses to gather objective evidence of validity and reliability. After empirical validation, items that meet acceptable technical quality indicators are included in an item bank, from which specific tests are assembled for each required administration (Moreira et al., 2022; Martínez et al., 2006).

The validity of an instrument, in its modern conception, refers to the degree to which the inferences drawn from its results are appropriate (AERA et al., 2014; Messick, 1989a, 1989b, 1995). This definition of validity, now internationally accepted, is scientifically more robust and replaces the earlier, almost tautological, definition that an instrument is valid when it measures what it is intended to measure (Kerlinger & Lee, 2002).

According to modern notions, validity is not a specific trait of the instrument per se; rather, it depends on the measurement's purpose, the target population, and the intended interpretations of the scores. Furthermore, validity is now conceived as a matter of degree, not as a dichotomous attribute, and there is broad consensus that the validation of an instrument should be understood as a continuous and ongoing process, like any other type of scientific research (Messick, 1989a, 1989b, 1995; Montero, 2013).

It is also widely and generally recognized that the consequences of test administration, including its social repercussions, are an integral part of the concept of validity. Thus, assessment teams must also be concerned with the uses of instruments and the consequences arising from their application, not only with technical and scientific aspects (Montero, 2013).

Reliability, for its part, is defined (since Anastasi, 1982) as the precision of the instrument in a given population and under normal administration conditions (AERA et al., 2014). As with validity, reliability is not absolute and depends not only on the content of the items but also on the test-takers, the conditions of administration, the scorers, and the scoring methods. Moreover, some contemporary authors consider it highly useful to conceptualize reliability as another dimension of the unified concept of validity proposed by Messick (1989a, 1989b, 1995).

Thanks to advances in modern psychometrics, there are now multiple techniques and strategies for assessing instrument quality through quantitative and qualitative analyses. For example, validity evidence can be gathered based on: a) the content of the items, b) the response process, c) the internal structure of the test, d) the associations of the test scores with external variables, and e) the consequences of its application. Reliability evidence can be gathered based on: a) score stability, b) internal consistency, and c) inter-rater agreement (AERA et al., 2014).

The most commonly used psychometric analysis methods are Exploratory and Confirmatory Factor Analysis, Classical Test Theory, Differential Item Analysis, Item Response Theory, and, particularly, the Rasch Model with its various extensions (Moreira-Mora et al., 2022; Wilson, 2005; Muñiz, 2003; Bond & Fox, 2001; Nunnally & Bernstein, 1995).

More recently, procedures derived from more qualitative approaches have been incorporated, such as the so-called "one-to-one tests," Cognitive Task Analysis, and Cognitive Interviewing. These methods allow for a closer examination of examinees' response processes and provide information on item quality and potential improvements. These qualitative methods are also recommended if, for any reason, it is not feasible to conduct a pilot administration with a relatively large sample of examinees (100 or more) (Domingo & Domingo, 2015; Smith & Molina, 2016).

Thus, if a test is intended for decision-making purposes regarding examinees, it is critical that, before its final administration, the items undergo pilot testing and technical quality analysis using the aforementioned theories and methods. For this reason, the assessment teams should include at least one specialist in psychometrics or statistics, who should be familiar with the most widely used measurement models and those recommended by the scientific community for analyzing instrument quality in relation to their purposes and contexts of use.

High-Stakes Standardized Tests in Costa Rica: Current Situation

In Costa Rica, few high-stakes standardized tests meet the standards and recommendations previously cited. The first test developed under these principles was the Academic Aptitude Test (PAA in Spanish) for admission to UCR. This test led to the creation of the IIP in the early 1960s. Currently, the test is developed within this research unit by an interdisciplinary team of specialists in assessment, psychometrics, education, philology, linguistics, statistics, and mathematics, among others.

The historical roots of this test can be traced back to the Scholastic Aptitude Test (SAT) in the United States during the 1950s, developed by the Educational Testing

Service (ETS) (Mainieri, 2008). However, the current PAA differs significantly from the SAT, focusing on reasoning in verbal and mathematical contexts. Within the verbal context, items assess the ability to solve problems using strategies such as supposing, presupposing, paraphrasing, contrasting, deducing, and reducing. On the other hand, the mathematical reasoning items measure the ability to manage and apply strategies such as generalizing, verifying, investigating, and representing, together with the understanding of basic mathematical concepts for problem-solving (IIP, 2022).

The current PAA consists of 45 items arranged in increasing order of difficulty, all single-choice with four response options. It is administered under strict, standardized conditions, with a maximum completion time of 1.5 h. Each year, the test includes experimental items that are not used for student scoring, as they are being tested for the first time in the operational administration solely to obtain their technical quality parameters and to introduce them into the item bank if they meet acceptable standards (Smith-Castro, 2014). The total score (simple percentage of correct answers) is one of the two equally weighted components used to calculate the "Admission Average" indicator, which is the measure by which applicants compete for entry to the UCR. The other component of the "Admission Average" is the grade point average from the core curriculum subjects of the final 2 years of secondary education. The selection process follows a norm-referenced model; that is, applicants' scores are ranked from the highest to the lowest, and as many students are admitted as there are available places in each program at the University (Smith-Castro, 2014). Currently, the test is administered to over 60,000 applicants to the UCR and the National University of Costa Rica (UNA in Spanish), both of which have few vacancies (9000 and 4000, respectively). The test has robust validity evidence. Factor analyses indicate a single dimension despite the two contexts (mathematical and verbal) in which reasoning is assessed (Rojas-Torres, 2014a), and predictive validity studies show that the test score is an important predictor of university academic achievement, even when controlling for other predictors of academic performance (Rojas-Torres, 2013).

Another high-impact test developed by the IIP is the Quantitative Skills Test (PHC in Spanish) (PHC, 2022) for admission to programs with high mathematical demands. Construction of this test began in the 2000s in response to the need for a complementary entrance test to the PAA for programs with curricula that included several mathematics courses. Quantitative reasoning (QR) is defined as the ability to analyze quantitative information and determine which strategies and procedures can be applied to solve a particular problem. QR is observed in skills such as the ability to use the properties of mathematical objects to arrive at a conclusion, to design strategies for applying a mathematical concept to problem-solving, to determine the validity of mathematical propositions, and to appropriately interpret a representation necessary to arrive at a solution (Rojas & Ordoñez, 2019).

This test consists of 40 single-choice items, evenly distributed across the main content topics: data analysis, arithmetic, algebra, and geometry. The content used in each subject is based on the Costa Rican primary and secondary education curricula. Examinees complete the test without a calculator, within a maximum time of

2 h (PHC, 2022). Currently, the test is used for admission to programs in Pharmacy, Chemistry, Physics, Meteorology, Mathematics, Actuarial Science, Geology, Statistics, and Mechanical Engineering, among others. Each year, it is administered to around 5000 candidates for these programs. Since university admission depends on the PAA, this test is used as a complementary requirement, with passing determined by a threshold based on the percentage of correct answers, set by sensitivity and specificity analyses (PHC, 2022). In terms of construct validity evidence, the most recent data confirm the test's one-dimensionality, with excellent internal consistency indicators above 0.90 and adequate discrimination coefficients. Furthermore, predictive validity analyses indicate that the test scores are the main predictors of students' performance in the initial courses of their respective majors (Rojas-Torres, 2013, 2014b).

It is important to note that both the PAA and PHC provide access arrangements for students with special educational needs, provided these do not compromise the validity of construct measurement, following the principle of reducing construct-irrelevant variance caused by disability or specific need. Table 6.3 presents the range of adjustments offered by the PAA as an example of the type of reasonable accommodations currently provided. The specific recommendations and strategies followed in the provision of adaptations for both the PAA and the PHC are described very clearly and didactically by Villareal-Galera et al. (2015) in their manual on the construction of standardized tests in educational contexts, which can be downloaded free of charge at the following link: https://iip.ucr.ac.cr/es/publicaciones/serie-cuadernos-metodologicos.

In addition to these two tests, the IIP is currently testing a measure to strengthen the admissions process for programs that require advanced reading comprehension skills. The Reading Comprehension Test (CL in Spanish) is a diagnostic tool that assesses the ability to understand the relationships among words, phrases, and sentences within a text, as well as to identify its main idea or theme (Brizuela-Rodríguez et al., 2019). The preliminary instrument consists of 60 single-choice items, in which students must select the correct answer from 4 options, with a time limit of 1 h and 30 min. The 60 items are divided into groups of 10, each of which must be answered based on the reading of 6 texts. Furthermore, the items measure four possible levels of textual comprehension: words, statements, paragraphs, and the text. For each of the six texts, ten questions cover all textual levels (Brizuela-Rodríguez et al., 2019).

The initial results from the pilot administration of this test to Law students confirm a desirable unidimensional structure, optimal levels of item discrimination and difficulty, but only moderate levels of internal consistency, meaning the test is still under analysis at present. The instrument is intended to be used as an initial diagnostic measure to determine whether students require additional reading support to complete courses in programs that demand significant reading effort (Brizuela et al., 2019).

In the field of knowledge assessments, it is worth mentioning the General Medical Knowledge Test (PCGM in Spanish). The test is used in the preselection of applicants to the medical specialization training programs offered by the CCSS in

Table 6.3 Examples of reasonable adjustments in the application of the University of Costa Rica Academic Aptitude Test by area of need

	Areas of need						
Reasonable adjustment	Learning	ADHD	Motor	Visual	Auditory	Systemic	Multiple
Extra time to complete the test	x	x	x	x	x	x	x
Adaptation of test booklets (e.g., enlarged print or Braille)				x			
Modifications to response formats			x	x		x	x
Specific seating arrangement in the testing room (e.g., front rows or near the door)	x	x	x	x	x	x	x
Support from sign language interpreters					x		
Administration of the test in accessible facilities			x	x		x	x
Adapted furniture			x	x		x	x
Technical aids (e.g., lamps, magnifier)				x			
Support from a reader or the use of screen readers			x	x		x	x
Individual or small-group administration	x	x	x	x	x	x	x

conjunction with the UCR (Postgraduate Program in Medical Specialities UCR [PPEM in Spanish], 2022). It is designed to assess the knowledge required of a professional in General Medicine and Surgery who wishes to enter a medical, surgical, or pediatric specialization. It is a single-choice instrument comprising 150 items, distributed across 6 topics: Surgery, Gynecology and Obstetrics, Family and Community Medicine, Internal Medicine, Pediatrics, and Psychiatry. The test is based on a specific syllabus and a mandatory bibliography defined for each of the six aforementioned topics (PPEM, 2022).

The most recent efforts in standardized assessment currently being undertaken at UCR are performance-based tests for programs that require specific skills, such as Fine Arts, Graphic Design, and Architecture (Montero-Rojas, personal communication, 3 October 2022). These are assessment procedures in which candidates are required to perform tasks that demonstrate their ability to apply knowledge and skills in situations similar to those they will encounter in their future profession, and which are subsequently evaluated by a panel of judges (Martínez-Arias, 2010).

It is also worth mentioning that other institutions in Costa Rica develop high-stakes tests of this kind, including the Costa Rica Institute of Technology, with a test similar to the PAA-UCR for university admissions; the Ministry of Public Education, responsible for administering certification exams at the end of secondary education;

and the Costa Rican Bar Association, which administers an entry examination for its members.

In 2015, these institutions, together with the CPPCR and the Directorate General of Civil Service (responsible for recruitment and selection of Central Government staff), joined forces to form the first Interinstitutional Commission on High-Stakes Testing in Costa Rica. The aim was to provide the various test development teams operating in Costa Rica with a set of minimum quality standards for the construction, validation, administration, and interpretation of high-stakes tests. The intention was to establish a common reference point to guide the work and improvement plans of institutions that wish to implement such tests in academic, employment, and professional contexts nationwide.

As a result of this collaborative network, the first "Quality Standards for High-Stakes Tests in the Costa Rican Academic and Professional Context" (Morerira et al., 2022) has recently been published as a practical manual. The document outlines the main recommendations for each stage of the process of constructing, validating, administering, and interpreting these tests. Unlike other standards, ours are designed to be accessible to nonspecialist audiences, decision-makers, interested members of the public, and professionals in training, providing concrete examples of best practices for the development, validation, and administration of such instruments, along with recommendations for key literature and useful software packages. Interested readers can find the document at the following link: https://iip.ucr.ac.cr/es/publicaciones/serie-cuadernos-metodologicos.

In summary, the high-stakes standardized tests described here are examples of the application of psychometrics to the development of instruments in a particular context, highlighting one of the distinctive features of assessment development in Costa Rica. These tests have their origins in tasks assigned to psychologists in the 1950s. Still, over time, they have been revisited by professionals from other disciplines to the extent that the construction teams for these tests today would be unimaginable without the interdisciplinary collaboration that enables their successful application in accordance with the principles of scientific excellence, equity, and justice.

Psychological and Educational Assessment in Costa Rica: Future Perspectives

Costa Rica presents an interesting particularity regarding assessment and measurement. Given the circumstances of the discipline's development both academically and professionally, psychology in our country has utilized tools for the assessment and measurement of psychological constructs not only in clinical and forensic settings, which are more typical of our field, but has also developed a tradition of work in the area of educational assessment, specifically concerning high-stakes standardized tests for the selection of candidates for higher education. In both fields, we observe significant progress, but also critical challenges that require improvement.

In terms of psychological assessment practices in high-impact professional settings, such as clinical and forensic contexts, significant advances have been made. However, recent data clearly indicate the need for greater joint efforts between academia and professional associations to reduce several existing gaps in psychometrics and best practices in psychological assessment.

The CPPCR requires the development of guidelines for best practices in different assessment settings, as well as adherence to international standards in the use of psychometric assessment instruments. It is necessary to adapt the guidelines reviewed in this chapter on best practices in psychological assessment to the particularities of Costa Rican professional culture and to the specific conditions of the various professional environments, in accordance with national legislation (see Saborío & Miranda, 2021). The data from the professional survey show a firm adherence to assessment principles based on best practices; however, there was no evidence of systematic strategies that facilitate their application in everyday professional practice.

Concerning high-stakes standardized tests, significant progress has been made in meeting the highest psychometric standards, but there is also a need for better training in psychometrics within curricular programs and greater national awareness of the importance of evidence-based decision-making.

The examples of tests reviewed in this chapter demonstrate that interdisciplinary work is essential for the development of such assessments. The teams that develop these tests should include professionals with expertise in measurement and psychometrics, as well as experts in the construct being measured, depending on the content of each test (Moreira et al., 2022). At the same time, it is crucial to recognize that, even when a psychological research unit manages these processes, psychologists are increasingly less likely to lead the development of such tests in Costa Rica. A future challenge will be to promote awareness of the importance of psychologists' participation in assessment teams for these types of tests, since psychometrics is, without doubt, one of the most successful scientific approaches providing valuable tools for undertaking the measurement of constructs in education and psychology (Nunnally & Bernstein, 1995; Martínez et al., 2006).

In summary, the future of assessment and measurement in Costa Rica can be strengthened through joint research processes in which universities and various public and private institutions promote a culture of excellence, rigor, equity, and justice in assessment and measurement. These stakeholders can foster the development and validation of specialized instruments tailored to the particularities of the Costa Rican population and different assessment contexts, as well as promote the conduct of normative studies that provide psychometric evidence on the instruments most widely used in academic and professional practice in the country.

Acknowledgments The authors acknowledge the support of the Institute for Psychological Research at UCR and its Aptitude Test Department for providing access to key information for the writing of the present chapter.

Competing Interests The authors declare that they have no known competing financial interests or personal relationships that could have influenced the work reported in this chapter.

References

Adis, G. (1975). Psicoterapia en Costa Rica. *Revista Interamericana de Psicología, 9*(1), 23–28. https://journal.sipsych.org/index.php/IJP/article/view/717

Adis, G. (1991). Sobre la historia de la psicología clínica en Costa Rica. *Revista Cúpula, 27*, 30–34. https://www.binasss.sa.cr/bibliotecas/bhp/cupula/n271991

American Educational Research Association, American Psychological Association, and National Council on Measurement in Education [AERA, APA, NCME]. (2014). *Standards for educational and psychological testing*. American Educational Research Association.

American Psychological Association [APA]. (2013). Specialty guidelines for forensic psychology. *American Psychologist, 68*(1), 7–19. https://psycnet.apa.org. https://doi.org/10.1037/a0029889

American Psychological Association, APA Task Force on Psychological Assessment and Evaluation Guidelines. (2020a). *APA guidelines for psychological assessment and evaluation*. https://www.apa.org/about/policy/guidelines-psychological-assessment-evaluation.pdf.

American Psychological Association, Board of Educational Affairs Task Force on Education and Training Guidelines for Psychological Assessment in Health Service Psychology. (2020b). *APA guidelines for education and training in psychological assessment in health service psychology.* https://www.apa.org/about/policy/guidelines-assessment-health-service.pdf.

Anastasi, A. (1982). *Psychological testing* (5th ed.). Macmillan.

Arbisi, P. A., & Beck, J. G. (2016). Introduction to the special series "empirically supported assessment". *Clinical Psychology: A Publication of the Division of Clinical Psychology of the American Psychological Association, 23*(4), 323–326. https://psycnet.apa.org. https://doi.org/10.1111/cpsp.12182

Archer, R. P., Buffington-Vollum, J. K., Stredny, R. V., & Handel, R. W. (2006). A survey of psychological test use patterns among forensic psychologists. *Journal of Personality Assessment, 87*(1), 84–94. https://doi.org/10.1207/s15327752jpa8701_07

Archer, R. P., Wheeler, E. M. A., & Vauter, R. A. (2016). Empirically supported forensic assessment. *Clinical Psychology: Science and Practice, 23*(4), 348–364. https://doi.org/10.1111/cpsp.12171

Baltodano-Chacón, M., Marín-Picado, B., Alpízar-Rojas, H., & Marín-Villalobos, R. (2021). Situación laboral de las personas graduadas y egresadas de las carreras de Psicología y Enseñanza de la Psicología de la Universidad de Costa Rica. *Wimb Lu, 16*(1), 51–73. https://doi.org/10.15517/wl.v16i1.46664

Boccaccini, M. T., & Brodsky, S. L. (1999). Diagnostic test usage by forensic psychologists in emotional injury cases. *Professional Psychology: Research and Practice, 30*, 253–259. https://doi.org/10.1037/0735-7028.30.3.253

Bond, T., & Fox, C. (2001). *Applying the Rasch model: Fundamental measurement in the human sciences*. Psychology Press. https://doi.org/10.4324/9781410600127

Bornstein, R. F. (2017). Evidence-based psychological assessment. *Journal of Personality Assessment, 99*(4), 435–445. https://doi.org/10.1080/00223891.2016.1236343

Brizuela-Rodríguez, A., Pérez-Rojas, N., & Rojas-Rojas, G. (2019). Validación de una prueba de comprensión lectora para estudiantes universitarios. *Revista Educación, 44*(1), 1–14. https://doi.org/10.15517/revedu.v44i1.34983

Campos, D., Pérez, R., & Rosabal, M. (1990). Identidad profesional e institucionalización de la psicología en Costa Rica: Crítica e interpretación histórica. *Revista de Ciencias Sociales, 47*, 81–92. https://www.iip.ucr.ac.cr/sites/default/files/contenido/Identidad%20profesional%20campos%20perez%20rosabal%20cs%2090.pdf

Carragher, N., Krueger, R. F., Eaton, N. R., & Slade, T. (2015). Disorders without borders: Current and future directions in the meta-structure of mental disorders. *Social Psychiatry and Psychiatric Epidemiology, 50*, 339–350. https://doi.org/10.1007/s00127-014-1004-z

Colegio de Profesionales en Psicología en Costa Rica [CPPCR]. (1 de agosto 2022). *Código de Ética y Deontológico del Colegio Profesional de Psicólogos de Costa Rica.* https://psicologiacr.com/sdm_downloads/codigo-de-etica-y-deontologico-del-cppcr-reforma-2019/

National Council of Rectors [Consejo Nacional de Rectores, CONARE]. (15 de octubre 2019). Radiografía Laboral 2019. https://radiografia.conare.ac.cr/radiografia-laboral-iii-2019/.
National Council of Rectors [Consejo Nacional de Rectores, CONARE]. (15 de octubre 2022). *Oferta Académica*. http://infoues.conare.ac.cr/web/infoues/carreras.
National Council for Private University Higher Education [Consejo Nacional de Educación Superior Privada, CONESUP]. (16 de octubre 2022). *Carreras por área y subárea*. http://www.ws.mep.go.cr/CONSULTAS/frmConsultas/frmConsultasVarias.aspx.
Domingo Segovia, J. & Domingo Martos, L. Análisis de tareas para preparar y seguir procesos de aprendizaje. En Domingo y M. Pérez Ferra (coords.) (2015). *Aprendiendo a enseñar. Manual práctico de didáctica (*Vol. 1, pp. 169-178). Pirámide.
Downing, S. M., & Haladyna, T. M. (Eds.). (2006). Handbook of test development. Lawrence Erlbaum Associates Publishers. https://doi.org/10.4324/9780203874776.
School of Psychology [Escuela de Psicología de la Universidad de Costa Rica, EPS]. (2 de agosto 2022). *¿Quiénes somos*. https://www.psico.ucr.ac.cr/index.php/es/quienes-somos/sobre-la-escuela/quienes-somos1.
Heilbrun, K. (2001). *Principles of forensic mental health assessment*. Kluwer Academic/Plenum. https://doi.org/10.1007/b100329
Heilbrun, K., Grisso, T., & Goldstein, A. (2009). *Foundations of forensic mental health assessment*. Oxford University Press. https://doi.org/10.1093/med:psych/9780195323092.001.0001
Instituto de Investigaciones Psicológicas [IIP]. (1 de agosto 2022). *Historia*. https://www.iip.ucr.ac.cr/es/sobre-el-iip/historia.
Kerlinger, F. N., & Lee, H. B. (2002). *Investigación del comportamiento*. McGraw-Hill.
Kotov, R., Krueger, R. F., Watson, D., Achenbach, T. M., Althoff, R. R., Bagby, R. M., Brown, T. A., Carpenter, W. T., Caspi, A., Clark, L. A., Eaton, N. R., Forbes, M. K., Forbush, K. T., Goldberg, D., Hasin, D., Hyman, S. E., Ivanova, M. Y., Lynam, D. R., Markon, K., et al. (2017). The hierarchical taxonomy of psychopathology (HiTOP): A dimensional alternative to traditional nosologies. *Journal of Abnormal Psychology, 126*(4), 454–477. https://doi.org/10.1037/abn0000258
Kotov, R., Krueger, R. F., Watson, D., Cicero, D. C., Conway, C. C., DeYoung, C. G., Eaton, N. R., Forbes, M. K., Hallquist, M. N., Latzman, R. D., Mullins-Sweatt, S. N., Ruggero, C. J., Simms, L. J., Waldman, I. D., Waszczuk, M. A., & Wright, A. G. C. (2021). The hierarchical taxonomy of psychopathology (HiTOP): A quantitative nosology based on consensus of evidence. *Annual Review of Clinical Psychology, 17*(1), 83–108. https://doi.org/10.1146/annurev-clinpsy-081219-093304
Krishnamurthy, R., Hass, G. A., Natoli, A. P., Smith, B. L., Arbisi, P. A., & Gottfried, E. D. (2022). Professional practice guidelines for personality assessment. *Journal of Personality Assessment, 104*(1), 1–16. https://doi.org/10.1080/00223891.2021.1942020
Lally, S. J. (2003). What tests are acceptable for use in forensic evaluations? A survey of experts. *Professional Psychology: Research and Practice, 34*, 491–498. https://psycnet.apa.org. https://doi.org/10.1037/0735-7028.34.5.491
López Core, R. (2013). Desarrollo de la especialidad en Psicología clínica en Costa Rica: perspectivas futuras. *Revista Costarricense de Psicología, 32*(1), 43–60. http://www.rcps-cr.org/openjournal/index.php/RCPs/article/view/18
Mainieri, A. (2008). Reseña Histórica de la Prueba de Aptitud Académica (PAA-U.C.R.). *Diálogos: Revista Electrónica de Historia, 9*. https://doi.org/10.15517/dre.v9i0.31204
Martínez-Arias, R. (2010). La evaluación del desempeño. *Papeles del Psicólogo, 31*(1), 85–96. https://www.papelesdelpsicologo.es/pdf/1799.pdf
Martínez, M. R., Hernández, M. J., & Hernández, M. V. (2006). *Psicometría*. Alianza Editorial.
McLaughlin, J. L., & Kan, L. Y. (2014). Test usage in four common types of forensic mental health assessment. *Professional Psychology: Research and Practice, 45*(2), 128–135. https://psycnet.apa.org. https://doi.org/10.1037/a0036318
Melton, G. B., Petrila, J., Poythress, N. G., Slobogin, C., Otto, R. K., Mossman, D., & Condie, L. O. (2018). *Psychological evaluations for the courts: A handbook for mental health professionals and lawyers* (4th ed.). The Guilford Press.

Messick, S. (1989a). Meaning and values in test validation: The science and ethics of assessment. *Educational Researcher, 18*(2), 5–11. https://doi.org/10.3102/0013189X018002005

Messick, S. (1989b). Validity. In R. L. Linn (Ed.), *Educational measurement* (3rd ed., pp. 13–103). American Council on Education and Macmillan.

Messick, S. (1995). Standards of validity and the validity of standards in performance assessment. *Educational Measurement: Issues and Practice, 14*(4), 5–8. https://doi.org/10.1111/j.1745-3992.1995.tb00881.x

Miranda, J. C., & Prado, J. E. (2014). Estado actual de la evaluación psicométrica en Costa Rica. Ponencia en el V Congreso ULAPSI, Ciudad de Antigua Guatemala, Guatemala, Centro América del 14 al 17 de mayo del 2014.

Montero, E. (2013). Referentes conceptuales y metodológicos sobre la noción moderna de validez de instrumentos de medición: implicaciones para el caso de personas con necesidades educativas especiales. *Actualidades en Psicología, 27*(114), 113–128. https://doi.org/10.15517/ap.v27i114.7900

Moreira-Mora, T. E., Alfaro-Rojas, L., Brizuela-Rodríguez, A., Chacón-Vega, C., Gómez-González, E., Jiménez-Alfaro, K., Jiménez-Segura, F., Mena-Castillo, P., Montero-Rojas, E., Picado-Barrantes, H., Rojas-Rojas, G., Rojas-Torres, L., Smith-Castro, V., Solórzano-Salas, M. J., & Villarreal-Galera, M. P. (2022). Estándares de calidad para pruebas estandarizadas de alto impacto en el contexto académico y profesional costarricense. Serie Cuadernos Metodológicos, Cuaderno 9. Instituto de Investigaciones Psicológicas. https://iip.ucr.ac.cr/index.php/es/publicaciones/series-cuadernos-metodologicos/cuaderno-9-estandares-de-calidad-para-pruebas.

Muñiz. J. (2003). Teoría Clásica de los Tests. Ediciones Pirámide, S.A.

Nunnally, J. C., & Bernstein, I. J. (1995). *Teoría psicométrica* (3rd ed.). Editorial McGraw-Hill Latinoamericana.

Otto, R. K., DeMier, R. L., & Boccaccini, M. T. (2014). *Forensic reports and testimony: A guide to effective communication for psychologists and psychiatrists*. Wiley.

Programa de Posgrado en Especialidades Médicas [PPEM]. (2 de noviembre 2022). *Proceso de Admisión al PPEM*. https://www.sep.ucr.ac.cr/ppem-ucr-inicio.html.

Prueba de Habilidades Cuantitativas [PHC]. (5 de noviembre 2022). *Historia de la PHC*. https://www.hc.iip.ucr.ac.cr/historia/

Rodríguez-Seijas, C., Eaton, N.R., y Krueger, R.F. (2015). How transdiagnostic factors of personality and psychopathology can inform clinical assessment and ióntervention. Journal of Personality Assessment, 97, 425–435. https://doi.org/10.1080/00223891.2015.1055752.

Rojas-Torres, L. (2013). Validez predictiva de los componentes del promedio de admisión a la Universidad de Costa Rica utilizando el género y el tipo de colegio como variables control. *Actualidades Investigativas en Educación, 13*(1). https://doi.org/10.15517/aie.v13i1.11707

Rojas-Torres, L. (2014a). Evidencias de validez de la Prueba de Aptitud Académica de la Universidad de Costa Rica basadas en su estructura interna. *Actualidades En Psicología, 28*(116), 15–26. https://doi.org/10.15517/ap.v28i116.14889

Rojas-Torres, L. (2014b). Predicción de la reprobación de cursos de matemática básicos en las carreras de Física, Meteorología, Matemática, Ciencias Actuariales y Farmacia. *Revista Electrónica Educare, 18*(3), 3–15. https://doi.org/10.15359/ree.18-3.1

Rojas-Torres, L., & Ordóñez-Gutierrez, G. (2019). Proceso de construcción de pruebas educativas: El caso de la Prueba de Habilidades Cuantitativas. *Revista Evaluar, 19*(2), 15–29. https://revistas.unc.edu.ar/index.php/revaluar/index

Roman, R., & Pawlowski, J. (2019). Reseña histórica del surgimiento de la psicología en Costa Rica: De la atención a la salud hacia su situación actual. *Boletim da Sociedade Brasileira de História da Psicologia, 2*(4), 6–27. https://sbhpsi.com.br/wp-content/uploads/2014/09/BOLETIM-SBHP-V2N4-SET2019.pdf

Saborío, C., & Miranda, J. C. (2021). Manual orientativo del proceso de evaluación psicológica de idoneidad mental para portar y poseer armas de fuego y laborar en seguridad privada. Colegio de Profesionales en Psicología de Costa Rica.

Sellbom, M., & Hopwood, C. J. (2016). Evidence-based assessment in the 21st century: Comments on the special series papers. *Clinical Psychology: A Publication of the Division of Clinical Psychology of the American Psychological Association, 23*(4), 403–409. https://psycnet.apa.org. https://doi.org/10.1111/cpsp.12183

Sibaja-Molina, J., Prado-Calderón, J. E., & Vindas-González, A. (2016). Análisis de la demanda laboral de profesionales en Psicología en Costa Rica durante el periodo 2012-2014. *Revista Costarricense De Psicología, 35*(1), 47–65. https://doi.org/10.22544/rcps.v35i01.04

Smith-Castro, V. (comp.) (2014). Compendio de Instrumentos de Medición IIP-2014. *Serie Cuadernos Metodológicos. Cuaderno 6*. Instituto de Investigaciones Psicológicas.https://www.iip.ucr.ac.cr/sites/default/files/contenido/cuamet6.PDF.

Thomas, P. (1970). La situación de la psicología en Costa Rica. *Revista Latinoamericana de Psicología, 2*(1), 9–13. http://www.redalyc.org/pdf/805/80502102.pdf

Thomas, P. (1975). La evolución de la psicología en Costa Rica. *Anuario de Psicología/The UB Journal of Psychology, 13*(2), 99–118. https://www.raco.cat/index.php/AnuarioPsicologia/article/view/59683/88098

Viljoen, J. L., McLachan, K., & Vincent, G. M. (2010). Assessing violence risk and psychopathy in juvenile and adult offenders: A survey of clinical practices. *Assessment, 17*, 377–395. https://doi.org/10.1177/1073191109359587

Villareal-Galera, M. P., Alfaro-Rojas, L., & Brizuela-Rodíguez, A. (2015). Construcción de pruebas estandarizadas en el ámbito de medición psicológica y educativa. *Serie Cuadernos Metodológicos. Cuaderno 8*. Instituto de Investigaciones Psicológicas. https://www.iip.ucr.ac.cr/sites/default/files/contenido/Cuadernometodologico8%20IIP.pdf.

Wilson, M. (2005). *Constructing measures: An item response modelling approach*. Lawrence Erlbaum.

Wright, A. J., Pade, H., Gottfried, E. D., Arbisi, P. A., McCord, D. M., & Wygant, D. B. (2022). Evidence-based clinical psychological assessment (EBCPA): Review of current state of the literature and best practices. *Professional Psychology, Research and Practice, 53*(4), 372–386. https://psycnet.apa.org. https://doi.org/10.1037/pro0000447

Chapter 7
Psychological Assessment in Ecuador: Past, Present, and Future Challenges

Claudio López-Calle, Manuel Capella, and Andrea Freire Pesántez

Introduction

Ecuador currently has a population of about 17 million (Instituto Nacional de Estadísticas y Censos, 2023). Of these, 78% self-identify as mestizo; 8% as montubio; 8% as Indigenous; 5% as Afro-Ecuadorian; and 2% as white. The median age is 29 years, with 63% of the population residing in urban areas. The poverty rate is around 24%, and extreme poverty is at 10% ((Instituto Nacional de Estadísticas y Censos, 2025). Ecuador is also a country where numerous psychology professionals study and work. The training of psychologists began in the second half of the twentieth century, which also fostered the development of psychological assessment, already practiced since at least the 1930s. In this chapter, drawing on documentary sources and key informants, we present a brief history of psychological assessment in Ecuador, exploring its past, analyzing its present, and reflecting on its future.

C. López-Calle (✉)
Universidad de Cuenca, Cuenca, Ecuador
e-mail: claudio.lopez@ucuenca.edu.ec

M. Capella
Universidad Católica del Uruguay, Montevideo, Uruguay
e-mail: mcapella@ucu.edu.uy

A. Freire Pesántez
Universidad del Azuay, Cuenca, Ecuador
e-mail: afreire@uazuay.edu.ec

S. V. Pugliese et al. (eds.), *Origins and Challenges of Psychological Assessment in Ibero-American Countries*, https://doi.org/10.1007/978-3-032-21380-8_7

The Historical Development of Psychological Assessment in Ecuador

Liberalism, together with positivism —understood as utilitarianism, scientism, and a drive for progress (Ossenbach, 2018)— shaped the country's history at the beginning of the twentieth century. This influenced the world of ideas and fields such as medicine, psychiatry, sociology, pedagogy, and, of course, psychology. The first theories and methods of local psychology were imported from what was considered the "holy trinity" of science: England, France, and Germany (De Veintimilla, 1906). Below, we briefly outline the main features of the development of psychological assessment in Ecuador by periods.

The First Three Decades of the Twentieth Century

Psychiatry had a significant influence on the initial development of psychology and psychological assessment. An important milestone was the creation of the first psychiatry chairs in the training of physicians at public universities: at the *Universidad Central del Ecuador* (Central University of Ecuador) (1913), the *Universidad de Cuenca* (University of Cuenca) (1917), and the *Universidad de Guayaquil* (University of Guayaquil) (1934) (Cueva Tamariz, 1965). These chairs, in addition to addressing psychiatric and mental health issues, indirectly enabled reflection on psychological matters, as they were up to date with the knowledge and methods of psychiatry, psychoanalysis, and psychology of the time.

The first professor of the psychiatry chair at the Central University of Ecuador was Carlos Alberto Arteta García, followed by Julio Endara Moreano in 1926 (Cueva Tamariz, 1965). Endara Moreano gave a significant boost to the field and became the most prominent figure in the development of psychiatry from a positivist perspective in Ecuador (Landázuri, 2008). He also worked at the *Hospicio y Manicomio San* Lázaro (San Lázaro Hospice and Asylum) in Quito, where, in 1926, the first "registration forms" for patients were introduced (Landázuri, 2008). These forms can be considered an initial precursor of psychological assessment, still closely tied to psychiatry. They included several sections (family, arithmetic, intelligence) and served as a space for psychiatrists to record patient data, evaluated according to the psychiatrist's "clinical judgment." These forms represented a type of psychological assessment closely linked to psychiatry. In 1910, the *Hospital Lorenzo Ponce* (Lorenzo Ponce Hospital) was established in Guayaquil (Instituto de Neurociencias, 2022), and it is possible that practices related to psychological assessment, also connected to psychiatry, were developed there as well.

On the other hand, psychology and psychological assessment were also advanced by the development of Education, which was likewise influenced by the Liberal Revolution and its positivist philosophy. As part of the process of secularizing society and separating Church and State, the liberal government founded educational institutions to train primary school teachers. In Quito, in 1901, the *Escuela Normal Juan Montalvo* (Juan Montalvo Normal School) for boys and the *Escuela Normal Manuela Cañizares* (Manuela Cañizares Normal School) for girls were established (Paladines-Escudero, 1998). To properly train teachers (known as "normalistas"), several *pedagogical missions* from abroad were hired, the most renowned being the German pedagogical missions of 1913 and 1922 (Tobar, 1954). Psychology was considered essential for teacher training and was incorporated into the curriculum (Goetschel, 2007). Its instruction in normal schools also enabled the development of materials and environments for its teaching; for example, the Juan Montalvo Normal School had a small "Experimental Psychology Laboratory" equipped with apparatus and some tests (Carbo-Bravo & Velasco-Mogollón, 1976, p. 93). For many decades, tests were taught and administered in normal schools.

Psychological and educational assessment was also influenced by the development of *hygienism*. In 1916, the *Dirección de Higiene Escolar* (School Hygiene Directorate) was created in Quito, attached to the *Dirección de Estudios* (Directorate of Studies), with the aim of safeguarding children's health and promoting physical development through physical activity. "School records" were implemented in schools to document children's health data (Chilig & Enma, 2017). Hygiene in general, and school hygiene in particular, were strengthened after the Juliana Revolution of 1925 (Sinardet, 1999), especially under President Isidro Ayora (1879–1978), who governed the country from 1926 to 1931. From physical hygiene emerged mental or psychological hygiene, which created a favorable environment for psychological assessment. This enabled, first, anthropometric studies, and subsequently, educational and psychological studies.

The adoption of the New School or Active School movement in the Ecuadorian educational system in the second half of the 1920s was also significant. Ecuador was the first American country to join the International Bureau of New Education in Geneva, and Adolphe Ferrière visited the country in 1930 (Fernández-Rueda, 2018). This event contributed to the development of psychological assessment, as it became necessary to evaluate students from this new educational perspective.

The 1930s

In the 1930s, interest began to grow in the assessment of intelligence and academic achievement (then referred to as *instructional achievement*). The assessment of intelligence also sparked debates about normality and abnormality, and, in an era of school hygiene and eugenic ideas, the issue of *special education* emerged, later known in inclusive education as the segregation stage (Parrilla Latas, 2002). At this time, the argument was already being made that "tests developed in other countries are not suitable for our own context" (Carbo-Bravo & Velasco-Mogollón, 1976, p. 23).

According to Carbo-Bravo and Velasco-Mogollón (1976), in 1930, the first test related to reading and writing acquisition (later known as the maturity test for reading and writing) was administered at the *Escuela Leopoldo Chávez* (Leopoldo Chávez School), affiliated with the Juan Montalvo Normal School. It was a test developed by the German Herbert Winkler, published in 1925, and brought to Ecuador by Professor Manuel Utreras Gómez, who had studied in Germany. Professors César Sylva and Ernesto Guevara Wolf administered the test and published the results. Herbert Winkler's tests served as the basis for the well-known ABC Test by Professor Lourenzo Filho in Brazil.

In 1935, another milestone occurred in the history of psychological and educational assessment: the first large-scale administration of tests. According to Carbo-Bravo and Velasco-Mogollón (1976), that year Carlos Zambrano Orejuela assumed the position of Minister of Education and created a technical section called the *Dirección de Higiene Escolar* (School Hygiene Directorate), which in turn had several divisions: Physiological Culture, Socioculture, and Psychoculture. The latter promoted psychological studies. The minister appointed Fernando Chávez Reyes as Director General of Education, who proposed administering academic achievement tests in Quito.

Ermel Velasco Mogollón (López-Calle & Cedillo-Quizhpe, 2022), who had begun training as a quantitative researcher, worked with Bolívar Druet under the supervision of Celso Jarrín, and in 1935–1936 they administered the Ballard Group Test, which measured intelligence, in 32 schools in Quito. This event was possibly the first large-scale administration of an intelligence test in the country. At the end of the 1930s, the Kuhlmann-Anderson Group Mental Test, which measured intelligence and had been provisionally translated and adapted by César Mora and J.B. Diefferding in 1933 (Carbo-Bravo & Velasco-Mogollón, 1976), was also administered in 12 schools in Guayaquil.

In 1938, Ermel Velasco and Edmundo Carbo —the authors who contributed most to the study of intelligence and academic achievement tests— administered an ad hoc knowledge test in Quito schools, based on the curricula of the time (Carbo-Bravo & Velasco-Mogollón, 1976). The same authors published *Pruebas Mentales: con Normas Obtenidas para Nuestro Medio* (Carbo-Bravo & Velasco-Mogollón, 1939), in which they presented the B.D. Test, the Concordia Group Test, and the Pieron Group Test; for the latter, they reported the results of its administration in Quito schools. During this period, there is also evidence of the presence of the Binet-Simon Test (Terman revision), as it was called at the time. In 1937, Carlota Félix de Garcés —who studied psychology in London on a scholarship from the Ecuadorian government (Fernández-Rueda, 2018)— published the *Manual de Inteligencia*, a text reflecting on the use of tests during those years.

During this period, Julio Endara Moreano turned to psychoanalysis, which he taught in his chairs at the Faculty of Medicine and later at the Faculty of Philosophy and Letters of his *alma mater*. Endara became an international expert in the Rorschach inkblot method. In 1936, he also founded the Institute of Criminology, which was later annexed to the Central University of Ecuador, and in 1937, he founded the journal *Archivos de Criminología, Neuro-Psiquiatría y Disciplinas Conexas*, initiating studies in criminology (López-Calle & León, 2020). By the late 1930s, studies based on Rorschach psychodiagnostics were already being conducted in prison and Indigenous populations (Rosero Padilla, 2019). In subsequent decades, research using this test increased.

The 1940s

In the 1940s, psychological assessment was carried out mainly in the context of education, the legal system, and medicine (Hall, 1946); for example, psychological tests were administered under the supervision of a psychiatrist to "juvenile delinquents," or used in schools with children and adolescents experiencing educational difficulties. During this period, the measurement of intelligence and academic achievement gained prominence. At the beginning of this decade, Carbo-Bravo et al. (1940) published *Pruebas de Rendimiento Instructivo: Constrastadas y Libres*. This was followed by the influential work *Pruebas de Instrucción ACV* (Carbo-Bravo et al., 1942), which served as a manual for the administering educational achievement tests.

During this decade, the Pintner-Cunningham Test, which assessed intelligence, the Otis Intelligence Test, the Decroly-Buyse Test to classify children in reading and writing, and the Maurice Debesse Questionnaire, which assessed vocational interests in adolescents, were also used.

The 1950s

In 1950, the renowned Ecuadorian educator Emilio Uzcátegui (1899–1986) (Bustamante-Torres & Velázquez-Seiferheld, 2022) founded the *Instituto de Psicología* (Institute of Psychology) within the Faculty of Philosophy, Letters, and Educational Sciences at the Central University of Ecuador, as a way to centralize the teaching of psychology, which had already been part of secondary teacher training since the 1930s. The training offered at the Institute was equivalent to current postgraduate studies, with two additional years of study for students from certain fields (pedagogy, medicine, law, and social work) who already held undergraduate degrees and wished to obtain the title of Professor of Psychology to work in secondary schools. The curriculum of the Institute of Psychology included subjects related to psychological assessment; in the first year, these were Biotypology and Mental Hygiene, Psychotechnics, and Mental Test Techniques, while in the second year, Statistics was included (Universidad Central del Ecuador, 1950). Uzcátegui also purchased a psychotechnical laboratory to enhance training (Uzcátegui, 1975), which was possibly the first laboratory of its kind established at an Ecuadorian university.

In the mid-1950s, the Institute was transformed into the *Escuela de Psicología* (School of Psychology). The program was extended to 4 years and became an undergraduate degree. The qualification for psychology teachers continued to be awarded for many more years. This curriculum also included subjects related to psychological assessment: Statistics in the second year; and Psychopathology and School Hygiene, Mental Tests: Personality, and Mental Tests: Aptitudes, in the third year (Universidad Central del Ecuador, 1956).

An important book at the beginning of this decade was *Psicometría Escolar* by Jacinto Bastidas (1950). During these years, records show the use of the Goodenough Human Figure Test; the Binet-Simon Test (Terman version); the Otis Group Test; the Concordia Test; the Vermeylen Psychographic Intelligence Examination; the Pieron Test; and the Thurstone Test (Carbo-Bravo & Velasco-Mogollón, 1976). Until 1950, research and adaptation of mental tests were conducted sporadically; with the creation of the Department of Educational Research in the Ministry of Education that same year (attached to the Statistics and Ranking section where Ermel Velasco worked), more tests were developed (Carbo-Bravo & Velasco-Mogollón, 1976). An example of this was the publication *Ensayo de Aplicación del Test de Inteligencia de Pieron* (Carbo-Bravo, 1957), which was administered to 1025 students from schools in Quito.

Another major milestone in psychological and educational assessment was the evaluation of 673 candidates for admission to the Central University of Ecuador during the 1956–57 academic year, conducted by the School of Psychology (Carbo-Bravo & Velasco-Mogollón, 1976; "Informe de Cómo se Realizó la Investigación de la Prueba Mental Canada", 1957). Knowledge and intelligence tests were administered; for the latter, provisionally adapted tests were used: the Canada Test, Otis Gamma Test, and Thurstone Test.

The 1960s

In this decade, the School of Psychology was founded at the University of Guayaquil in 1962, which established a specialization in educational psychology and vocational guidance (Facultad de Ciencias Psicológicas, 1984). During these years, at the University of Guayaquil, the importance of tests was also emphasized, for example, in the context of measuring interests and in the field of vocational guidance (Asociación de Escuela de Psicología, 1967). Among those mentioned —and considered at the time by some of the institution's psychology professionals to have greater validity— are: the Vocational Interest Blank, the Vocational Interest Inventory, similar questionnaires developed by other authors such as Suttleworth, Thurstone's Record of Professional Interests, the Kuder Questionnaire, and Lee and Thorpe. The questionnaire developed by Brainard was regarded by some of the institution's psychology professionals at the time as "the best constructed and validated" (Asociación de Escuela de Psicología, 1967, p. 26).

During these same years in Guayaquil, tests criticized for validity issues included: the Agricultural Engineering Test (Butt); Children's Play Interests (Terman); Children's Reading (Wissler); College Women's Occupational Interests (McHale); Girl's General Trade Interests (Troops); Men's Mechanical Interests (O'Rourke);

Social Interests (Ream); the Wyman Word Association Test (1926), based on Jungian theory; and Burtt's Hobbies Test (1926) (Asociación de Escuela de Psicología, 1967).

In the 1960s, vocational guidance gained prominence, along with the focus on interests and aptitudes. This professional activity had already been underway since the 1950s. In Quito, records show the use of the Gertrudis Hildreth Inventory of Professional Interests and Personality Traits (Hildreth Personality Inventory); the Differential Aptitude Test (DAT); the Lee-Thorpe Occupational Interests Test; the Angeline Interests Test; Raven's Progressive Matrices; the Domino Test; and the California Test (Carbo-Bravo & Velasco-Mogollón, 1976). Additionally, university entrance exams since 1956 and the interest in vocational guidance during those years led to the creation of the *Departamento de Orientación Profesional* (Department of Vocational Guidance) at the Central University of Ecuador. The faculty of the School of Psychology were responsible for administering and scoring the exams; later, the journal *Archivos Ecuatorianos de Orientación* was also established.

Another aspect worth mentioning is the contribution of Father Emilio Gambirasio, an Italian Salesian priest, to the development of psychological assessment. Since the 1960s, he promoted psychological assessment in Salesian schools. He began with what was called the *Centro Psicológico Salesiano* (Salesian Psychological Center), which initially operated at the *Colegio Don Bosco de la Tola* (Don Bosco School of La Tola), Quito, and later became part of the *Instituto Superior Salesiano* (Salesian Higher Institute) (García, 2008), which is the origin of today's *Universidad Politécnica Salesiana* (Salesian Polytechnic University). He equipped the center with a psychometric laboratory containing various assessment instruments. Later, in the 1970s, he also worked at the *Pontificia Universidad Católica del Ecuador* (Pontifical Catholic University of Ecuador) as a psychometrics professor. The center continues to operate today at the Salesian Polytechnic University, Quito campus, and is now called the *Centro Psicológico Salesiano "P. Emilio Gambirasio"* (Salesian Psychological Center "P. Emilio Gambirasio").

The 1970s

At the beginning of this decade, psychology schools were established within the two Catholic universities: the Pontifical Catholic University of Ecuador and the Catholic University of Santiago de Guayaquil. From their inception, these universities were oriented toward psychoanalysis, and consequently, psychological assessment also followed this approach. The first director of the School of Psychology (1970) at the Pontifical Catholic University of Ecuador was the Jesuit Jaime Malo Borrero (Pontificia Universidad Católica del Ecuador, 1996), who was also a professor of Rorschach Psychodiagnostics, a technique he had learned at Harvard University (Ewald Utreras, personal communication, September 2, 2022).

On the other hand, in 1972, the Faculty of Psychological Sciences was established at the Central University of Ecuador. The orientation of this new faculty, influenced by medicine and psychiatry, was toward the biological. In psychology, the focus was on the Russian school, mainly reflexology (Facultad de Ciencias Psicológicas, 1988). In the new faculty, everything related to psychoanalysis was discarded, and psychological assessment followed the same trend.

In Cuenca, Leopoldo Peñaherrera Mosquera (López-Calle & Ortiz-Ochoa, 2022), a former Salesian, was the founder of the first specialization in educational psychology at the University of Cuenca (1977) and the founder of the clinical psychology specialization at the Catholic University of Cuenca (1978); he was also among the first psychodiagnostics professors in the city, having learned it in a self-taught manner. Leopoldo Peñaherrera met and was in contact with Father Emilio Gambirasio, from whom he requested tests for his psychodiagnostics chair. Additionally, as dean, he purchased one of the best psychology laboratories from *Casa Takei* (Takei House) in Japan, which unfortunately did not function due to a lack of trained personnel. The devices and instruments from this laboratory were stored for decades and are now exhibited as part of the history in the *Laboratorio de Psicometría, Psicología Comparada y Etología del Centro de Investigación, Innovación y Transferencia Tecnológica* (Laboratory of Psychometrics, Comparative Psychology, and Ethology at the Center for Research, Innovation, and Technology Transfer, CIITT) of the Catholic University of Cuenca (Universidad Católica de Cuenca, 2021).

An important book from the seventies, and possibly the first book on statistics applied to psychology and education in Ecuador, is *Estadística para Educadores y Psicólogos* (Velasco-Mogollón, 1971). The first volume was devoted to descriptive statistics; a second volume on inferential statistics was planned but never published. In the seventies, there are also reports on the Wechsler Intelligence Test; the Gates-MacGinitie Reading Tests; the Terman-Merrill Test; the Bender Visual-Motor Gestalt Test; and the Raven Progressive Matrices Test (Carbo-Bravo & Velasco-Mogollón, 1976).

According to Rosero-Padilla (2019), in the seventies there was a strong dissemination and application of tests in the clinical area, mainly at the San Lázaro Psychiatric Hospital in Quito, such as: the Rorschach Test; Karl Koch's Tree Test; Karen Machover's Human Figure Test; and the Louis Corman's Family Drawing Test. Intelligence tests were also administered, such as: the Kent E-G-Y Test; Otis Test; Bender Visual-Motor Gestalt Test; Raven Progressive Matrices Test; and Goodenough Test.

Let us look at an example of assessment from those times at the Catholic University of Santiago de Guayaquil, which leaned toward psychoanalysis. A clinical psychologist trained at that university and working at a private school in Guayaquil in the late seventies provides insight into how "clinical" psychological assessment of children with "learning problems" was conducted (Escuela de Psicología, 1979, pp. 91–94). The diagnostic process involved two therapists and took place in both individual and group contexts, emphasizing "the search for meaning or significance in the symptom, in this case, learning problems," prioritizing "the qualitative, the affective, the relational" in diagnostic evaluations. The "model" of work included: an interview with the parents (clarifying the referral, conducting an anamnesis); an interview with the child, or "play hour" (analyzing all forms of expression, including games, drawings, words, etc.); and a "diagnostic" family interview (to clarify doubts of the evaluator, for example, missing or contradictory data, or when "serious distortions in family relationships are suspected"). The data analyzed led to an "assessment regarding": types of anxieties, level of anxiety, defenses, unconscious fantasies, ego states and capacities, roles, explicit and implicit ideology.

One of the characteristics of psychology training in Ecuador from its beginnings was specialization at the undergraduate level, a trend that continues in some universities to this day. The first specializations were: educational psychology and vocational guidance, clinical psychology, and industrial psychology, later called organizational psychology. From this decade onward, psychology programs established in the country adopted the training curricula created in Quito, and possibly also in Guayaquil, imprinting the same trend in psychological assessment.

The 1980s and the 1990s

Regardless of the theoretical orientations of the universities, places of work, and professionals, most of the instruments used for assessment during the 1970s and 1980s appear to be local adaptations of those developed between the 1940s and 1960s in the United States and Europe. A brief exploratory interview with a professional who studied at the University of Guayaquil and practiced clinical and industrial psychology during the 1970s and 1980s provides insight into the types of instruments apparently most commonly used locally at the time. Among these are intelligence tests such as the Wechsler, Raven, and Domino; and projective tests based on psychodynamic principles, such as the Sacks Sentence Completion Test, Philipson Plates, Rorschach Test, Murray's Thematic Apperception Test (TAT), as well as the Family Drawing Test and the House-Tree-Person (HTP) Drawing Test. In clinical settings, the use of these and other instruments was usually accompanied by a clinical history. In organizational and business contexts, an interview was also included in certain personnel selection or evaluation situations. In these contexts, a battery of 12 tests was also used, known by its two versions: Colombian Industrial Psychology (PIC) and/or Venezuelan Industrial Psychology (PIV). This battery included three particularly relevant tests, used to measure aspects related to personality (also applied in other contexts, such as clinical or educational): the 16 Personality Factors (16PF) created by Cattell; the Contact Factors of Personality, Introversion-Extraversion (CPF); and the Neurotic Factors of Personality, Psychological Stability and Emotional Balance (NPF). The latter two corresponded to two of the scales from the Eysenck Test. Since at least the 1990s, the battery of Tests for the Selection of Administrative Personnel (SET) created by Benett and Gelink in 1985 has also been used.

In the 1980s and 1990s, educational psychology and vocational guidance remained strong, and psychological assessment followed this trend. The evaluation of intelligence, aptitudes, and interests continued to be important. In the clinical area, personality assessment and projective techniques became consolidated. Tests focused on personnel evaluation were also used in industrial psychology, which gradually shifted toward organizational psychology. In the 1990s and early 2000s, the number of psychology programs increased, especially at private universities.

The Beginning of the Twenty-First Century

In the first decade of the twenty-first century, private higher education institutions and psychology programs expanded. Psychological assessment remained tied to specializations. As a result, in practice, many educational psychology professionals tended to limit themselves to assessing intelligence and learning, clinical psychology professionals to personality and intrapsychic variables, and organizational psychology professionals exclusively to personnel selection assessments. Conflicts sometimes arise when the (artificial and arbitrary) boundaries set largely by specializations are crossed; this is one of the consequences of psychology training with undergraduate specializations.

Since 2014, due to the *Reglamento de Armonización de la Nomenclatura de Títulos Profesionales y Grados Académicos* (Regulation for the Harmonization of the Nomenclature of Professional Degrees and Academic Titles) issued by the *Consejo de Educación Superior* (National Council of Higher Education) (CES, 2019), demand has also increased for the Bachelor's degree in Psychology (without specialization). Students in this new program study a broad range of tests used in different contexts.

Current State of Psychological Assessment

In all psychology programs in the country, psychological assessment and the use of specific tests are taught in one form or another. Training in quantitative and qualitative techniques that contribute to assessment is also considered important. However, some gaps remain in knowledge essential for correctly applying and interpreting tests, such as training in statistics and psychometrics.

There are several names or designations for the courses that deal with psychological assessment. Currently, the most common term is *psychological assessment*. The term *psychodiagnostics* is still used, but the term *psychotechnics* has practically disappeared. In any case, regardless of the name, the purpose of these courses is the same: to train students in one of the psychologist's core competencies, which is assessment.

Table 7.1 presents information on the tests most commonly used in the training of psychology students in the country, based on a review of curricula, study plans, and consultations with faculty who teach these courses at the main universities: Central University of Ecuador, University of Guayaquil, University of Cuenca, Pontifical Catholic University of Ecuador, Catholic University of Santiago de Guayaquil, and University of Azuay.

The aforementioned inquiry also revealed the following information: 1) most tests are acquired from the publishers TEA Ediciones, Manual Moderno, and Pearson; 2) the majority of tests have not been validated or adapted in Ecuador; 3) most tests are still administered using paper and pencil; 4) the tests in circulation are copies of the originals, meaning that in most cases commercial versions are not used, but rather photocopies are made. On the other hand, it should also be noted that projective tests continue to be widely used in psychological practice, despite ongoing criticism and debates regarding their validity evidence.

Shortcomings and Future Challenges

After this general and, of course, incomplete overview, several aspects are presented for reflection and improvement in psychological assessment in the country. Psychological assessment should be approached from a pluralistic perspective, with sufficient epistemological, theoretical, and methodological rigor. In the case of psychometric approaches, there is a clear need for reliable psychological assessment instruments, with robust validity evidence and norms developed for the Ecuadorian population. It is also important to address the cultural validity of instruments in relation to the Ecuadorian context and its marked diversity (Capella & Andrade, 2017; Jadhav, 2009). That is, techniques and instruments should be grounded in the real meanings and needs of the local populations and individuals being "assessed." A further step in terms of reflexivity and positionality would involve, for example, considering the psychopolitical validity of assessment techniques and instruments (Prilleltensky, 2008). This entails examining the extent to which certain asymmetric power relations have been considered in the process of designing and/or applying instruments, the purposes for which they are used, and which social groups are benefited or excluded. This will be especially relevant if we incorporate into the assessment process contemporary debates regarding the risks of coloniality in psychology in Ecuador (Capella & Andrade, 2017; Capella & Jadhav, 2020), among other critical academic perspectives.

There are at least two ways to address these shortcomings. One is to adapt and validate the instruments we use when they originate from other countries. Another approach, with greater cultural validity, would be to move toward developing our own assessment instruments, so that they respond to our contexts and cultural diversity. For both approaches, and any others, historical, epistemological, theoretical, and psychometric training, as well as knowledge of the characteristics of our population, will be essential. One area that could assist in this regard is, for example,

Table 7.1 Assessment areas and tests used in psychology training in Ecuador (2022)

Assessment Areas	Specific Tests
Cognitive	• Wechsler Intelligence Scale (for preschoolers [WPPSI], children [WISC-V], and adults [WAIS-IV]) • Raven's Progressive Matrices • Kaufman Brief Intelligence Test (K-BIT) • Bender Visual-Motor Gestalt Test (B.G.) • Toulouse-Piéron Test (Revised, TP-R) • d2 Test of Attention
Neuropsychology	• School Neuropsychological Maturity Questionnaire (CUMANES) • Child Neuropsychological Maturity Questionnaire (CUMANIN) • Brief Neuropsychological Assessment in Spanish (NEUROPSI) • Boehm Test of Basic Concepts (BOEHM) • Illinois Test of Psycholinguistic Abilities (ITPA) • Luria-Nebraska Neuropsychological Battery (LNNB) • Halstead-Reitan Neuropsychological Test Battery (HRNTB)
Personality	• Minnesota Multiphasic Personality Inventory (MMPI-2) • Millon Clinical Multiaxial Inventory III (MCMI III) • Revised NEO Personality Inventory (NEO-PI-R) • Sixteen Personality Factor Questionnaire (16 PF-5) • Eysenck Personality Questionnaire (EPQ) • Mini International Neuropsychiatric Interview (MINI)
Anxiety and Depression	• State-Trait Anxiety Inventory (STAI) • Symptom Checklist (SCL-90-R) • Zung Self-Rating Anxiety Scale (SAS) • Zung Self-Rating Depression Scale (SDS) • Beck Anxiety Inventory (BAI) • Beck Depression Inventory (BDI) • Liebowitz Social Anxiety Scale (LSAS) • Children's Anxiety Scale (CAS) • State-Trait Anxiety Inventory for Children (STAIC) • Children's Depression Scale (CDS) • Children's Depression Inventory (CDI)
Projective	• Human Figure Drawing Test (HFD) • Family Drawing Test (FDT) • Person in the Rain Test (PIRT) • House-Tree-Person Test (HTP) • Thematic Apperception Test (TAT) • Children's Apperception Test (CAT) • Sacks Sentence Completion Test (SSCT) • Rorschach Test
Others	• Battelle Developmental Inventory. • Self-Concept Form 5 (AF5) • Goldstein Social Skills Scale • Coopersmith Self-Esteem Inventory (SEI) • Lucy Reidl Self-Esteem Scale • Family Satisfaction Adjective Scale (ESFA) • School Bullying and Violence Test (AVE) • Interpersonal Risk Factors for Adolescent Drug Use Test (FRIDA) • Overeating Assessment Questionnaire (OQ)

what Isabel Reyes Lagunes termed *etnopsicometría* (ethnopsychometrics) (Reyes-Lagunes, 2011).

In Ecuador, we do not have evaluation of undergraduate or graduate psychology programs, nor do we have accreditation or certification. There is also no Psychological Association or similar body to regulate, accredit, and certify the profession, or to sanction practices that are inconsistent with both science and ethics. We suggest moving toward the evaluation and certification of the instruments used in the country, so that they are as reliable as possible and have strong validity evidence.

Training in psychological assessment and, above all, the use of tests in psychological practice should be based on international standards and best practices, such as those recommended by the *International Test Commission* (ITC, 2022) and the *American Educational Research Association* (AERA), *American Psychological Association* (APA), and the *National Council on Measurement in Education* (NCME) (Eignor, 2013). All these recommendations should be known by instructors and included in student training.

The training of instructors who teach psychological assessment must also be improved. In addition to mastering the instruments and having experience in their administration, they should have solid training in Statistics and, above all, in Psychometrics, so that they understand the logic behind tests, how they are constructed and function; otherwise, they will teach only the mechanical aspects of administration, scoring, and interpretation, without deeper reflection.

Along the same lines, student training in psychological assessment should be enhanced both as a theoretical and applied field, since assessment is a key competency for psychology professionals, alongside intervention. Students should be well-versed in theory and receive adequate training in the use of tests. To support this competency, they must also receive proper instruction in statistics and psychometrics, which will prevent the mechanical application and interpretation of tests, a problem that unfortunately still occurs. Likewise, it is crucial that they learn to contextualize and compare data collected through quantitative tests with qualitative techniques such as observation and interviews, as well as with the life history of the individuals being assessed.

The issue of psychological assessment using projective tests, where the evaluator's interpretation plays a central role, must be addressed with the seriousness it deserves, especially regarding the validity evidence for such instruments. The scientific community has made efforts to advance in this area, seeking to ensure that these instruments have sufficient validity. Therefore, training and education should address these issues so that assessment and intervention are grounded in scientific evidence and not merely in subjective speculation. When qualitative techniques are used for assessment, such as observation and interviews, validity criteria must be respected, which can be readily identified, for example, in qualitative research design manuals (Maxwell, 2019).

We still use paper-based instruments, even though in many contexts it would be feasible to transition to online formats, a practice that has grown significantly since the COVID-19 pandemic. Despite existing digital divides, efforts should be made to move toward assessment using electronic devices whenever possible, as a way to save time in administration, scoring, and generating automated reports, allowing greater focus on psychological intervention, which remains a relative weakness in training in several cases. To achieve this, training in Information and Communication Technologies must be improved, as well as proficiency in various types of software. Training in the use of current Artificial Intelligence, which will influence psychological assessment and intervention, should also be enhanced.

It is also recommended to form research groups in psychological assessment to investigate the realities of our context as a way to help solve the problems our society faces. Whenever possible, research should not be conducted solely to increase the number of publications by researchers. We should also have associations focused on this topic and, above all, conferences and other academic spaces where experiences can be shared and collective learning can take place.

The challenges currently facing psychological assessment in Ecuador can only be understood by looking back at its history. In this chapter, we have sought to contribute in this regard and, from our particular perspectives, have suggested some possibilities for future directions. Of course, this is an unfinished history, open to other interpretations, and the suggestions for improvement are open to dialogue and constructive debate at both local and regional levels. It will be up to the various communities engaged in psychology in Ecuador to decide the next steps we can and wish to take.

References

Asociación de Escuela de Psicología. (1967). *En el primer centenario de la Universidad de Guayaquil (1867-1967)*. Universidad de Guayaquil.

Bastidas, J. (1950). *Psicometría Escolar*. Talleres Gráficos Nacionales.

Bustamante-Torres, J., & Velázquez-Seiferheld, D. (2022). Uzcátegui García, Emilio. In J. Ana, K. Hugo, & R. Ardila (Eds.), *The Palgrave biographical encyclopedia of psychology in Latin America*. Springer/Palgrave Macmillan. https://doi.org/10.1007/978-3-030-38726-6_156-1

Capella, M., & Andrade, F. (2017). Hacia una psicología ecuatoriana: una argumentación intergeneracional sobre la importancia de la cultura y la glocalidad en la investigación. *Teoría y Crítica de la Psicología*, (9), 173–195. http://teocripsi.com/ojs/index.php/TCP/article/view/178

Capella, M., & Jadhav, S. (2020). How coloniality shapes the making of Latin American psychologists: Ethnographic evidence from Ecuador. *International Review of Psychiatry, 32*(4), 348–358. https://doi.org/10.1080/09540261.2020.1761777

Carbo-Bravo, E. (1957). *Ensayo de aplicación del test de inteligencia "Pieron"*. Casa de la Cultura Ecuatoriana.

Carbo-Bravo, E., & Velasco-Mogollón, E. (1939). *Pruebas mentales: con normas obtenidas en nuestro medio*. Editorial Escuela Central Técnica.

Carbo-Bravo, E., & Velasco-Mogollón, E. (1976). *Antecedentes y realizaciones de la investigación psicopedagógica en el Ecuador*. Editorial Universitaria.

Carbo-Bravo, E., Larrea, G., & Velasco-Mogollón, E. (1940). *Pruebas de rendimiento instructivo: contrastadas y libres*. Editorial Escuela Central Técnica.

Carbo-Bravo, E., Abad-Grijalva, G., & Velasco-Mogollón, E. (1942). *Pruebas de instrucción ACV: guía para su corrección, valoración e interpretación de los resultados*. Imprenta del Ministerio de Educación Pública.

CES. (2019). *Reglamento de Armonización y Nomenclatura de los Títulos Profesionales y Grados Académicos que confieren las Instituciones de Educación Superior del Ecuador*. CES [Consejo de Educación Superior].

Chilig, C., & Enma, P. (2017). *"Los seres débiles son la causa de la decadencia de las naciones". Control y protección de la infancia en el marco de la institucionalización de la higiene en Quito entre 1914-1937* [Tesis de licenciatura, Pontificia Universidad Católica del Ecuador]. http://repositorio.puce.edu.ec/handle/22000/13344.

Cueva Tamariz, A. (1965). *Evolución de la psiquiatría en el Ecuador*. Casa de la Cultura Ecuatoriana núcleo del Azuay.

De Veintimilla, M. (1906). Conferencia sobre psicología moderna. *Revista de la Sociedad Jurídico-Literaria*, 9(51), 81–128.

Eignor, D. R. (2013). The standards for educational and psychological testing. In K. F. Geisinger (Ed.), *APA handbook of testing and assessment in psychology* (Vol. 1, pp. 245–250). American Psychological Association. https://doi.org/10.1037/14047-013

Escuela de Psicología. (1979). *Memorias. II Jornadas Nacionales de Psicología*. Universidad Católica Santiago de Guayaquil.

Facultad de Ciencias Psicológicas. (1984). *El psicólogo: aspectos generales fundamentales de su formación*. Departamento de publicaciones de la Facultad de Ciencias Psicológicas [Universidad de Guayaquil].

Facultad de Ciencias Psicológicas. (1988). *Memorias: 15 años de vida institucional*. Instituto de Investigaciones de la Facultad [Universidad Central del Ecuador].

Fernández-Rueda, S. (2018). *La escuela que redime. Maestros, infancia escolarizada y pedagogía en Ecuador, 1925-1948*. Universidad Andina Simón Bolívar/Corporación Editora Nacional.

García, E. M. (2008). El Centro Psicológico Salesiano "Dr. P. Emilio Gambirasio". Trayectoria y perspectivas. *Alteridad, Revista de Educación*, *3*(1), 78–81. https://doi.org/10.17163/alt.v3n1.2008.07.

Goetschel, A. (2007). *Educación de las mujeres, maestras y esferas públicas: Quito en la primera mitad del siglo XX*. FLACSO Ecuador/Abya Yala. https://digitalrepository.unm.edu/cgi/viewcontent.cgi?article=1173&context=abya_yala.

Instituto Nacional de Estadísticas y Censos. (2023). *Boletín Técnico Nacional*. Censo Ecuador: cuenta conmingo 2022; Instituto Nacional de Estadísticas y Censos. https://www.censoecuador.gob.ec/.

Instituto Nacional de Estadísticas y Censos. (2025). *Encuesta Nacional de Empleo y Subempleo (ENEMDU)*. Ecuador en cifras. https://www.ecuadorencifras.gob.ec

Informe de cómo se realizó la investigación de la prueba mental Canadá. (1957). *Anales*, *86*(341), 413–423.

Instituto de Neurociencias. (2022). *Historia*. Instituto de Neurociencias / Junta de Beneficencia de Guayaquil. https://institutoneurociencias.med.ec/nosotros/historia.

ITC. (2022). *Guidelines*. International Test Commission. https://www.intestcom.org/page/28.

Jadhav, S. (2009). What is cultural validity and why is it ignored? The case of expressed emotions research in South Asia. In S. van der Geest & M. Tankink (Eds.), *Theory and action: Essays for an anthropologist* (pp. 92–96). Diemen. https://discovery.ucl.ac.uk/id/eprint/136529/2/136529.pdf

Landázuri, M. (2008). *Salir del encierro: Medio siglo del Hospital Psiquiátrico San Lázaro*. Banco Central del Ecuador. http://www.marianalandazuri.com/Hospital_San_Lazaro.pdf.

López-Calle, C., & Cedillo-Quizhpe, C. (2022). Velasco Mogollón, Ermel Neptalí. In A. Jacó-Vilela & R. K. H. Ardila (Eds.), *The Palgrave biographical encyclopedia of psychology in Latin America*. Springer/Palgrave Macmillan. https://doi.org/10.1007/978-3-030-38726-6_605-1

López-Calle, C., & León, R. (2020). Endara Moreano, Julio César. In A. Jacó-Vilela & R. K. H. Ardila (Eds.), *The Palgrave Biographical Encyclopedia of Psychology in Latin America*. Springer/Palgrave Macmillan. https://doi.org/10.1007/978-3-030-38726-6_153-1

López-Calle, C., & Ortiz-Ochoa, W. (2022). Peñaherrera Mosquera, Gerardo Leopoldo. In A. Jacó-Vilela, H. Klappenbach, & R. Ardila (Eds.), *The Palgrave biographical encyclopedia of psychology in Latin America*. Springer/Palgrave Macmillan. https://doi.org/10.1007/978-3-030-38726-6_402-1

Maxwell, J. A. (2019). *Diseño de investigación cualitativa. Un enfoque interactivo*. Gedisa.

Ossenbach, G. (2018). *Formación de los sistemas educativos nacionales en Hispanoamérica. El caso ecuatoriano, 1895-1912* (Vol. 37). Universidad Andina Simón Bolívar sede Ecuador/ Corporación Editora Nacional.

Paladines-Escudero, C. (1998). Rutas al siglo XXI. Aproximaciones a la historia de la educación en el Ecuador. Aula XXI/Santillana.

Parrilla Latas, Á. (2002). Acerca del origen y sentido de la educación inclusiva. Revista de Educación, 327(1), 11–29.

Pontificia Universidad Católica del Ecuador. (1996). *Libro de oro: Pontificia Universidad Católica del Ecuador 1946/1996*. Imprenta Mariscal.

Prilleltensky, I. (2008). The role of power in wellness, oppression, and liberation: The promise of psychopolitical validity. Journal of Community Psychology, 36(2), 116–136. https://doi.org/10.1002/jcop.20225.

Reyes-Lagunes, I. (2011). Conceptualización y desarrollo de la etnopsicometría en México. In A. D. Espinoza (Ed.), *Lecturas Introductorias a la Psicología Cultural, Transcultural y Etnopsicología*. Universidad Iberoamericana.

Rosero Padilla, A. P. (2019). *Emergencia de la Psicología en Ecuador. Un estudio de las condiciones históricas de posibilidad e institucionalización* [Tesis de maestría]. http://hdl.handle.net/10469/15613.

Sinardet, E. (1999). La preocupación higienista en la educación ecuatoriana en los años treinta y cuarenta. *Bulletin de l'Institut Français d'Études Andines, 28*(3), 411–432. https://www.redalyc.org/pdf/126/12628308.pdf.

Tobar, J. (1954). *Evolución de las ideas pedagógicas en Ecuador*. Universidad Central del Ecuador.

Universidad Católica de Cuenca. (2021). Laboratorios de Investigación. Universidad Católica de Cuenca. https://investigacion.ucacue.edu.ec/laboratorios-de-investigacion/.

Universidad Central del Ecuador. (1950). *Actas de las sesiones del H. Consejo Universitario*. Universidad Central del Ecuador.

Universidad Central del Ecuador. (1956). *Actas de las sesiones del H. Consejo Universitario*. Universidad Central del Ecuador.

Uzcátegui, E. (1975). *Medio siglo a través de mis gafas*. s.e.

Velasco-Mogollón, E. (1971). *Estadística para educadores y psicólogos* (Vol. 1). Editorial Santo Domingo.

Chapter 8
Development and Challenges of Psychological Assessment in El Salvador

Carlos Marcel Weil Cruz

Origins and Historical Milestones of Psychology in El Salvador

On April 16, 1956, just 5 years after the founding of the *Interamerican Society of Psychology* (SIP) in 1951, the *School of Psychology in the Faculty of Humanities* at the *University of El Salvador* was established. From that date, psychology professionals have faced conditions and challenges in their pursuit to consolidate a professional identity and organizational unity that would facilitate their contributions. This historical milestone stands as the starting point for the formal establishment of psychology in the country. However, the configuration of this event is rooted in the sociocultural dynamics of Salvadoran reality, a context in which El Salvador was emerging as a dynamic and prosperous society in various industrial, economic, and sociocultural spheres. In the following decades, however, the country would be shaken by a civil war and deep political and military conflicts, during which the contributions of psychology were distorted and even severely undermined due to its critical and reflective nature.

The historical foundations of psychology's development in El Salvador date back to 1928, when German psychologist Carlos Garbe assumed the directorship of the Normal Schools, together with a team of educators who adopted a scientific approach oriented toward education and experimentation. This team implemented psychometric tools, specifically the Binet-Simon scales, in Salvadoran normal schools, which led to the organization of the *Psychoeducational Office* in 1938. This development enabled a new conceptualization and perspective on psychophysiology and pedagogy under the jurisdiction of the so-called *Ministry of Public*

C. M. W. Cruz (✉)
Dr. José Matías Delgado University, La Libertad, El Salvador
e-mail: cmweilc@ujmd.edu.sv

S. V. Pugliese et al. (eds.), *Origins and Challenges of Psychological Assessment in Ibero-American Countries*, https://doi.org/10.1007/978-3-032-21380-8_8

Instruction. The *Psychoeducational Office* operated until 1945, and its influence contributed to strengthening education in El Salvador, particularly in the training and development of teachers. The momentum generated by these efforts culminated in the creation of the *Superior Normal School* in 1952, where a group of education professionals graduated and went on to conduct interventions and assessments in special education. These professionals also played a role in the establishment of the *Psychology Office* and the psychology degree program in 1956 (Calderón de Orellana, 2006).

Beginning in the 1950s, a period of stability and development in psychology emerged at the scientific, technical, and human levels, as a result of demographic, social, academic, and governmental conditions that fostered an environment conducive to the implementation of educational and social policies. This favorable context enabled psychology professionals to enter a field of practice with growing professional demand.

In 1964, the *Salvadoran Society of Psychology* was founded as an effort to establish the legal and ethical foundations regulating the profession. This initiative, led by graduates, faculty, and students, would eventually enable the academic expansion of Psychology within a broader academic reorganization, with Rodolfo José Semsch Aguilar becoming the first individual to earn a degree in Psychology. That same year saw the *First University Seminar on Psychology,* organized by students from the *University of El Salvador*, with participation in the *10th Central American Medical Congress* held in San Salvador. In 1967, at the *11th Interamerican Congress of Psychology* in Mexico, proposals from the field of Psychology were also included at the level of socioeconomic development in the region. These significant efforts, part of a prolific period of academic activity, established an interprofessional dynamic that showed great promise but was later interrupted and distorted during the difficult decades that followed (Calderón de Orellana, 2006).

In June 1967, the first statutes were published in the Official Gazette, granting legal status and establishing the legal framework for the formation, implementation, and regulation of the professional practice of Psychology in El Salvador. The ongoing advancement and technical improvement of Psychology reflected the dynamism of Salvadoran society at scientific, sociocultural, and academic levels. Just 3 years before the outbreak of armed conflict, on September 15, 1977, the *Dr. José Matías Delgado University* was founded, consolidating new private higher education options and later incorporating a psychology program with a clinical and integrative approach across various professional fields. This private initiative in professional training was soon joined by the *Francisco Gavidia University* (UFG) and the *Technological University of El Salvador* (UTEC). However, the subsequent period, from 1970 to 1985, was marked by sociopolitical crises that had major repercussions on academic administration and organization. Despite the looming conflicts, the prior organizational groundwork enabled the establishment of the foundations later adopted by the College of Psychologists in 1973, which subsequently led to the drafting and founding of the Professional Practice Law Project between 1977 and 1978.

Following a series of budget cuts, academic quality suffered a significant decline, further exacerbated by a context shaken by political conflict and social violence.

Many lives were lost in a bloody war, with the academic sector deeply affected. Professional and student associations were dissolved, and various academic efforts and achievements faded into obscurity. The impact of this period left a profound mark on the research culture within academic training, as well as on the development and perception of psychology and psychometrics in El Salvador.

During the civil war, particularly throughout the 1980s and up to 1992, academic life was severely disrupted nationwide. Many students and faculty members became direct victims of persecution, imprisonment, exile, forced desertion, and even disappearances and assassinations. The *University of El Salvador*, alma mater of psychology professionals during this period and a pioneer in higher education, gradually became a center of uprisings, persecution, and social unrest. Nevertheless, psychologists demonstrated resilience and commitment, adopting stances far removed from indifference amid the Salvadoran civil war, especially regarding the inequalities and vast social and economic gaps that hindered access to the comprehensive well-being so strongly advocated by Psychology and related disciplines.

The *José Simeón Cañas Central American University*, founded in 1965, established itself as an alternative in higher education, with a critical approach and distinguished Jesuit scholars. These academics became key figures in political advocacy, the development of the armed conflict itself, and as national and regional references in Psychology. The academic contributions arising from the work of faculty and researchers at this new institution profoundly influenced Psychology, leading to a new understanding of its scientific role and core identity. This is reflected in the various processes of training and development of Psychology within a turbulent context of civil war, forced migration, human rights violations, and humanitarian crisis.

The academic work "Action and Ideology: Social Psychology from Central America" by Spanish psychologist, philosopher, and priest Ignacio Martín Baró became a benchmark for understanding the complex social reality of El Salvador from the perspective of the social sciences. With a distinctly critical approach from Social Psychology, he systematically guided the field of Psychology in El Salvador, influencing various academic institutions, research centers, and generations of psychology professionals in the decades to come. In particular, the critical spirit of his work and the tragic assassination of its author, along with other key figures during the complex social situation in 1989, shaped the identity of Psychology and its role in understanding and intervening in the psyche of Salvadoran citizens.

As the armed conflict dragged on, and even after it concluded through the peace accords, academic training opportunities expanded between 1986 and 2005. Within the context of a growing population demanding psychological services, this demand remains shaped by widespread misunderstandings, taboos, and myths specific to the national idiosyncrasy, as well as by the profound aftermath of the war embedded in the collective imagination and unconscious of the nation.

After a period of significant political instability, the *Board of Oversight of the Psychology Profession* was established in 1987, later becoming part of the *Superior Council of Public Health* in 2003. During this period, the scope of psychology was officially and systematically expanded, thanks to international cooperation. Between

1999 and 2003, with the support of the *National Institute of Sports* in El Salvador (INDES), a Specialist Course in Sport Psychology was conducted. Partnerships between the *University of El Salvador* and foreign universities, particularly Spain's *University of Barcelona* and the *Catalan Association for International Cooperation* enabled the creation of a Master's program in Psychology, focusing on Childhood and Adolescent Difficulties, Diagnosis, and Intervention.

The formal implementation of academic specializations marked the beginning of ongoing professional development and opened psychology to new schools of thought and models for a new century. By the mid-2000s, nine higher education institutions offered a Bachelor's degree in Psychology, each implementing training programs with different approaches, emphasizing social and clinical areas. These programs integrated aspects of assessment, psychometrics, and psychodiagnosis, with training strongly influenced by psychodynamic and behavioral roots, adopting an eclectic and integrative approach.

By 2004, with a new organizational structure and optimism for promising institutional, regulatory, and professional stability, there were 3291 graduates with a Bachelor's degree in Psychology; of these, only 2850 had completed the required registration process with the *Board of Oversight of the Psychology Profession* as of June 2005. By mid-2008, the number of professionals registered with the regulatory body was approaching 5000. The growth of the profession and the dynamics of registration continued to pose challenges for the promotion and regulation of registered professionals at the beginning of the 2020s.

Despite the turbulent dynamics of Salvadoran society, psychology continues to develop at the start of this century, attracting young people eager to make an impact on the nation's mental health. Nevertheless, many challenges remain in the scientific implementation of psychology in a context deeply influenced by myths and misconceptions about the field, including both superstition and prescientific notions.

Advances and Challenges in Psychological Assessment

El Salvador underwent a rapid process of technological adaptation during the 1990s and the early years of the current century. This occurred after the peace accords, in a context of openness and strong influence from the United States, closely linked through a constant flow of migration and remittances. However, access to technology—particularly that intended for basic and higher education—was markedly unequal due to a significant gap in purchasing power and access to education in El Salvador. This gap was reflected in both cultural and academic production, resulting in a relatively insufficient adaptation of psychological tools and resources for their application in intervention, study, and research on the complex transformative phenomena being experienced.

The implementation of psychometrics through standardized tests was a gradual process that, as in the early days of the professionalization of psychology in El Salvador, was closely tied to educational processes. Higher education institutions were the first to introduce technological tools in their teaching and training processes, and progressively in the measurement of psychological variables. The *Technological University of El Salvador* systematized much of the sociological and psychological dynamics experienced by thousands of Salvadorans in the post-peace accords context, with the academic study by Orantes and Gutierrez (2010) standing out as a research compilation reflecting the complex daily life marked by violence, overcrowding, migration, and limited urban development—factors that created a series of adverse conditions fostering the emergence and consolidation of gangs and organized crime within the so-called "marginal" urban areas. These areas became belts of poverty and underdevelopment, further deepening existing inequalities.

Beginning in 2011, scientific projects and academic studies gained greater prominence within educational institutions. This allowed research activities to become increasingly consolidated as part of the various university missions and visions. This also influenced national and regional accreditation processes, which were incorporated into institutional agendas for their progressive design and implementation, albeit in a heterogeneous and sometimes irregular manner. One of the most significant efforts in test standardization in recent years was part of a project led from Spain with Ibero-American reach. The research directed by Juan Carlos Arango-Lasprilla, Ph.D., included El Salvador in an ambitious project to standardize a series of neuropsychological instruments. The project began in September 2013 as a coordinated effort between the *University of Deusto* in Spain and the School of Psychology at the *Dr. José Matías Delgado University* applying a series of neuropsychological tests for clinical use in differentiated samples for subsequent publication and follow-up in professional practice and assessment (Rivera et al., 2015). Among the most notable tests are the Boston Naming Test, the Barthel Index, the Stroop Test, and the Rey-Osterrieth Complex Figure Test, among others.

In this context, academic institutions and research centers, where psychology training was already inherent and well established, progressively began to integrate new information technologies (ICTs). Initially, this trend emerged from computer science-related fields and gradually extended into the humanities, with psychology being a discipline whose practitioners demonstrated openness and willingness to adopt these innovations.

In psychology education, ICTs were systematically implemented to integrate available tools across various higher education institutions and to adapt to evolving trends and training needs. The School of Psychology at *Dr. José Matías Delgado University* has implemented virtual content for foundational courses since 2013, in accordance with the current and approved curriculum. As these materials were systematically hosted and delivered through educational platforms *Learning Management System* (LMS), based on Moodle and Chamilo, this experience facilitated the rapid transition to virtual learning during the COVID-19 pandemic in 2020. This added value to the training of students, especially by enhancing knowledge in areas related to monitoring and research on the measurement of psychoeducational variables (Rodríguez, 2016).

In the case of *Technological University of El Salvador*, as a result of the pandemic and the home quarantine implemented in El Salvador in March 2020, existing resources were utilized to create and deliver virtual classes. LMS tools, Moodle, and Blackboard Learn Ultra were used to establish a virtual learning environment, enabling the institution to continue offering its full range of academic programs previously delivered in person (Noticias de El Salvador, September 21, 2020). Similarly, *Francisco Gavidia University* (Noticias de El Salvador, May 24, 2021) implemented its training processes through specialized mobile platform applications and the use of cloud-based solutions.

By the end of 2022, psychology training programs systematically incorporated information technologies. These programs continually seek to expand the boundaries and scope of traditional training in line with new government policies in the education and health sectors. In terms of advances in Psychological Assessment, several targeted initiatives have been undertaken to standardize, validate, and implement psychometric tests from various perspectives and higher education institutions, as well as from research and assessment centers.

In addition to formal teaching and instruction, psychometrics in El Salvador has been strengthened through the *Pro Education Foundation of El Salvador* (FUNPRES), an institution founded in 1989 as a civil and professional initiative. Among its founders and professional staff were experts in psychology and related fields, who aimed to contribute to improving education and mental health in El Salvador. Initially, its projects focused on special education, but gradually expanded to include professional training and the design and development of behavioral scales. These training programs covered socio-emotional aspects, inclusive education, and mental health consulting, resulting in a series of studies and publications with significant theoretical and technical contributions to Psychological Assessment. Since 2010, FUNPRES has operated its own *Center for Psychological Assessment and Care* (CEAP), which continues to provide professional resources and tools, as well as specialized technical assessment services to the Salvadoran population both nationally and internationally.

These resources have been of great technical and professional value, serving as primary sources for subsequent research processes, whether in specific populations or as a baseline for research activities during the COVID-19 pandemic (Mena et al., 2022).

Accessibility of Psychology in a Globalized World

As part of the response to the pandemic, the *Board of Oversight*, since 2021, undertook a comprehensive update of the code of ethics and guidelines for online psychological care in 2021 and 2022, respectively. Drawing on the pandemic experience and new government policies, new programs have been launched, such as the "Born with Love" law and other educational initiatives targeting early childhood, in which psychology professionals are required to join interdisciplinary teams for both assessment and professional intervention processes.

Psychology professionals in El Salvador cannot remain indifferent. The impact on our ethics, professional practice, and research is critical and often goes unstudied and undiscussed. Contemporary events, the pandemic, political circumstances, and technology demand new competencies and present challenges for these phenomena, which are inherent to human history and the study of behavior.

Challenges in Psychological Assessment

The previously described historical background and this entire foundation, set within a complex global reality, constitute in themselves a challenge for academia and particularly for Psychology. This is because they influence mental health and the development of life projects for citizens. Psychology, therefore, must play a role in strengthening assertive public policies regarding educational, demographic, health, and social aspects, as well as in all spheres of Salvadoran reality in which the perception of Psychology and the role of professionals remain largely absent from citizens' daily lives.

Historical research on the academic development of psychology, and particularly psychological assessment, suffers from deficiencies and limited access to studies and works that provide optimal systematization of primary sources and research standards. As a reference for the scientific implementation background, the only available work is Leticia Calderón de Orellana's "The History of Psychology in El Salvador" (2006), which itself presents challenges in terms of access and indexing in the current digital landscape. There is a noticeable lack of Psychology professionals in indexed higher education platforms, and this reality is reflected in the current state of Psychology and its challenges.

In light of the aforementioned background and the current complex dynamics, the field of Psychometrics in El Salvador faces several challenges, among which the following stand out:

1. The general lack of awareness and understanding of the importance of psychological tests and assessments in El Salvador, as many people do not understand how these tools can be used to improve education, employment, and other areas of life.
2. Cultural differences, since many standardized tests used in other countries may not accurately measure the skills and knowledge of Salvadorans, and such psychometric tests must be culturally sensitive and appropriate for the local context.

In addition to all the above, it is important to emphasize the need to continue and advance the professionalization of Psychology through: strengthening professional associations, integrating into existing health infrastructure in other disciplines, and accessing available financial policies such as the provision of services within the framework of public and private social security. Likewise, it is necessary to expand academic specialization opportunities and enhance scientific research and evaluation.

Conflicts of Interest The authors declare that the research was conducted in the absence of any commercial or financial relationships that could be construed as a potential conflict of interest.

References

Calderón de Orellana, L. (2006). The history of psychology in El Salvador, 1928–2005. Impr. Criterio.

Mena, F. J., Molina, C., & Castillo, Y. E. (2022, April 8). Research Report: Mental Health of Salvadorans and Associated Factors—Funpres. https://funpres.org.sv/informe-de-investigacion-salud-mental-de-los-salvadorenos-y-factores-asociados/.

Noticias de El Salvador. (September 21, 2020). *UTEC strengthens its virtual education structure.* https://historico.elsalvador.com/historico/755026/uteceducacion-virtual-superior-el-salvador.html.

Noticias de El Salvador. (May 24, 2021). *Training the creators of the future.* https://historico.elsalvador.com/historico/840893/universidad-francisco-gavidiaufg-inicio-ciclo-carreras-tecnologia.html.

Orantes, B. R., & Gutiérrez, J. R. (2010). *Research compilation 2009.* Universidad Tecnológica de El Salvador.

Rivera, D., Perrin, P. B., Stevens, L. F., Garza, M. T., Weil, C., Saracho, C. P., Rodríguez, W., Rodríguez-Agudelo, Y., Rábago, B., Weiler, G., García de la Cadena, C., Longoni, M., Martínez, C., Ocampo-Barba, N., Aliaga, A., Galarza-del-Angel, J., Guerra, A., Esenarro, L., & Arango-Lasprilla, J. C. (2015). Stroop color-word interference test: Normative data for the Latin American Spanish speaking adult population. *NeuroRehabilitation, 37*(4), 591–624. https://doi.org/10.3233/NRE

Rodríguez, A. L. (2016). Development of digital educational content to support learning processes at Dr. José Matías Delgado University. [mimeo] https://recursos.educoas.org/sites/default/files/VE16.561.pdf.

Chapter 9
Psychological Assessment and Psychometrics in Spain

Paula Elosua and Juan Carlos Sierra

Introduction

Psychological Assessment and Psychometrics are fields of unquestionable value within Psychology. From an applied perspective, they are essential for obtaining empirical evidence to support psychologists in the decision-making process. Although Psychometrics encompasses much more than the development and use of tests, in this brief overview of the history and current state of both disciplines, we will focus primarily on this more applied aspect, which is closely linked to professional practice and has a strong connection to Psychological Assessment. As will be demonstrated throughout this chapter, their current status in Spain is the result of ongoing work and the commitment of individuals, associations, and universities, which over the course of their 100-year history have forged an environment that can be described as both solid and promising.

In analyzing the evolution and current state of both fields, this chapter will focus on three key aspects: academic training, professional development, and scientific output. Regarding academic training, we will highlight the integration of both disciplines into undergraduate programs offered by Spain's Faculties of Psychology. In terms of professional development, we will describe the most relevant national associations, international connections, and the adoption of guidelines related to the construction/adaptation and use of assessment tools. Finally, we will examine the current situation in terms of scientific output, which can be

P. Elosua (✉)
University of the Basque Country, San Sebastián, Spain
e-mail: paula.elosua@ehu.eus

J. C. Sierra
University of Granada, Granada, Spain
e-mail: jcsierra@ugr.es

S. V. Pugliese et al. (eds.), *Origins and Challenges of Psychological Assessment in Ibero-American Countries*, https://doi.org/10.1007/978-3-032-21380-8_9

attributed to the impact of intense training, active professional associations, and strategic internationalization.

As a brief historical prelude, Psychological Assessment and Psychometrics took formal shape—professionally with the founding of the Instituto Nacional de Psicotecnia (National Institute of Psychotechnics) in 1928 and academically with the opening of the Escuela de Psicología y Psicotecnia (School of Psychology and Psychotechnics) in 1954–1955 at the University of Madrid (Buela-Casal et al., 2002). The initial curriculum for the first year included the following courses: Psychometrics and Statistics, taught by Mariano Yela, and Test Theory and Psychodiagnostics, taught by María Eugenia Romano. In the second year, the course School Diagnosis was offered, taught by Juan García Yagüe (Bandrés & Llavona, 2004).

The Emergence of Psychology in Spain

The formal beginning of the university degree in Psychology is generally considered to have taken place in the 1960s, when the transition to an official degree was implemented. Until then, and since the late nineteenth century, various Psychology courses had been institutionalized in the faculties of the *Universidad Española*, allowing Psychology to develop a relatively regular academic life. As noted in the "White Paper on Psychology" (Agencia Nacional de Evaluación de la Calidad y Acreditación, 2005), in the nineteenth century, Psychology studies were structurally part of Metaphysics, lacking doctrinal and institutional autonomy. Psychology's absolute independence from Metaphysics occurred with the reform of the curricula in the Faculties of Science, Medicine, and Philosophy and Letters. In the latter, the course Advanced Studies in Psychology was established, which was soon split into two courses: Experimental Psychology and Advanced Psychology. Experimental Psychology was immediately established as a separate department in the *Faculty of Science* at the *Central University of Madrid*. It was intended for doctoral students in the Natural Sciences and Medicine, as well as for undergraduate students in the *Faculty of Philosophy and Letters*. The Advanced Psychology course, in turn, was intended for students of this latter degree. With the reform of university curricula during the Republic in 1931, Experimental Psychology ceased to be taught in the *Faculty of Philosophy and Letters*, and Advanced Psychology was renamed simply Psychology.

Parallel to this official university psychology, in the 1920s and 1930s, a movement emerged to apply psychology to the professions, centered on the so-called *Escuela de Barcelona* (*Barcelona School; Instituto de Orientación Vocional*—Institute of Vocational Guidance of Barcelona-, since 1919) and the *Escuela de Madrid* (*Madrid School*) (*Sección de Orientación Profesional del Instituto de Reeducación de Inválidos del Trabajo*—Vocational Guidance Section of the Institute for the Rehabilitation of Disabled Workers, since 1922). After a short period, both the Madrid and Barcelona centers were transformed into *Institutos de Orientación Profesional* (Institutes of Vocational Guidance) in 1927, and in 1931, into the *Instituto Nacional de Psicotecnia* (National Institute of Psychotechnics) and the *Instituto de Barcelona* (Institute of Barcelona), respectively. *Instituto Nacional de*

Psicotecnia required university graduation for enrollment and was primarily oriented toward practice in various sectors of applied psychology. The creation of this supplement to the undergraduate degree was not immediately accompanied by the formal definition of Psychology as a degree program. However, it served as the foundation for the subsequent academic development of the discipline.

Thus, beginning in 1968, Psychology attained the status of a university degree, and instruction began in the *Facultades de Filosofía y Letras (Schools of Philosophy and Letters)* at the University of Madrid and the University of Barcelona. Shortly thereafter, in the early 1970s, the Psychology degree began to separate from the academic oversight previously exercised by the schools of Philosophy. The growing presence of Psychology in Spanish universities led to a dramatic increase in student enrollment, representing one of the most significant growths experienced by any degree program in the recent history of Spanish higher education (the number of enrolled students rose in just 7 years from 160 in the 1968–1969 academic year to 13,484 in 1975–1976). By the late 1970s, core psychology content began to be incorporated into the early years of the curriculum, while common content was phased out. These new curricula generally consisted of a set of core content blocks that have since defined the areas of knowledge currently taught in the undergraduate Psychology program. In the 1980s, the structure of the Psychology degree curriculum underwent a profound transformation, establishing six areas of knowledge: (1) Methodology of Behavioral Sciences; (2) Personality, Psychological Assessment, and Intervention; (3) Psychobiology; (4) Basic Psychology; (5) Developmental and Educational Psychology; and (6) Social Psychology (Agencia Nacional de Evaluación de la Calidad y Acreditación, 2005).

Any analysis of the facts related to the establishment and development of Psychological Assessment in Spain must necessarily begin with a general overview of Psychology, in which no specialties are recognized. Over the course of more than a hundred years in the history of psychology, 72 higher education institutions have been established, offering Psychology programs. Regarding psychological assessment, four well-defined stages can be identified (see Buela-Casal & Sierra, 1997). The first spans from the early twentieth century to 1936 (the start of the Civil War), coinciding with the period of scientific Psychology's formation. The second stage, corresponding to the postwar period and the early 1950s, marks the reconstruction of Psychology. The third stage begins with the founding of the School of Psychology and Psychotechnics, during which psychological assessment and measurement became university disciplines. The final stage begins in the mid-1970s, with the introduction of behavioral Psychology in Spain, and is characterized by the consolidation and significant development of Psychological Assessment.

Training

Seventy-two universities offer a Bachelor's degree in Psychology, with half of these institutions being public. The Psychology degree program lasts 4 years, during which students complete 240 credits. Each credit, measured according to the

European system (ECTS, *European Credit Transfer System*), represents a unit that quantifies the estimated amount of work, in hours, required to achieve the learning objectives established as competencies in the curriculum (1 ECTS = 25 h of student work) (Real Decreto 1393/2007, 2007).

In current Psychology curricula, courses in assessment/psychological diagnosis and psychometrics are mandatory components; this means that all universities are required to offer these subjects. Furthermore, the term "assessment" is part of the name of the knowledge area that includes courses in Psychological Assessment: Personality, Assessment, and Psychological Intervention. Until the mid-1990s, the term psychodiagnosis was commonly used to refer to this area; it was reintroduced in current curricula, combining the terms assessment and diagnosis. The vast majority of universities have opted for the term "assessment," which encompasses diagnosis, so that the most widely used term for this subject is currently Psychological Assessment (Sierra et al., 2025).

Depending on the university, courses in Psychological Assessment may have different names, credit values, and sequencing; regarding Psychometrics, this term is used in virtually all curricula, although there are variations in terms of timing and number of credits. To provide a clearer picture of the presence of assessment and measurement courses, the curricula of all 72 Psychology degree programs currently offered in Spain have been reviewed. Across Spanish universities, more than one hundred courses include the terms "assessment" and/or "diagnosis" in their titles. Depending on the university: (1) students may take one or more courses (up to four at some institutions); (2) there is variation in the number of credits assigned to each course, and although most are six-credit courses, there are also courses worth 3, 4, 5, 9, or 12 ECTS; and (3) these courses are scheduled in different years, mainly from the second to the fourth year, although some are also offered in the first year.

The situation regarding the Psychometrics course is somewhat more stable: (1) the number of credits ranges from 4 to 6, with the 6-credit option being the most common; and (2) It is taught in the second or third year of the undergraduate program. Credits are distributed among theoretical classes, practical sessions, laboratory work, and tutorials; additionally, students are expected to engage in both independent and group work. Furthermore, schools often offer additional required and elective courses related to Psychometrics, such as Statistics and Data Analysis, Experimental Design, Survey Development, and Multivariate Techniques. Although there are variations among different universities, students have the opportunity to acquire a reasonable basic methodological training.

At the same time, test publishers operating in Spain (e.g., CEPE, GiuntiEOS Psychometrics, Pearson, and TEA Hogrefe) offer specialized training related to the proper use of the tests included in their catalogs. Additionally, it is worth noting that the General Council of Psychology provides its members with a Continuing Distance Education Program (FOCAD) that covers, among other topics, test construction and use, as well as Psychological Assessment. For example, Godoy and Gavino (2011) developed the course "Case Formulation in Clinical Settings"; Jiménez González and Uceda Espigares (2015) offered training in "Forensic

Assessment of Gender-Based Violence: Evaluation of Psychological Harm in Victims"; Muñiz and Fonseca (2017) taught a course on "Construction of Measurement Instruments in Psychology"; Pérez García (2012) developed the module titled "Neuropsychological Assessment"; Arch Marín (2019) prepared materials on "Forensic Psychological Assessment in Family Contexts," and Elosua (2019) was responsible for a specific section entitled "Psychological Tests in Professional Practice." As an example of the training offered at Spanish universities, below is a list of the competencies to be acquired in the courses on Psychometrics and Psychological Assessment according to the syllabi for the 2025/26 academic year at the universities where the authors of this work hold their respective professorships (Table 9.1).

There are various training opportunities in the field of assessment and Psychometrics. Of course, there is room for improvement in several areas. One such area could be the implementation of a certification system for professionals in test

Table 9.1 Learning outcomes for the courses psychometrics (six credits), fundamentals of psychological assessment (six credits), and psychological assessment: techniques and applications (six credits)

Learning outcomes
• Understand the characteristics associated with measurement in psychology • Become familiar with the principles related to the construction and validation of measurement instruments (reliability, validation, and standardization) • Develop the ability to prepare technically rigorous reports on the psychometric properties of items • Acquire the knowledge and skills necessary to critically understand and evaluate the psychometric information provided by assessment instruments (tests, questionnaires, etc.) • Be able to select and evaluate the most appropriate tests for a given assessment situation • Become familiar with national and international guidelines regarding the use of tests • Know the most important resources related to tests
Fundamentals of psychological assessment
• Understand the historical, conceptual, and methodological framework in the study of Psychological Assessment • Understand the functions, characteristics, and limitations of different theoretical models of Psychological Assessment • Understand the procedures for formulating and testing hypotheses, as well as interpreting the results • Be able to formulate hypotheses in a clinical case and select the most appropriate assessment techniques for their testing • Understand the steps of the psychological process and carry them out in response to a client's request • Be able to prepare a psychological report in response to a client's request • Be able to plan and conduct an observation and self-observation process • Be able to conduct a psychological interview • Understand and apply self-report techniques effectively • Understand the methodological and scientific requirements that an assessment technique must meet in relation to the objective being pursued • Understand the ethical standards that govern the profession of psychology

(continued)

Table 9.1 (continued)

Psychological assessment: techniques and applications
• Understand the general characteristics of the primary psychological assessment techniques • Know how to classify Psychological Assessment techniques • Know how to apply the main Psychological Assessment techniques, as well as properly carry out the Psychological Assessment process • Know how to administer, score, interpret, and integrate results from the main Psychological Assessment techniques • Be able to conduct an actual assessment in each of the different areas of application and write the corresponding assessment report • Know how to select the most appropriate Psychological Assessment techniques in response to a specific request from an individual or group • Know how to properly prepare a psychological report based on data obtained from appropriate psychological techniques, providing a comprehensive response to the individual or group, taking into account their reason for consultation • Recognize the importance of proper selection of assessment techniques based on their reliability, validity, and utility • Utilize psychological assessment techniques in strict compliance with the ethical standards of the profession • Maintain an up-to-date perspective on Psychological Assessment • Promote scrupulous respect for the Psychological Assessment process in all areas of application

use, with multiple levels of specialization—similar to those already in place in some European countries (Muñiz et al., 2021).

A relevant indicator of the status of Psychological Assessment and Psychometrics at the academic level is the number of textbooks published by Spanish authors that serve as essential tools for training future psychologists, as well as reference materials for professionals. Over the past two decades, more than 40 monographs on psychological assessment and measurement authored by Spaniards have been published (Quevedo-Blasco, 2023), underscoring the interest of Spanish professors in ensuring that up-to-date works on these disciplines are accessible to psychology students and professionals. Since Álvarez Villar published *Psicodiagnóstico Clínico* in 1972, numerous books on psychological assessment and measurement have been written originally in Spanish, both general (manuals or textbooks) and specialized. An analysis of the content of assessment books, conducted by the authors of this chapter, reveals the presence of: (1) conceptual and methodological aspects (i.e., concept, models, process, scientific guarantees, etc.); (2) assessment techniques (i.e., interview, observation, self-reports, tests, psychophysiological records, etc.); (3) applications in different fields (i.e., clinical, health, educational, occupational, etc.); (4) populations (i.e., children, adults, etc.). Regarding volumes dedicated to Psychometrics, these basically cover the following topics: (1) construction of measurement instruments; (2) models for estimating reliability; (3) validation, standardization of scores; (4) test adaptation from theoretical and applied perspectives.

National Associations and International Relations

The analysis of psychologists' professional activity helps understand the status of psychological assessment and measurement. A study conducted three decades ago by Díaz and Quintanilla (1992) among Spanish licensed psychologists revealed the great relevance of Psychological Assessment in professional practice, with tasks such as diagnosis, report writing, personnel selection, forensic assessment, and psychotechnical evaluation taking on particular importance. A decade later, Santolaya Ochando et al. (2002) confirm that assessment is one of the most important tasks performed by psychologists in their professional practice. Furthermore, psychologists themselves consider themselves as qualified as psychiatrists, for example, to conduct psychological expert evaluations in the legal field (Buela-Casal, Bretón-López et al., 2005), an opinion also shared by the majority of psychology students (Sierra et al., 2005). Likewise, among the general Spanish population, the idea that assessment is one of the fundamental tasks performed by psychologists is also widespread (Berenguer Contri & Quintanilla Pardo, 1994), with more than 70% of the population believing that psychologists are qualified to diagnose mental health problems (Buela-Casal, Teva, et al., 2005).

Regarding the use of tests, the most recent study on psychologists' attitudes toward tests, conducted in 2020 (Muñiz et al., 2020), revealed the following results: (1) Spanish psychologists show a positive attitude toward tests when they are used appropriately, with an average rating of four points on a scale from 1 to 5; (2) There is recognition of areas for improvement regarding tests, with an average rating of 2.93, slightly below the theoretical mean of the scale, which is 3; (4) There is a favorable attitude toward increasing oversight and regulation of test use by relevant institutions, such as the European Federation of Psychologists' Associations (EFPA), the International Test Commission (ITC), and the *Consejo General de la Psicología*, with an average rating of 4.07; (5) The need for ongoing training in all matters related to tests is emphasized.

In the professional sphere, it is essential to acknowledge the crucial role of scientific and professional associations. Regarding psychological assessment, the initial meetings of faculty in the field laid the foundation for the *Sociedad Española de Evaluación Psicológica* (SEEP). SEEP, founded in Madrid in 1986, was responsible, among other tasks, for publishing the journal *Evaluación Psicológica/Psychological Assessment*, which had been created a year earlier, and for organizing the *Congresos de Evaluación Psicológica* in 1985 and 1987. In 1990, SEEP became the European Association of Psychological Assessment, and the journal was renamed the European Journal of Psychological Assessment (Buela-Casal & Sierra, 1997). As a result, Spain lost two key references in Psychological Assessment in Spanish.

At the 2016 faculty meeting in Málaga, the foundation of the *Sociedad Española para el Avance de la Evaluación Psicológica* (SEAEP) was proposed, and it was established in Madrid in 2017. This addressed the need for a forum to facilitate the exchange of knowledge between academics and professionals, following the dissolution of SEEP. As stated on its website, the objectives of SEAEP are: (1) to increase scientific interest and advance the study, research, and best practices in psychological assessment and evaluation in Spain, as well as to contribute to the training of its members; and (2) to create opportunities for scientific exchange and for sharing academic and professional resources among its members, and between them and other academics and professionals (Sociedad Española para el Avance de la Evaluación Psicológica, 2025). In the more applied field of Psychometrics, particularly focused on test development and use, the establishment of associations and active participation in international organizations have had a significant impact on both academic and professional training. One of the most important milestones in this regard was undoubtedly the creation, in 1995, of the *Comisión de Test* by the Spanish Psychological Association. This commission serves as an advisory body to the governing board, the former *Colegio Oficial de Psicólogos* (established in 1979), which was later renamed the *Consejo General de la Psicología*. Its main objective is to undertake a range of activities and projects aimed at enhancing the quality and utilization of tests in Spain (Hernández et al., 2022). Over its more than 25 years of existence, the Test Commission has developed various initiatives aimed at improving these three aspects: (1) test quality, (2) appropriate use, and (3) training for test users. To incorporate all perspectives involved in test quality and use, the Commission has consistently included experts in Psychometrics and Psychological Assessment, as well as representatives from Spanish test publishing companies. This convergence of professional and academic experts, as well as publishers, is essential for enhancing the quality and utility of tests. Additionally, the commission includes a representative from the *Consejo General de la Psicología*, as many of the Commission's decisions have professional and institutional implications. To achieve its objectives, the *Comisión de Test* proposes and undertakes numerous initiatives, collaborating with international organizations that share similar goals, such as the Test Commission of the European Federation of Psychologists' Associations (EFPA) (currently known as the Board of Assessment), or the International Test Commission (ITC), in whose governing body Spanish professionals regularly participate (Elosua, 2017; Elosua & Muñiz, 2013).

Scientific Output

As a natural consequence of intense training and professional development, Spain has a notable scientific output related to Psychological Assessment and Psychometrics. To examine scientific productivity in psychological assessment and measurement within the Spanish context from 2001 to 2024, the authors of this chapter analyzed: (1) the content indexed in the Scopus database from the four Spanish journals in the top quartile of the most recent year published in the Journal

Citation Reports (JCR 2024), which included: *European Journal of Psychology Applied to Legal Context, International Journal of Clinical and Health Psychology, Psychosocial Intervention, Psicothema* and *Revista Iberoamericana de Psicología y Salud*; (2) the presence of articles authored by Spanish researchers in several leading English-language journals on psychological assessment and measurement included in the JCR: *Applied Psychological Measurement, Assessment, Educational and Psychological Measurement, European Journal of Psychological Assessment, Journal of Personality Assessment, Journal of Psychoeducational Assessment*, and *Psychological Assessment*, as well as in the only Latin American journal specific to the field: *Revista Iberoamericana de Diagnóstico y Evaluación-e Avaliaçao Psicológica*; and (3) the overall productivity of Spanish authors in psychological assessment and measurement.

First, in the content analysis of the four Spanish journals with the highest impact factor, the number of articles indexed in *Scopus* from 2001 to 2024 was quantified, focusing on those whose titles included any of the following terms and truncations: "test," "testing," "measur*", "psychodiagnos*", "diagnos*", "assessment," "evaluation," "validation," "adaptation," "psychometr*", "reliability," "validity," or "invariance." In descending order, 25%, 21%, 17%, 16%, and 13% of the articles published in the *Psicothema, International Journal of Clinical and Health Psychology, Revista Iberoamericana de Psicología y Salud, Psychosocial Intervention*, and *the European Journal of Psychology Applied to Legal Context*, respectively, contained at least one of these search terms in their titles. These results clearly indicate that psychological assessment and measurement have a significant presence in the highest-impact Spanish scientific journals, both in those focused on specific areas (e.g., *European Journal of Psychology Applied to Legal Context*) and in more generalist journals (e.g., *Psicothema*).

Second, to analyze the productivity of Spanish authors in the field of psychological assessment and measurement from 2001 to 2024, the authorship of articles published in several leading journals in the field, as indexed in the *Journal Citation Reports*, was examined. The percentages of articles authored by Spanish researchers during this period in the analyzed journals, in descending order, were as follows: *European Journal of Psychological Assessment* (11%), *Psychological Assessment* (5%), *Applied Psychological Measurement* (4%), *Assessment* (4%), *Educational and Psychological Measurement* (4%), *Journal of Personality Assessment* (2%), and *Journal of Psychoeducational Assessment* (2%). The presence of Spanish authors in these prominent English-language journals appears limited. The trend observed in recent decades, where Spanish authors have published in English-language journals included in the JCR (see Musi-Lechuga et al., 2009; Olivas-Ávila & Musi-Lechuga, 2010), does not seem to be clearly reflected in psychological assessment journals. However, it should be noted that many works in the field are published in generalist journals, so it cannot be concluded, by any means, that Spanish scientific output in this area is scarce. In comparison with the aforementioned journals, the percentage of Spanish authors increases considerably in the *Revista Iberoamericana de Diagnóstico y Evaluación-e Avaliaçao Psicológica*, reaching 37%.

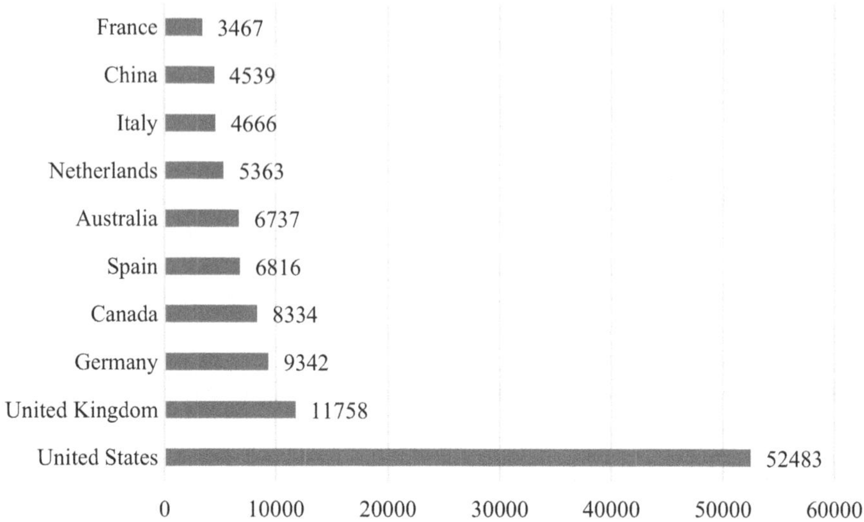

Fig. 9.1 Top ten most productive countries in psychological assessment and measurement, 2001–2024. Source: Scopus

Third, to compare the productivity of Spanish authors from 2001 to 2024, the countries of authors of publications indexed in Scopus in the Psychology subject area were examined, focusing on titles containing the previously described search terms. As shown in Fig. 9.1, Spain ranks among the top ten most productive countries, with 6816 publications.

A more detailed analysis enables a comprehensive description of the current scientific landscape of psychological assessment and measurement in Spain. The evolution of scientific productivity over the past two decades exhibits a marked upward trend, with the number of publications increasing nearly ninefold from 2001 to 2024 (Fig. 9.2).

Secondly, the previously mentioned fact that Spanish authors tend to prefer publishing their work on psychological assessment and measurement in generalist journals rather than in specialized journals becomes evident when examining Fig. 9.3, which includes the 20 journals that have published the most articles by Spanish authors on this topic during the period 2001–2024. It can be seen that among the journals most frequently chosen by Spanish authors to publish their work on psychological assessment and measurement, there are only two journals specifically dedicated to the field: *Revista Iberoamericana de Diagnóstico y Evaluación Psicológica* and *European Journal of Psychological Assessment*. It is worth noting that, of the 20 journals, more than half (12) are Ibero-American, with the majority being Spanish.

Finally, a list was compiled of the ten most productive Spanish universities in this field over the past two decades. The University of Valencia leads this ranking with 585 publications. Figure 9.4 shows the top ten universities.

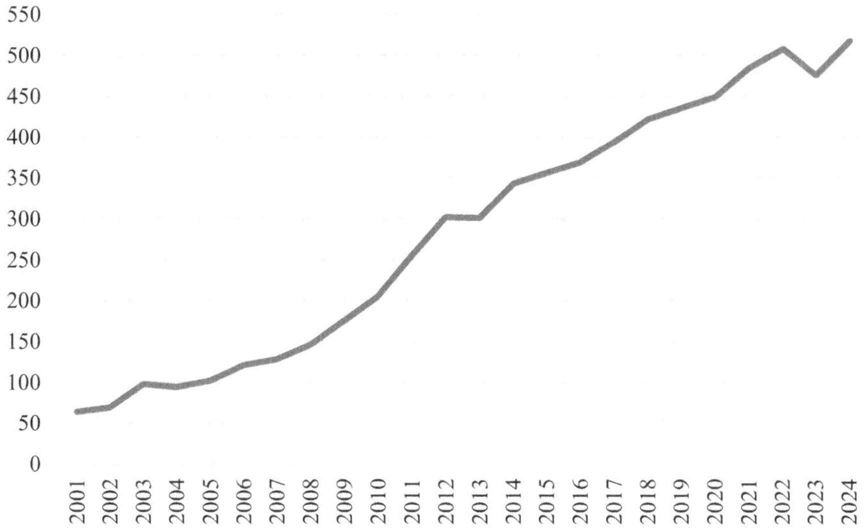

Fig. 9.2 Evolution of Spanish authors' output in psychological assessment and measurement. Source: Scopus

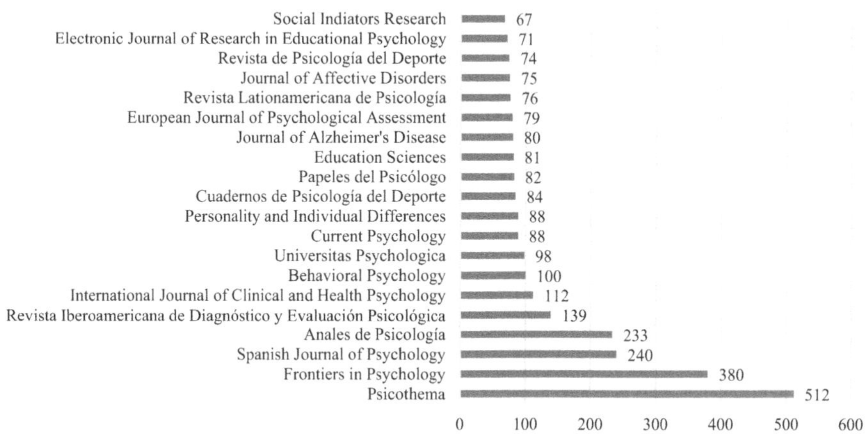

Fig. 9.3 Top 20 journals with the most articles on psychological assessment and measurement authored by Spanish researchers during 2001–2024. Source: Scopus

Challenges

This brief overview of the history and current state of the fields of Psychological Assessment and Psychometrics in Spain highlights the upward trajectory of two disciplines that share connections and areas of standard practice, and that have become two of the cornerstones of scientific psychology. When considering the

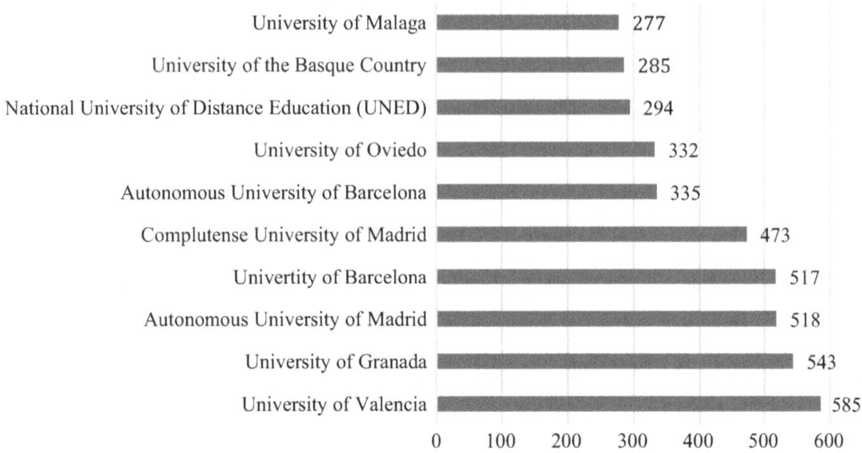

Fig. 9.4 Top ten most productive universities in psychological assessment and measurement during 2001–2024. Source: Scopus

factors that have driven their development and consolidation, we would essentially cite the sections into which this chapter is divided: (1) training, (2) association and internationalization, and (3) scientific output. These are the three pillars underpinning the development of our disciplines. Without training and association, there is no productive capacity, and internationalization provides a perspective that directly impacts both areas. This chapter has outlined the progress made thus far; however, in the twenty-first century, we face challenges that the pioneers could not have imagined (Elosua, 2022a, 2022b; Elosua et al., 2023). The introduction and development of digital technology have broadened and enriched the concept of testing, and assessment environments are now diverse, complex, and dynamic. The penetration of digital technology in assessment has brought us into a new territory, where contributions from fields such as engineering, computational linguistics, computer science, and artificial intelligence are opening up new avenues for exploration. "Data" has emerged as a unit of analysis and has become a new reference point, originating from applications, mobile devices, and social networks, enabling the analysis, classification, and prediction of behavior. Several questions arise in this context, among which two stand out: (1) Are psychologists prepared to take on this task?; and (2) Do more technology-oriented professionals (engineers, computer scientists, etc.) have sufficient substantive *background* to address it?

Coordination between fields, such as training psychologists in languages like R or *Python* (Elosua, 2011), and teamwork (Adjerid & Kelley, 2018; König et al., 2020; Oswald, 2020), may be helpful strategies to address the diversity and dynamism of this era. The experience psychologists have gained in the fields of assessment and measurement is an asset that psychology contributes, and from which *big data* can clearly benefit. Just as we succeeded in building and consolidating Assessment and Psychometrics, we will continue to work rigorously and equitably to meet the new challenges posed by the paradigm shift associated with the digital revolution.

References

Adjerid, I., & Kelley, K. (2018). Big data in psychology: A framework for research advancement. *The American Psychologist, 73*(7), 899–917. https://doi.org/10.1037/amp0000190

Agencia Nacional de Evaluación de la Calidad y Acreditación. (2005). *Libro blanco del título del grado en Psicología [White paper on the undergraduate degree in Psychology]*. http://www.aneca.es/var/media/150356/libroblanco_psicologia_def.pdf

Arch Marín, M. (2019). *La evaluación psicológica forense en el ámbito de la familia [Forensic psychological assessment in the family context]* (2nd updated edition). FOCAD. Consejo General de Colegios Oficiales de Psicólogos.

Bandrés, J., & Llavona, R. (2004). La escuela de Psicología y Psicotecnia de la Universidad de Madrid (1954–1989) [The School of Psychology and Psychotechnics of the University of Madrid (1954–1989)]. *Psicothema, 16*, 173–180. https://www.psicothema.com/pdf/1179.pdf

Berenguer Contri, G., & Quintanilla Pardo, I. (1994). La imagen de la psicología y los psicólogos en el estado español [The image of psychology and psychologists in Spain]. *Papeles del Psicólogo, 58*, 41–68. https://www.papelesdelpsicologo.es/resumen?pii=618

Buela-Casal, G., Bretón López, J., Agudelo, D., Bermúdez, M. P., Sierra, J. C., Teva, I., & Gil Roales-Nieto, J. (2005). Imagen de la Psicología como profesión sanitaria en psicólogos españoles [The image of psychology as a health profession among Spanish psychologists]. *Papeles del Psicólogo, 26*, 16–23. https://www.papelesdelpsicologo.es/pdf/1241.pdf

Buela-Casal, G., & Sierra, J. C. (1997). Evolución histórica de la evaluación psicológica en España [Historical evolution of psychological assessment in Spain]. In G. Buela-Casal & J. C. Sierra (Eds.), *Manual de evaluación psicológica. Fundamentos, técnicas y aplicaciones* (pp. 49–70). Siglo XXI Editores.

Buela-Casal, G., Sierra, J. C., Carretero-Dios, H., & De Los Santos-Roig, M. (2002). Situación actual de la evaluación psicológica en lengua castellana [Current situation of psychological assessment in Spanish]. *Papeles del Psicólogo, 22*(83), 27–33. https://www.papelesdelpsicologo.es/resumen?pii=894

Buela-Casal, G., Teva, I., Sierra, J. C., Bretón-López, J., Agudelo, D., Bermúdez, M. P., & Gil Roales-Nieto, J. (2005). Imagen de la Psicología como profesión sanitaria entre la población general [The image of psychology as a health profession among the general population]. *Papeles del Psicólogo, 26*, 30–38. https://www.papelesdelpsicologo.es/pdf/1243.pdf

Díaz, R., & Quintanilla, I. (1992). La identidad profesional del psicólogo en el Estado Español [The professional identity of psychologists in Spain]. *Papeles del Psicólogo, 52*, 22–74. https://www.papelesdelpsicologo.es/resumen?pii=522

Elosua, P. (2011). *Introducción al entorno R [Introduction to the R environment]*. Universidad del País Vasco. https://www.researchgate.net/publication/264697893_Introduccion_al_entorno_R

Elosua, P. (2017). Avances, proyectos y retos internacionales ligados al uso de test en Psicología [Advances, projects and international challenges related to the use of tests in psychology]. *Revista Estudos de Psicologia (Campinas), 34*(2), 201–210. https://periodicos.puc-campinas.edu.br/estpsi/article/view/7632

Elosua, P. (2019). *Los test psicológicos en la práctica profesional [Psychological tests in professional practice]* (2ª ed. actualizada). FOCAD. Consejo General de Psicología de España.

Elosua, P. (2022a). Impacto de la TIC en el entorno evaluativo. Innovaciones al servicio de la mejora continua [Impact of ICT on the assessment environment: Innovations for continuous improvement]. *Papeles del Psicólogo, 43*(1), 3–11. https://doi.org/10.23923/pap.psicol.2985

Elosua, P. (2022b). Tecnología digital, test y evaluación [Digital technology, tests, and assessment]. *Papeles del Psicólogo, 43*(1), 1–2. https://doi.org/10.23923/pap.psicol.2987

Elosua, P., Aguado, D., Fonseca-Pedrero, E., Abad, P., & Santamaría, P. (2023). New trends in digital technology-based psychological and educational assessment. *Psicothema, 35*(1), 50–57. https://doi.org/10.7334/psicothema2022.241

Elosua, P., & Muñiz, J. (2013). Proyectos españoles para una mejora en el uso de los tests [Spanish projects to improve test use]. *Psiencia. Latin American Journal of Psychological Science, 5*(2), 139–143. https://www.redalyc.org/pdf/3331/333129928012.pdf
Godoy, A., & Gavino, A. (2011). *Formulación de casos clínicos [Case formulation in clinical psychology]*. FOCAD. Consejo General de Colegios Oficiales de Psicólogos.
Hernández, A., Elosua, P., Fernández-Hermida, J. R., & Muñiz, J. (2022). Comisión de Test: Veinticinco años velando por la calidad de los test [Test commission: Twenty-five years ensuring test quality]. *Papeles del Psicólogo, 43*(1), 55–62. https://doi.org/10.23923/pap.psicol.2978
Jiménez González, E. M., & Uceda Espigares, M. S. (2015). *Evaluación forense de la violencia de género: Valoración del daño psíquico en la víctima [Forensic assessment of gender-based violence: Evaluation of psychological harm in victims]*. FOCAD. Consejo General de Colegios Oficiales de Psicólogos.
König, C., Demetriou, A., Glock, P., Hiemstra, A., Iliescu, D., Ionescu, C., Langer, M., Liem, C., Linnenbürger, A., Siegel, R., & Vartholomaios, I. (2020). Some advice for psychologists who want to work with computer scientists on big data. *Personnel Assessment and Decisions, 6*(1), 17–23. https://doi.org/10.25035/pad.2020.01.002
Muñiz, J., & Fonseca, E. (2017). *Construcción de instrumentos de medida en psicología [Construction of measurement instruments in psychology]* (2nd updated edition). FOCAD. Consejo General de Colegios Oficiales de Psicólogos.
Muñiz, J., Hernández, A., Elosua, P., & Wechsler, S. (2021). El uso de los test en España y Latinoamérica: Perspectivas actuales y retos futuros [The use of tests in Spain and Latin America: Current perspectives and future challenges]. *Anuario Internacional de Revisiones en Psicología, 1*(2020), 67–94. https://www.researchgate.net/publication/350033500_El_Uso_de_los_Test_en_Espana_y_Latinoamerica_Perspectivas_actuales_y_retos_futuros
Muñiz, J., Hernández, A., & Fernández-Hermida, J. R. (2020). La utilización de los test en España: El punto de vista de los psicólogos [The use of tests in Spain: Psychologists' perspectives]. *Papeles del Psicólogo, 41*, 1–15. https://doi.org/10.23923/pap.psicol2020.2921
Musi-Lechuga, B., Olivas-Ávila, J. A., & Buela-Casal, G. (2009). Producción científica de los programas de doctorado en Psicología Clínica y de la Salud en España [Scientific production of doctoral programs in clinical and health psychology in Spain]. *International Journal of Clinical and Health Psychology, 9*, 161–173. https://www.aepc.es/ijchp/articulos_pdf/ijchp-316.pdf
Olivas-Ávila, J., & Musi-Lechuga, B. (2010). Análisis de la profesión de los profesores funcionarios de Psicología en España en artículos de revistas de la Web of Science [Analysis of the profession of tenured psychology professors in Spain in Web of Science journals]. *Psicothema, 22*, 909–916. https://www.psicothema.com/pdf/3819.pdf
Oswald, F. L. (2020). Future research directions for big data in psychology. In S. E. Woo, L. Tay, & R. W. Proctor (Eds.), *Big data in psychological research* (pp. 427–441). American Psychological Association. https://doi.org/10.1037/0000193-020
Pérez García, M. (2012). *La evaluación neuropsicológica [Neuropsychological assessment]* (2nd updated edition). FOCAD. Consejo General de Colegios Oficiales de Psicólogos.
Quevedo-Blasco, R. (2023). Síntesis bibliográfica sobre la evaluación psicológica durante los siglos XX y XXI [Bibliographic synthesis of psychological assessment during the 20th and 21st centuries]. In J. P. Roberti Junior (Ed.), *Psicología: história e(m) contexto(s) de atuaçao* (pp. 9–24). Editora BAGAI.
Real Decreto 1393/2007, De 29 De Octubre. (2007). Por el que se establece la ordenación de las enseñanzas universitarias oficiales [Royal Decree 1393/2007 of 29 October, which establishes the regulation of official university education]. *Boletín Oficial del Estado* (n.° 260, 30 de octubre de 2007). https://www.boe.es/buscar/act.php?id=BOE-A-2007-18770
Santolaya Ochando, F., Berdullas Terres, M., & Fernández Hermida, J. R. (2002). La década 1989–1998 en la psicología española: Análisis del desarrollo de la psicología profesional en España [The decade 1989–1998 in Spanish psychology: Analysis of the development of the professional field]. *Papeles del Psicólogo, 22*, 65–82. https://www.redalyc.org/pdf/778/77808205.pdf

Sierra, J. C., Bermúdez, M. P., Teva, I., Agudelo, D., Bretón-López, J., Gutiérrez, O., González Cabrera, J., León Jaime, J., Gil Roales-Nieto, J., & Buela-Casal, G. (2005). Imagen de la Psicología como profesión sanitaria entre estudiantes de Psicología [The image of psychology as a health profession among psychology students]. *Papeles del Psicólogo, 26*, 24–29. https://www.papelesdelpsicologo.es/pdf/1242.pdf

Sierra, J. C., Sánchez, A. I., & Quevedo-Blasco, R. (2025). *Evaluación psicológica: Técnicas y aplicaciones [Psychological assessment: Techniques and applications]* (6th ed.). Editorial Técnica Avicam.

Sociedad Española Para El Avance De La Evaluación Psicológica. (2025). ≃Quiénes somos? [Who we are]. https://seaep.es/quienes-somos/

Chapter 10
Development and Paradigms of Psychological Assessment: A Perspective from Guatemala

Sandra Luna-Sánchez, Claudia García de la Cadena, and Patricia Rodas

Historical Background

Assessment in Latin America

Psychological assessment is a tool used for measurement, while also imparting a scientific character to psychological work, the field of educational pychology was the origins in the early twentieth century in France, with Binet's work; however, its scope soon extended to other disciplines. Its use in diverse sociocultural contexts reinforced the emerging importance of its scientific value and its application across various fields of psychology (Cohen & Swerdlik, 2000; Ureta, 2022). During the 1960s, the role of the Latin American psychologist emphasized assessment skills, as the prevailing view was that their expertise should focus on conducting psychodiagnosis (Ardila, 1968; Schulmeyer, 2016).

In contrast, American psychology employs various types of tests, such as projective, intelligence, and personality tests, all of which are used exclusively for psychodiagnosis (Piotrowski et al., 1985). In the first decades of the twenty-first century in Latin America, especially in Southern Cone countries—Peru, Argentina, Chile, and Colombia—publications emerged to showcase the development of assessment in their respective countries (Schulmeyer, 2016). The development of psychometrics and assessment has been shaped by multiple perspectives. On one hand, there is its use in the diagnostic process; on the other, the validity of tests,

S. Luna-Sánchez (✉)
Universidad Francisco Marroquín, Guatemala, Guatemala
e-mail: seliluna53@gmail.com

C. García de la Cadena · P. Rodas
Universidad del Valle de Guatemala, Guatemala, Guatemala
e-mail: claudigd@uvg.edu.gt; prodasdr@uvg.edu.gt

S. V. Pugliese et al. (eds.), *Origins and Challenges of Psychological Assessment in Ibero-American Countries*, https://doi.org/10.1007/978-3-032-21380-8_10

particularly projective ones, which have sparked debate regarding the objectivity of results obtained in several countries across the Americas (Piotrowski & Keller, 1984).

Throughout Latin America, psychology congresses have debated the training of psychologists and the development of a professional profile, including the knowledge areas in which students should be educated. Training areas include the fundamentals of psychometrics as well as skills in psychological assessment, as this has been a central field from the mid-twentieth century to the present (Alarcón, 2004). The contexts in which psychological assessment has become indispensable have increased in recent decades, with the challenge that in some countries they have limited access to tests due to their nonexistence or high cost (Schulmeyer, 2016).

The historical development of psychological testing indicates that many of the instruments used in assessment work have been employed for extended periods. Many of these have not had their norms updated, nor have they undergone the necessary standardization for application to different populations (Carpintero et al., 2011). Psychometrics was initially used in psychological research by psychiatrists, but it was psychologists who, through exhaustive research, succeeded in establishing new fields within Psychology such as Assessment (Gallegos de San Vicente, 2021).

The debate over the use of tests adapted for different cultures began in the 1970s, as did conceptual and psychometric issues of equivalence or comparability. Tests were translated for use in various social and cultural groups, which called into question the validity of the resulting scores. This led to an anti-testing movement. Currently, among psychologists, this has changed; there is greater credibility in the use of tests and the results they yield. The test market has grown; the most widely used are intelligence tests, specifically the Wechsler Scales (Leong et al., 2020).

Historical Background of Psychology in Guatemala

Psychology was closely linked to politics in the country for a long time. Student uprisings were frequent from the 1940s to the 1980s. These were considered mass youth movements and played a significant role in popular struggles to demand better living conditions, defend democracy, and protest military dictatorships (Del Valle Cóbar, 1991).

Within these student movements emerged an academic leader, the physician and psychologist Jaime Barrios Peña, who participated in the revolutionary conflicts that culminated in the Revolution of October 20, 1944. The then-president Juan José Arévalo awarded him a scholarship to study at the *National Autonomous University of Mexico* (Luna-Sánchez et al., 2020). His initiatives led to works such as the book "Considerations on the Szondi Test," which demonstrates the deep roots of the psychoanalytic model in early twentieth-century Psychology (Barrios Peña, 1952). This work was pioneering in the study of personality, highlighting the importance of assessment in the country and the need for its use. As previously mentioned, the psychometric tests used throughout most of the twentieth century were contextualized for other populations, especially North American. Similarly, other tests arrived in the country from South America (Alarcón, 2004).

The first Faculty of Humanities was founded at the *University of San Carlos of Guatemala* in 1945, because of sociopolitical movements in the country. Psychology initially was only a course taught as general, experimental, and child and adolescent psychology, included in the philosophy section of the curriculum. The history of Guatemala recognizes Emilio Mira López, of Spanish origin, who, during his time in Guatemala, gave lectures on career guidance, job analysis, and psychotechnics (Gallegos de San Vicente, 2021). These activities inspired the creation of the *Institute of Psychology and Psychological Research*, which served as a training institute in psychology and led to the establishment of the Psychology degree program (Gallegos de San Vicente, 2021).

The first curriculum for the Psychology degree included statistics courses, called "Statistics and Measurement Practices," taught in the first semester of the second year. In the third year, the courses "Psychotechnics and Career Guidance I and II" were offered, one in each semester. The curriculum underwent many and frequent modifications until it became more stable. In 1954, on the tenth anniversary of the faculty, the department's leadership indicated that one of the academic achievements of the program had been the vocational guidance of students (Gallegos de San Vicente, 2021).

In 1957, within the *Ministry of Education of Guatemala* (Mineduc), the *Department of School and Vocational Guidance* was created. In 1959, the *Department of Student Welfare* was established, with psychologists working in the areas of Guidance and Career Selection. Later, in 1966, the *Department of Student Welfare* was formed, which included the *Department of School and Vocational Guidance*, where interest and aptitude tests were used (Quevedo, 2003; Rodas, 1988).

In the 1970s, José González and Otto Gilbert developed a creativity test and measured its reliability. The study was conducted with secondary school students from a private school in Guatemala City. This effort demonstrates the need for innovation in the field of psychometrics and for placing it on the international map, as the results were published in the "Interamerican Journal" of the *Interamerican Society of Psychology* (González & Gilbert, 1979).

Intervention within the field of Educational Psychology in Guatemala, emphasizes individualized for student, the identification of learning difficulties, and implementation of remedial programs designed to address academic challenges. Similarly, in private practice, assessments are conducted upon referral from educational centers or parents seeking a diagnosis. Among the most frequently requested types of assessments are neuropsychological evaluations, psychoeducational assessments, and neurological evaluations (Ureta, 2022).

Even in the early twenty-first century, reproductions of manuals and answer sheets were still in use until companies such as *TEA Ediciones* and *Manual Moderno* made tests more accessible to professionals. Among the most widely used tests for evaluating various clinical, developmental, educational, and forensic domains, psychologists in Guatemala have relied on tests available in the market or accessible online. Instruments used across all settings have included interviews, observation checklists, rating scales, and tests to assess deficits or disabilities in neurodevelopment, psychomotor skills, or academic performance (Ureta, 2022). Recently, specialized tests requiring additional training, such as neuropsychological batteries, have also been used.

In Guatemala, standardized tests from other regions that lack normative data for the Guatemalan population are still in use. The development of psychological or neuropsychological instruments has been very limited in the country, partly due to limited funding and little interest from research groups. This has necessitated the use of instruments that are often not appropriate because they lack local norms. This gap allowed a research group in 2014 to participate in a first international collaborative project (Arango-Lasprilla et al., 2015). These studies have made it possible to generate data by obtaining normative data for neuropsychological tests for adults and children, carried out through cooperative agreements with the participation of undergraduate Psychology students and graduate students in Neuropsychology at the *Universidad del Valle de Guatemala* (UVG). The generation of normative data for neuropsychological tests coincided with the academic project to train neuropsychologists in the first formal program in Central America, the master's in clinical Neuropsychology and currently Applied Neuropsychology at UVG. Thus, the UVG group, led by García-Egan and García de la Cadena in 2014, initiated a collaborative project to standardize neuropsychological tests in adult, child, and adolescent populations.

Normative data for adults and children were obtained thanks to the participation of different countries, and the data were published for each instrument. The tests standardized to measure attention and working memory included the Trail Making Test (TMT) A and B for adults (Arango-Lasprilla et al., 2015); the TMT A and B for those under 15 years in the pediatric version; the Brief Test of Attention (BTA) (Rivera, Perin, Aliaga, et al., 2015); the D2 Test of Concentration (Rivera, Salinas, et al., 2017); memory and learning with the Hopkins Verbal Learning Test (HVLT) (Arango-Lasprilla et al., 2015); the Verbal Learning and Memory Test TAMV-I (Rivera, Olabarrieta-Landa, 2017; Rivera, Salinas, et al., 2017), to assess visuoconstructional processes and visual memory with the Rey-Osterrieth Complex Figure Test in adults (Rivera, Perrin, Morlett-Paredes, et al., 2015) and in children (Arango-Lasprilla, Rivera, Ramos-Usuga, et al., 2017); to assess language with the short version of the Token Test (Olabarrieta-Landa, Rivera, Rodríguez-Lorenzana, et al., 2017); the Verbal Fluency Test, which included the semantic category "animals" and the phonological categories F, A, and S (Olabarrieta-Landa, Rivera, Galarza-del-Angel, et al., 2015) and the pediatric version (Olabarrieta-Landa, Rivera, Lara, et al., 2017); subsequently, data were analyzed for the semantic categories of fruits and occupations (Rivera et al., 2019, the Boston Naming Test (Olabarrieta-Landa, Rivera, Morlett-Paredes, et al., 2015) and for children, the Peabody Picture Vocabulary Test (Olabarrieta-Landa, Rivera, Ibáñez-Alfonso, et al., 2017).

To assess executive functions, the modified Wisconsin Card Sorting Test (M-WCST) was standardized (Arango-Lasprilla et al., 2015). The Stroop Test in adults (Rivera, Perrin, Stevens, et al., 2015); for children, the M-WCST (Arango-Lasprilla, Rivera, Nicholls, et al., 2017). Finally, to assess processing speed, the Symbol Digit Modalities Test (SMDT) in adults (Arango-Lasprilla et al., 2015) and in children (Arango-Lasprilla, Rivera, Trapp, et al., 2017).

Progress has been made in the standardization of tests in pediatric populations. In 2019, in collaboration with the research group at Loyola University, led by Dr. Joaquín Ibáñez and his research team from Spain, along with professionals from Guatemala, the sample of Guatemalan children living in vulnerable conditions was increased (Ibáñez-Alfonso et al., 2021). This work has enabled neuropsychological intervention in Guatemalan children for more relevant approaches.

The history of psychology in Guatemala is only beginning to be written. There are few documents that support its development, especially in specialized areas such as Psychometric Assessment, which is further divided into the following subspecialties: (1) Clinical, (2) Educational, and (3) Forensic, among others. There are few references regarding training in psychometric assessment, clinical evaluation, psychodiagnostics, and statistics, as well as the work carried out by evaluators.

Methodology

In Guatemala, there is little documented and published information, making the use of Oral History methodology an alternative tool for constructing information. This type of methodology serves to reconstruct sociohistorical processes through the oral testimony of key participants. This approach allows the researcher to access the subject of history by collecting data through semi-structured interviews, which provide a conversational dialogue that builds the information (Lara & Altunes, 2014). Once transcribed, the testimonies become written documents that provide information. For this purpose, Fig. 10.1 shows the steps used in data collection.

Study Participants

The sample was non-probabilistic, as is common in qualitative studies. For this study, criterion sampling was used, since participants had to meet specific conditions to be included and to provide the necessary information (Hernández-Sampieri et al., 2014). Additionally, the assistance of specialists recognized for their professional trajectory in Guatemala was sought. To delve into the history of psychological assessment in Guatemala, eight highly experienced professionals and two professionals with intermediate experience were interviewed, who provided and

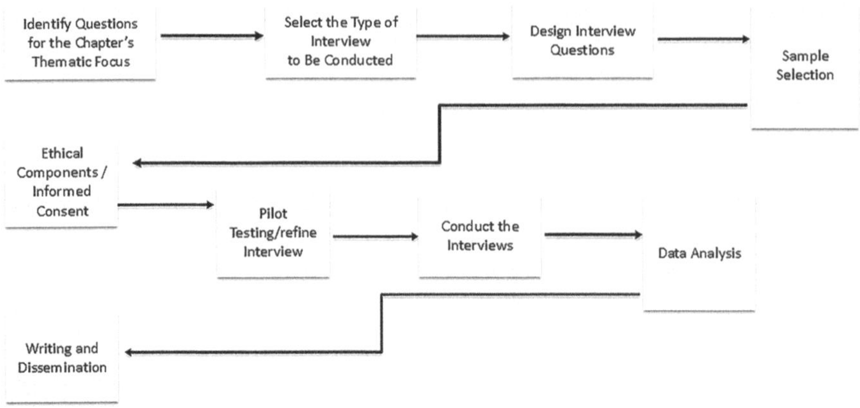

Fig. 10.1 Representation of the methodology. Adapted from Young et al. (2018)

shared their experiences. The selection criteria for the sample were as follows: (a) psychologists who are graduates and practicing professionals; (b) with recognized professional practice; (c) professionals who studied between the 1970s and 2000s to provide testimony on the development of the history of psychometric assessment; (d) individuals over 40 years of age; and (e) recognized for their experience in the use of psychometric tests and assessment practice.

Participant Data

Ana María Jurado Golón, graduated in the 1970s from the *Universidad de San Carlos de Guatemala*, holds a master's degree in medical sciences from the *Universidad Francisco Marroquín*, and has professional experience in clinical, hospital, and university teaching settings.

Arturo Alejos, graduated in the 1960s–1970s from the *Universidad de San Carlos de Guatemala*, holds a master's degree in medical psychology from the *Universidad Francisco Marroquín*, and has experience in clinical practice and university teaching.

Bárbara Mejía, graduated in the 2000s from the *Universidad del Valle de Guatemala*, with professional experience in the clinical field.

Javier Álvarez Vassaux, graduated in the 1970s from the *Universidad del Valle de Guatemala*, holds a master's degree in medical sciences from the *Universidad Francisco Marroquín*, and has experience in organizational settings.

Marlenne Molina de Kesler, graduated in the 1980s from the *Universidad Rafael Landívar*, holds a bachelor's degree in psychology, and has experience in clinical practice and university teaching.

María del Pilar Grazioso, graduated in the 1970s from the *Universidad del Valle de Guatemala*, holds a doctorate in Psychology from the *Universidad*

Nacional de San Luis, Argentina, and has experience in clinical practice and university teaching.

Mónica Laugerud, graduated in the 2000s from the *Universidad del Valle de Guatemala*, with experience in clinical and educational practice.

Nineth Alburez de von Ahn, graduated in the 1970s from the *Universidad Rafael Landívar*, is a psychometrics technician, licensed in Psychology, with a master's degree in clinical psychology and Mental Health, with clinical practice in the private sector and mental health management in the public sector.

Rosa Amalia de Camacho, graduated in the 1960s from *Universidad Rafael Landivar*, with experience in university teaching.

Sara Pereira, graduated in the 1970s from *Universidad de San Carlos de Guatemala*, holds a master's degree in medical sciences from *Universidad Francisco Marroquín*, with clinical hospital practice and university teaching experience.

Each participant signed an informed consent form in which they voluntarily agreed to participate in the virtual interview via the Zoom platform, which was recorded and transcribed.

Instrument

In the qualitative model used for this historical review, a semi-structured interview instrument was employed. The interview is a method used for multiple purposes, including obtaining sociocultural ecological information on specific topics. It is highly useful for understanding the knowledge, values, beliefs, or decision-making processes of stakeholders and for strengthening research design and outcomes (Young et al., 2018).

The questions for the instrument were developed to gather information that supported the reconstruction of a segment of the history of Psychological Assessment in Guatemala. To this end, the process began with the historical background of each interviewee's training, followed by exploration of their training in the use of tests and the settings in which they specialized. Additionally, information was collected on the populations they serve and the objectives of Assessment in their professional practice. Subsequently, the tests used were discussed. Furthermore, participants were asked whether they used tests for research purposes and about the lessons learned.

The final topics addressed the challenges faced in their practice with the use of Assessment. Their perspectives on the evolution of Assessment in Guatemala today were also explored. The same script was used for each interview separately, which allowed for comparison across the different transcripts (Punch, 2005, cited in Young et al., 2018).

For the analysis, the Dedoose program was used, a web application designed for mixed methods research. It was developed by academics at the *University of California Los Angeles* (UCLA), with support from the *William T. Grant Foundation*. It is a cloud-based research and data analysis platform. Evaluators, market researchers, psychologists, sociologists, students, professors, and political scientists can use it for qualitative and mixed methods research. The analysis can incorporate text, audio, video, images, and spreadsheets; for this study, the videos and audios of the interviews were used. Both qualitative and quantitative data are managed to create interactive visualizations with graphs, diagrams, and tables. The version used in this study was Dedoose Desktop Win Portable 9.0.82 (2021).

Findings

The interviews were structured around a questionnaire of nine questions (two were combined in the writing for practical purposes) centered on the topic (see Fig. 10.2). In addition, this questionnaire was accompanied by the informed consent form. The conceptual map (see Fig. 10.2) emerged from the qualitative analysis of the interviews conducted with the professionals and the categories generated from the information collected. The findings are described below:

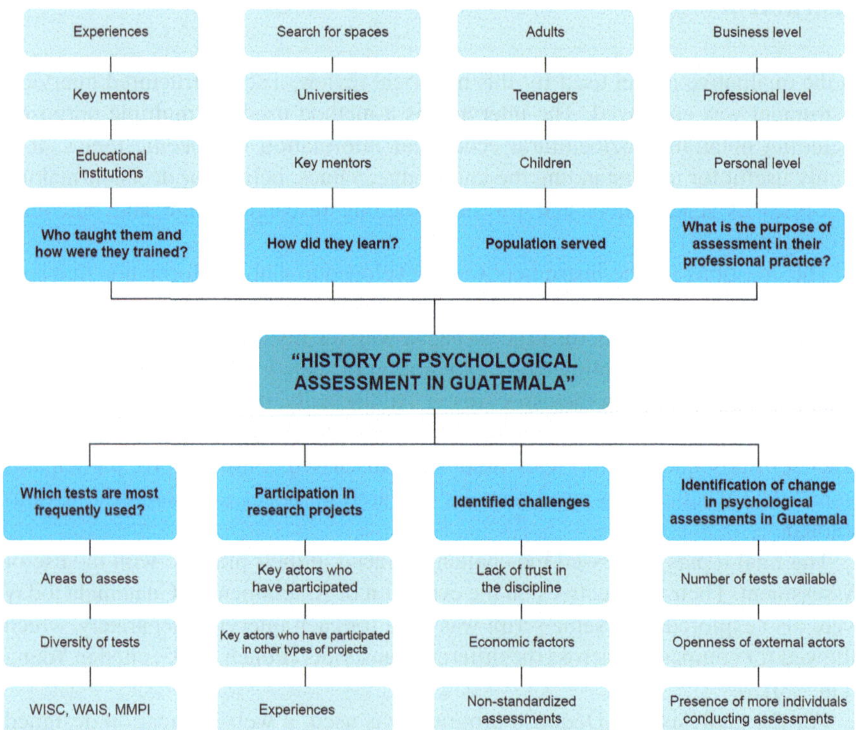

Fig. 10.2 Conceptual map of themes. Authored by the researchers

Training and Teaching

The participants highlighted the role of universities in the country as centers for training and education. The *Universidad del Valle* was one of the key institutions for many assessors in training. The collaboration between this university and the *American School of Guatemala* allowed participants to complete supervised practicums with children at the institution as researchers or counselors. This, together with the ongoing training opportunities offered by the university, enabled students and interested staff to deepen their knowledge in psychometrics.

At UVG and the *American School of Guatemala*, the professionals most widely recognized were Lilian Rodríguez, Arturo Alejos, and María del Pilar Grazioso. They are identified by their students as their instructors in assessment. Laugerud shares that her training in psychological assessment began at the *Universidad del Valle* under the guidance of Grazioso, who began teaching about the Cognitive Assessment System (CAS) in 2000. Molina de Kestler also expresses her appreciation for Lilian Rodríguez for having trained her. Alejos is remembered for his openness toward his students and for the cutting-edge knowledge he provided them.

Álvarez acknowledges that *Universidad del Valle* provided him with professional training in administering and learning how to standardize certain assessment instruments, under the mentorship of Blanca Soler Mendizábal and Rosamalia de Camacho. Both worked alongside Robert McVean, Francisco Nieves, and Beatriz Molina at the *American School of Guatemala* on the topic of Psychological Assessment.

Alburez de von Ahn notes that the Psychometrics Technician program covered topics in general psychology, child and personality development, where students acquired the foundational knowledge necessary to interpret test results. Within this framework, students learned about both individual and group test administration, as well as topics related to intellectual abilities, personality, learning disabilities, personnel selection, and interests. The Thurstone Mira, Kuder, Wechsler Intelligence Scale for Children (WISC), Gesell, and Otis Gamma tests were used during their training.

Jurado recalls from her years of training at Universidad Rafael Landívar, María Luisa Vivar, who taught her the administration of the Otis and WISC tests. She also mentions Elsa Asturias de Vadillo, with whom she learned the Bender Koppitz and Bender Hutt tests. For her part, Alburez de von Ahn remembers university professors such as Fidelio Swana, Montenegro, Margarita Urrutia, Blanca Delia López Pedroza, Tomas Martínez, and Rolando Del Valle.

Finally, at the graduate level, *Universidad Francisco Marroquín* contributed to the training of evaluators in Guatemala through its master's in clinical and medical psychology. Elsa Asturias de Vadillo taught her students how to prepare, administer, and interpret reports.

Psychological Practice and Assessment

The participants agree that the universities provided them with the theoretical foundations necessary to administer tests. They expanded their knowledge in various branches of psychometrics. The professional experiences to which they were exposed took place both in the country and abroad.

While working as a primary school teacher in the public system with children with learning difficulties in the early 1980s, Alburez de von Ahn became concerned about having to administer tests that were not adapted to her students' reality. For this reason, while studying for the Psychometrics Technician degree at *Universidad Rafael Landívar*, she developed a pilot test using more suitable and functional assessment tools and techniques for first-grade students in the public system. *"At that time, there was no mandatory preschool education, and we administered the Pintner Cunningham forms A and B, as well as Pintner K and L (...), so I felt that was not ideal because those psychometric tests had been developed for a different population"* (Alburez de von Ahn, 2022, personal communication).

Laugerud learned by working alongside various individuals in test standardization. In 2006, she worked with Yetilu de Baessa, Enriqueta Salazar, and Álvaro Fortín on statistics and test standardization. The experience was highly educational.

Population Served

The following three population groups were identified as those with whom the interviewed professionals have worked: (1) children, (2) adolescents, and (3) adults (see Fig. 10.3).

Jurado and Alburez de von Ahn share that they have had the opportunity to work specifically with these three groups. Grazioso, in her psychotherapeutic work during the assessment phase, administers neurodevelopmental, psychoeducational, clinical, and personality batteries, focusing on child populations (infants and preschoolers), school-age children (children and adolescents), and adults (individuals and couples).

Paz de Camacho has worked with children, adolescents, and adults. In the educational field, she has used tests of cognitive development, reading, and skills. She has also worked in the field of human resources. She emphasizes her work in Vocational Guidance, with experience in both group and individual test administration.

The interviewed experts who primarily work with children and adolescents include Mejía, Laugerud, Molina de Kestler, and Pereira. Mejía shared her experience working with children and adolescents and described the areas she assesses. She focuses on learning difficulties, which she considers every day and practical, as well as neurodevelopmental disorders and child development.

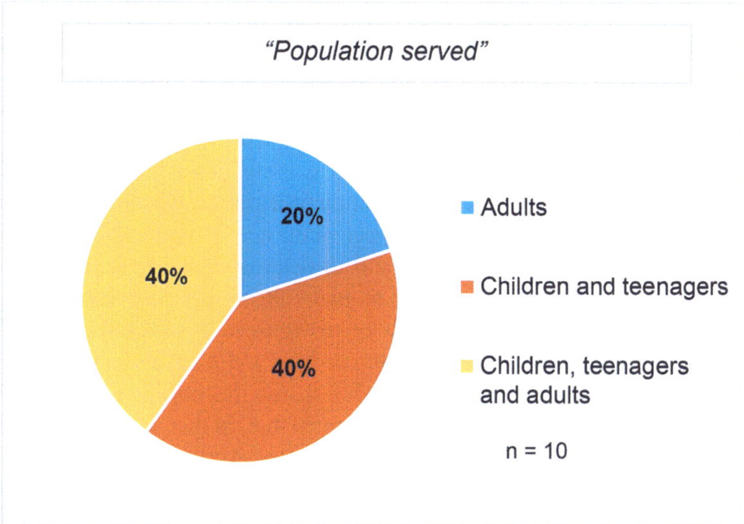

Fig. 10.3 Assessment services by population

In the case of Molina de Kestler, she dedicated herself to and specialized in children and adolescents. She also assessed young adults, but only during their early university years. Molina de Kestler explains that she begins assessment with a formal evaluation, where she mainly advises the parents of children aged 4 and older. She also mentions that she assesses children as young as 3. Laugerud reports that the population she serves consists of preschool and school-age students, and to a lesser extent, adolescents.

The adult population has received limited attention in psychological assessment. In the case of adults, referrals are made when needs identified by themselves, their work environment, or family. In recent years, referrals have also come from other professionals in the medical field.

Alejos mentions that he had the opportunity to work with children, but due to the pandemic, she now works with private sector populations and adults. In Álvarez's case, he provides insight into the corporate world and how, over time, within the company where he worked, he has come to value the importance of psychology and psychometrics applied in the workplace. In these settings, he worked with adults, specifically with candidates seeking to enter the workforce at the company where he was employed.

Professional Practice

When addressing the objectives of Psychological Assessment in each expert's professional field, their responses indicate that these objectives are a significant part of their daily work. Based on these objectives, they can better structure their work and define the goals for each case. Jurado shares that the objectives of assessment in her professional practice are to present to teachers and professionals working with a child the strengths and weaknesses of their general functions and abilities. At the same time, she aims to clarify what can be expected and which areas should be developed. For Jurado, the purpose of the tests is to collaborate, to be brief, concise, and considerate, and to understand the intended audience.

Laugerud states that one of her objectives in assessment is to analyze the patient's strengths and weaknesses, so that a remediation process can subsequently be implemented. She also identifies as a second objective the need to understand the patient's status prior to their emotional process and to determine which areas will be the focus of intervention. *"The objective of an assessment, especially in children and adolescents, is to understand the profile of strengths and weaknesses in order to identify areas where improvement is still possible..."* (Molina de Kestler, 2022, personal communication). Alburez de von Ahn shares the objective she had when working at the *Mental Health Hospital.* She notes that, in that setting, the objective was at the request of psychiatry and the justice system. Authorities requested a diagnosis of the cognitive domain. Pereira explains that the objective of psychological assessment in her professional practice is to understand the child's emotional state, intellectual capacity, or whether there is a learning problem. In short, to determine what is happening with the child to provide appropriate support. *"The objective is to understand the child's emotional state, the reasons for low academic performance, or whether there is a learning problem, in order to help them"* (Pereira, 2022, personal communication).

For Molina de Kestler, the objective of an assessment in children and adolescents is to identify the profile of strengths and weaknesses of the individual. This helps determine which areas still offer opportunities for improvement, as well as whether there is a specific diagnosis that requires intervention. However, her main goal is to gather more information and understand the patient's functional profile, including abilities, strengths, and weaknesses.

Paz de Camacho, for her part, identifies two objectives: one at the personal level and another at the institutional or community level. For her, the personal objective is essential because it helps individuals recognize their strengths and opportunities and become aware of potential threats. In other words, the aim is for the person to gain better self-understanding in terms of abilities, skills, and competencies, and to overcome their deficiencies. At the institutional or community level, the goal is to provide the necessary resources for support. Finally, for Grazioso, the primary objective is to enable screening, psychological and psychoeducational diagnosis, outcome evaluation, follow-up, and monitoring of change during intervention processes.

Instruments

In the context of assessment, there is a wide range of test batteries that professionals in the field have used over the years. These vary according to the specifics of each assessment and the objectives of the process. Based on this, Grazioso notes that batteries are designed using different instruments. Alburez de von Ahn shares that her experience is in the academic, emotional, and cognitive domains. All of this depends primarily on the type of population or the profile of the person being assessed. She also emphasizes the importance of thoroughly exploring these aspects before conducting an assessment, as failure to do so can compromise the success of the evaluation.

Paz de Camacho notes that in the field of measurement, an important figure was Mr. McVean. Around the 1960s, when he worked at the *American School of Guatemala*, many of the tests had already been translated, adapted, and even developed within the country. Today, there is still a legacy of this experience and training. Mr. McVean was committed to assessment and to having appropriate instruments for each student's needs. She also mentions that, for conducting an assessment, it is most advisable to start with a general abilities test, to understand the individual's experience or cognitive background, and that currently, the best practice is to use a test battery.

Among the tests used, several are mentioned repeatedly by our ten interviewees. As shown in Fig. 10.4, the test most frequently used by the experts interviewed is the WISC, with 60%, followed by the Wechsler Adult Intelligence Scale (WAIS), the Minnesota Multiphasic Personality Inventory (MMPI), and the Bender Test, each with 30%, and finally the Revised Reading Processes Assessment Battery (PROLEC-R) with 20%. Different universities use and teach different instruments. Universidad del Valle de Guatemala has been a pioneer in the acquisition, use, and development of tests and scales in the psychological, socio-emotional, cognitive, and neuropsychological domains.

According to Laugerud, various private assessment centers use the Wechsler series, WAIS, WISC, and the Wechsler Preschool and Primary Scale of Intelligence (WPPSI). Among the tests and inventories, the Behavior Rating Inventory of

Fig. 10.4 Word cloud of identified challenges. Author's own work

Executive Function (BRIEF) and the System for the Evaluation of Children and Adolescents (SENA) are also utilized. Neuropsychological tests include the Neuropsychological Battery of Executive Functions and Frontal Lobes (BANFE), the Neuropsychological Battery for the Assessment of Learning Disorders (BANETA), the Child Neuropsychological Assessment (ENI), the Neuropsychological Battery (NEUROPSI), and projective tests such as the Draw-a-Person, House-Tree-Person, Person-in-the-Rain, Human Figure, and Family Drawing, among others. The professionals interviewed reported using the following instruments: WISC and WAIS, Reading Processes Assessment Battery (PROLEC), Writing Processes Assessment Battery (PROESC), MMPI, Bender-Hutt Test, ABC Test, MMPI for adults, Rotter for adults and children, Conners Scale, Bayley Scales of Infant Development, McCarthy Scales of Children's Abilities, Preschool Language Scale, Peabody Developmental Motor Scales, Symbolic Play, State-Trait Anxiety Inventory (STAI), Beck Depression Inventory (BDI), Beck Anxiety Inventory (BAI), Outcome Questionnaire-45 (OQ-45), Working Alliance Inventory (WAI), Personality Assessment Inventory (PAI), Millon Clinical Multiaxial Inventory (MCMI-IV), and the NEO Personality Inventory (NEO).

Álvarez reports having used the Differential Aptitude Tests (DAT) in the corporate sector. He also implemented the DISC Personality Styles Test. He concludes that the use of these assessments made a significant difference in evaluations within the business context.

Research

Psychological assessment is an important element in research and serves as a tool for its development and implementation. Among the participants, only 50% reported having worked on research projects, while the rest stated they had not. The main projects in which they were involved included the standardization of the RANSA and PROFONSA tests led by Enriqueta Salazar, the norming of the Otis Test led by *Rafael Landívar University*, the development of a test for first-grade children in special education coordinated by the *Ministry of Education of Guatemala*, and the assessment of child neurodevelopment in vulnerable populations using the Bayley Scales of Infant and Toddler Development (BSID-III). Additionally, a longitudinal study on child development was conducted, following three generations. Various cognitive domains, reading development, and anthropometric measurements were evaluated for norming with Guatemalan populations. One of the interviewees also participated in a project assessing neurodevelopment in Guatemalan infants in rural populations, a prospective study on Zika infection during pregnancy, and its effects on maternal and child health in the southwestern region of Guatemala.

In the occupational field, Álvarez highlights the importance of assessments for reducing staff turnover and increasing employee satisfaction, emphasizing the relevance of sustainable outcomes within companies. He notes that assessment has been an important tool in the organizational context.

Challenges

In the interviews conducted, participants indicated that one of the oldest and ongoing challenges in psychological assessment is the stigma toward psychology and the lack of trust in the discipline. This lack of trust, as noted by Jurado and Álvarez, stems from misinformation about the work psychologists do. According to Pereira, this lack of trust and credibility still creates problems for collaborative work between schools and even with parents. *"I would say that the main challenge at the beginning was credibility, right? I remember they used to call us, saying we were like people who read horoscopes..."* (Álvarez, 2022, personal communication).

Alejos and Molina de Kestler point to economic factors. Both report that there is difficulty in paying the actual cost of an assessment, which limits access to this service. Considering the cost of the test, its administration, scoring, obtaining results, and report writing, it becomes an expensive service. Molina de Kestler addresses the issue of low-cost assessments, referring to colleagues who conduct assessments but lack the training to recognize the associated costs. It is worth noting that they use tests that are not standardized in or for the Guatemalan population, as shown in Fig. 10.4, which presents the elements agreed upon by participants regarding the challenges they have faced in their professional experience as evaluators.

These challenges open the discussion on the need to adapt assessments to specific populations to address the sociocultural challenges posed by population diversity. Within this diversity, there is also polarity in socioeconomic classes, neurodiversity, and gender diversity. According to Mejía, this is one of the greatest challenges for psychological assessment in Latin America. This is a rapidly evolving topic, and it is not yet clear whether psychological assessment takes it into account or supports it.

In the educational field, Alburez de von Ahn points out the lack of training for interpreting results. On the other hand, there is a need for supervised practice to apply the theory learned. These shortcomings affect the quality of assessment.

Álvarez notes that, in the business sector, there are challenges, one of the most significant being the overemphasis on psychometrics. He also shares how a company may purchase rights from a provider, and in the absence of limits on the number of tests or their use, the human resources department applies everything to everyone. This results in poor management of assessments and, consequently, discrepancies in the results.

Paz de Camacho highlights that the hybrid modality in assessment can be a challenge. The difficulty arises from the lack of direct contact with the client or patient, which prevents the observation of attention spans and body language, as well as other skills that are difficult to perceive.

Future and Changes

Regarding the question posed to participants about their perspective on whether psychological assessment in Guatemala has changed or evolved, most confirm that there has been positive progress, particularly in economic aspects, recognition of professional fees, and diversification of assessments. However, they also share some of their fears or concerns for the future that warrant greater attention. *"There is now a proliferation of tests. There are many types of tests, especially in the neuropsychological field"* (Jurado, 2022, personal communication).

Among these positive factors of change in assessment in Guatemala is the increasing number of tests currently available. Both Laugerud and Pereira, as well as Alburez de von Ahn, emphasize that today there is easier access to more tests in Spanish, which positively impacts Spanish-speaking evaluators. Another important factor in this change is moving away from the practice of reproducing tests and respecting copyright. Today, there is greater openness, education, and trust in assessment processes, both for referring and conducting assessments, as well as for participating in an assessment and receiving results.

Mejía describes this as a boom in psychology, as the discipline is now taken much more seriously. Likewise, the need to seek diagnosis and professional help is growing every day. This cultural shift in the population, as Mejía calls it, is strongly associated with the emergence and evolution of technology.

Technology has been a driver of change, helping to break down barriers and fears surrounding assessment. Mejía and Paz de Camacho also consider access to social networks and information on the internet as key elements within technology. However, within this same topic, there is also concern about dependency, as virtual assessments and manuals may lead to a tendency not to read them, raising concerns about how this could affect future professionals.

Therefore, a possible solution is proposed: combining tools and methods from both virtual and in-person settings and teaching these skills from university training onward. Paz de Camacho stresses the importance of not neglecting populations without access to technology, as there is a tendency to focus on privileged areas that do have such access. *"I feel very proud; I see people who are much better prepared, people more focused on specialization, and I like that"* (Mejía, 2022, personal communication).

Finally, another key element for change in Guatemala is the presence of more individuals conducting assessments. Grazioso notes that there are now more trained professionals, as well as ethical standards applied to assessment included in the Guatemalan Psychologists' Code of Ethics. The increase in people conducting assessments requires professionals with solid training. However, Álvarez recommends strengthening the training of those who use assessments, as this area is currently underestimated.

Final Reflections

Psychological assessment is an essential part of psychological practice in Guatemala. It plays a fundamental role in identifying, intervening, and providing follow-up in clinical, educational, and occupational settings. The study of the history of assessment has highlighted how its core principles have been managed over time in the country. The main aspects reflected upon in this work concern the development of tests and the consolidation of the discipline within Guatemalan society. Likewise, access to services, training and instruction in the use of tests, their interpretation, and the preparation of reports have been considered. In constructing this chapter, other topics addressed included research, test standardization, and supervision as factors that have influenced the advancement and transformation of assessment in Guatemala.

The motivation for test standardization has changed from generation to generation. The drive to introduce psychological assessment initially led to the use of intelligence tests, vocational and career guidance instruments, as well as personality tests. Over the years, other areas and resources have been incorporated into assessment.

On the one hand, the development of assessment has been accompanied by the consolidation of the discipline in our country. Professional training programs have undergone various transformations in the pursuit of updating and responding to the needs of each era. Aguilar and Recinos (1996) noted the need to consolidate to Psychology as a profession in which the credibility of the discipline was necessary for the development of this science (Aguilar & Recinos, 1996).

Another component is access to assessment services, which is restricted according to the participants. On one hand, this is linked to the costs involved in Psychological Assessment, mainly in the private sector, since the public sector currently has a very limited capacity to conduct assessments. Fortunately, there are university clinics that offer these services, such as: *Universidad del Valle de Guatemala, Universidad Francisco Marroquín, Universidad Rafael Landívar, and Universidad del Istmo*. All of them offer a range of services at more affordable prices, while also providing training opportunities for undergraduate and master's students. Based on the results from the consulted experts, it can be said that many of these instruments are expensive and not easily accessible to most psychologists in this country.

In recent years, a key factor has been the development and acquisition of normative data for neuropsychological tests in the Guatemalan population. Clinical neuropsychology focuses its efforts on the assessment of individuals suspected of having functional impairments or deficiencies due to congenital, neurodevelopmental, or acquired conditions that cause brain damage in different populations. This science is of recent development in Guatemala (García de la Cadena et al., 2009); however, in the last decade, there has been growth not only in the training of professionals in the discipline, but also in the development of normative data for neuropsychological tests in both adult and pediatric populations across various domains such as attention, memory, language, visuospatial processes, processing speed, and executive functions (Arango-Lasprilla, 2015; Arango-Lasprilla, et al., 2015; Arango-Lasprilla & Rivera, 2017; Arango-Lasprilla, Rivera, Ertl, et al., 2017; Arango-Lasprilla, Rivera, Ramos-Usuga et al., 2017).

Considering the training of psychologists, the participants in this sample indicated the need for more systematic training in Assessment and the development of greater competencies. An analysis of the various Psychology programs in Guatemala shows that most include principles of Psychometrics and Psychological Assessment, but there remains a gap in training in Assessment.

Regarding the use and availability of assessment instruments, most participants reported the use of certain instruments as the most employed. Among these are: Wechsler intelligence scales (WISC, WAIS, WPPSI); personality scales (Minnesota Multiphasic Personality Inventory-2 Restructured Form [MMPI-2RF], SENA, PAI, Personality Assessment Inventory for Adolescents [PAI-A], Brief Symptom Inventory [LSB-50], Symptom Checklist [SCL-90], Big Five, Children's Personality Questionnaire [CPQ], Children's Depression Scale [CDS], BDI, BAI); projective instruments (Thematic Apperception Test [TAT], Children's Apperception Test [CAT], Family Drawing Test, Human Figure Drawing Test, Tree Test, House-Tree-Person Test, Rain Test); instruments for detecting learning problems (PROLEC and PROESC, Cognitive Assessment System [CAS-2], ENI-2, ENI-preschool, BANETA, BANFE-3, NEUROPSI, Woodcock-3 Achievement and Cognitive Test, BANPE) and tests of executive functions. However, there is insufficient training for their use.

The oral histories of the interviewees indicate challenges in the development of psychological tests relevant to the Guatemalan population. This also affects the review and processes of norming and standardization. There is no clear evidence of the different types of initiatives and actors involved in this area: researcher, publisher, collaboration between researcher and publisher, and leadership by a responsible institution.

However, across the different decades, there is no evidence of interest in formally reviewing or standardizing scales until 2015, when the professional responsibility to do so emerged. The professionals who have undertaken this work in recent years have collaborated with academia to carry it out. Other actions have been implemented through research projects in collaboration with nonprofit institutions and small collaborations within project groups funded by donations and supported by elite specialists.

Leadership in the development and/or standardization of psychological tests should be a collaborative effort between academia and publishing houses. In this way, researchers can take the initiative so that, at the end of the exploration, materials and resources are produced that benefit psychological assessment.

The study did not address the issue of supervision in assessment. It is worth nothing that this type of supervision exists in university institutions; however, when professionals begin their private or public practice, this support is discontinued. Supervision sessions among professionals offer the opportunity to discuss, disagree, and provide feedback on findings, diagnoses, and recommendations.

Understanding the timeline in some way allows us to discuss and conclude the social impact that Psychological Assessment has or has not had from a historical perspective. The time devoted to these interviews with oral histories of psychological assessment in Guatemala is significant. This work offers the potential to make an important contribution to the future of Psychological Assessment.

References

Aguilar, G., & Recinos, L. A. (1996). History and current state of psychology in Guatemala. *Latin American Journal of Psychology, 28*(2), 197–232. https://www.redalyc.org/pdf/805/80528202.pdf

Alarcón, R. (2004). Half a century of Latin American psychology: An overview. *Interamerican Journal of Psychology, 38*(2), 307–316. https://www.redalyc.org/articulo.oa?id=28438217

Arango-Lasprilla, J. C. (2015). Commonly used neuropsychological tests for Spanish speakers: Normative data from Latin America. *NeuroRehabilitation, 37*(4), 489–491. https://doi.org/10.3233/NRE-151276

Arango-Lasprilla, J. C., & Rivera, D. (2017). Normative data for Spanish-language neuropsychological tests: A step forward in the assessment of pediatric populations. *NeuroRehabilitation, 1*, 577–580. https://doi.org/10.3233/NRE-001479

Arango-Lasprilla, J. C., Rivera, D., Ertl, M. M., Muñoz Mancilla, J. M., García-Guerrero, C. E., Rodriguez-Irizarry, W., Aguayo Arelis, A., Rodríguez-Agudelo, Y., Barrios Nevado, M. D., Vélez-Coto, M., Yacelga Ponce, T. P., Rigabert, A., García De La Cadena, C., Pohlenz Amador, S., Vergara-Moragues, E., Soto-Añari, M., Peñalver Guia, A. I., Saracostti Schwartzman, M., & Ferrer-Cascales, R. (2017). Rey-Osterrieth Complex Figure—Copy and immediate recall (3 minutes): Normative data for Spanish-speaking pediatric populations. *NeuroRehabilitation, 41*(3), 593–603. https://doi.org/10.3233/NRE-172241

Arango-Lasprilla, J. C., Rivera, D., Nicholls, E., Aguayo Arelis, A., García De La Cadena, C., Peñalver Guia, A. I., Vergara-Moragues, E., Rodriguez-Lorenzana, A., Marín-Morales, A., Soto-Añari, M., Lara, L., Rodríguez-Agudelo, Y., Alcazar Tebar, C., Galarza-Del-Angel, J., Rodriguez-Irizarry, W., Ibañéz-Alfonso, J. A., García-Guerrero, C. E., Delgado-Mejía, I. D., Pohlenz Amador, S., & Sánchez-San Segundo, M. (2017). Modified Wisconsin Card Sorting Test (M-WCST): Normative data for Spanish-speaking pediatric population. *NeuroRehabilitation, 41*(3), 617–626. https://doi.org/10.3233/NRE-172242

Arango-Lasprilla, J. C., Rivera, D., Ramos-Usuga, D., Vergara-Moragues, E., Montero-López, E., Adana Díaz, L. A., Aguayo Arelis, A., García-Guerrero, C. E., García De La Cadena, C., Llerena Espezúa, X., Lara, L., Padilla-López, A., Rodriguez-Irizarry, W., Alcazar Tebar, C., Irías Escher, M. J., Llibre Guerra, J. J., Torales Cabrera, N., Rodríguez-Agudelo, Y., & Ferrer-Cascales, R. (2017). Trail making test: Normative data for the Latin American Spanish-speaking pediatric population. *NeuroRehabilitation, 41*(3), 627–637. https://doi.org/10.3233/NRE-172247

Arango-Lasprilla, J. C., Rivera, D., Rodríguez, G., Garza, M. T., Galarza-Del-Angel, J., Rodríguez, W., Velázquez-Cardoso, J., Aguayo, A., Schebela, S., Weil, C., Longoni, M., Aliaga, A., Ocampo-Barba, N., Saracho, C. P., Panyavin, I., Esenarro, L., Martínez, C., García De La Cadena, C., & Perrin, P. B. (2015). Symbol digit modalities test: Normative data for the Latin American Spanish-speaking adult population. *NeuroRehabilitation, 37*, 625–638. https://doi.org/10.3233/NRE-15128

Arango-Lasprilla, J. C., Rivera, D., Trapp, S., Jiménez-Pérez, C., Hernández Carrillo, C. L., Pohlenz Amador, S., Vergara-Moragues, E., Rodríguez-Agudelo, Y., Rodriguez-Irizarry, W., García De La Cadena, C., Galvao-Carmona, A., Galarza-Del Angel, J., Llerena Espezúa, X., Torales Cabrera, N., Flor-Caravia, P., Aguayo Arelis, A., Saracostti Schwartzman, M., Barranco

Casimiro, R., & Albaladejo Blázquez, N. (2017). Symbol Digit Modalities Test: Normative data for Spanish-speaking pediatric population. *NeuroRehabilitation, 41*, 639–647. https://doi.org/10.3233/NRE-172243

Ardila, R. (1968). Psychology in Latin America. *American Psychologist, 23*(8), 567–574. https://doi.org/10.1037/h0026430

Barrios Peña, J. (1952). *Considerations on the Szondi test*. Editorial del Ministerio de Educación Pública.

Carpintero, H., González Calderón, M. J., & Del Barrio Gándara, M. V. (2011). Bela Szekely: his book Los Tests in the Latin American context. *Revista Latinoamericana de Psicología, 43*, 357–368.

Cohen, R. J., & Swerdlik, M. E. (2000). Psychological testing and assessment.

Del Valle Cóbar, D. (1991). *The student movement in Guatemala, 1973-1981*. Bachelor's thesis, Universidad Autónoma de México. https://www.usfx.bo/nueva/vicerrectorado/citas/ECONOMICAS_6/Administracion_Publica/51%20%20drdelv%20cobar.pdf

Gallegos De San Vicente, M. (2021). The professionalization of psychology in Guatemala in the mid-twentieth century. *Revista Psicólogos, 27*.

García de la Cadena, C., Henriquez, J. L., Sequeira, E., Cortés Ojeda, A. L., De Obaldía, Y. R., & Judd, T. (2009). Neuropsychology in Central America. *Revista Neuropsicología, Neuropsiquiatría y Neurociencias, 9*(2), 1–19. https://dialnet.unirioja.es/descarga/articulo/3988008.pdf

González, J. M., & Gilbert, O. (1979). The measurement of creativity: development of an instrument and study of its reliability. *Revista Latinoamericana de Psicología, 11*(3), 363–381.

Hernández-Sampieri, R., Fernández, C., & Baptista, M. (2014). *Research methodology*. Editorial McGraw Hill.

Ibáñez-Alfonso, J. A., Company-Córdoba, R., García De La Cadena, C., Simpson, I. C., Rivera, D., & Sianes, A. (2021). Normative data for ten neuropsychological tests for the Guatemalan pediatric population updated to account for vulnerability. *Brain Sciences, 11*(7), 842. https://doi.org/10.3390/brainsci11070842

Lara, P., & Altunes, A. (2014). Oral history as a methodological alternative for the social sciences. *Revista de Teoría y Didactics of Social Sciences, 20*, 45–62. https://www.redalyc.org/pdf/652/65247751003

Leong, F., Bartram, D., Cheung, F., Geiseinger, K., & Iliescu, D. (2020). *International handbook of testing and assessment by the ITC*. Editorial Manual Moderno.

Luna-Sánchez, S. E., Juárez Estrada, R., & Mejía Palencia, N. (2020). The power of scientific publications: Psychology in Guatemala. *Revista Psicólogos, 26*, 5–10.

Olabarrieta-Landa, L., Rivera, D., Galarza-Del-Angel, J., Garza, M. T., Saracho, M. T., Rodríguez, W., Chávez-Oliveros, M., Rábago, B., Leibach, G., Schebela, S., Martínez, C., Luna, G., Longoni, G., Ocampo-Barba, G., Rodríguez, G., Aliagao, A., Esenarro, L., García De La Cadena, C., Perrin, P. B., & Arango-Lasprilla, J. C. (2015). Verbal fluency tests: Normative data for the Latin American Spanish-speaking adult population. *NeuroRehabilitation, 37*, 515–561. https://doi.org/10.3233/NRE-151279

Olabarrieta-Landa, L., Rivera, D., Ibáñez-Alfonso, J. A., Albadalejo-Blázquez, N., Martín-Lobo, P., Delgado-Mejía, I. D., Lara, L., Rabago Barajas, B. V., Rodríguez Salgado, A. M., Paredes Quispe, L. A., Romero-García, I., Velázquez-Cardoso, J., García De La Cadena, C., Fernández-Agis, I., Padilla-López, A., Hernández Agurcia, G. P., Marín-Morales, A., San Jose, A. C., & Arango-Lasprilla, J. C. (2017). Peabody Picture Vocabulary Test-III: Normative data for Spanish-speaking pediatric population. *NeuroRehabilitation, 41*(3), 687–694. https://doi.org/10.3233/nre-172239

Olabarrieta-Landa, L., Rivera, D., Lara, L., Rute-Pérez, S., Rodríguez-Lorenzana, A., Galarza-Del-Ángel, J., Peñalver Guia, A. I., Ferrer-Cascales, R., Velázquez-Cardoso, J., Campos Varillas, A. I., Ramos-Usuga, D., Chino-Vilca, B., Aguilar Uriarte, M. A., Martín-Lobo, P., García De La Cadena, C., Postigo-Alonso, B., Romero-García, I., Rabago Barajas, B. V., Irias Escher, M. J., & Arango-Lasprilla, J. C. (2017). Verbal fluency tests: normative data for Spanish-speaking pediatric population. *NeuroRehabilitation, 41*(3), 673–686. https://doi.org/10.3233/nre-172240

Olabarrieta-Landa, L., Rivera, D., Morlett-Paredes, A., Jaimes-Bautista, A., Garza, M. T., Galarza-Del-Angel, J., Rodríguez, W., Rábago, B., Schebela, S., Perrin, P. B., Luna, M., Longoni, M., Ocampo-Barba, N., Aliaga, A., Sarachom, C. P., Bringas, M. L., Esenarro, L., García-Egan, P., & Arango-Lasprilla, J. C. (2015). Standard form of the Boston Naming Test: Normative data for the Latin American Spanish speaking adult population. *NeuroRehabilitation*, 501–513. https://doi.org/10.3233/NRE-151278

Olabarrieta-Landa, L., Rivera, D., Rodríguez-Lorenzana, A., Pohlenz Amador, S., García-Guerrero, C. E., Padilla-López, A., Sánchez-Sansegundo, M., Velázquez-Cardoso, J., Díaz Marante, J. P., Caparros-González, R. A., Romero-García, I., Valencia Vásquez, J., García De La Cadena, C., Muñoz Mancilla, J. M., Rabago Barajas, B. V., Barranco Casimiro, R., Galvao-Carmona, A., Martín-Lobo, P., Saracostti Schwartzman, M., & Arango-Lasprilla, J. C. (2017). Shortened version of the Token Test: Normative data for Spanish-speaking pediatric population. *NeuroRehabilitation, 41*(3), 649–659. https://doi.org/10.3233/nre-172244

Piotrowski, C., & Keller, J. W. (1984). Psychodiagnostic testing in APA-approved clinical psychology programs. *Professional Psychology: Research and Practice, 15*(3), 450–456. https://doi.org/10.1037/0735-7028.15.3.450

Piotrowski, C., Sherry, D., & Keller, J. W. (1985). Psychodiagnostic test usage: A survey of the Society for Personality Assessment. *Journal of Personality Assessment, 49*(2), 115–119. https://doi.org/10.1207/s15327752jpa4902_1

Quevedo, M. (2003). *The academic guidance service and counseling in higher education and its importance in professional development*. Master's thesis, Universidad San Carlos de Guatemala. http://biblioteca.usac.edu.gt/tesis/07/071315

Rivera, D., Olabarrieta-Landa, L., Rabago Barajas, B. V., Irias Escher, M. J., Saracostti Schwartzman, M., Ferrer-Cascales, R., Martín-Lobo, P., Calderón, J. A., Aguilar Uriarte, M. A., Peñalver Guia, A. I., Camlla Ynga, R., García-Guerrero, C. E., Fernández-Agis, I., García-Gómez-Pastrana, A., Ibañez-Alfonso, J. A., Gómez, H., Galarza-Del-Ángel, J., García De La Cadena, C., & Arango-Lasprilla, J. C. (2017). Newly developed Learning and Verbal Memory Test (TAMV-I): Normative data for Spanish-speaking pediatric population. *NeuroRehabilitation, 41*(3), 695–706. https://doi.org/10.3233/NRE-172249

Rivera, D., Olabarrieta-Landa, L., Van Der Elst, W., Gonzalez, I., Rodriguez-Agudelo, Y., Aguayo Arelis, A., Rodríguez-Irizarry, W., García de la Cadela, C., & Arango-Lasparilla, J. C. (2019, March). Normative data for verbal fluency in healthy Latin American adults: Letter M, and fruits and occupations categories. *Neuropsychology, 33*(3), 287–300. https://doi.org/10.1037/neu0000518

Rivera, D., Perrin, P. B., Aliaga, A., Garza, M. T., Saracho, C. P., Rodríguez, W., Justo-Guillen, E., Aguayo, A., Schebela, S., Gulin, S., Weil, C., Longoni, M., Ocampo-Barba, N., Galarza Del-Angel, J., Rodriguez, D., Esenarro, L., Garcia-Egan, P., Martinez, C., & Arango-Lasprilla, J. C. (2015). Brief Test of Attention: Normative data for the Latin American Spanish-speaking adult population. *NeuroRehabilitation, 37*(4), 663–676. https://doi.org/10.3233/NRE-151283

Rivera, D., Perrin, P. B., Morlett-Paredes, A., Galarza Del Angel, J., Martínez, C., Garza, M. T., Saracho, C. P., Rodriguez, W., Rodríguez-Agudelo, Y., Rábano, B., Aliada, A., Schebela, S., Luna, M., Longoni, M., Ocampo-Barba, N., Fernández, E., Esenarro, L., García-Egan, P., & Arango-Lasprilla, J. C. (2015). Rey–Osterrieth Complex Figure—Copy and immediate recall: Normative data for the Latin American Spanish-speaking adult population. *NeuroRehabilitation*, 677–698. https://doi.org/10.3233/NRE-151285

Rivera, D., Perrin, P. B., Stevens, L. F., Garza, M. T., Weil, C., Saracho, C. P., Rodríguez, W., Rodríguez-Agudelo, Y., Rábago, B., Weiler, C., García De La Cadena, C., Longoni, M., Martínez, C., Ocampo-Barba, N., Aliaga, A., Galarza Del-Angel, J., Guerra, A., Esenarro, L., & Arango-Lasprilla, J. C. (2015). Stroop Color-Word Interference Test: Normative data for the Latin American Spanish-speaking adult population. *NeuroRehabilitation, 37*, 591–624. https://doi.org/10.3233/NRE-151281

Rivera, D., Salinas, C., Ramos-Usuga, D., Delgado-Mejía, I. D., Vasallo Key, Y., Hernández Agurcia, G. P., Valencia Vásquez, J., García-Guerrero, C. E., García De La Cadena, C., Rabago Barajas, B. V., Romero-García, I., Campos Varillas, A. I., Sánchez-Sansegundo, M., Galvao-Carmona, A., Lara, L., Granja Gilbert, E. J., Martín-Lobo, P., Velázquez-Cardoso, J., Caracuel, A., & Arango-Lasprilla, J. C. (2017). Concentration Endurance Test (d2): Normative data for Spanish-speaking pediatric population. *NeuroRehabilitation, 41*(3), 661–671. https://doi.org/10.3233/NRE-172248

Rodas, O. P. (1988). *Establishment of a guidance department in an educational center*. Bachelor's thesis, Universidad del Valle de Guatemala. https://repositrio.uvg.edu.gt/handle/123456789/2472#:~:text=http%3A//repositorio.uvg.edu.gt/xmlui/123456789/2472

Schulmeyer, M. (2016). Training in psychological assessment in psychology programs in Bolivia. *Interamerican Journal of Psychology, 50*(2), 288–300.

Ureta, F. (2022). Psychology in Guatemala: Fields, currents, and collectives. In M. González (Ed.), *Educational psychology in Guatemala* (pp. 15–64). Universidad de San Carlos de Guatemala, School of Psychological Sciences. Professional Research Unit.

Young, J., Rose, D., Mumby, H., Benitez-Capistros, F., Derrick, C., Finch, T., Garcia, C., Home, C., Marwaha, E., Morgans, C., Parkinson, S., Shah, J., Wilson, K., & Mukherjee, N. (2018). A methodological guide to using and reporting on interviews in conservation science research. *Methods in Ecology and Evolution, 9*(1), 10–19. https://doi.org/10.1111/2041-210X.12828

Chapter 11
Advances and Challenges in Psychological Assessment in Mexico

Rosa Angélica Torres Marmolejo

Introduction

The contribution of this chapter to the book "Origins and Challenges of Psychological Assessment in Ibero-American Countries" is the result of work carried out as a member of the Psychological Assessment and Measurement Working Group of the Interamerican Society of Psychology. It represents an attempt to share some historical facts about psychological assessment in Mexico, some achievements, and above all, the challenges currently present in the practice of psychological assessment. Valuable information obtained from interviews with faculty members who have trained several generations of psychologists is shared. I hope that readers will find something of interest in these lines that will strengthen their desire for knowledge and enrich their work as psychology professionals.

I would like to thank Dr. Marigú González Garza, educational psychologist, and Dr. Juana Angélica Salgado, clinical psychologist, for sharing their professional experience as psychologists and as professors who have trained many generations of psychology graduates from the University of Guanajuato, the Universidad Iberoamericana, and Universidad La Salle Bajío in León, Guanajuato.

Psychological assessment is one of the main activities carried out by psychologists in their professional practice. It involves various processes aimed at obtaining sufficient information about the individual or situation through the use of reliable tools such as interviews and psychological tests.

Psychological assessment is conducted in order to generate a synthesis derived from the analysis of data collected during the process. The goal is to reach a result that may be formulated as a qualitative description, reflecting an understanding of

R. A. Torres Marmolejo (✉)
Universidad La Salle Bajío, León, Guanajuato, Mexico
e-mail: rtm103349@lasallebajio.edu.mx

S. V. Pugliese et al. (eds.), *Origins and Challenges of Psychological Assessment in Ibero-American Countries*, https://doi.org/10.1007/978-3-032-21380-8_11

aspects of a person's or group's life and their interactions with the context, or as a formal diagnosis, or as a final recommendation for intervention, care, or treatment (Nunes-Baptista et al., 2006).

Recognizing the importance of psychological assessment, various national and international organizations such as the International Test Commission (ITC), the Official College of Psychologists (COP), the American Psychological Association (APA), the European Federation of Professional Psychologists' Associations (EFPPA), among others, have taken steps to develop ethical and legal guidelines, as well as those based on respect for the individual. These actions provide a foundation for conducting professional psychological assessment in accordance with professional standards (Muñiz & Hernández, 2015).

The practice of psychological assessment is anchored in the scientific method, sharing several of its steps: (1) observation of the behaviors under study; (2) experimentation through the application of instruments to broaden the collection of information; (3) generation of hypotheses based on the identification of indicators derived from the information obtained; and (4) testing of theories through diagnostic formulations and drawing conclusions from the process.

From this perspective, psychological assessment is not limited to the administration of tests or measurement instruments, which is the domain of the more specific field of psychometrics. The latter is just one of the tools used within the broader set of actions that comprise the assessment process. According to Nunes-Baptista (2006), the purpose of psychological assessment is not to label individuals with a diagnostic nomenclature; rather, its broader aim is to communicate, using appropriate language, the best understanding of the different aspects of an individual's or a group's life.

Conceptualizing psychological assessment in our country in this way was the result of a historical process that has enabled us to understand its transformation over time, from its origins linked to the field of philosophy to its professionalization as a science.

Historical Overview of Psychology and Psychological Assessment in Mexico

First Period: Origins of Psychology as a Science

The origins of psychology in Mexico date back to the fifteenth century, with events related to the way life events and behavior were understood through religious beliefs. In the cultures of the great indigenous peoples, the gods were consulted to find answers and explain natural phenomena. The period of conquest that Mexico experienced between the fifteenth and eighteenth centuries brought about major changes in religious practices, which also impacted the way natural events and daily life were conceived; religious practice shifted from the worship of multiple gods to monotheistic worship, with Catholicism becoming predominant. During this period, the understanding of human behavior was governed by the prevailing Aristotelian philosophical and religious principles, and the interpretation of mental illness was based on supernatural phenomena and magical explanations, viewing it as divine punishment or warning.

In this context, around 1567, Fray Bernardino Álvarez, a devout Christian, founded the country's first hospital for the mentally ill, "Hospital San Hipólito," which became the first psychiatric hospital in Latin America and one of the earliest asylums in the world (Quijano Pitman, 1997).

This first period concluded in the mid-nineteenth century with the influence of positivism, which led to psychology being considered a discipline and also advanced the study of mental illness with a focus on care and treatment.

Second Period: The Emergence of Psychology as a Science

The second period began in the last decade of the nineteenth century with the emergence of modern psychology. Several events marked this second historical phase of psychology and psychological assessment in Mexico; one of the first was the introduction of the study of psychological phenomena through courses on Psychology and Ethics taught by Ezequiel Chávez around 1893, as part of the curriculum at the National Preparatory School of the National Autonomous University of Mexico (UNAM) (Zanatta Colín & Camarena, 2012). These courses, included independently in the curriculum, proposed a scientific training approach different from the prevailing positivist thought, emphasizing the intellectual and moral development of students and highlighting the scientific and experimental nature of psychology.

As a result of this effort and to support the establishment of experimental psychology in the country, Enrique Aragón and Daniel Vergara founded the first Experimental Psychology Laboratory in 1916 at the National Autonomous University of Mexico (UNAM). Various projects were inspired by this laboratory, which played a key role in the development of experimental psychology in Mexico (Escobar, 2016).

Another major development at the beginning of the twentieth century was the creation of the first intelligence test by Alfred Binet and Theodore Simon in 1905 in Paris, designed to identify children in the educational system who were unable to benefit from the standard curriculum. This instrument became the first test for measuring and detecting intellectual disability and was introduced in Mexico for use in the educational field.

It was Dr. Rafael Santamarina, working as a resident physician at the La Castañeda Psychiatric Hospital, founded in Mexico in 1910, who became interested in normal and abnormal cognitive processes and their measurement in patients. Around 1914, he made the first attempts to adapt and use the Binet-Simon intelligence test in his practice. Years later, in 1921, he translated and adapted this test for Mexican schoolchildren, presenting it at the First Mexican Child Congress in 1921 (Colotla, 1984).

This work was continued from 1920 by Dr. David Boder, who opened an important field for experimental and applied psychology in the country and contributed to psychometrics through the translation, adaptation, and application of various instruments for assessing cognitive processes, including the Binet-Simon Test in 1925.

In the following years, Dr. Santamarina led various projects focused on the adaptation and standardization of mental tests, serving as head of the Biometric Calculation Section of the Department of Psychopedagogy and Hygiene of the Ministry of Public Education, founded in 1925. Later, in 1937, this department became the National Institute of Psychopedagogy and then the National Institute of Pedagogy. Through the work of this department, a battery of tests[1] adapted for the Mexican population was developed to assess the mental abilities of schoolchildren and to carry out classification and selection processes for students of that era (Colotla, 1984).

From this perspective, the adaptation and application of various psychological assessment instruments was supported by agencies such as the Ministry of Public Education, created in 1921. Within this educational context and in support of children, the introduction of psychological tests in this field was facilitated. However, rather than focusing on innovating educational programs or fostering the development of those assessed, the prevailing evolutionary approach emphasized the importance of identifying students with high intelligence quotients (IQ), so psychological assessment processes were oriented toward evaluating the cognitive abilities of students subjects for study and grouping purposes (Gregory, 2001).

Undoubtedly, the work of Dr. Santamarina and Dr. Bode provided a solid foundation for the advancement of applied psychology and the introduction of psychometrics in our country. Evidence of this is the interest shown in subsequent decades to continue the work of translating, adapting, standardizing, and validating various psychological tests, among which the Army Beta intelligence test, the Dominoes Test, Raven's Progressive Matrices Test, the Goodenough Test, and, years later, the adaptation of the Wechsler Adult Scale stand out (Colotla, 1984).

As a result of these advances in the study of experimental and applied psychology and contributions to psychometrics, in 1928 UNAM opened the School of Psychology as part of the Faculty of Philosophy and Letters. Shortly thereafter, the Institute of Psychology and Psychiatry was established, linking the teaching of psychology to psychiatry—a development that was not particularly favorable for the construction of a professional identity for psychologists, who, in practice, began to be seen as assistants in the psychiatrist's assessment tasks.

It was not until 1959 that the first undergraduate program in Psychology was launched, offered by UNAM with the right to a professional degree, and it was not until 1974 that the Psychology degree received official recognition and graduates obtained the right to a professional license as a Psychologist (Zanatta Colín & Camarena, 2012).

[1] This battery included the FAY TEST, the DESCOUDRES scale, the EBBINGHAUS test, and application norms for Mexican boys and girls for the VERMEYLEN scale, among others (Colotla, 1984).

It is worth noting that in Mexico, 66 years passed from Ezequiel Chávez's first seminars to the opening of the first undergraduate program in Psychology. During this period, the academic training profile in psychology and its practice in psychological assessment were guided by the medical-psychiatric model, which reinforced trends toward measurement, quantitative research, and psychometrics, as well as the psychoanalytic theories of Freud and Erich Fromm, which at that time still enjoyed broad acceptance in the academic community. This community was largely composed of philosophers, lawyers, psychiatrists, and psychoanalysts, significantly impacting both the content and approach to patient assessment and intervention.

Among the faculty involved in training psychologists in this program was Ramón de la Fuente, considered the leading figure of modern psychiatry in Mexico and founder, in 1970, of the first open psychiatric service at the Spanish Hospital of Mexico (Capetillo-Hernández, 2012).

With the official recognition of the undergraduate degree in Psychology, university training programs in Psychology began to expand. From the two programs registered by 1950 with the National Association of Universities and Higher Education Institutions (ANUIES)—those of UNAM and Universidad Iberoamericana—the number grew to 11 programs in 1960, 54 in 1970, and 82 in 1990. This expansion led to the need to review the curricula for this degree and to develop accreditation processes to ensure the proper professional preparation of psychology students, as well as their integration into the fields of psychological assessment and intervention (Zanatta Colín & Camarena, 2012).

Third Period: The Professionalization of Psychology and Practice of Psychological Assessment

At the end of the 1940s, the social needs arising from the First and Second World Wars prompted changes in the curricula of UNAM's university programs. The new programs were oriented toward strengthening science, research, and their application to solving social problems. In this context, the 1949 undergraduate curriculum in Psychology was no exception, incorporating research, methodology, and instrumental courses such as Psychometrics, and making professional practice a mandatory activity.

During this period, the training of psychologists in Mexico continued to be guided by the medical, psychoanalytic, and psychometric models, with an emphasis on knowledge of the main tests and instruments for psychometric assessment and measurement. These training orientations were decisive in the practice of students and the professional work of psychology graduates, who found fertile ground in the application of intelligence and personality tests as assistants in the field of psychiatry.

In the 1960s, Psychology began an important period of expansion and consolidation as an academic discipline. During this growth, the Faculty of Psychology at Universidad Veracruzana, Xalapa region, was founded in 1963, and 10 years later, in 1973, the Faculty of Psychology at UNAM was established as an independent entity from the Faculty of Philosophy. The study of human behavior from the perspective of experimental psychology continued to attract the interest of researchers of the time, leading to the founding of the Center for Behavioral Science Research, along with the opening of the first laboratory for behavioral analysis at UNAM in 1972 (Covarrubias, 2003).

During this same period, in 1971, the National Council for the Teaching and Research of Psychology (CNEIP) began operations, from which studies on compensatory education emerged as a proposal in the educational field to address disadvantages faced by individuals due to genetic and sociocultural factors. In these studies, psychological assessment gained great importance, and assessment tasks within educational organizations increased, benefiting psychologists (Consejo Nacional para la Enseñanza e Investigación de la Psicología, 2000).

This approach to assessment continued to be based on the application of intelligence or personality tests, with the aim of evaluating behavior through indicators that would allow for the measurement of the subject's performance based on IQ or the presence of other factors related to performance issues identified in students within the educational process.

By the late 1970s, psychological research on intelligence and its application in the field of special education gained momentum. Researchers' interest continued to focus on information processing at the cognitive level and the role these processes play in knowledge acquisition (Gregory, 2001).

This perspective integrated contributions from various theories that had been present in the country's scientific community for decades, broadening the understanding of intelligence development. Among these were Piaget's constructivist approach, with his concepts of assimilation, accommodation, and the construction of knowledge schemas (Piaget, 1984), and Vygotsky's sociocultural approach, particularly his contributions regarding the Zone of Proximal Development as an essential space to traverse in advancing the development of higher mental functions (Fariñas, 2017).

Years later, the studies of Reuven Feuerstein and Sternberg began to be incorporated into the curricula of psychologists interested in psychological assessment within educational contexts. These authors focused on the dynamic assessment of learning potential and research on cognitive structural modifiability, marking a significant shift in the understanding and practice of psychological assessment. This new approach emphasized a more qualitative, integrative, and preventive perspective on the state of cognitive processes, behavior, and personality.

They sought to move beyond the traditional assessment model, which was primarily centered on the administration of tests and the calculation of IQ and performance indicators, toward a more dynamic evaluation focused on exploring the individual's learning potential across all areas of life and on a careful analysis and interpretation of the information obtained.

Integrating this approach to psychological assessment into everyday professional practice from a dynamic perspective primarily aimed to deepen the analysis of the processes each individual uses to arrive at answers and to use the results to discover the person's maximum potential regarding a given task. Most importantly, it sought to identify, through assessment, how each person can reach their highest learning potential (Noguez, 2002; Gregory, 2001).

In connection with these changes, psychologists have maintained an interest in adapting or designing new psychological assessment instruments that contribute to the understanding of cognitive or mental processes. Notable contributions include the successful revisions and adaptations of the Wechsler scale in its 1974, 1991, and 2011 versions, as well as the development of various scales, inventories, and instruments constructed with appropriate precision, validity, and reliability criteria. These have resulted from independent research or from graduate theses in various fields of psychology (Calleja, 2011).

Finally, in the early decades of the twenty-first century, psychology has established a professional presence distinct from philosophy and psychiatry, strengthened by the professional practices of psychology students in training across different fields of application: clinical, educational, occupational, research, and social intervention.

During this period, 250 psychology programs remain active throughout Mexico, and in most of them, the influence of this historical process in psychology is evident. Among these programs are the Bachelor's in Psychology at the University of Guanajuato, Universidad Iberoamericana, and Universidad La Salle Bajío—programs that, in their consolidation, have followed a trajectory similar to that of UNAM since its inception. Some programs have adopted a generalist professional training profile in psychology, others have maintained areas of semi-specialization, and some offer training in a single area (Zanatta Colín & Camarena, 2012).

In recent decades, the training profile offered by universities has been strengthened through the updating of psychology programs, but above all, by seeking to balance professional practice with theoretical learning. The aim is to address current social and contextual demands, which require not only a broad theoretical understanding but also that psychologists be able to "solve problems within their area and professional competence" (Zanatta Colín & Camarena, 2012, p. 161). Among these professional competencies are those related to strengthening theoretical foundations, diagnostic assessment, intervention, and research.

To date, the domains of knowledge and forms of intervention, even in the practice of psychological assessment, remain highly diverse. Therefore, in addition to improving the academic training quality of psychology graduates, it is necessary to regulate assessment practices. For this reason, the Ethical Code for Mexican Psychologists, developed by the Mexican Society of Psychology in 2016, specifies criteria to be followed for the use, administration, scoring, and interpretation of assessment instruments, emphasizing the psychologist's responsibility for the management of the instruments they use and for their reliability and validity (Sociedad Mexicana de Psicología, 2016).

Regarding the diversity in current psychological assessment practices, a common factor is the use of psychological tests. Intelligence assessment tests, maturational tests, personality scales or inventories, and projective tests continue to be part of the assessment battery used with children, adolescents, and adults. It is worth noting that, although projective tests maintain a qualitative approach and some have questionable validity, their use remains very high in psychological assessment practice (Pérez-Aguero et al., 2019).

Current Challenges and Dilemmas in Psychological Assessment from the Perspective of Experts

Up to this point, a brief historical overview of the emergence of psychology in Mexico has been presented, aiming to identify the main events that have shaped its evolution. Undoubtedly, the introduction of a paradigm distinct from the prevailing positivist and evolutionist thought of the time opened the door to the introspective study of mental processes, alongside the emergence of psychometrics as a tool that initiated the measurement and assessment of various mental processes and functions.

From these foundations, psychological assessment has gone through various stages in order to achieve greater validity and reliability in the results provided by its procedures. As a result, it has become an essential task for psychologists, enabling them to understand, identify, categorize, explore, diagnose, or make decisions that are useful for individuals or groups. In this sense, assessment in psychology is a process that goes beyond the mere administration of tests (Fernández-Ballesteros, 1999).

However, due to the changes brought about in recent years by the modernization and streamlining of processes resulting from technological advances, new questions have arisen:

1. What challenges have psychologists faced in their training to be able to conduct reliable psychological assessments today?
2. What knowledge and skills do psychologists need to develop during their professional training in order to conduct reliable psychological assessments?
3. How is psychological assessment taught and learned from the perspective of formative experience?
4. What challenges does psychological assessment face at present?

To address these questions, I highlight some relevant ideas shared by two experts in the field of psychological assessment, Mtra. Juana Angélica Salgado Frías and Mtra. Ma. Guadalupe Minerva González Garza. It is important to emphasize their generosity in sharing their experience, as well as their extensive professional and teaching careers—one in the field of clinical psychology[2] and the other in the field of educational psychology.[3]

Professional Training of Psychologists and the Learning of Psychological Assessment

Analyzing the data gathered from the experiences of the interviewed instructors and relating them to the findings reported in the various reviewed articles revealed commonalities in these professional training histories in the field of psychology and psychological assessment, as well as in the events reported regarding the transitions this discipline and its practices have undergone in our country.

One point of agreement among the participating psychologists was the way the emergence of psychology was experienced in Mexico and in other states of the Republic. Although psychology was officially recognized as a science in Mexico in 1970, in other states such as Guanajuato, the opportunity to train as a psychologist did not arise until 1978, when the University Council of the University of Guanajuato authorized the inclusion of a Bachelor's Degree in Psychology among its academic offerings, under the direction of Dr. Manuel Torres Madrazo (Salgado, personal communication, August 11, 2022).

Given the development of psychology programs at the national level, it is not surprising that this professional option emerged in the provinces under the auspices of the Faculty of Philosophy and the Faculty of Medicine, and was supported by the teaching staff of UNAM, who continued the training tradition of new psychologists based on the medical, psychiatric, psychoanalytic, experimental psychology, behaviorist, constructivist, and innovative instrumental enrichment models prevalent at the time. In the first decades of the twenty-first century, the influence of humanism, the systemic model, and the complexity model has also become prominent (González, personal communication, August 4, 2022).

---

[2] Ms. Juana Angélica Salgado, a clinical psychologist with more than 30 years of experience, taught for 28 years in various courses related to Psychological Assessment in the Bachelor's in Psychology at the University of Guanajuato, coordinated the Bachelor's in Psychology at this university from 2010 to 2015; head of Psychology services and coordinator of clinical and organizational practice. In private universities, she taught in the Psychology program at Universidad de la Salle, Bajío. Throughout her professional career, she has coordinated and taught various courses on psychological assessment with an emphasis on the clinical field.

[3] Ms.Guadalupe Minerva González Garza (Marigu), an educational psychologist and Master in Educational Research, with more than 30 years of experience, taught for 28 years in various courses related to psychoeducational assessment in the Bachelor's in Psychology at the University of Guanajuato, coordinated the practice center for this program in the clinical and educational area CITELAC from 1983 to 1993, was thesis advisor for more than 25 years at the University of Guanajuato and master's thesis advisor at the University of La Salle Bajío and the Ibero-American University of León. Throughout her professional career, she has coordinated and taught various courses on psychological assessment with an emphasis on the educational field.

In this context, the construction of professional identity among psychologists in Mexico has, from its origins, been shaped by the different theoretical approaches of their instructors,[4] who share with their students both the what and the how of their work, based on the theoretical frameworks that define them and the experience they have gained in their respective fields of practice (Salgado, personal communication, August 11, 2022).

Another aspect to consider in this training is that, since the emergence of psychology as a science of behavior, the specific task of psychological assessment has been a central function of psychologists. However, in Mexico, it was not until the consolidation of psychology training programs by UNAM in 1959 that assessment was formally integrated as an area of teaching and learning, with courses covering measurement theory, instrument construction, psychometrics, assessment of developmental processes, personality, and knowledge of diagnostic classifications.

Within this framework, psychological assessment in the country has become a fundamental activity across the various fields of psychology—clinical, educational, organizational, social, legal, among others.

In practice, two main approaches have been identified: (a) Assessment considered as traditional, supported by the principles of psychometrics, a process that begins with the administration, scoring, and interpretation of tests, yielding quantitative data that reflect what the individual is able to accomplish; and (b) dynamic assessment, developed from R. Feuerstein's approach, which aims to understand, through analytical thinking, how an individual's performance is constructed when faced with a task—not how much they know, but how they know it—and to identify their potential and the means to achieve it (González, 2003).

This form of dynamic assessment has been widely disseminated in the educational field, seeking a radical change in the evaluation process so that the results obtained from psychological assessment can be used to implement "cognitive structural modification" programs, based on evaluating the individual's true potential and providing a diagnosis that supports decision-making to guide developmental progress (Noguez, 2002).

This approach to psychological assessment has been well received in both clinical and educational settings, as it seeks to deepen the understanding of what is being assessed and how it is assessed. However, as González notes (personal communication, August 4, 2022), its application requires more than just theoretical understanding; it demands that the trainee psychologist be willing to make the effort to study each case in depth, going beyond what the traditional psychometric approach requires.

---

[4] Special thanks to the founders of the first psychology program established at the University of Guanajuato in the city of León, Gto. in 1978: Dr. Manuel Torres Madrazo and collaborators Dr. Ángel Ortiz Escudero, Dr. Arroyo, and Dr. Aranda, as well as the faculty team of the first cohort, including Dr. Carmen Badillo, Dr. Augusto Vázquez, psychotherapist Salvador Aguilar, M.A. Lolita Hernández, Dr. Antonio Hinojosa, for their willingness to share their knowledge and support the training of the first generations of psychologists in the state of Guanajuato.

In this regard, learning to conduct psychological assessments from this dynamic perspective involves a process of guidance and supervision by the instructor, in order to develop the trainee psychologist's exploratory skills.

The Teaching–Learning Process of Psychological Assessment from a Formative Experience

According to Salgado (personal communication, August 11, 2022), the university training experience that helps consolidate the knowledge required to strengthen learning in dynamic psychological assessment is, above all, professional practice in various settings. This formative practice consists of the prior knowledge that trainees acquire about different assessment instruments—what they are, what tests and materials they include, how they are administered, scored, and interpreted—followed by the integration of information. In addition, it requires the modeling provided by instructors in each course of the curriculum for trainee psychologists, as well as the guidance offered by the instructor through supervision during the student's practical experience.

In this sense, providing students with supervised and feedback-based experiences in psychological assessment practice is considered essential for better training of psychology students and a closer alignment with the desired graduate profile. In this context, "the creation of university practice centers aims to offer students a formative opportunity in controlled environments and, for those who use these centers, access to low-cost services" (Salgado, personal communication, August 11, 2022).

Another opportunity that supports the consolidation of knowledge and the development of skills for psychological assessment is the involvement of psychology trainees in institutional practice centers, such as family development centers (DIF), hospitals, schools, health centers, companies, and various organizations, ensuring that the work is carried out under the conditions required by the psychologist's assessment and intervention model, with ethics, attentive listening, privacy, and confidentiality.

Thus, as Salgado points out (personal communication, August 11, 2022), psychoeducation is of great importance as a task of raising awareness and providing guidance to the authorities of the various institutions involved in the development of practice, in order to clarify the role of the trainee psychologist, the psychological assessment and intervention model, and the ethical requirements and scope necessary for practice.

Regarding the psychological assessment instruments most commonly used in practice, there is consensus that psychology training programs tend to teach the administration and interpretation of well-recognized assessment tools, even though some of these instruments have not been recently updated or adapted for use with the Mexican population.

In this regard, the most frequently used tests in psychological assessment in the region include: the Wechsler Intelligence Scale in its versions for children and adults, the Terman-Merrill Intelligence Test, the Raven's Progressive Matrices, the Beta Intelligence Test, the Bender Visual-Motor Gestalt Test, the Frostig Test, the Machover Human Figure Drawing Test, the Draw-a-Person-in-the-Rain Test, the Family Drawing Test, the Thematic Apperception Test (TAT and CAT), the House-Tree-Person Test (HTP), the Sacks Sentence Completion Test; among personality inventories, the Minnesota Multiphasic Personality Inventory (MMPI) and the 16 Personality Factor Questionnaire (16PF) are frequently used. In recent years, neuropsychological tests such as the ENI or Neuropsi, the BANFE scale for assessing executive functions, the BANETA test for learning disabilities, and other scales for evaluating anxiety, depression, state-trait scales, scales for assessing communication skills, neurodevelopmental disorders, or scales for evaluating psychosocial and socioemotional variables, among others, have been incorporated into assessment (González, personal communication, August 4, 2022; Salgado, personal communication, August 11, 2022).

Regarding the procedure for conducting psychological assessment, whether in an individual or one-on-one format,[5] it is recommended to begin by identifying the needs that lead the individual to request the assessment, followed by the integration and administration of a battery of tests that will provide the necessary data to address the referral question. Above all, it must be considered that the Psychological Assessment process takes place within an agreement or contract, in which both parties—the client and the evaluator—commit to providing a response in order to achieve the intended objective.

In this regard, it is essential to encourage psychology trainees to use the various assessment tools and instruments appropriately, ensuring that, during the administration of tests, scales, or inventories in practice, the characteristics of the individuals being assessed are taken into account, standardized conditions and procedures are maintained, and protocols, scoring tables, and norms appropriate to the target population are used, in order to guarantee the reliability and validity of the results obtained (FENANPSIME, 2018, Art.56).

In this way, the necessary conditions are preserved to enable accurate psychological diagnoses, incorporating psychometric, descriptive, and psychodynamic criteria in their formulation. An appropriate diagnostic formulation integrates the evaluation of the individual's weaknesses and strengths, avoiding the stereotyping of the person based solely on deficiencies or pathology.

To this end, it is essential that the psychological tests used in assessment processes correspond to the most current and contextually relevant versions, and are preferably standardized for the Mexican population.

[5] It is important to note that psychological assessment can be conducted individually or in groups; however, the reason for the assessment will determine the procedure to be followed, the selection of instruments to be used, and the conditions that must be maintained to achieve its objective.

Knowledge and Skills Required for Psychological Assessment Practitioners

Psychological assessment is a specialized activity, carried out by psychologists who are trained and equipped with a set of knowledge, skills, and aptitudes that form the foundation of their professional identity and practice. In this sense, it is crucial to incorporate the following throughout their academic and professional training:

Knowledge

Knowledge provides the theoretical foundation that students must acquire through the courses included in the curriculum; the proper integration of this knowledge distinguishes those who administer a test from a purely quantitative perspective from those who use this foundation to understand the explanatory reasons behind an individual's behavior. This comprehensive training includes theoretical foundations on theories of normal and pathological personality, the neurophysiological and sociocultural bases of behavior, cognitive, intellectual, psycholinguistic, socioemotional, and perceptual-motor development processes, as well as an understanding of the various paradigms underlying the comprehension of human nature, normality, and psychopathology. Academic training in assessment and diagnosis is also considered, including interview techniques, psychometrics, knowledge of various psychological assessment instruments, conditions for individual, group, and large-scale administration, and the integration of various intervention approaches (González, personal communication, August 4, 2022).

Skills

Observation and attention are fundamental skills for a competent psychologist; these abilities allow for the perception and integration of the quality of events that arise during the Psychological Assessment process. Also emphasized are analysis, synthesis, abstraction, the ability to integrate collected information, and to make correlations between what is heard and what is observed. Tolerance for fragmentation is required to engage in the analytical process and identify correlations among the information obtained; as well as the ability to communicate results assertively within a framework of responsibility, honesty, confidentiality, and respect for the individual, in addition to empathy and the capacity to connect with human suffering, to engage with the discourse of feelings, intuition, and common sense (Salgado, personal communication, August 11, 2022).

Aptitude

Psychological assessment requires professionals with an interdisciplinary perspective, strong listening skills, a willingness to work collaboratively, to conduct research, to tolerate waiting, initiative in problem definition and resolution, the ability to formulate hypotheses in accordance with scientific methodology, and above all, respect and ethical responsibility inherent in working with people (González, personal communication, August 4, 2022).

Strengthening knowledge about the teaching and learning of Psychological Assessment requires the committed participation of faculty who, drawing on their professional experience, guide and support students as they navigate the challenges of transitioning from classroom learning to practical application.

Current Challenges in Psychological Assessment

In the first decades of the twenty-first century, the field of psychological assessment has been characterized by the increasing complexity of human processes and social interactions, resulting from major advances in neuroscience, technology, and science, the transformation of communication processes, and, to top it off, the impact of a pandemic,[6] which has affected the way individuals develop as persons with distinct identities.

These transitions require psychology professionals to develop a broader, more human, and holistic understanding of psychological processes in order to assess and intervene from a perspective of diversity, with emotional well-being and mental health as central reference points.

From this perspective, the tradition of face-to-face Psychological Assessment remains relevant today, as does the importance and richness of what is observed during the evaluator–evaluee interaction; however, the use of technology to streamline the processes of administration, scoring, and generation of global performance profiles through the creation of digitized versions of assessment instruments has gained ground, aiming to deliver evaluations in less time, not only in research or organizational settings, but also in individual practice and large-scale group assessment (Salgado, personal communication, August 11, 2022).

Psychological Assessment has not been exempted from the influence of virtual evaluation and should not distance itself from new trends; the challenge is to ensure the reliability and validity of results by adjusting the standardization of the assessment process. To achieve this, it is necessary to conduct research that documents what occurs in these approaches, identifies biases that arise when assessing under

[6] In Mexico, the Covid-19 pandemic required people to remain at home from March 17, 2020, until the gradual return to classrooms and workplaces between January and March 2022. This period mandated the use of face masks, social distancing as a health precaution, and the transition of education and work activities in all sectors to virtual formats.

these conditions, addresses behavioral issues stemming from individuals' interactions on social networks, and leverages these not only as challenges but also as opportunities for growth in psychological practice. This involves substantiating findings and strengthening the assessment process under new conditions, thereby contributing to the updating of psychology curricula and programs in the country (González, personal communication, August 4, 2022).

Conclusions

In conclusion, several recommendations are proposed based on the significant interaction between psychology students, their instructors, the examinee, and the context in which the assessment takes place. The following key points are presented:

1. It is important to recognize that Psychological Assessment is not limited to the administration and scoring of psychological tests; all measurement instruments serve as auxiliary techniques within the set of actions undertaken by the psychologist in this evaluation process, which is governed by the scientific method.
2. The central task of Psychological Assessment involves an integrative process that goes beyond quantitative aspects and requires the application of various skills to formulate a diagnosis that can be communicated based on a comprehensive understanding of the different facets of an individual's or group's life.
3. In every field of application of Psychology and Psychological Assessment, it is essential to keep in mind the purpose of the assessment, as this determines the feasibility of its application, the required procedures, and the type of instruments to be used in order to obtain accurate results. This process is established within the context of a professional evaluator-examinee relationship, with specific roles and tasks.
4. Given the population, contextual, and modality variations—whether individual, group, or large-scale—in which Psychological Assessment is conducted, it is recommended to review and update undergraduate psychology curricula offered in the country, promoting the strengthening of these programs through research and the accreditation criteria set by regulatory bodies such as the National College of Psychologists, the National Council for the Teaching and Research of Psychology, and regulatory organizations for Psychological Assessment such as the International Test Commission, the College of Psychologists, among others.
5. Assessment through virtual platforms presents a challenge and therefore necessitates research, analysis, and the establishment of new approaches to address it. It is advisable to identify, analyze, and document successful outcomes in these new assessment practices in order to make informed decisions about necessary adjustments and aspects to be considered in remote assessment processes.
6. It is necessary to strengthen psychology students' foundational knowledge, skills, and aptitudes to ensure sound Psychological Assessment practices and

foster interdisciplinarity. In this endeavor, the guidance of instructors, drawing on their professional experience, is essential to support psychology trainees as they transition from academic activities in the classroom to professional practice settings, ensuring the integrity of the Psychological Assessment process (Fernández-Ballesteros, 2013).

7. This guided practice, combined with a well-structured educational pathway grounded in current knowledge that addresses the needs of individuals and their contexts, enables the achievement of a strong graduate profile in the discipline.
8. In this educational process, it is necessary to guide students regarding the ethical standards governing Psychological Assessment (APA, 2002) and the preparation and safeguarding of assessment records in accordance with the guidelines set forth in the current national Code of Ethics for psychologists.
9. It is important to encourage, from the educational stage, the development of research projects that support the creation or adaptation of assessment instruments and promote the generation of norms and standardization processes tailored to the country and its diverse contextual conditions.
10. In all areas of practice—whether assessment, diagnosis, intervention, or research—psychologists must maintain a humanistic perspective that guides their interventions with ethics, honesty, and professionalism, always remembering that the individual is at the center of the entire process and that their rights, dignity, and personal integrity must be respected.

Acknowledgments To my teachers. For sowing the seeds of my professional development as a psychologist.

References

American Psychological Association. (2002). Principios éticos de la psicológica y código de conducta. http://www.apa.org/ethics

Calleja, N. (2011). *Inventario de escalas psicosociales en México, 1984–2005*. Facultad de Psicología. Universidad Nacional Autónoma de México.

Capetillo-Hernández, J. (2012). *La emergencia del psicoanálisis en México*. Biblioteca.

Colotla, V. (1984). Rafael Santamarina y los orígenes de la Psicometría en México. *Revista de Historia de la Psicología, 5*(4), 163–170.

Consejo Nacional para la Enseñanza e Investigación de la Psicología en México. (2000). Memorias de Asambleas Anuales.

Covarrubias, P. (2003). *Currículum, disciplina y profesión, desde la perspectiva de los académicos de Psicología de Iztacala*. Tesis. Doctorado en Pedagogía. UNAM

Escobar, R. (2016). El primer laboratorio de Psicología experimental en México. *Revista Mexicana de Análisis de la Conducta, 42*(2), 116–144.

Fariñas, G. (2017). *Aprendizaje y desarrollo humano desde la perspectiva de la complejidad*. Educare y De la Salle Ediciones.

Federación Nacional de Colegios, Sociedades y Asociaciones de Psicólogos de México. A.C. (2018). *Código de ética de las y los psicólogos mexicanos*, FENAPSIME.

Fernández-Ballesteros, R. (1999). Psychological assessment: Futures, challenges and progresses. *European Psychologist, 4*(4), 248–262. https://doi.org/10.1027/1016-9040.4.4.248

Fernández-Ballesteros, R. (2013). *Evaluación Psicológica. Conceptos, métodos y estudio de caso* (2nd ed.). Pirámide.
González, M. (2003). *Evaluación psicoeducativa*. Material inédito, no publicado.
González, M. (2022). Entrevista, comunicación personal. 4 de agosto de 2022.
Gregory, R. (2001). *Evaluación Psicológica. Historia, principios y aplicaciones*. Manual Moderno.
International Test Commission. (2013). *International guidelines quality control in scoring, Test análisis and reporting of test scores*. ITC.
Muñiz, J., & Hernández, A. (2015). Nuevas directrices sobre el uso de los test: Investigación, control de calidad y seguridad. *Papeles del Psicólogo, 36*(3), 161–173. http://www.papelesdelpsicologo.es
Noguez, S. (2002). El desarrollo potencial de aprendizaje. Entrevista a Reuven Feuerstein. *Revista Electrónica de Investigación Educativa, 4*(2), 132–147. http://redie.uabc.mx/vol4no2/contenido-noguez.html
Nunes-Baptista, M., García-Capitao, C., & Alba-Scortegagna, S. (2006). Evaluación Psicológica en Salud: Contextos actuales. *Estudios Sociales, 15*(20), 138–116.
Pérez-Aguero, M., Cabrera-Zamora, I., & Meza-Alejos, A. (2019). Utilización de las pruebas psicológicas en México. Un análisis exploratorio. *Revista de Iniciación Temprana. Ciencia y Tecnología Preludio, 1*(1), 49–58. Facultad de Psicología. https://doi.org/10.22402/j.ritcyt%20preludio.unam.1.1.2020.247.49-58
Piaget, J. (1984). *Seis estudios de Psicología*. Ed. Seix Barral.
Quijano Pitman, F. (1997). El primer hospital psiquiátrico de América, 1567. *Primicias Médicas Nacionales, Gaceta Médica de México, 133*(4), 351.
Salgado, J. (2022). Entrevista. Comunicación Personal. 11 de agosto de 2022.
Sociedad Mexicana de Psicología A.C. (2016). Una vida dedicada al desarrollo humano. *Revista Mexicana de Psicología, 33*(1), 5–6.
Zanatta Colín, E., & Camarena, T. Y. (2012). La formación profesional del psicólogo en México. *Enseñanza e Investigación en Psicología, 17*(1), 151–170. Recuperado de: https://www.redalyc.org/artículo.oa?id=29223246010

Chapter 12
An Overview of the Past, Present, and Future of Psychological Assessment in Paraguay: Current Reality and Challenges

Norma Coppari

Introduction

The aim of this chapter is modest: to provide an overview of the most significant milestones in the past, present, and future of Psychological Assessment in Paraguay, describing and analyzing its current realities and forthcoming challenges. Addressing the topic of the "Origins and Challenges of Psychological Assessment in Ibero-American Countries," specifically focusing on Paraguayan Psychological Assessment, is a challenging and, above all, still developing task. For this reason, the intention is not to delve deeply, given the lack of bibliographic resources and records that would allow for a more detailed and accessible approach. The challenge lies in the scarcity of references and official documents that account for its history, present, and future. Given the limited literature and systematization of data documenting these events, it was decided to collect them using a methodology that would provide such information.

This initial sample of reconstructed tables is based on the accounts and perceptions of those who teach in various areas, such as psychometrics, measurement theory, instrument training, and others, within what is commonly referred to as Psychological Assessment. It draws on the memories, experiences, and knowledge of the interviewees—experts who describe the historical development of assessment across three time periods. Once again, it is hoped that this overview will be engaging and shed initial light on this scarcely explored topic within our psychology as a science, discipline, and profession, which undoubtedly has much to reveal about our Paraguayan context.

N. Coppari (✉)
Catholic University of Assumption, Assumption, Paraguay
e-mail: normacopparipy@gmail.com

S. V. Pugliese et al. (eds.), *Origins and Challenges of Psychological Assessment in Ibero-American Countries*, https://doi.org/10.1007/978-3-032-21380-8_12

Methodology

This study is framed within a qualitative approach, using in-depth interviews and analysis of records from invited experts, as well as references from selected articles and books that, in isolated instances, mention aspects of the history of Psychological Assessment in our country.

Ten faculty representatives specializing in Psychological Assessment from the two largest universities in Paraguay—the National University of Asunción and the Catholic University of Asunción—were invited to participate. Invitations were sent via email between March and June 2022.

The interviews, which included a statement of purpose, instructions, and informed consent, were sent to the participants. Responses were awaited until the beginning of July. Of the initial group invited, only three responded.

The interviews consisted of semi-structured guiding questions, such as: (1) What historical milestones, figures, and contributions do you know of in the development of Psychological Assessment in Paraguay?; (2) What knowledge and skills are taught and practiced in the professional training of psychologists in Paraguay regarding Assessment?; (3) What theoretical and methodological approaches are addressed in Psychological Assessment in Paraguay?; (4) Which instruments are most commonly used in academic practice, research, theses, and diagnostic assessment across various fields (clinical, health, educational, occupational, social, forensic)?; (5) What critical evaluation would you make of current teaching—what gaps and deficiencies do you observe?; (6) What proposals would you make in response to current and future demands for psychologists in the field of assessment?; (7) Are you aware of contributions in the area of Psychological Assessment regarding the creation, adaptation, validation, or reliability of instruments for use with local and foreign populations?; (8) Please add any other topics you consider relevant to the present and future of Paraguayan Psychological Assessment—realities and challenges you can reference.

Many of these questions went unanswered due to lack of knowledge or experience in the areas consulted.

The analysis and systematization of the responses form the basis for the following sections.

Some Historical Milestones of Psychology in Paraguay

The history of Psychology in Paraguay can be studied across a very extended period, with its earliest antecedents found in the colonial education provided in seminaries for priestly formation. From those distant origins, Psychology underwent several fundamental changes, evolving up to the present day. To facilitate understanding, the study of this field can be divided into: (1) a pre-university period; and (2) a university and professional period. The first period spans from approximately 1610 to

1960, during which psychology was taught in seminaries and secondary schools, especially in religious training centers where basic psychology courses were offered. From those times, there was a clear interest in the application of Psychological Assessment in educational settings. Our focus, however, will be on the second period—the university and professional era—which began with the establishment of the first psychology degree program at the Catholic University of Asunción in 1963 and continues to the present day (García, 2009).

According to Opening Act No. 13, dated April 26, 1962, the institutionalization of Psychology occurred only in the 1960s, when the first Bachelor's degree in Psychology in the country was offered at the Catholic University of Asunción (UC) in 1963, with a 4-year curriculum. The National University of Asunción (UNA) launched a second program in 1967, with similar content and duration (Martínez Cáceres, 2008). Both universities held a monopoly on undergraduate psychology education until the late 1980s.

The fall of the dictatorship in 1989, and continuing to the present, marked a period of rapid expansion in training opportunities throughout the country, with the establishment of new higher education institutions. This increase in offerings led to the emergence of programs of questionable quality. Currently, both UNA and UC, which were historically the only institutions providing psychology training, have numerous campuses across the country offering psychology programs. Additionally, more than 20 private universities, with multiple campuses in various regions, have been authorized. This scenario makes it very difficult to determine the current number of public and private higher education institutions involved in psychology training at the local level. However, it can be stated that most psychology degree programs last between 4 and 5 years, and there are very few postgraduate psychology programs in the country (Coppari, 2015; Martínez Cáceres, 2008).

During the 1990s, several Mercosur agreements were established to ensure that psychology training would be mutually recognized across all member countries. These agreements also aimed to improve the quality of educational offerings through a professionalizing, inter- and transdisciplinary, multiparadigmatic curriculum based on competencies, with an emphasis on research, professional practice, and internships, balanced with theoretical development. At that time, there was already debate about the need to create quality assurance and control institutions in the member countries of Mercosur Academia (Plenary of Committees of the Paraguayan Society of Psychology, 2009).

The auditing institutions would be responsible for certifying quality and quantity through evaluation processes, for accreditation by independent bodies, with local and foreign peer reviewers, requiring each country to establish the relevant agency. In Paraguay, Law 2072 (2003) created the National Agency for the Evaluation and Accreditation of Higher Education (ANEAES) in 2003. However, to date, only two institutions (UNINORTE and UNA) have official ANEAES accreditation; others, such as UC, are currently undergoing the process. ANEAES is the technical body responsible for evaluating and accrediting the academic quality of higher education institutions under Law 4995 (2013) "On Higher Education" in Paraguay.

In retrospect, the recommendations of the Mercosur Academic Agreements (Plenary of Committees of the Paraguayan Society of Psychology, 2009), specifically regarding the psychology degree, show that although some progress has been made in certain institutions, these have not been structural changes, nor have they addressed the future demands of a globalized world. The content remains outdated and encyclopedic. Programs are not mutually recognized, as there is no single national training proposal for all universities, making student mobility between programs within the country impossible. Even less feasible is mobility to Mercosur countries, the United States, or the European Union. The curriculum continues to emphasize classical theories and mentalist, intrapsychic paradigms, with a notable lack of research, practical training, and internships.

Above all, there remains a significant deficiency in training in basic, applied, and technological psychological science, lacking a scientist-practitioner, evidence-based profile, which results in deficient and largely irrelevant scientific output, despite the recommendations of the 1990s Mercosur Training Agreement (Plenary of Committees of the Paraguayan Society of Psychology, 2009). There are no cutting-edge research lines addressing emerging topics in Psychology to guide undergraduate theses and dissertations. The courses offered do not encourage research from the early years of training, which is essential for the scientific validation of professional practice. Scientific activity is relegated to insufficient or sporadic postgraduate training, and is viewed as a means of acquiring specific skills and knowledge that were absent from undergraduate education.

Although the undergraduate curriculum claims to be professionalizing, there is no evidence of a consistent plan or program for practical training and internships, nor the provision of tutoring and supervision at the various stages of its fulfillment. There is not always a close relationship between the development of the content in courses described as theoretical-practical and professional practice in applied fields such as clinical and health, occupational, educational, community, or forensic settings, nor is there continuity. Internships are subject to the availability of access to professional settings for their completion. This results in internships being inconsistent, lacking significance, and varying from year to year. The consequence for generations of interns is that they experience a wide range of options, not always of high quality, nor related to the course content, and often without supervision for feedback and assessment of their contribution to the development of professional procedural competencies.

Regarding internships, always within the context of professional training, the Ministry of Public Health and Social Welfare (MSPBS) established several years ago, through Resolution No. 426, dated July 4, 2007, and regulated by Circular No. 04/08, dated June 25, 2008, the mandatory Rural Internship for all university graduates in the health field, whether from public, private, or foreign institutions. This requirement is understood to apply to psychologists with a focus on clinical and health training, but not to other areas of application such as educational, occupational, community, forensic, or others. To date, it is difficult to determine, due to lack of data, whether this criterion is being met, under what procedures, what it contributes to the professional development of psychologists, and above all, to the quality, effectiveness, and efficiency of the services provided to the rural population that seeks them.

With regard to attitudinal competencies, which are intrinsic to the ethical training of psychologists, there is also no plan or program in place to reinforce components such as emotional intelligence, self-efficacy, resilience, and adaptive coping for the challenges inherent in professional practice in any applied area. In this respect, although there is a Code of Ethics (Paraguayan Society of Psychology, 2004) developed and approved by the Paraguayan Society of Psychology (SPPs), in force since November 10, 2004, its limited dissemination and application remain merely anecdotal in the practice of psychology in Paraguay.

Historically, legislation governing the professional practice of psychology in Paraguay has only required a university degree in Psychology, validated by the National University, and registration with the MSPBS. If the degree is from a foreign country, the process and associated costs are far from user-friendly; it could be said that those seeking education at foreign universities ranked for excellence—which our universities do not participate in or are insignificantly ranked—are penalized.

The most significant recent development is the enactment of Law 6293 (2019) on the Professional Practice of Psychology in Paraguay, passed on May 3, 2019. This law establishes the regulations governing the work of psychologists in any field of practice. However, professional registration falls under the jurisdiction of the MSPBS, raising questions about how other areas, beyond clinical and health, will be addressed, given the lack of specific regulations for each area of professional work.

In this overview, which is not exhaustive and therefore incomplete, it is difficult to focus on the role of Psychological Assessment, as there are very few and scattered published data referencing specific aspects of training, key figures, contributions, and advances made in the country regarding this topic. The following section presents the accounts obtained from the three interviews conducted for this work, based on the guiding questions provided to the invited faculty members. These are professionals holding academic management positions, who also teach courses on topics related to Psychological Assessment and its history.

Psychological Assessment from the Perspective of Interviewed Psychologists

Interview 1

– What historical milestones, figures, and contributions do you know of in the development of Psychological Assessment in Paraguay?

> My relative youth and limited training in the history of psychology in Paraguay do not allow me to identify figures and contributions to Psychological Assessment in our country,

except for the distinguished professors I have had the opportunity to meet during my academic life. First, I mention the late Professors Jesús Ramírez and Oscar Serafini. I especially emphasize the latter for his work in the construction and validation of assessment instruments and the measurement of psychological constructs. Although I have been fortunate to have other professors, I am not aware of many works in the field of instrument development carried out by professionals from our country. Nevertheless, I would like to highlight the significant contribution made during my time as a student by having Professor Enrique Morosini as a teacher, who was responsible for my shift toward psychometrics, statistics applied to psychology, and the use of computer tools for instrumental research. Likewise, I highlight Professor Nicolás Garcete and his extensive experience in forensic assessment, as well as his guidance in preparing for an assessment session, selecting instruments, verbal and nonverbal communication, empathy, the use of the Guaraní language, and other practices I experienced during a student internship at the Tacumbú prison (Asunción), specifically regarding the assessment of individuals deprived of their liberty, thanks to the help of this colleague. Finally, I do not want to fail to mention Professor Oscar Gaona, who was my thesis advisor, and whose guidance was focused precisely on a process of adaptation and scale validation.

– What knowledge and skills are taught and practiced in the professional training of psychologists in Paraguay regarding Assessment?

I believe that the teaching is mainly oriented toward the administration, scoring, and interpretation of psychological tests in most of the faculties where professionals are trained in our country. I do not see much difference in terms of practice, considering that it is more common to see colleagues seeking to acquire the "best" assessment instruments to use them as diagnostic tools in their clinical, educational, and forensic practices.

– What theoretical and methodological approaches are addressed in Psychological Assessment in Paraguay?

With regard to assessment, I believe that the Classical Test Theory and its principles are strongly predominant, with some occasional introduction to Item Response Theory. Nevertheless, I think the approach is, by far, more theoretical than practical.

– Which instruments are most commonly used in academic practice, research, theses, and diagnostic assessment across various fields of application (clinical, health, educational, occupational, social, forensic)?

Without going into specific instruments, I believe that intelligence tests, aptitude tests, cognitive assessment tools, career guidance instruments, projective techniques, and standardized personality tests are the most prominent. There is also significant use of neuropsychological tests. All of these, and likely others, are used regardless of the area of specialization.

– What critical evaluation would you make of what is currently taught, and what shortcomings and deficits do you observe?

I believe that teaching in courses labeled as Psychometrics is, for the most part, still conducted in a mechanical manner, under the mistaken notion that it is a practical discipline and, therefore, students must repeatedly practice the protocols for administration, scoring, and interpretation of instruments with several subjects. In this sense, students are asked to obtain copies of tests and protocols so that they can receive training that, without exaggeration, requires little more effort than reading the test manual, understanding it, and putting it into practice. I assume not much wisdom is needed for this. More training is required on construction, adaptation, and validation of instruments, but from the perspective of instrumental research, with research teams and groups, where the instructor, specialized in this area, acts as a tutor and instructor in the use of software tools for the corresponding statistical analyses. Likewise, there is a need for practical application of the assumptions of test theories.

– What proposals would you make in response to current and future demands for professional psychologists?

In general, I believe that in Paraguay it is necessary to look at what is being taught at the world's leading universities, the most up-to-date content, applications of experimental psychology, training in neuroscience—in other words, to seriously strive to offer a modern education. We cannot continue teaching as we did 20 years ago. In fact, the COVID-19 pandemic and the resulting virtualization of education have shown that we were in a comfortable and repetitive position regarding teaching. Technology must be incorporated, as well as reading articles rather than just old manuals and textbooks, virtual means of knowledge dissemination (such as podcasts, for example), and other resources.

– Are you aware of contributions in the field of assessment regarding the creation, adaptation, and validation of instruments for use with local and foreign populations?

In Paraguay, there are some published articles on this subject, but it is an area that, considering our sociolinguistic characteristics, has vast potential for instrumental research. It is also possible that there is more work, but as always, conducting research, such as a thesis or dissertation, and not publishing it is unfortunately quite common.

Interview 2

– What historical milestones, figures, and contributions do you know of in the development of Psychological Assessment in Paraguay?

Professor Carlos de Jesús Ramírez was the country's first psychometrician; he went to the United States for training and, upon his return, worked for the Ministry of Education in that area, conducting research, and since then we have had national "norms." He worked for both the Catholic University and the National University in the Psychology program in the area of Psychological Assessment. Father Dr. José de Jesús Aguirre published a book on "Character and Intelligence," where he presents a comparative table between the Dutch and Paraguayan populations. Another comparative point he presents is between character and intelligence, the latter measured by the D48 or Dominoes Test. From this comparison, the following points emerge:

(a) The difference in average intelligence between men and women, at both the secondary and university levels.
(b) The variation in average intelligence in men and women when moving from secondary to university studies.
(c) The similarities in the classification of character, according to the Heymans test as assessed by physicians who responded to the survey, and the classification obtained using the average intelligence resulting from the application of an intelligence test to the examined subjects.

– What knowledge and skills are taught and practiced in the professional training of psychologists in Paraguay regarding Assessment?

I do not have sufficient knowledge to comment on the entire training provided in the country. However, I do have experience with students from private universities located in the Asunción area. During my work as a psychologist at a prestigious private school, I accepted third- and/or fourth-year psychology students, but upon observing their inadequate preparation in handling, for example, a "norm table," interpolation, or even the use of a basic template such as the Raven's Progressive Matrices, I spoke with the level director and expressed my refusal to continue accepting interns from private universities. It should be understood that UCA is not part of that group; moreover, they never requested to send students for such purposes.

My experience with students from the National University of Asunción and the National University of Itapúa was very satisfactory during the internships they completed to fulfill academic requirements. They handled assessment materials competently, and the technical terms related to the use of psychometric instruments were not unfamiliar to them. The student who came from Encarnación to Asunción fully met all requirements without delaying the work that the school's Psychology Department needed to carry out, such as vocational guidance, which includes psychometric assessment among other activities. The population involved consisted of 135 students distributed across 5 technical programs, and 108 students from basic education who had to decide which high school track to pursue and then take entrance exams if interested in available spots.

– What theoretical and methodological approaches are addressed in Psychological Assessment in Paraguay?

No response.

– Which instruments are most commonly used in academic practice, research, theses, and diagnostic assessment across various fields of application (clinical, health, educational, occupational, social, forensic)?

Psychotherapeutic approaches: CBT, holistic, humanistic. As for research: quantitative, non-experimental, descriptive, and correlational studies.

– What critical evaluation would you make regarding current teaching? What shortcomings and deficits do you observe?

From the perspective of my role, my criticism is that students today do not want to study or conduct research; they want everything 'summarized'. From the coordination side, I have more professors who wish to teach in depth and with seriousness, but they encounter students who do not share the same standards.

– What proposals would you make in response to current and future demands for psychology professionals?

No response.

– Are you aware of contributions in the field of Psychological Assessment regarding the creation, adaptation, validation, or reliability of instruments for use with local and foreign populations?

Yes, I am aware, but I do not have them on hand; they are at the Faculty of Philosophy at UNA.

– Please add any other topics you consider relevant.

Psychological Assessment is the tool or instrument that psychologists have to obtain data that may not emerge through interviews alone. This is why we still need these tools to effectively carry out therapeutic interventions. What I have observed is a decline in the seriousness required for assessments, such as controlling variables that may influence the administration of an instrument. Also, the proper use of measures or corresponding norms according to the population, since a population from the northern hemisphere is not the same as ours. The modification of standardization to support the use of an instrument merely for the convenience of the practitioner, without any scientific basis, is also an issue.

Interview 3

- What historical milestones, figures, and contributions do you know of in the development of Psychological Assessment in Paraguay?

The pioneer of psychometrics was Professor Ramón Indalecio Cardozo, who introduced the Stanford-Binet test in the 1920s while serving as Director General of Schools. In the 1950s, the Ecuadorian educator Emilio Uzcátegui was also important, introducing some psychological tests in the context of the Ministry of Education. Personality (and characterological) tests were introduced by Father José de Jesús Aguirre in the 1960s.

- What knowledge and skills are taught and practiced in the professional training of psychologists in Paraguay regarding Assessment?

Usually, the greatest emphasis is placed on specific skills in administering each individual test, although the quality of this instruction and the relevance of the content vary greatly from one institution to another. There is a significant deficit in understanding statistical analysis tools. The most notable shortcomings are in the methodological processes for constructing original psychometric tests and in neuropsychological assessment.

- What theoretical and methodological approaches are addressed in Psychological Assessment in Paraguay?

Predominantly, psychometric assessment based on the calculation of the intelligence quotient (IQ). In some cases, training is provided in the use of instruments for personality assessment, although generally within the intrapsychic modality of psychoanalysis. Trait-based tests in the field of personality are not widely used. Psychophysiological assessment, such as the study of evoked potentials of the brain, for example, are hardly mentioned at all.

- Which instruments are most commonly used in academic practice, research, theses, and diagnostic assessment across various fields of application (clinical, health, educational, occupational, social, forensic)?

Primarily, I believe the most frequently used are the different versions of the Wechsler test, as well as the Raven, for measuring intelligence. Several tests are also used to assess attitudes, generally following the Likert scale model. In personality assessment, the most commonly used projective tests are the Rorschach, Murray's T.A.T., the man-in-the-rain test, the family test, and similar instruments, despite their questionable reliability. Some psychologists use the Eysenck test and the McCrae and Costa test. Le Senne's characterological questionnaire continues to be used in certain settings, such as primary schools.

- What critical assessment would you make regarding current teaching practices? What shortcomings and deficits do you observe?

The main problem is the lack of up-to-date materials; the instruments used and the literature are outdated. The material infrastructure of universities is insufficient, and there are no well-designed facilities for the practice of Psychological Assessment in all its forms. The faculty are also out of date and lack feedback. With the two previous years of the pandemic, training has become even more theoretical, and these problems have intensified.

– What proposals would you make in response to current and future demands for psychologists in the field of assessment?

Training for psychologists in this area must be improved. Likewise, public and private institutions should raise their standards to prevent cases of malpractice, which are currently very frequent.

– Are you aware of contributions in the field of Psychological Assessment regarding the creation, adaptation, validation, or reliability testing of instruments for use with local and foreign populations?

Dr. Oscar Serafini developed a cognitive screening test titled 'El Robot' during his residency at the University of Minho, Portugal. He also produced other works along the same lines. Serafini is the only researcher worthy of that title in contemporary Paraguayan psychology.

– Please add any other topics you consider relevant regarding the present and future of Paraguayan Psychological Assessment. Realities and challenges you can reference.

I believe one point that is never addressed is the need to introduce an intercultural component into psychological assessments. Tests must be adapted to our culture and, more importantly, produced from within our own culture. When that happens, we will be able to make contributions to the world. Beyond that, I would add the topics mentioned in the previous questions.

Psychological Assessment, in Summary: Perspectives and Challenges

The information gathered allows us to identify some points of consensus in the accounts of the interviewees, as well as from the data collected in the literature and references consulted.

The author is aware of the inaccuracies, biases, and gaps that this approach may contain, and thus the reader will understand that this area still requires, in our country, much more sustained, organized, and in-depth research to provide more objective and comprehensive evidence. Here lies fertile ground for undergraduate and postgraduate thesis research lines that can be suggested as a derivation from the current state of the art.

Regarding the pioneers in the early days of Psychological Assessment in our country, it is possible to recognize the contributions and teachings of Professor Ramón Indalecio Cardozo (García, 2008), the Ecuadorian educator Emilio Uzcátegui, Father Dr. José de Jesús Aguirre, Licentiate Carlos de Jesús Ramírez as the first psychometrist, Dr. Oscar Serafini, and surely others whose careers are unknown to us. These national and foreign figures (García, 2003, 2008, 2014, 2016), whose work in the field of Psychological Assessment is scarcely documented—except for articles by Lic. José Emilio García Noce—would require individual treatment (Aguirre, 1966, 1990, 1995) to learn about, record, and appreciate their work in teaching psychometrics, in research on instruments applied to Paraguayan samples, in the development of local norms, and in the creation and adaptation of tests for measuring variables in areas such as personality, education, maturity, and clinical settings, within local samples.

Regarding the approach to teaching assessment, there is consensus that the Classical Test Theory and its principles are strongly emphasized, with only occasional introduction to Item Response Theory. It is worth noting that the undergraduate psychology curriculum spans 5 years, and in various semesters, courses related to Psychological Assessment cover the teaching of psychometrics in several chapters, as well as specific tests (intelligence, maturity, projective, assessment and diagnosis, and methodology and instruments). However, the approach is, by far, more theoretical than practical, with a marked absence of training in skills for the creation and/or adaptation of instruments for national samples. In most faculties where professionals in our country are trained, teaching is not a scientific endeavor (Coppari, 2008, 2011, 2015) of research and development of proprietary assessment instruments. This is rather oriented toward the application, scoring, and interpretation of psychological tests in a mechanical manner, with a lack of analysis and explanation based on the theoretical framework underlying the instruments. It is common to see students and professionals crafting traditional assessment tests in an improvised way for use in clinical, educational, and forensic settings. There is consensus regarding the perceived deficiencies in the theoretical and practical training of future psychologists, particularly concerning current foundations related to the construction, validation, and reliability of instruments with local samples. There is a significant dependence on foreign instruments, which are often used with little or no adaptation. Transcultural variables and local idiosyncrasies—such as bilingualism (Spanish-Guarani), indigenous cultures, and regional diversity—are not taken into account. Additionally, regarding the instruments taught in academic settings and required in practical training to develop application skills, there is a noticeable lack of updates; the classics persist, with no research directed toward the development of new tools supported by sufficient theoretical and psychometric evidence to ensure their validity and reliability. There is an increasing online supply of pseudo-resources for Psychological Assessment, lacking psychometric and theoretical quality control, which students commonly used for their undergraduate and graduate research projects. In this context, several challenges are currently being raised and projected for the future, which, within the framework of accreditation processes for psychology programs at various private and national universities, should be considered priorities to improve the quality of training in Psychological Assessment, regarded as a fundamental competency for professional practice. This scenario is shared by other Latin American countries. This evaluative perception of the local situation of Psychological Assessment as a discipline and professional competency is not foreign to what has historically been reported as the Latin American psychometric movement, which has focused more on technological dependence on foreign sources, the use of foreign tests with minimal updating, and a lack of creativity in the production of original, national instruments. Among the limitations that must be acknowledged in this presentation is the very small sample (3) of interviews received and the fact that some questions in the requested questionnaire were not answered by the participants. It is possible that the brevity of this review does not meet the reader's expectations, and thus we appeal to the understanding of those who consult it. Finally, with an optimistic outlook, we outline three viable proposals to improve the current situation of Psychological Assessment at the level of local professional training. First, in the context of recent legislation regulating (Law 6293, 2019) the professional practice of psychologists in Paraguay, it should be a priority in its regulation to establish specialized certification (Law 836 of the Health Code, 1980), enabling professionals trained in the appropriate use of Psychological Assessment instruments in areas such as neuropsychology, forensic, social, community, and the traditional fields of clinical, health, occupational, and educational psychology, with the aim of making ethical and appropriate decisions when the well-being and quality of life of those assessed depend on it. Second, in the current context of accreditation processes (Law 2072 of 2003) for psychology programs in the country, it is essential and urgent to update the curriculum in courses that provide theoretical and practical training in Psychological Assessment. Emphasis should be placed on the selection and study of Psychological Assessment instruments that currently meet international standards supporting theoretically and psychometrically grounded decision-making. It is very important to deepen the theoretical foundations of the measurements to be used with Paraguayan populations, to train in the knowledge of idiosyncratic cultural variables, and to move beyond the use of foreign tests referenced to the native culture of adoption, as the results obtained with them do not reflect the actual level of functioning of behaviors in local populations. Third, and emphasizing the need for improvements in the quality and rigor of training, it is necessary to strengthen the teaching of scientific research. Research lines and teams should be created at both undergraduate and graduate levels (Coppari, 1997a, 1997b, 2011) to develop local instruments needed to assess specific populations, as well as to adapt foreign tools that can meet the criteria of validity, reliability, and norms adjusted to our local population. It is necessary to have appropriate instruments to carry out applied work, such as measurements of intelligence, vocational interests, personality, and attitudes, for psychoeducational and diagnostic purposes. Observing the experiences of countries in the region, and Latin America in general, it is evident that the lack of creativity in past psychometrics is being overcome by basic theoretical research to support the construction of psychological tests that address the absence of original theories regarding the behaviors to be measured in the development of equally original tests. In recent years, there has been a persistent interest in subjecting the constructs underlying foreign tests to rigorous review using statistical methods, such as factor analysis, to determine whether they correspond to the behavioral characteristics of individuals in the culture of adoption; these procedures are essential before using them indiscriminately. Based on these statistical verifications, rigorously valid and reliable tests and scales are being developed in several Latin American countries. This positive experience should serve as a model for our country, which still remains outside these regional efforts. In closing this chapter, there is positive news to share. The Psychology programs at the Universidad de Itapúa, at the National University of the East, Centro Médico Bautista University, Ibero-American University, UNINORTE, UNA of Asunción (the last two already announced), and the Catholic University of Asunción were accredited.

References

Aguirre, J. J. (1966). *Character and Intelligence. A study of Paraguayan typology*. El Ateneo.

Aguirre, J. J. (1990). *Rorschach interpretation manual* (2nd ed.). Editora Litocolor.

Aguirre, J. J. (1995). *Character and intelligence (A study of Paraguayan typology)* (2nd ed.). Distribuidora Montoya SJ.

Coppari, N. B. (1997a). *Research in the university setting: Development versus unproductivity*. EDUNA.

Coppari, N. B. (1997b). *Research in the university setting: Development and proposed solutions*. EDUNA.

Coppari, N. B. (2008). Psychology. One science, diverse arts. Challenges for defining and accrediting the degree in our country and in MERCOSUR. *EUREKA, 5*(1), 111–121.

Coppari, N. B. (2011). An approach to research and graduate programs in Paraguayan psychology. *Estudos de Psicologia (Natal) [online], 16*(1), 05–15. ISSN 1413-294X. https://doi.org/10.1590/S1413-294X2011000100002

Coppari, N. B. (2015). An approach to Paraguayan psychology as a discipline, science, and profession. *Informacio Psicologica, 109*, 97–110. https://doi.org/10.14635/IPSIC.2015.109.1

García, J. E. (2003). Central issues in academic training and professional development of psychologists in Paraguay. In J. F. Villegas & J. P. Toro (Eds.), *Central issues in academic training and professional development of psychologists in the Americas* (Vol. 2, pp. 205–279). Interamerican Society of Psychology.

García, J. E. (2008). Ramón Indalecio Cardozo as a pioneer of psychology in Paraguay. *Interamerican Journal of Psychology, 42*(1), 171–180.

García, J. E. (2009). Brief history of psychology in Paraguay. *History of Psychology, 17*.

García, J. E. (2014). Paraguayan psychology as represented in the work of James O. Whittaker and Sandra J. Whittaker. *Interamerican Journal of Psychology, 48*(2), 265–282.

García, J. E. (2016). The introduction of the Stanford-Binet intelligence scale in Paraguay. *Interactions, 2*(1), 65–83.

Law 836 of 1980. (1980, December 4). Health code.

Law 2072 of 2003. (2003, February 13). Creation of the National Agency for Evaluation and Accreditation of Higher Education.

Law 4995 of 2013. (2013, August 2). On higher education.

Law 6293 of 2019. (2019, May 3). On the professional practice of psychology in Paraguay.

Martínez Cáceres, M. R. (2008). Psychology in Paraguay, Historical context: Challenges for integration in Latin American scenarios. *Interamerican Journal of Psychology, 42*(3), 472–480.

Opening Act 13 of 1962 [Catholic University of Asunción]. (1962, April 26). Establishing the opening of the Bachelor's Degree in Psychology.

Paraguayan Society of Psychology. (2004). Code of ethics for the professional practice of psychology in Paraguay

Plenary of Committees of the Paraguayan Society of Psychology. (2009). Manifest: Training of psychologists in Mercosur. *EUREKA, 6*(1), 5–6.

Further Reading

Coppari, N. B. (2002). *Current scientific training of Paraguayan psychologists in the university setting*. FFCH-UCA.

Coppari, N. B. (2008). Psychology. One science, diverse arts. Challenges for defining and accrediting the degree in our country and in MERCOSUR. *EUREKA, 5*(1), 111–121.

García, N. J., & Coppari, N. B. (2013). Fifty years of the psychology program at the Catholic University: A retrospective view. *EUREKA, 10*(2), 137–146.

Law 136 of 1993. (1993, March 29). University Council.

Ministry of Education and Worship. (1997). National report on higher education in Paraguay

Chapter 13
Psychological Assessment in Peru: History, Psychometric Research, and Perspectives

Walter Lizandro Arias Gallegos, Carlos Renzo Rivera Calcina, Miguel Ángel Vallejos Flores, and José Livia Segovia

Introduction

Alarcón (1968) noted that the development of psychology in Peru has followed three main orientations: a philosophy-spiritual trend, a scientific-experimental line, and a psychoanalytic approach. Within the second line, research using psychological tests was promoted, as well as their application in professional practice. Alarcón et al. (1976) established that Honorio Delgado and Walter Blumenfeld can be considered the founders of Peruvian psychology, having contributed to the development of psychology as both a science and a profession. It is within this context that psychometrics and psychological assessment emerged in the early twentieth century, but only became a systematic and scientific process in the 1930s, with the arrival of Walter Blumenfeld (1882–1967) in Lima, when he took charge of the Instituto de Psicología y Psicotecnia (Institute of Psychology and Psychotechnics) at the Universidad Nacional Mayor de San Marcos (Major National University of San Marcos) (Alarcón, 1994). In the following section, we will briefly review the origins of psychological assessment in Peru and its process of institutionalization, and then analyze psychometric research in the country, as well as the challenges and limitations for the development of this branch of applied psychology.

W. L. A. Gallegos · C. R. R. Calcina (✉)
Universidad Católica of San Pablo, Arequipa, Peru
e-mail: warias@ucsp.edu.pe; crrivera@ucsp.edu.pe

M. Á. V. Flores
Universidad Nacional Federico Villarreal, Lima, Peru
e-mail: miguelvallejos.universidad@gmail.com

J. L. Segovia
Federico Villarreal National University, Lima, Peru
e-mail: jlivia@unfv.edu.pe

S. V. Pugliese et al. (eds.), *Origins and Challenges of Psychological Assessment in Ibero-American Countries*, https://doi.org/10.1007/978-3-032-21380-8_13

Origins and Development of Psychological Assessment in Peru

Alarcón (2000) pointed out that, in Peru, psychiatrists were the first to apply psychological tests. However, Orbegoso (2016), in a recent historiographic study, established that it was Joseph Mac Knight, a psychologist trained at Columbia University, who took charge of the Normal School for Boys in Lima and, together with the educator Humberto Luna (1887–1926), conducted the first intelligence assessments between 1909 and 1913 among schoolchildren in Lima, Arequipa, Cuzco, and Puno.

Certainly, psychiatrists conducted more diversified assessments, going beyond the administration of intelligence tests. Among the Peruvian psychiatrists who applied the first psychological tests in the first half of the twentieth century, we have Victoria Izcue (1919), who assessed memory in children; Felipe Chueca (1920), who applied the Binet and Simon Intelligence Scale to 388 schoolchildren in Lima; Hermilio Valdizán (1925), who also evaluated the intellectual capacity of Peruvian Indigenous people; and Segisfredo Luza (1954), who administered the Wartegg test to patients with schizophrenia. Other authors such as Ethel Bazán, Pedro Aliaga, and José Donayre administered the Tsedek tests, the Rorschach Psychodiagnostic, and the Szondi Test, respectively (Alarcón, 2000; Livia, 2008).

On the other hand, after an initial phase of introductory use of tests, there was a transition to a stage of standardization of psychological tests, which became the responsibility of psychologists in the proper sense, who were trained by Walter Blumenfeld and constituted the first generation of Peruvian psychologists. With Blumenfeld's arrival in Peru in 1935, systematic research in psychometrics began, with several studies conducted both at the Instituto de Psicología y Psicotecnia (Institute of Psychology and Psychotechnics) and at the Instituto Psicopedagógico Nacional (National Psychopedagogical Institute), which, according to Alarcón (2020), is where psychometric research was consolidated. Furthermore, it was the psychologists trained by Blumenfeld who carried out the first standardizations of psychological tests in the country.

Studies with national or regional scope were established by Blumenfeld (1946); for example, he conducted the first Peruvian standardization of the Terman Intelligence Test, while Reynaldo Alarcón (1951) standardized the Theodore Simon Intelligence Test and the California Test of Mental Maturity in 1960 (Alarcón, 1961). Later, in 1985, Cecilia Thorne standardized the administration and scoring criteria for the Anstey Dominoes Test (Thorne et al., 1985), and Alegría Majluf standardized the Goodenough-Harris Drawing Test (Majluf, 1999). Thus, it can be said that there has been a notable interest in the standardization of psychological tests that assess intelligence, since, as in the United States, the criteria of these instruments met the needs for student placement according to intellectual ability. Other tests that have also been standardized include the Boehm Test of Basic Concepts, standardized in Lima by Cecilia Thorne and Alicia Narváez (1987), and the Kolb Learning Style Inventory, adapted by Luis Miguel Escurra (1992), while the Beck Hopelessness Scale was standardized by Aliaga et al. (2006), and more recently, the Cell Phone Dependency Test was standardized among university students in Arequipa (Gamero et al., 2016). Evidently, many more psychological tests have been standardized, especially for the purpose of obtaining the psychologist's degree through thesis work, both in universities in Lima (Lazo & Zanolo, 1996) and Arequipa (Chávez, 2014). However, psychological tests in the educational and clinical fields have attracted the most interest from Peruvian psychologists, clearly due to their practical applications. It is in these fields that several tests have been consistently validated for psychological assessment, with a more noticeable increase in recent years.

For instance, a recent systematic review by Vega-Dienstmaier (2022) has reported that Peru is one of the Ibero-American countries where tests evaluating variables related to mental health have been validated, such as the *General Health Questionnaire*, the *Self Reporting Questionnaire*, and the Kessler Psychological Distress Scale. In the field of educational psychology, the Peer Aggression Scale has been validated in a sample of 3978 adolescents in the city of Arequipa (Rivera et al., 2015), as well as the Purpose in Life Test (Huamani & Arias, 2018) and the Satisfaction with Life Scale (Arias et al., 2018a) in students from public educational institutions, and the Academic Achievement Motivation Test in university students (Arias et al., 2018b). In Lima, Sergio Dominguez has validated the Academic Procrastination Scale (Dominguez, 2016) and the Self-Efficacy Scale for Academic Situations (Dominguez-Lara et al., 2012), while Alberto Alegre (2013) validated a test to assess self-efficacy and another to assess procrastination in university students.

In this regard, Peru has been characterized more by the application, validation, or standardization of psychological tests, and very little by the development of new instruments. The first psychological test created in the country dates back to 1955: the Noetic-Perceptual Integration Test, developed by Leopoldo Chiappo to assess patients with schizophrenia through language and from a humanistic-existential perspective (Chiappo, 1957). Regarding the creation of instruments, it is worth highlighting the Vocational and Occupational Interests Inventory-CAMS 83 developed by Vicuña in 1983, and a Technical Career Choice Inventory designed by Vivanco in 1995, as well as the Disposition Toward Critical Thinking Scale by Escurra and Delgado (2008), the Thinking Skills Test by Tapia and Luna (2010), the Teacher Self-Efficacy Scale by Burga (2015), the Social Networks Addiction Questionnaire by Escurra and Salas (2014), and the Behavioral Assessment Scale for Emotional Disorders (API), created and validated from a behavioral perspective by Anicama (2008).

This scarcity of tests originally developed in Peru is due, in part, to the limited psychometric training of Peruvian psychologists, who tend not to favor psychostatistics, psychometrics, and mathematics—disciplines essential for the validation and construction of psychological tests. Moreover, the importance of psychometric studies is not sufficiently valued, with greater interest placed on the application of tests, given the pragmatic orientation of the majority of Peruvian and Latin American psychologists (Arias, 2011). Although the majority of psychological tests used in Peru measure intelligence and personality, there is little scientific evidence regarding their ecological validity and other psychometric properties, which should be tested in various regions of the country given its ethnic and cultural diversity (Wechsler et al., 2022). In this regard, some tests developed in the country, in our opinion, lack sufficient evidence of validity and reliability, either because there is only one supporting study with unrepresentative samples or because they are based on classical psychometric models (Palma, 1999; Pereira, 1992).

Thus, most psychometric studies conducted in Peru are based on classical test theory (Livia, 1990) and do not adequately address the behavior of the items used to measure specific variables. In comparison, other psychometric models based on differential item functioning or item response theory have not been systematically or widely introduced in the country (Cortada de Kohan, 2002; Gómez-Benito & Hidalgo-Montesinos, 2003). Consequently, few Peruvian psychologists have training in psychometrics to work with these theoretical models. Among these authors, we can mention Luis Miguel Escurra, Jorge Bazán, Andrés Burga, César Merino, José Livia, Sergio Dominguez, José Luis Ventura, Tomás Caycho, and Renzo Rivera, who have published various methodological articles in the field of psychometrics (Burga, 2006; Domínguez, 2012; Escurra, 1988; Merino & Livia, 2007, 2009; Ventura-León & Caycho-Rodríguez, 2017), as well as multiple studies analyzing the validity and reliability of psychological tests based on different theoretical models.

Noteworthy in this regard is the psychometric research conducted by Miguel Escurra on various psychological tests using the Rasch model, such as the Honey-Alonso Learning Styles Questionnaire (Escurra, 2011), the advanced form of the Raven's Progressive Matrices Test (Escurra & Delgado, 2010), the CES-D Depression Scale (Escurra & Delgado, 2012), and the Bery Test (Escurra et al., 1993). It should be noted that Escurra is one of the few authors working with the Item Response Theory (IRT) model in Peru, followed by Andrés Burga León, who has analyzed the psychometric properties of the Stress Response Scale (Burga, 2012) and the Parental Stress Questionnaire (Burga & Sánchez-Griñán, 2016), as well as an analysis of the Teacher Self-efficacy Scale using the Rasch model (Burga, 2015), among other instruments under the psychometric assumptions of IRT.

The issue of the misuse of psychological tests in Peru is reflected in certain directives issued for the psychological evaluation of vehicle drivers, as stated in Ministerial Resolution 718–2017, which indicates that areas such as organicity, intelligence, personality, and psychopathological traits must be assessed. The recommended tests include the Wechsler Block Design, the Benton Retention Test, the Raven's Progressive Matrices Test, the Otis Intelligence Test, the Dominoes Test, the Person in the Rain Test, the Neurotic Personality Factors Test, the Eysenck Personality Inventory, the AUDIT Alcoholism Test, the Armed Person Test, and the Neurological Personality Change Questionnaire. Another aspect is the approval of the Clinical Practice Guidelines in Mental Health and Psychiatry by RM 648–2006, which recommends the use of the Personal Health Scale, the SRQ-18 Symptom Questionnaire, and the Hamilton Depression Scale. However, the aforementioned tests lack validity evidence for their use at the national level.

On the other hand, it is necessary to move from an individual to a social space to build networks that bring together efforts, creating an organized psychology (Livia & Ortiz, 2014), which should be strengthened in Ibero-America. At the international level, we see relevant institutions in psychological assessment such as the *European Association of Psychological Assessment* and the *Brazilian Institute of Psychological Assessment*. In this context, the creation of the Sociedad Peruana de Evaluación Psicológica (*Peruvian Society of Psychological Assessment)* and the Sociedad Peruana de Psicometría (*Peruvian Society of Psychometrics)* has been proposed in Peru, as well as initiatives to organize through research groups at universities, such as the Advances in Psychological Measurement Group at the Major National University of San Marcos and the Psychological Assessment Research Group at the Universidad Nacional Federico Villarreal (National University Federico Villarreal).

Within this context, some initiatives have been developed to raise awareness about the proper use of psychological tests. For this reason, the Colegio de Psicólogos del Perú (Peruvian College of Psychologists) held the First International Symposium on Tests, with participants including José Muñiz from Spain, Susana Urbina from the United States, and Acacia Dos Santos from Brazil, along with prominent Peruvian psychologists. This led to the creation of the National Commission of Psychological Tests, whose current board (2021–2024) is set to be implemented.

There have also been efforts by universities such as the Universidad San Ignacio de Loyola, which has held international events on psychological assessment, while the Universidad Nacional Federico Villarreal (National University Federico Villarreal) has organized several Conferences on Psychological Assessment and Psychometrics. It is worth highlighting the leadership of Cecilia Thorne at the Pontificia Universidad Católica del Perú (Pontifical Catholic University of Peru), Irma Altez at the Universidad Femenina del Sagrado Corazón (Women's University of the Sacred Heart), and Juan Quijano at Universidad César Vallejo (Cesar Vallejo University), who have promoted psychometric research at their respective institutions.

Psychometric Research Lines in Peru

Most psychometric studies conducted in Peru have taken place in the cities of Lima, Arequipa, and Trujillo, and more recently in Puno. However, many of these studies have not used representative samples nor have they established a sustained line of research over time. Thus, it can be said that research lines in Peru are quite limited, and few authors have carried out exhaustive and ongoing analyses of the psychometric properties of specific psychological tests.

One author who has developed a prolific line of research through the analysis of the psychometric properties of the Bender Visual-Motor Gestalt Test is César Merino Soto, who was awarded the 2018 National Psychology Prize by the Colegio de Psicólogos del Perú (College of Psychologists of Peru). Merino has conducted several studies reviewing the Bender scoring system and its psychometric properties, in its various versions and with samples of different sociodemographic characteristics (Merino, 2009, 2010a, 2010b, 2011a, 2011b, 2011c, 2011d, 2012, 2013a, 2013b, 2014, 2018; Merino & Allen, 2013; Merino & Benites, 2009; Merino et al., 2016). In this regard, it would be desirable for other psychological tests, as with the Bender, to have systematic and consistent evidence of their validity and reliability over time.

Another line of psychometric research addresses studies on the family, a recurring research topic in the country, notable for the examination of the psychometric properties of various instruments that assess family-related variables such as parenting styles and parental practices (Merino & Arndt, 2004; Merino et al., 2004), the Family Interaction Quality Scale (Dominguez & Alarcón, 2017; Dominguez et al., 2013), the various versions of Olson and Wilson's FACES (Arias et al., 2019c; Bazo-Alvarez et al., 2016; Copez-Lonzoy et al., 2016; Villarreal-Zegarra et al., 2017), the Family Life Satisfaction Scale (Caycho-Rodríguez et al., 2018), and the Family Apgar Scale (Castilla et al., 2014a). Additionally, within this line of research, a particularly noteworthy contribution is led by Walter Arias, who, after creating the Family Integration Inventory, has conducted various psychometric analyses of the validity and reliability of this instrument over a period of 10 years (Arias et al., 2013; Arias et al., 2019a; Arias et al., 2022).

Another line of psychometric research developed in Peru is situated in the field of occupational health, specifically regarding the analysis of the internal structure and reliability of the Maslach Burnout Inventory (MBI), which is used to assess burnout syndrome—a topic that has been the subject of various studies in the country. In this context, Manuel Fernández and César Merino have published several psychometric studies on the test's cut-off points, social desirability, and factorial invariance with samples of workers from Lima (Fernández & Merino, 2014, 2016; Fernández et al., 2015); while in Arequipa, Walter Arias has analyzed the construct validity and reliability of the MBI in teachers and healthcare personnel (Arias et al., 2019b; Arias & Velásquez, 2025). In Arequipa, the psychometric properties of instruments used to measure psychological variables in organizational contexts have also been analyzed, such as organizational climate (Arias & Jiménez, 2016), job satisfaction (Arias et al., 2017), and job involvement (Arias & Jiménez, 2017), among others.

In the field of assessment within the spectrum of addictions, it is necessary to contrast numerous sources of information in conjunction with the use of valid and reliable psychological instruments (Levounis et al., 2017). In the Peruvian context, there has been a predominant focus on the validation of psychometric instruments rather than the creation and development of new measures. Regarding drug use and dependence, validated measures include questionnaires that assess abusive and dependent alcohol consumption, such as the Münchner Alkoholismus Test—MALT (Gorenc et al., 1990; Llanos et al., 1993) and the *Alcohol Use Disorders Identification Test—AUDIT* (Colán & Rosario, 2022). For tobacco use assessment, the Fagerström Test for Nicotine Dependence is available (Arias et al., 2018c), and for marijuana use, validated instruments include the *Cannabis Abuse Screening Test—CAST* (DEVIDA, 2014), and for motives for marijuana use, the brief version of the *Marijuana Motives Measure—MMM-P15* (Vallejos et al., 2023). Regarding other factors associated with the use of psychoactive substances, there are validated instruments that assess stages of change, such as the Confidence Questionnaire for Risk Situations for Use (Vigo, 2003), the University of Rhode Island Change Assessment Scale—URICA (Vallejos et al., 2007), the AWARE Questionnaire for Relapse Warning Signs (Solano & Copez-Lonzoy, 2017), and the Drug Use Refusal Self-Efficacy Scale—DURSE (Olivo et al., 2021).

On the other hand, in the past decade, the scientific community's interest has focused on the development and validation of instruments that assess behavioral addictions (Cía, 2014). In this regard, psychometric studies related to the construction of instruments at the national level have been based on identifying mechanisms underlying the interaction of adolescents and university students, particularly with respect to social networks, resulting in measures with optimal evidence of validity and reliability for instruments that assess, for example, internet addiction (Arias et al., 2025; Lam-Figueroa et al., 2011; Matalinares et al., 2014; Tafur-Mendoza et al., 2020), social networks addiction (Escurra & Salas, 2014; Melgar et al., 2022; Vilca & Vallejos, 2015), and other psychometric studies that have focused on the detection of addiction to specific social networks, such as the assessment of Instagram addiction using the Bergen Instagram Addiction Scale—BIAS (Chávez & Vallejos, 2021). Regarding Facebook use, the Bergen Facebook Addiction Scale—BFAS was validated (Vallejos et al., 2018), and for smartphone addiction, the Smartphone Dependence and Addiction Scale—EDAS was developed (Sánchez-Villena et al., 2021). There are also validated instruments that assess pathological gaming, especially video game addiction, such as the Video Game Dependence Test—TDV (Salas et al., 2017). All these instrument proposals were developed following recommendations for adaptation and validation, including semantic and cultural modifications of psychometric tests, which have enabled the creation of an increasingly optimal and efficient repertoire of instruments for the assessment of addictions (Salas et al., 2020).

Within the epistemological framework of Positive Psychology as an emerging field, it is important to highlight the work of Reynaldo Alarcón (1924–2020), who made significant contributions to psychometrics, not only through the validation and standardization of various psychological measurement instruments between the 1960s and 1980s (León, 2009), but also by introducing the courses "Theory of Psychological Measurement" and "Intelligence Testing" in 1965, and organizing the "Seminar on the Construction of Psychological Tests" in 1969, all at the National University of San Marcos (Caycho, 2013). Furthermore, since 2000, he introduced Positive Psychology in Peru, which led him to create three measurement instruments: the Lima Happiness Scale (Alarcón, 2006), the Attributional Optimism Scale (Alarcón, 2013), and the Gratitude Scale (Alarcón, 2014). These instruments have been used to assess the aforementioned variables at both national and international levels and initiated a psychometric movement focused on the validation of tests measuring happiness (Arias et al., 2016), gratitude (Arias & Huamani, 2023), hope (Arias et al., 2018d; Castilla et al., 2014b), optimism (Caycho et al., 2017), forgiveness (Arias & Velásquez, 2022; Caycho et al., 2018a), resilience (Castilla et al., 2013; Tomas et al., 2021), life satisfaction (Arias et al., 2018a; Caycho et al., 2018b), love (Arias et al., 2023; Ventura & Caycho, 2016), sense of humor (Caycho-Rodríguez et al., 2019), and many other constructs related to positive emotions, virtues, and human strengths. This line of psychometric research has been prolifically developed in populations of children, adolescents, adults, and older adults in Lima, Arequipa, and Trujillo by Tomás Caycho, José Luis Ventura, and Walter Arias.

Likewise, in the context of the COVID-19 pandemic, which has generated a variety of psychological and mental health impacts on the population, Tomás Caycho and a team of Latin American researchers have led a line of psychometric research involving the analysis of the psychometric properties of newly developed instruments to assess fear of COVID-19 or coronaphobia, grief due to COVID-19-related deaths, stress from COVID-19 infection, psychological impact of COVID-19, conspiracy beliefs about COVID-19 vaccination, and other related variables (Caycho-Rodríguez et al., 2021a, 2021b, 2022a, 2022b; Noe-Grijalva et al., 2022). This line of research is setting an important precedent in Latin America, not only due to the novelty of the topics and the utility of the adapted and validated instruments, but also because, in several cases, it involves samples from up to 13 countries in the region, including Argentina, Bolivia, Brazil, Chile, Colombia, Cuba, Ecuador, Guatemala, Mexico, Paraguay, Peru, Uruguay, Venezuela, among others.

These and other initiatives demonstrate the progress that psychometrics and psychological assessment have made in the country. However, there are various limitations that must be overcome for better consolidation and critical dissemination of this field, which is of vital importance for the work of professional psychologists, researchers, and especially for the psychological training of future professionals.

Limitations and Future Perspectives of Psychological Assessment in Peru

We have observed that there is a substantial and diverse national output in relation to psychometrics and psychological assessment, but it is still limited. Although we cannot mention all the psychological tests that have been created and validated in Peru, it is clear that psychometric production has improved significantly in recent years; however, it remains insufficient compared to other countries in the Americas or Europe. Nevertheless, the fact that several psychologists are dedicating their efforts to psychometric production and that various regions of the country have begun to join the psychometric research being conducted in the capital are indicators that this branch of psychology will gain greater relevance in the coming years. In this regard, we believe that one factor driving the growth of psychometrics in Peru is the digitalization of psychological tests and the limited number of applications authorized by companies that develop and offer these materials. Added to this is the multicultural population of Peru, which requires us to develop psychometric tests with rigorous standards, tailored to each region according to its sociocultural particularities. However, despite the fact that a large sector of the Peruvian population is Quechua-speaking, there are still no instruments adapted and validated for all Quechua variants in Peru.

Nevertheless, there is a deficient psychometric training in the country's universities, especially in the interior regions. In this regard, the training in psychological assessment for Peruvian psychologists is often limited to teaching the administration and scoring of psychological tests, with no postgraduate policies for the construction and adaptation of instruments.

Another indicator of the limited development of psychometrics as a specialized discipline in the country is the publication of psychometrics books, among which we can mention the text by Esther Delgado et al. (2006) entitled "Measurement in Psychology and Education: Theory and Applications" or "Construction of Psychometric Tests" by José Livia and Mafalda Ortiz (2014), or "Statistical methods in psychometrics" edited by Tomás Caycho and José Luis Ventura-León (2024), and as well as texts that serve as catalogs documenting the norms of various psychological tests validated in Peru (Aliaga & Giove, 1993; Chan & Quezada, 2013; Universidad Femenina del Sagrado Corazón, 1997). In this context, the teaching of psychometrics is hindered by the lack of sufficient materials for proper instruction.

This explains why, in many cases, the validation of psychological instruments used in the country is also flawed. Nevertheless, these instruments, with statistical deficiencies in their validation processes, are used indiscriminately. Therefore, as is the case in other countries, it would be advisable to establish certain technical criteria to assess the quality of the processes of adaptation, validation, and standardization of psychological tests (Herrera & León, 2022).

In summary, it can be said that a major issue in psychological assessment in the country is the lack of properly constructed or validated instruments. This, combined with the indiscriminate and poorly informed use of the tests that are administered, could have serious consequences for the diagnosis and evaluation of the target populations, whether in clinical, educational, or organizational contexts. For this reason, it would be important to develop an updated catalog of psychological tests that can be used in the country and that have adequate validity and reliability indices, properly obtained. The Peruvian College of Psychologists could play a significant role in raising awareness about the sensitive nature of using psychological instruments for diagnostic purposes.

In this context, the reactivation of the Peruvian Society of Psychometrics would also be a key element, as it could greatly contribute to the process of raising awareness and screening of psychological tests used in the country, based on rigorously calculated psychometric evidence. Finally, it should be noted that one of the psychologist's main activities is assessment, where the use of psychological tests must be supported by evidence of validity and reliability. It is therefore urgent to evaluate the instruments used in Peru and to establish a standardization policy, as well as to develop an evaluation system, similar to what has been implemented in Spain according to the proposals of Prieto and Muñiz (2000), or to follow the model of the

Brazilian Psychological Test Evaluation System (SATEPSI). Likewise, it is important to develop a publishing industry that invests in research and formally markets psychological tests, as is done by TEA in Spain, Manual Moderno in Mexico, and Casa del Psicólogo and Vetor in Brazil.

References

Alarcón, R. (1951). Results of the application of the collective P.V. Test by Dr. Th. Simon, in 185 primary school students. *Revista de Educación Nacional, 5*, 267–294.

Alarcón, R. (1961). Standardization of the California mental maturity test. Intermediate series, 150-S. *Boletín del Instituto Psicopedagógico Nacional, 16*(4), 3–35.

Alarcón, R. (1968). *Panorama de la Psicología en el Perú*. Universidad Nacional Mayor de San Marcos.

Alarcón, R. (1994). *The psychological thought of Walter Blumenfeld*. Concytec.

Alarcón, R. (2000). *History of psychology in Peru: From the colonial period to the republic*. Universidad Ricardo Palma.

Alarcón, R. (2006). Development of a factorial scale to measure happiness. *Interamerican Journal of Psychology, 40*(1), 99–106.

Alarcón, R. (2013). Construction and validation of a scale to measure optimism. In J. C. Alchieri & J. Barreiros (Eds.), *Proceedings of the XXXIV Interamerican congress of psychology* (pp. 377–389). SBPOT.

Alarcón, R. (2014). Construction and psychometric properties of a scale to measure gratitude. *Acta de Investigación Psicológica, 4*(2), 1520–1534.

Alarcón, R. (2020). Historical overview of psychometrics in Peru. *Revista Peruana de Historia de la Psicología, 6*, 7–26.

Alarcón, R., Infante, J., Ponce, P., & Bibolini, A. (Eds.). (1976). *Psychological research in Peru*. Peruvian Society of Psychology.

Alegre, A. A. (2013). Self-efficacy and academic procrastination in university students from metropolitan Lima. *Purposes and Representations, 1*(2), 57–82.

Aliaga, J., & Giove, A. (1993). *Norms for psychological tests used in Peru*. Amauta.

Aliaga, J., Rodríguez, L., Ponce, C., Frisancho, A., & Enríquez, J. (2006). Escala de desesperanza de Beck (BHS): adaptación y características psicométricas. *Revista de investigación en Psicología, 9*(1), 69–79. https://doi.org/10.15381/rinvp.v9i1.4029

Anicama, J. (2008). A behavioral assessment scale for emotional disorders: API. *Peruvian Journal of Psychometrics, 1*(1), 1–26.

Arias, W. L. (2011). Common threads in the history of Latin American psychology. *Arequipa Journal of Psychology, 1*(1), 27–47.

Arias, W. L., Castro, R., Dominguez, S., Masías, M., Canales, F., Castilla, S., & Castilla, S. (2013). Development of a family integration inventory. *Advances in Psychology, 21*(2), 195–206.

Arias, W. L., Castro, R. J., & Rivera, R. (2022). Psychometric properties of the family integration inventory for couples with and without children in Arequipa. *Latin American Journal of Family Studies, 14*(1), 92–116. https://doi.org/10.17151/rlef.2022.14.1.6

Arias, W. L., Castro, R. J., Rivera, R., & Ceballos, K. (2019a). Exploratory factor analysis of the family integration inventory in a sample of workers from the city of Arequipa. *Psychological Science, 13*(2), 367–377. https://doi.org/10.22235/cp.v13i2.1893

Arias, W. L., Caycho, T., Ventura, J. L., Maquera, C., Ramírez, M., & Tamayo, X. (2016). Exploratory analysis of the Lima happiness scale in university students from Arequipa (Peru). *Psychologia: Advances in the Discipline, 10*(1), 13–24.

Arias, W. L., & Huamani, J. C. (2023). Gratitude in students and workers from the city of Arequipa: A psychometric and comparative analysis. *CES Psychology Journal, 16*(3), 1–15. https://doi.org/10.21615/cesp.6956
Arias, W. L., Huamani, J. C., & Caycho, T. (2018a). Life satisfaction in schoolchildren from the city of Arequipa. *Purposes and Representations, 6*(1), 389–410. https://doi.org/10.20511/pyr2018.v6n1.206
Arias, W. L., Huamani, J. C., & Ceballos, K. D. (2019b). Burnout syndrome in school and university teachers: A psychometric and comparative analysis in the city of Arequipa. *Purposes and Representations, 7*(3), 143–176. https://doi.org/10.20511/pyr2019.v7n3.390
Arias, W. L., Huamani, J. C., & Choque, R. (2018b). Psychometric analysis of the Fagerström test for nicotine dependence in a sample of university students from Arequipa, Peru. *Peruvian Medical Act, 35*(3), 174–179.
Arias, W. L., & Jiménez, N. A. (2016). Psychometric analysis of the Likert organizational profile. *Journal of Psychology (Catholic University of Santa María), 13*, 46–58.
Arias, W. L., & Jiménez, N. A. (2017). Psychometric analysis of the Lodhal and Kejner job involvement scale in workers from Arequipa. *Industrial Data, 20*(1), 47–54. https://doi.org/10.15381/idata.v20i2.13946
Arias, W. L., Rivera, R., & Ceballos, K. D. (2017). Psychometric analysis of the Warr, cook, and wall job satisfaction scale in a multi-occupational sample from Arequipa, Peru. *Interacciones, 3*(2), 79–85. https://doi.org/10.24016/2017.v3n2.74
Arias, W. L., Rivera, R., & Ceballos, K. D. (2025). Psychometric analysis of the internet addiction test (IAT) in university students from Arequipa, Peru. *Psychological Files, 25*(1), 26–42. https://doi.org/10.18566/infpsic.v25n1a02
Arias, W. L., Rivera, R., Ceballos, K. D., Maquera, C., Melgar, C., Sota, A., & Díaz Cano, M. (2018c). Achievement motivation in university psychology students: A psychometric and comparative data analysis. *Revista Peruana de Investigación Educativa, 10*, 159–178.
Arias, W. L., Rivera, R., Laurie, P., & Ceballos, K. D. (2019c). Psychometric properties of the Olson and Wilson family satisfaction scale in university students. *Perspectiva de Familia, 4*, 47–66.
Arias, W. L., Rivera, R., & Núñez, A. L. (2023). Psychometric analysis of Sternberg's triangle love scale in a sample from Arequipa. *Acta de Investigación Psicológica, 13*(1), 64–75. https://doi.org/10.22201/fpsi.20074719e.2023.1.479
Arias, W. L., & Velásquez, D. (2022). Psychometric analysis of the forgiveness capacity scale in Arequipa. *Avances en Psicología, 30*(2), e2647. https://doi.org/10.33539/avpsicol.2022.v30n2.2647
Arias, W. L., & Velásquez, D. (2025). *Validity and reliability of the Burnout Maslach inventory in a multioccupational sample from Arequipa, Peru*. Manuscript submitted.
Arias, W. L., Ventura, J. L., Caycho, T., Román, A., Ceballos, K., Zúñiga, C., Díaz Cano, M., & Lovón, E. (2018d). Internal structure and internal consistency of the Herth Hope index in residents of the city of Arequipa. *Revista Argentina de Ciencias del Comportamiento, 10*(3), 1–11.
Bazo-Alvarez, J. C., Bazo-Alvarez, O. A., Aguila, J., Peralta, F., Mormontoy, W., & Benett, I. M. (2016). Psychometric properties of the FACES-III family functioning scale: A study in Peruvian adolescents. *Revista Peruana de Medicina Experimental y Salud Pública, 33*(3), 462–470. https://doi.org/10.17843/rpmesp.2016.333.2299
Blumenfeld, W. (1946). The mental level of male and female students as determined by the Terman group test. *Boletín del Instituto Psicopedagógico Nacional, 5*(1), 3–64.
Burga, A. (2006). The unidimensionality of a measurement instrument: A factorial perspective. *Revista de Psicología (Pontificia Universidad Católica del Perú), 24*(1), 53–80.
Burga, A. (2012). Fit of a multidimensional Rasch model to the abbreviated MNC stress response scale. *Persona, 12*, 53–67–53–90.
Burga, A. (2015). Analysis of the teacher self-efficacy scale using classical test theory and the Andrich rating scale Rasch model. In D. Jaúregui, R. León, & M. A. Rodríguez (Eds.), *Homenaje a Reynaldo Alarcón* (pp. 265–307). Universidad Ricardo Palma.

Burga, A., & Sánchez-Griñán, G. (2016). Fit to the Rasch rating scale model of the parental stress questionnaire, abbreviated version. *Persona, 19*, 77–90.

Castilla, H., Caycho, T., Shimabukuro, M., & Valdivia, A. (2014a). Perception of family functioning: Psychometric analysis of the APGAR-family scale in adolescents from Lima. *Propósitos y Representaciones, 2*(1), 49–63. https://doi.org/10.20511/pyr2014.v2.1.53

Castilla, H., Caycho, T., Shimabukuro, M., Valdivia, A., & Torres-Calderón, M. F. (2013). Exploratory analysis of the Wagnild and young resilience scale in a sample of adolescents, young adults, and university students from metropolitan Lima. *Revista de Psicología de Arequipa, 4*(1), 80–93.

Castilla, H., Urrutia, C. M., Shimabukuro, M., & Caycho, T. (2014b). Psychometric analysis of the Herth Hope index in a non-clinical Peruvian sample. *Psicología desde el Caribe, 31*(2), 187–206.

Caycho, T. (2013). An overview of the psychological work of Reynaldo Alarcón and his contribution to scientific psychology in Peru. *Revista de Historia de la Psicología, 34*(3), 7–24.

Caycho, T., Ventura, J. L., Arias, W. L., Azabache, K., Rodríguez, L. M., & Moreno, J. E. (2018a). Forgiveness likelihood scale: Initial evidence of validity and reliability in the Peruvian context. *Revista Argentina de Ciencias del Comportamiento, 10*(3), 12–21.

Caycho, T., Ventura, J. L., & Castilla, H. (2017). Confirmatory factor analysis of an attributional optimism scale in a Peruvian sample. *Revista de Psicología (Universidad Católica San Pablo), 7*(1), 13–29.

Caycho, T., Ventura, J. L., García, C. H., Barboza, M., Arias, W. L., Domínguez, J., Azabache, K., Cabrera, I., & Samaniego, A. (2018b). Psychometric evidence of the Diener's satisfaction with life scale in Peruvian elderly. *Revista Ciencias de la Salud, 16*(3), 473–491.

Caycho, T., & Ventura-León, J. L. (2024). *Statistical methods in psychometrics*. Universidad Ricardo Palma.

Caycho-Rodríguez, T., Vilca, L. W., Vivanco, A., Saroli, D., Carbajal, C., Arias, W. L., White, M., & Lee, S. (2021a). Assessment of dysfunctional grief due to death from COVID-19 in Peru: Adaptation and validation of a Spanish version of the pandemic grief scale. *Trends in Psychology, 29*(4), 595–616. https://doi.org/10.1007/s43076-021-00091-1

Caycho-Rodríguez, T., Reyes-Bossio, M., Ventura-León, J., Arias, W. L., Domínguez, J., & Azabache, K. (2019). Psychometric evidence of a brief version of the *coping humor scale* in older Peruvian adults. *Revista Española de Geriatría y Gerontología, 54*(4), 230–236. https://doi.org/10.1016/j.regg.2018.09.012

Caycho-Rodríguez, T., Valencia, P. D., Ventura-León, J., Vilca, L. W., Carbajal-León, C., Reyes-Bossio, M., et al. (2022a). Design and cross-cultural invariance of the COVID vaccine conspiracy beliefs scale (COVID-VCBS) in 13 Latin American countries. *Frontiers in Public Health, 10*, 908720. https://doi.org/10.3389/fpubh.2022.908720

Caycho-Rodríguez, T., Valencia, P. D., Vilca, L. W., Cervigni, M., Gallegos, M., Martino, P., Bares, I., Calandra, M., Rey Anacona, C. A., Lopez-Calle, C., Moreta-Herrera, R., Chacon-Andrade, E. R., Lobos-Rivera, M. E., Del Carpio, P., Quintero, Y., Robles, E., Panza Lombardo, M., Gamarra Recalde, O., Buschiazzo Figares, A., White, M., & Burgos Videla, C. (2021b). Cross-cultural measurement invariance of the fear of COVID-19 scale in seven Latin American countries. *Death Studies, 46*, 1–15. https://doi.org/10.1080/07481187.2021.1879318

Caycho-Rodríguez, T., Ventura-León, J., Barboza-Palomino, M., Reyes-Bosio, M., Arias, W. L., García, C., Cabrera-Orosco, I., Ayala, J., Morgado-Gallardo, K., & Huamani, J. C. (2018). Validity and factorial invariance by sex of a brief measure of family life satisfaction in schoolchildren from Lima (Peru). *Universitas Psychologica, 17*(5), 1–17. https://doi.org/10.11144/Javeriana.upsy17-5.vifm

Caycho-Rodríguez, T., Vilca, L. W., Carbajal-León, C., Reyes-Bossio, M., Delgado-Campusano, M., Gallegos, M., Carranza, E., & Noe-Grijalva, M. (2022b). Psychometric evidence of a new short Spanish version of the COVID-19 impact scale: A study based on confirmatory factor analysis, graded response model, multigroup analysis, and path analysis. *Electronic Journal of General Medicine, 19*(6), em407. https://doi.org/10.29333/ejgm/12388

Chan, L. A., & Quezada, J. Z. (2013). *Norms for psychological tests: Children and adolescents*. UNIFE.
Chávez, A., & Vallejos-Flores, M. A. (2021). Design and validity of the Bergen Instagram addiction scale (BIAS) in Peruvian adults. *Propósitos y Representaciones, 9*(1), e973. https://doi.org/10.20511/pyr2021.v9n1.973
Chávez, Y. (2014). Psychological instruments in Arequipa. *Psychology Today, 1*(1), 18–19.
Chiappo, L. (1957). Noetic-perceptual integration test in chronic schizophrenics. *Annals of the Faculty of Medicine, 40*(1), 108–129.
Chueca, F. (1920). Study on the intellectual capacity of children in Lima schools. *Annals of the Faculty of Medicine, 6*, 46–57.
Cía, A. H. (2014). Non-substance-related addictions (DSM-5, APA, 2013): A first step toward the inclusion of Behavioral addictions in current categorical classifications. *Journal of Neuro-Psychiatry, 76*(4), 210–217. https://doi.org/10.20453/rnp.v76i4.1169
Colán, A., & Rosario, F. (2022). Psychometric analysis of the alcohol use detection questionnaire—AUDIT in Peruvian university students. *Veritas et Scientia, 11*(2), 168–179. https://doi.org/10.47796/ves.v11i2.688
Copez-Lonzoy, A., Villarreal-Zegarra, D., & Paz-Jesús, A. (2016). Psychometric properties of the family communication scale in university students. *Costa Rican Journal of Psychology, 35*(1), 31–46.
Cortada de Kohan, N. (2002). Importance of psychometric research. *Latin American Journal of Psychology, 34*(3), 229–240.
Delgado, A. E., Escurra, L. M., & Torres, W. (2006). *Measurement in psychology and education: Theory and applications*. Editorial Hozlo.
Dominguez, S. (2012). Proposals for the calculation of ordinal alpha and Armor's theta. *Journal of Research in Psychology, 15*(1), 213–217.
Dominguez, S. (2016). Normative data for the academic procrastination scale in psychology students in Lima. *Evaluar, 16*, 20–30.
Dominguez, S., & Alarcón, D. (2017). Structural analysis of the family interaction quality scale in schoolchildren in Lima. *Family Perspective, 2*, 9–26.
Dominguez, S., Aravena, S., Ramírez, F., & Yauri, C. (2013). Psychometric properties of the family interaction quality scale in schoolchildren in Lima. *Journal of Psychology (César Vallejo University), 15*(1), 55–77.
Dominguez-Lara, S., Villegas, G., Yauri, C., Mattos, E., & Ramírez, F. (2012). Psychometric properties of a self-efficacy scale for academic situations in Peruvian university students. *Journal of Psychology (San Pablo Catholic University), 2*, 29–39.
Escurra, L. M., & Delgado, A. E. (2008). Construction of a scale of disposition toward critical thinking using Samejima's model in university students from the City of Lima. *Theory and Research in Psychology, 18*(1), 41–72.
Escurra, L. M., & Delgado, A. E. (2010). Psychometric analysis of the raven's advanced progressive matrices test using the three-parameter item response theory model. *Persona, 13*, 71–97.
Escurra, L. M., & Delgado, A. E. (2012). Análisis psicométrico de la Escala de Depresión CES-D bajo el modelo de crédito parcial de Rasch. *Persona, 15*(15), 173–190. https://doi.org/10.26439/persona2012.n015.132
Escurra, L. M., & Salas, E. (2014). Construction and validation of the social networks addiction questionnaire (ARS). *Liberabit, 20*(1), 73–91.
Escurra, M. (1988). Quantification of content validity by expert judgment. *Journal of Psychology (Pontifical Catholic University of Peru), 6*(1–2), 103–111.
Escurra, M. (1992). Adaptation of Kolb's learning styles inventory. *Journal of Psychology (Pontifical Catholic University of Peru), 10*(1–2), 125–142.
Escurra, M. (2011). Psychometric analysis of the honey and Alonso learning styles questionnaire (CHAEA) using classical test theory and Rasch models. *Persona, 14*, 71–109.
Escurra, M., Delgado, A. E., & Aparcana, A. (1993). Study of the psychometric properties of the short form of the beery test using the Rasch model. *Journal of Psychology (Pontifical Catholic University of Peru), 11*(1), 31–43.

Fernández, M., Juárez, A., & Merino, C. (2015). Measurement and structural invariance of the MBI-GS in a multi-occupational Peruvian sample. *Liberabit, 21*, 9–20.
Fernández, M., & Merino, C. (2014). Measurement error around Cutoff points in the MBI-GS. *Liberabit, 20*(2), 209–218.
Fernández, M., & Merino, C. (2016). The socially desirable side of responses to the MBI-GS and UWES-S: A preliminary study. *Colombian Journal of Psychology, 25*(1), 83–94.
Gamero, K., Flores, C., Arias, W. L., Ceballos, K. D., Román, A., & Marquina, E. (2016). Standardization of the cell phone dependence test for university students. *Persona, 19*, 179–200.
Gómez-Benito, J., & Hidalgo-Montesinos, M. D. (2003). Recent developments in psychometrics. *Advances in Measurement, 1*(1), 17–36.
Gorenc, K. D., Villa, G., Bruner, C. A., Beltrán, J. E., Pacurucu, S., & Llanos, R. (1990). Trans-Hispano-American study of alcoholism. *Latin American Journal of Psychology, 22*(1), 83–109.
Herrera, A. N., & León, F. A. (2022). Development of an instrument to assess the technical quality of psychological tests. *Colombian. Journal of Psychology, 31*(2), 65–76. https://doi.org/10.15446/rcp.v31n2.93018
Huamani, J. C., & Arias, W. L. (2018). Psychometric analysis of the meaning in life test in schoolchildren from the City of Arequipa (Peru). *Journal of Research in Psychology, 21*(1), 51–66. https://doi.org/10.15381/rinvp.v21i1.15112
Izcue, V. (1919). On memory in children. *Journal of Psychiatry and Related Disciplines, 2*(4), 171–277.
Lam-Figueroa, N., Contreras-Pulache, H., Mori-Quispe, E., Nizama-Valladolid, M., Gutiérrez, C., Hinostroza-Camposano, W., et al. (2011). Internet addiction: Development and validation of an instrument in adolescent schoolchildren from Lima, Peru. *Peruvian Journal of Experimental Medicine and Public Health, 28*(3), 462–469.
Lazo, E., & Zanolo, B. (1996). *Psychological research and publications in Peru*. Editorial San Marcos.
León, R. (2009). The contribution of Reynaldo Alarcón to the development and strengthening of psychometrics in Peru. *Journal of Psychological Researches, 12*(2), 239–250.
Levounis, P., Zerbo, E., & Aggarwal, R. (2017). *Guide for the assessment and treatment of addictions*. Elsevier Health Sciences.
Livia, J. (1990). Psychological tests in Peru. *Current Psychology Journal, 8*(18), 23–32.
Livia, J. (2008). Scientific production and postgraduate studies in psychology in Peru. *Interamerican Journal of Psychology, 42*(3), 431–445.
Livia, J., & Ortiz, M. (2014). *Construction of psychological tests*. Universidad Nacional Federico Villarreal.
Llanos, R., López, R., Griebenow, W., & Gálvez, J. (1993). Diagnosis of alcoholism: Validation of the MALT inventory in a population from metropolitan Lima. *Psicoactiva, 11*, 97–145.
Luza, S. (1954). Wartegg test and acute episodes of schizophrenia. *Journal of Neuropsychiatry, 17*(4), 488–493.
Majluf, A. (1999). *Goodenough-Harris drawing test. Review and extension of the Goodenough test*. UNSA.
Matalinares, C., & M., Raymundo V., O., & Baca R., D. (2014). Psychometric properties of the internet addiction test (IAT). *Peruvian Journal of Psychology and Social Work, 3*(2), 45–66. http://revistas.uigv.edu.pe/index.php/psicologia/article/view/71
Melgar, G. G., Fuertes, Y. P., & Medina, E. M. (2022). Psychometric evidence of the adolescent addiction risk scale for social networks and internet in Peruvian students. *Journal of Clinical Psychology with Children and Adolescents, 9*(1), 62–71. https://doi.org/10.21134/rpcna.2022.09.1.7
Merino, C. (2009). A nonparametric item analysis of the modified bender gestalt test for primary school students. *Liberabit, 15*(2), 83–94.
Merino, C. (2010a). Normative data on psychomotor development: A reanalysis. *Peruvian Journal of Psychology, 1*(1), 30–41.

Merino, C. (2010b). The qualitative scoring system for the modified bender gestalt test: Preliminary study of its psychometric properties. *Advances in Latin American Psychology, 28*(1), 63–73.
Merino, C. (2011a). Comparative validity of three scoring systems for the modified bender visual-motor gestalt test. *Journal of Psychology (César Vallejo University), 13*(1), 90–102.
Merino, C. (2011b). Exploration of normative differences in the qualitative scoring system for the modified bender gestalt test. *Liberabit, 17*(2), 199–209.
Merino, C. (2011c). Modified bender visual-motor gestalt test and Faces test: An evaluation of construct validity. *Neuropsychology Notebooks, 5*(2), 129–143.
Merino, C. (2011d). Construct validity of the qualitative scoring system for the modified bender visual-motor gestalt test. *Electronic Journal of Research in Educational Psychology, 9*(3), 1245–1260.
Merino, C. (2012). Reliability of the bender gestalt test—2nd version, in an independent sample of raters. *Journal of Educational Research, 30*(1), 223–234.
Merino, C. (2013a). Modified bender gestalt test and VMI-4: Comparison of incremental validity. *Psicoperspectivas, 12*(1), 183–204.
Merino, C. (2013b). Dimensionality of the modified bender visual-motor gestalt test: A confirmatory factor analysis. *Psychological Assessment, 12*(3), 341–350.
Merino, C. (2014). Evidence of incremental validity of the modified bender gestalt test in first-grade children. *Advances in Latin American Psychology, 32*(2), 275–286.
Merino, C. (2018). The qualitative scoring system and the modified bender visual-motor gestalt test. *Journal of Psychology (Universidad Católica San Pablo), 8*(2), 85–91.
Merino, C., & Allen, R. A. (2013). Effects of inter-rater reliability on the construct validity of the bender gestalt test, 2nd version. *Interdisciplinaria, 30*(2), 253–264.
Merino, C., & Arndt, S. (2004). Confirmatory factor analysis of the Steinberg parenting styles scale: Preliminary evidence of construct validity. *Journal of Psychology (Pontifical Catholic University of Peru), 22*(2), 187–214.
Merino, C., & Benites, L. (2009). Reliability assessment in two age groups using the qualitative scoring system for the modified bender test. *Universitas Psicológica, 10*(1), 237–249.
Merino, C., Calderón, G., & Manzanares, E. (2016). Comparative study of inter-rater agreement and consistency in the Bender Visual-Motor Gestalt Test, 2nd edition. *Latin American Journal of Psychology, 48*, 175–182.
Merino, C., Díaz, M., & DeRoma, V. (2004). Validation of the parental behavior instrument: A confirmatory factor analysis. *Persona, 7*, 145–162.
Merino, C., & Livia, J. (2007). Rho, tau, and Pearson's r: A visual basic program for their transformation and confidence intervals. *Advances in Measurement, 5*, 145–152.
Merino, C., & Livia, J. (2009). Asymmetric confidence intervals for the content validity index: A visual basic program for Aiken's V. *Annals of Psychology, 25*(1), 169–171.
National Commission for Development and a Drug-Free Life—DEVIDA. (2014). *Problematic Marijuana use in the secondary school population (Validation of the CAST—Cannabis Abuse Screening Test Scale)*. www.devida.gob.pe
Noe-Grijalva, M., Polo-Ambrocio, A., Gómez-Bedia, K., & Caycho-Rodríguez, T. (2022). Spanish translation and validation of the COVID stress scales in Peru. *Frontiers in Psychology, 13*, 840302. https://doi.org/10.3389/fpsyg.2022.840302
Olivo-Chang, D. P., Chau Pérez-Aranibar, C., Otiniano-Campos, F., & Romero-Saletti, S. M. (2021). Adaptation of the marijuana subscale of the drug use refusal self-efficacy scale (DURSE) in adolescents. *Liberabit, 27*(2), e434. https://doi.org/10.24265/liberabit.2021.v27n2.02
Orbegoso, A. (2016). Joseph mac knight and his contribution to Peruvian psychology (1909–1915). *Peruvian Journal of the History of Psychology, 2*, 41–51.
Palma, S. (1999). Development and validation of a job satisfaction scale SL-SPC for workers in metropolitan Lima. *Theory and Research in Psychology, 9*(1), 27–34.
Pereira, J. L. (1992). *Profile of professional preferences*. UNSA.
Prieto, G., & Muñiz, J. (2000). Un modelo para evaluar la calidad de los tests utilizados en España. *Papeles del Psicólogo*, (77), 65–72.

Rivera, R., Bellido, F., Salas, J. C., Bellido, V., Peña, N., Villasante, G., Casapía, Y. M., & Paredes, G. (2015). Validation of the peer aggression scale for adolescents, cyberbullying factor, and victimization subscale in students from Arequipa. *Educationis Momentum, 1*, 11–32.

Salas, E., Copez-Lonzoy, A., & Merino-Soto, C. (2020). Is it really too short? Brief version of the social media addiction questionnaire (ARS-6). *Health and Addictions, 20*(2), 105–118. https://doi.org/10.21134/haaj.v20i2.536

Salas, E., Merino, C., Chóliz, M., & M. (2017). Psychometric analysis of the video game dependency test (TDV) in a Peruvian population. *Universitas Psychologica, 16*(4), 290–302. https://doi.org/10.11144/javeriana.upsy16-4.aptd

Sánchez-Villena, A. R., Domínguez-Lara, S., Aranda, M., Fuentes Gutiérrez, V., & García-Domingo, M. (2021). Structural analysis of the smartphone dependence and addiction scale (EDAS) in Peruvian university students. *Health and Addictions, 21*(2), 93–113. https://doi.org/10.21134/haaj.v21i2.572

Solano, C., & Copez-Lonzoy, A. (2017). Preliminary analysis of the AWARE relapse warning signs questionnaire in Peruvian drug addicts. *Interacciones, 3*(2), 87–94. https://doi.org/10.24016/2017.v3n2.65

Tafur-Mendoza, A. A., Acosta-Prado, J. C., Zárate-Torres, R. A., & Ramírez-Ospina, D. E. (2020). Assessing the psychometric properties of the internet addiction test in Peruvian university students. *International Journal of Environmental Research and Public Health, 17*(16), 1–19. https://doi.org/10.3390/ijerph17165782

Tapia, V., & Luna, J. (2010). Validation of a thinking skills test for fourth- and fifth-year secondary students and first-year university students. *Revista de Investigación en Psicología, 13*(2), 17–59.

Thorne, C., & Narváez, A. (1987). The Boehm test of basic concepts: Adaptation and development of norms for Lima and Callao. *Revista de Psicología (Pontificia Universidad Católica del Perú), 5*(2), 133–148.

Thorne, C., Villegas, O., Martínez, P., Rossel, Z., & Twanama, W. (1985). The dominoes test: Development of norms for the population of metropolitan Lima. *Revista de Psicología (Pontificia Universidad Católica del Perú), 3*(2), 163–181.

Tomas, J. M., Caycho, T., Ventura, J., Sancho, P., García, C. H., & Arias, W. L. (2021). Measurement invariance of the brief resilient coping scale in Peruvian and Spanish older adults. *Journal of Cross-Cultural Gerontology, 36*(4), 431–444. https://doi.org/10.1007/s10823-021-09441-z

Universidad Femenina del Sagrado Corazón. (1997). *Standardization of aptitude and intelligence tests in children: Thorndike and Cattell*. UNIFE.

Valdizán, H. (1925). Mental alienation in the indigenous race. *Anales de la Facultad de Medicina, 7*, 145–163.

Vallejos, M., Capa, W., Caycho, A., Chávez, A., Reyes, G., & Bello, C. (2023). Internal structure and invariance of a brief version of the marijuana motives measure (MMM-P15) in a Peruvian population of marijuana users. *Anales de Psicología, 39*(1), 39–50. https://doi.org/10.6018/analesps.509651

Vallejos, M., Orbegoso, C., & Capa, W. (2007). Rhode Island change assessment scale (URICA): Validity and reliability in drug-dependent individuals. *Revista de Psicología (Universidad César Vallejo), 9*, 52–59. https://revistas.ucv.edu.pe/index.php/revpsi/article/view/513

Vallejos, M. A., Copez-Lonzoy, A. J. E., & Capa-Luque, W. (2018). Is anyone online?: Validity and reliability of the Spanish version of the Bergen Facebook addiction scale (BFAS) in university students. *Health and Addictions, 18*(2), 175–184. https://doi.org/10.21134/haaj.v18i2.394

Vega-Dienstmaier, J. M. (2022). Psychometric studies of Spanish-language instruments for the detection of common mental disorders: A review. *Revista de Neuropsiquiatría, 85*(2), 127–138. https://doi.org/10.20453/rnps.v85i2.4230

Ventura, J. L., & Caycho, T. (2016). Exploratory analysis of the Sternberg love scale in Peruvian university students. *Acta de Investigación Psicológica, 6*, 2430–2439.

Ventura-León, J., & Caycho-Rodríguez, T. (2017). The omega coefficient: An alternative method for estimating reliability. *Revista Latinoamericana de Ciencias Sociales, Niñez y Juventud, 15*(1), 625–662.

Vigo, A. M. (2003). *Psychometric adaptation of the confidence in risk situations questionnaire for substance use in addicted patients [Undergraduate thesis]*. Universidad Nacional Federico Villarreal. http://repositorio.unfv.edu.pe/handle/UNFV/948

Vilca, L. W., & Vallejos, M. (2015). Construction of the risk of addiction to social networks scale (Cr. ARS). *Computers in Human Behavior, 48*, 190–198.

Villarreal-Zegarra, D., Paz-Jesús, A., Copez-Lonzoy, A., & Costa-Ball, C. D. (2017). Validity and reliability of the family satisfaction scale in university students from metropolitan Lima, Peru. *Actualidades en Psicología, 31*(123), 89–98. https://doi.org/10.15517/ap.v31i123.23573

Wechsler, S. M., Schulmeyer, M. K., Vinet, E. V., & Livia, J. (2022). Psychological assessment in South America: Perspectives from Brazil, Bolivia, Chile, and Peru. In S. Laher (Ed.), *International histories of psychological assessment* (pp. 295–323). Cambridge University Press.

Chapter 14
Psychological Evaluation in Uruguay

Evelina Kahan Kruchik and María Susana Martínez Ferreira

Introduction

This chapter describes the role that psychological assessment occupies in the work of professional practice of psychologists in Uruguay. To do so, it is necessary to take a historical review that situates the use of assessment techniques in the very prehistory of the profession. The use of tests predates the official establishment of Psychology, having been introduced primarily by educational disciplines and later by health sciences. This initial disciplinary core expanded into areas that later contributed to the foundation of other disciplines, which also found in the use of these techniques a basis for their scientific development. It is important to highlight here professions more closely related to the health sciences, such as Psychomotricity and Speech Therapy, as well as those linked to social sciences within the field of education, such as Psychopedagogy, and also those related to the workplace aimed at determining aptitudes for specific trades.

With the official introduction of Psychology in the University setting, it is possible to observe the role that assessment has played in the training of psychologists. Different moments can also be identified regarding the weight of the topic in the curricular structures, as well as the different names it has acquired, which bear witness to the underlying theoretical and epistemological shifts.

The prevailing theoretical models regarding mental functioning, as well as the epistemological stances, have influenced the forms that assessment has taken, even determining its very nomenclature. As a result, even today, there is a variety of terms used for this type of professional practice. Psychological assessment, psychodiagnosis, psychological diagnosis, psychological study, and psychotechnical

E. Kahan Kruchik (✉) · M. S. Martínez Ferreira
University of the Republic, Montevideo, Uruguay
e-mail: eve.kahan@gmail.com; licsumart@gmail.com

S. V. Pugliese et al. (eds.), *Origins and Challenges of Psychological Assessment in Ibero-American Countries*, https://doi.org/10.1007/978-3-032-21380-8_14

evaluation represent a semantic trajectory of concepts that, while related, cannot necessarily be considered synonyms, as they reveal different approaches to the subject matter.

Origins of Psychological Evaluation in Uruguay

The emergence of Psychology in Uruguay can be traced from the late 1800s to the mid-1900s, linked to the educational reform of the late nineteenth century led by José Pedro Varela, founder of Uruguay's modern public school system, which established positivism in teacher training and later in university education (Tuana, cited in Oiberman, 2001, p. 27). It was characterized by experimental, psychometric, and later, functionalist psychology, developed in areas related to education, medicine, and the research center founded by W. Radecki (1944). At that historical moment, delving into the functionalist aspects of Psychology emphasized the functional interpretation of tests, focusing on the refinement of criteria for the selection, adaptation, application, and evaluation of tests (Domínguez, 1948, p. 10). The author refers to the advantages of tests, as they reveal the functional modality, the potential capacity, developmental state of each function, as well as the feelings, interests, and values of the subject. She adds that both the application and the functional interpretation of the test must be conducted by a psychologist (Domínguez, 1948, p. 11).

The earliest precedents date back to the 1920s and 1930s, with several key figures interested in Psychology, including Carlos Vaz Ferreira, from the field of Philosophy, who established the first Psychology Laboratory. On the other hand, there were teachers concerned with pedagogy, with Sebastián Morey Otero standing out in 1925 for teaching the first course on Experimental Psychology and, in 1926, introducing Experimental Psychology as a subject in the professional training cycle for teachers at the María Stagnero de Munar Normal School for Girls (Tuana, cited in Oiberman, 2001, p. 27). In 1929, the Alfred Binet Association was founded, focusing on psychological research for pedagogical purposes, maintaining ties with the Société Alfred Binet-Psychologie de l'Enfant et Pédagogie Expérimentale, France.

In this context, education contributed to the growth of Psychology alongside Psychopedagogy, leading to the establishment of the Experimental Psychopedagogical Laboratory within the National Council of Primary and Secondary Education. The creation of this laboratory marked "the beginning of the evolutionary process of Psychology and indirectly and incipiently showed the start of the recognition of Psychology as a profession" (Carrasco, 2005, p. 3).

The task, approached from a psychometric and psychotechnical perspective, was aimed to improve teaching. It is worth noting that the psychological assessment techniques used included the Stanford Revision of the Binet-Simon Intelligence Scale (1937), the Goodenough Draw-A-Person Test (1991), as well as questionnaires on activities and interests, and pedagogical performance tests in reading comprehension and mathematics (Tuana, cited in Oiberman, 2001, p. 28). In the 1940s and 1950s, notable foreign scientists such as Dr. Emilio Mira y López participated in the Experimental Psychopedagogical Laboratory, which facilitated the introduction of the Rorschach Psychodiagnostic, the Myokinetic Psychodiagnostic (PMK), as well as personality inventories and other collective tests.

This laboratory enabled the training of the first Psychotechnicians, who attended the First Latin American Course for Psychotechnicians Training held in Rio de Janeiro, Brazil (Tuana, cited in Oiberman, 2001, p. 31). Dr. Horacio Rimoldi also contributed with his statistical insights in intelligence measurement, which led to the creation and adaptation of intellectual assessment techniques. This made it possible to have a battery to measure intelligence in adolescents, in line with the parameters of the g-factor Theory.

The techniques employed, whether pedagogical or intellectual, shifted toward vocational guidance at the Industrial School, a public educational institution that was the precursor to the current University of Work of Uruguay (UTU). It was an organization focused on vocational education, so aptitude tests also began to gain ground. This shift, which highlighted the utility of assessment to describe specific skills, facilitated the transition from education to occupational settings, and thus, the next area of application being the Uruguayan Air Force for pilot selection.

As can be observed, psychological evaluation began to expand, although not as a practice of psychologists, since the profession as such did not yet exist. Simultaneously, by the late 1940s and early 1950s, Psychology entered the health field, with the creation of the Psychology Laboratory at the Psychiatric Clinic of the Faculty of Medicine for the study of adult mental pathology, and the Medical-Psychological Clinic at the Pedro Visca Hospital, which focused on child psychology. During this period, "the activities developed were mainly academic, and when any practical application was made, it was psychotechnical in nature, often exclusively psychometric" (Carrasco, 2005, p. 4).

Therefore, even before the official existence of Psychology as an independent university profession, the three traditional fields of psychological evaluation—educational, vocational, and clinical—were established. It is evident that in Uruguay, the interest in this practice came before the profession, marking the origins of it. "In the early days of the profession, psychodiagnosis was the essential and almost exclusive task of the psychologist. Psychology, psychodiagnosis, and test administration were virtually synonymous" (Giorgi, 2002, p. 7).

It is, therefore, important to emphasize that psychological assessment predates psychology in Uruguay, contributing to its creation, being linked to the professional identity and its conflicts of demarcation with other professions.

> ...and in the beginning, it was psychodiagnosis... This statement—of undeniable biblical connotations—reflects upon an origin, something foundational, to transform, to overcome, but also to be reclaimed...; a place to return to. Something that includes both the old and the new through a continuous process of distancing and reunions, re-elaborations and re-significations (Giorgi, 2002, p. 7).

It becomes evident, in an eloquent manner, the role that psychological assessment has had in the history of Psychology in Uruguay, laying the foundations and even contributing to the creation of the profession.

Psychology and Psychological Evaluation: Their Beginnings in the University and Academia

In the 1950s, the discipline of Psychology entered the University of the Republic through the health sciences specifically the Faculty of Medicine. The Course of Applied Psychology for Childhood was incorporated into the Medical Auxiliary Courses offered by the School of Medical Assistants. This would become a university space that, in 1978, would be renamed as the School of Medical Technology. Shortly after, in 1956, Psychology would also enter through the social sciences, now as the Institute of Psychology and a Bachelor's degree in Psychology within the Faculty of Humanities and Sciences.

The official entry into academic life, represented by the university space and the recognition of its status as an independent discipline and not merely an auxiliary to medicine, fostered its scientific development, leading to the foundation in 1953, of the Uruguayan Society of Psychology. It is worth mentioning once again Dr. Waclaw Radecki, a Polish doctor and psychologist, who settled in Brazil in the 1920s, where he contributed to the development of Psychology in that country through a study center that was closed during the de facto regime of Getúlio Vargas. He moved to Uruguay and founded the Center for Psychological Studies of Montevideo, being responsible for a biannual publication, *La Hoja de Psicología*, which contained theoretical contributions about the new and emerging discipline.

Among the students of this center were recognized pioneers of Uruguayan Psychology, such as psychologists Juan Carlos Carrasco, Mercedes Freire de Garbarino, and María Esther Domínguez, among others. It was also from this center that the first job opportunities for psychologists emerged (Andrade, 2007, p. 16). In the aforementioned publication, it becomes evident the importance of psychotechnical studies (psychograms of children and adults, adaptation, guidance, and selection), and it specifies:

> Offering the National Medical Corps… a Psychotechnical laboratory and a Psychagogy Consultation… in all cases where the doctor addresses problems that are not predominantly somatic, will provide the necessary elements to sustain and clarify a diagnosis or orienting a therapeutic approach of the psyche (Domínguezet al., 1948/1949, p. 39). It is worth mentioning that, according to the Royal Spanish Academy (2022), Psychagogy refers to the "art of guiding and educating the soul."

And these authors add:

> The psychogram to be delivered when requested is nothing more than a detailed study, function by function, of all psychic aspects: functions of perception, accommodation, elaboration, and use in the intellectual realm, as well as affective and active modalities, which are then synthesized to highlight the correlations and compensations that typify the personality (Domínguez et al., 1948/1949, p. 39).

It is worth mentioning that the School of this Center became the Free Faculty of Psychology, according to the motion of the First Latin American Congress of Psychology (Radecki, 1950a, p. 29).

At that Congress, the first steps were taken to address issues related to: defining the field of practice, professional training, responsibility, and professional ethics. Regarding the formation of psychologists, the need for specialized professional psychologists' services was emphasized, recommending the creation of higher professional schools, similar to Faculties, in countries where such institutions did not exist. Concerning the psychologist's responsibility, it was raised the need to "clearly delimit the scope of the psychologist's practice and to define the professional responsibility of this professional when collaborating with other professionals or when working independently" (Radecki et al., 1950, p. 18). At the same time, the ethical aspects of the activity were established, "raising the need to create standards," for which a Permanent Commission was appointed, based in Montevideo, consisting of Uruguayan, Brazilian, and Argentinian psychologists (Radecki et al., 1950, p. 19).

Some of the papers presented at this First Latin American Congress of Psychology, held in July 1950, reveal the value attributed to various psychological techniques. One in particular stands out, related to the Rorschach Psychodiagnosis and its contribution to the diagnosis of schizophrenia. It referred to the longitudinal study of a case of hebephrenic schizophrenia, showing the evolution of the condition even before the appearance of clinical symptoms, up to its progressive deterioration and onset of dementia through the application of the aforementioned technique at different moments and after different biological treatments received, such as insulin shock, electroshock, and prefrontal lobotomy (Pascual del Roncal, 1950, p. 307).

Furthermore, another paper presented at the Congress addressed the importance of conducting psychodiagnostics assessments on candidates for teaching positions. This was proposed by a professor from the Teacher Training School of the Institute of Education of Porto Alegre, interested in understanding the personality and adaptability of the teacher to their work, in order to advise or discourage their entry into the teaching career (Flores Cabral, 1950, p. 313–314).

It is also worth highlighting that, in the 4-year course program offered by the Radecki Center (now as the Free Faculty) by the year 1951, in its third year, a course in Psychogogy was already taught, and in its fourth year, there was a course in Psychotechnics and Psychopedagogy, demonstrating the importance of psychological assessment in the educational field (Radecki, 1950b, p. 30–32).

In summary, in the early 1950s, psychological practice was carried out in isolated groups according to the specificity of its activities: Pedagogical psychology at Morey Otero; Vocational guidance at the Industrial School and the WMCA; pilot selection in the Uruguayan Air Force; clinical Psychology in the Psychology Laboratory, in the Psychiatric Clinic, and the Medical-Psychological Clinic at the Pedro Visca Hospital; research at the Institute of Psychology of the Faculty of Humanities and Sciences and teaching and specific forms of psychological diagnosis and practice at the center founded by Radecki (Carrasco, cited in Oiberman, 2001, p. 32).

Influence of Psychoanalysis in Psychological Evaluation and Psychodiagnosis

In the early years of the discipline and its subdiscipline, the theoretical frameworks were varied, reflecting the developments of the time derived both from Modern Psychometrics, represented by the contributions of Galton, Cattell, and Binet (Meneses, 2013), as well as from concepts related to general Psychology from various schools of thought.

In the 1950s, the rise of psychoanalysis began in the Río de la Plata region, with the foundation of the Argentine Psychoanalytic Association (APA) in 1942 and the Uruguayan Psychoanalytic Association (APU) in 1955. Laura Achard and Marta Lacava, founding members of the APU, were part of the Psychopedagogical Laboratory of Morey Otero and the Psychotechnical Section of the Medical-Psychological Clinic at the Pedro Visca Hospital, respectively (Mundell, 2022). As a result, the psychoanalytic theoretical framework began to influence psychological assessment, with the use of projective techniques in psychological evaluation becoming more central, as well as the value of diagnostic interviews. From this point on, other terms began to be used for this psychological practice, such as psychodiagnosis, psychological study, and psychological diagnosis, and this is how the activity would be referred to in specialized literature.

Up until today, this is the way in which professional practice in this area is commonly referred to. Frequently, in consultation requests made by other professionals in the Uruguayan setting, it is common to read: "request for psychological study," "request for intelligence test," "psychodiagnostic," "attentional assessment," "level and personality study," etc. In the clinical field, the hegemonic medical model is undoubtedly highly influential. However, even among groups of psychologists, there is no consensus on how to name this activity, making evidently the variety of epistemological positions. The expansion into other areas allows broadening this denominative spectrum, and thus, one can encounter a request for a psychotechnical study in the field of occupational psychology, associated with psychological evaluation within the context of personnel selection. In the educational field, there will be references to "vocational testing," among others, while in forensic Psychology, the specificity of the field will give rise to the term "psychological expert evaluation".

The value of the so-called "depth psychology," a term commonly used to refer to psychoanalytic thought in the Uruguayan psychological community, established a sort of dichotomous categorization of techniques. On the one hand, there are those where the measurement component and psychometric aspects are more relevant, and on the other, those where the focus is on understanding and explaining the uniqueness of the situation beyond normative data. The first group includes intelligence tests, aptitude tests, personality inventories, among others, and in the second, projective techniques in all their varieties.

The entry of institutionalized psychoanalysis through scientific organizations influenced psychological practice both in the areas of psychopathological diagnosis and psychotherapy. In a lecture given in 2005, Emeritus Professor Juan Carlos

Carrasco pointed out the concern raised within the Uruguayan Society of Psychiatry regarding psychologists' involvement in the fields of psychotherapy and psychopathology.

Up until that point, psychological activity was practically confined to diagnosis, through the use of techniques and discrete orientation activities, all of which was not only tolerated by doctors but also defined by them as the "legal" practice of Psychology (Carrasco, 2005).

The controversy over this dispute for disciplinary boundary territories culminated in an intrusion complaint by the Uruguayan Medical Union accusing psychologists of encroaching on their professional practice. The Uruguayan Psychological Society, founded just a few years earlier, managed to resolve this difference, at least until the establishment of the civic-military dictatorship, during which there was once again an attempt to subordinate psychological knowledge to medical knowledge. During the de facto regime that took place between 1973 and 1985, the health authorities of the time sought to limit professional practice exclusively to psychological assessment upon medical indication.

In the 1960s, there was significant development in both psychoanalysis and psychoanalytic-rooted social Psychology, with Enrique Pichón Rivière and his disciples and collaborators Bauleo, Bleger, Debrassi, Pavlovsky, Baremblit, Kesselman, and Caparrós standing out (Andrade, 2007, p. 17). This strong presence of psychoanalysis facilitated the introduction of projective techniques and the concept of psychodiagnosis, which, for a long period, replaced the term "evaluation" as the prevailing terminology.

Nevertheless, other documentary testimonies from the time show investigations conducted with psychometric techniques, such as the study "Validity and Reliability of Verbal and Non-Verbal Tests in Children from High Socio-Cultural Levels" (Artecona, 1969), in which the Kuhlmann-Anderson intelligence tests, the Detroit-Engel test, the Otis test, and the Raven Progressive Matrices were applied, or the "Psychological Study of 5,000 Primary School Students in the Maroñas District, Montevideo" (Desideri de Castiglioni & Migliarino de Motta, 1969), the results of which were presented at the XII Inter-American Congress of Psychology, organized by the Inter-American Society of Psychology (SIP), which took place in Montevideo. Therefore, it cannot be said that the growing influence of psychoanalysis as a model of mental functioning has displaced the use of non-projective techniques.

Psychology, Psychological Evaluation, and Psychodiagnosis During the Dictatorship (1973–1985)

Subsequently, during the dictatorship period in Uruguay, there was an intervention to the University from 1973 to 1984. The Bachelor's Degree in Psychology at the Faculty of Humanities and Sciences was definitively closed, losing its status as a bachelor's degree. Only the Child Psychology Course, dictated at the School of

Medical Technology, dependent on the Faculty of Medicine, remained, although it was closed for 2 years.

Martinez Sena (2016) suggests that in September 1973, just a few months after the start of the civil-military government, the collective of the Association of University Psychologists of Uruguay (APUU), composed of those who had earned the degree of Bachelor of Psychology at the Faculty of Humanities and Sciences before its closure, managed to publish an informational bulletin about the regulatory project for the profession.

It outlined the conditions that individuals would need to meet to be authorized to practice the profession and detailed the functions for which psychologists had competence. The professional was one who, with the use of specific methods and techniques, could operate in the fields of rehabilitation, psychopedagogical orientation, as well as vocational, occupational, and professional guidance. They were also qualified to study psychological phenomena in society, psychological and psychophysiological experimentation on behavior. The bulletin also mentioned the authority to direct Psychology services in the field of educational psychology and the teaching of psychology.

Note that the health field was not considered a place for holding hierarchical positions, likely because the medical hegemony of the time did not permit it. In fact, diagnoses, counseling, and individual, group, and institutional care activities in psychoprophylaxis and psychohygiene, as well as in psychotherapy, were expected to be preceded by a medical examination conducted by a specialist. Both theoretical and practical research were considered areas of competence in which it was permissible to perform roles of supervision or coordination, as well as to provide technical advice to organizations, conduct expert evaluations, and offer opinions on matters of Psychology (APUU, 1973). This framework of the psychologist's duties highlights the value of psychological evaluation techniques and diagnosis applied to various fields. It was the first initiative to regulate professional practice, but it did not succeed, as it was aborted when the Institute of Psychology and the Bachelor's Degree at the Faculty of Humanities were abolished by the dictatorship.

In 1975, during the university intervention, it was approved the creation of the University School of Psychology (USP), which began its courses in 1978, with the authority to grant the downgraded title of psychologist, compared to the bachelor's degree that was issued by the Faculty of Humanities and Sciences before its closure. This represented a demotion in university status, shifting from a faculty to a school, along with a decline in training quality, reducing the 5 years bachelor's program to 4 years. It also led to a change in both the conception and objectives of Psychology training, "becoming exclusively focused on the reproduction and technological application of psychodiagnostic tools, as the definition of the professional role, in accordance with the concept of medicalization" (Faculty of Psychology, n.d.). That is, during this period, there was an attempt to reduce the scope of Psychology, limiting it to diagnostic tasks, "stripping it of autonomy, submitting it to the directives of other professions, and attempting to dismantle the theoretical and epistemological coherence that university and Río de la Plata Psychology had built" (Giorgi, 2002, p. 8).

Once again, it became necessary to defend professional autonomy and, in particular, psychodiagnosis, which was intended to be one of the few technical activities that psychologists could perform under medical direction. Sobrado, defending professional identity, stated that "the monopoly of psychodiagnosis should be a claim from which no theoretical discussion can divert us" (Sobrado, 1993, p. 46). He also referred to diagnosis as "a scientific practice, which should begin with the theoretical review of tests, their methodological positioning in the diagnostic process, and their articulation with a theory of the psyche, which, in turn, specifies and coherently aligns an applicable psychopathology" (Sobrado, 1993, p. 46).

The USP curriculum included annual subjects related to the teaching of psychometric aspects (Psychostatistics and Psychometrics), techniques for intellectual and psychomotor assessment (Psychological Tests I), graphic and thematic projective techniques, and Rorschach Psychodiagnosis (Psychological Tests II), as well as comprehensive diagnosis (Psychodiagnosis). Meanwhile, the 4-year Child Psychology Course offered at the School of Medical Technology under the Faculty of Medicine, which awarded the title of Child Psychology Technician, included Psychological Techniques I and Statistics in the first year, Psychological Techniques II in the second year, Psychological Techniques III and Psychodiagnosis in the third year, and concluded with Clinical Practice A and Clinical Practice B in Psychodiagnosis in the fourth year.

During the period of military dictatorship, and prior to the return to democracy in 1984, due to the prevailing conditions, private training was promoted in both psychoanalytic-oriented psychotherapy and psychodiagnosis, in small groups led by professionals who, in many cases, had been dismissed from their teaching positions by the de facto authorities of the dictatorship. During this time, the Institute of Philosophy, Sciences, and Letters, an educational institution under the auspices of the Uruguayan church, also gained prominence. In 1979, the Jesuit Order was entrusted with the responsibility of overseeing official Psychology training in the private sector, becoming the immediate predecessor of the Catholic University of Uruguay. This program gave rise to the first private Faculty of Psychology authorized to grant the degree of Licentiate in Psychology. The curriculum structure here included Statistics in the first year, Development Assessment in the second, Level Assessment in the third, Graphic Tests, Phillipson Test, Rorschach, and Interview in the fourth, concluding with Psychodiagnosis in the fifth year. All of these were annual courses.

It is from 1984 onward that a process began in which the University regained its legitimate spaces and consolidated its fundamental principles of plurality and democracy. Simultaneously, during this period, there was an extensive debate on Psychology in the country, leading to the creation, through the organized inter-union activity of students, faculty, and graduates from various centers, of the Unified Center for Psychology Studies. This movement culminated in 1987 with the establishment of the Institute of Psychology of the University of the Republic (IPUR), where the previous curricula (USP and Child Psychology from the School of Medical Technology) are unified, becoming the sole training center at the University of the Republic, of a public nature. The Institute of Psychology of the University of the Republic became as Faculty, and the implementation of the new curriculum (1988) was authorized. Finally, on March 15, 1994, the Faculty of Psychology of the University of the Republic was created.

Creation of the Profession by Law: Another Milestone for Psychology and Psychological Evaluation

On August 17, 1999, Law No. 17,154 was enacted, establishing the profession of psychologist in Uruguay, which was regulated by Decree No. 361/002 on September 12, 2002. On May 3, 2001, the Professional Code of Ethics for Psychologists was approved, signed by the Coordinating Body of Psychologists of Uruguay, the Uruguayan Society of Psychology, the Faculty of Psychology of the University of the Republic (UdelaR), and the Faculty of Psychology of the Catholic University of Uruguay (UCU). It is important to highlight that Chap. 3 of this Code specifically addresses psychological assessment through the following articles:

Article 22: Psychological assessment, an exclusive task of psychologists, does not have an end in itself; it will always be embedded within an objective of prevention, intervention, and/or research.

Article 23: The techniques and instruments used by psychologists must be selected based on information regarding their reliability and validity, with a thorough knowledge of the instrument, its principles, the research supporting it, and the requirements for its use.

Article 24: Psychologists' evaluations, recommendations, reports, and diagnoses or evaluative judgments are based on the information and techniques necessary for an adequate foundation of the results obtained.

Returning to the situation of the Institute of Psychology, it was only in 1994 that it was officially recognized as a Faculty, and a few years later, the Law Regulating the Practice of the Psychology profession was approved in 1999.

The Role of Psychological Evaluation in Post-Dictatorship Curricula

Earlier paragraphs referred to the reunification of university Psychology training in 1987, which led to the establishment of IPUR and its curriculum, known as Plan 88. The academic structure of IPUR, later the Faculty of Psychology in 1994, was organized into Areas, Workshops, Courses not assigned to Areas, and Services, responsible for delivering the curriculum content over five annual training cycles. The content related to psychological assessment was overseen by the Area of Psychological Diagnosis and Intervention (APDI), with a significant weight in the curriculum in terms of courses. It spanned from the second to the fifth cycle with the following consecutive courses: Psychological Interview and Introduction to Diagnosis (First Cycle); Exploration of Intellectual, Psychomotor, and Developmental Aspects (Third Cycle); Basic Course in Projective Techniques, Advanced Projective Techniques, and Introduction to the Rorschach Test (Fourth Cycle); Basic Course in Psychological Diagnosis and Advanced Psychological Diagnosis (Fifth Cycle).

The Area was defined within the Plan 1988 as "a structure created for the purpose of developing a specific research field, as an outcome of the psychologist's activities and/or community demands." The APDI's main objective was to provide instruction in psychological diagnosis in its various forms and fields of application, including its theoretical foundations, technical aspects, and its integration with clinical practice in collaboration with various public institutions (educational, health, etc.), where students took responsibility for clinical cases under faculty supervision.

Cristóforo stated, "The aim should be to diagnose the consultation situation and resolve it, prioritizing the consultation and considering diagnosis as a tool for its resolution. Diagnostic techniques are thus included within the concept of consultation" (Cristóforo, 2005, p. 29). Following her ideas, she later adds, "It must be a practice within the framework of a psychological consultation, as it involves diagnosis-intervention and the resolution of the consultation" (Cristóforo, 2005, p. 29–30).

For her part, Muniz argues that interventions require the development of a strategy that "incorporates indications, exploration with techniques, testing hypotheses, and discarding others" (Muniz, 2005, p. 19). Regarding undergraduate training, Muniz stated at the time that, although there are challenges due to student massification, "the psychologist must be familiar with the basic guidelines of the techniques in order to use them in their professional practice if they so choose, or if their future work requires it" (Muniz, 2002, p. 74). Under the cited Plan, regarding the Rorschach technique specifically, a mandatory year-long course was offered in the undergraduate program; it was taught from the Klopfer approach, incorporating contributions from the Argentine School and the perspective of Dynamic Analysis. Additionally, there were training and advanced course with specialized instructors from Argentina (Passalacqua, 1994; Weigle, 1999).

The effect of the changes in university education between 2007 and 2010, framed within the second Reform process at the University of the Republic (UR), followed the guidelines of organizations and associations governing higher education in Latin America and in line with the Bologna process, aimed to address educational innovations in a globalized world that facilitated smoother exchange between countries. This has led to a new curriculum at the Faculty of Psychology at the University of the Republic (UdelaR). These transformations, which follow the principles of the Bologna Plan, include, among other points, the introduction of credits, the prioritization of skill acquisition over knowledge acquisition, meaning that undergraduate and postgraduate education will be strongly oriented toward meeting the labor needs of society, as well as accreditation through an internal and external evaluation system that monitors the quality of each institution. This approach seeks to construct more personalized academic pathways, promoting curricular flexibility and diversification.

According to Artigas (2014), this involves incorporating distance learning strategies, creating more open pathways that consider the students' interests, the emergence of new degree programs, some with intermediate qualifications, and interdisciplinary proposals involving multiple departments in their development (Artigas, 2014, p. 75). Additionally, the undergraduate degree is promoted as a step that should be articulated with postgraduate studies. Indeed, alongside the new undergraduate curriculum, specializations, master's degrees, and doctoral programs will begin to be developed.

In the new Curriculum of the Bachelor's Degree in Psychology (2013), there is a reduction in the duration of the undergraduate program, which is now 4 years. The curriculum is structured into three training cycles (Initial, Integral, and Graduation), and its contents are grouped into five modules: Psychology, Methodology, Referential, Knowledge Articulation, and Pathway Construction. Each of these modules includes Mandatory Curricular Units (MCUs), as well as Seminars, Pre-professional Practicums, and Research or Extension Projects, all addressing various topics that students must choose to fulfill their credit requirements. Furthermore, this new plan is based on a new academic structure that includes the creation of five Institutes: Clinical Psychology, Social Psychology, Health Psychology, Psychology and Education, and Foundations and Methods of Psychology, as well as two Research Centres: the Clinical Psychology Research Centre and the Basic Research Psychology Center.

As it can be observed in this new curricular structure, significant importance is given to the increasing degree of autonomy granted to students in their educational process. A flexible modality of semester-based courses enables the construction of a personalized academic pathway. This change is consistent with the transformations at the University of the Republic, associated with the integration of the functions of teaching, research, extension, knowledge, and interdisciplinarity.

These transformations resulted in a drastic reduction of mandatory content in undergraduate training related to psychological assessment and diagnosis. There is only the Mandatory Curricular Unit (MCU) of Psychological Interview, located in the second semester of the program, belonging to the Initial Training Cycle; the MCU of Clinical Psychology Tools in the fourth semester, corresponding to the Integral Training Cycle; and Theory and Technique of Interventions (fifth semester). The elective modalities in all their formats (seminars, practices, or projects) do not necessarily address these topics, leaving them to the discretion of the Institutes' Programs. The Programs are the component units of the five Institutes that carry out research and extension lines that feed back into teaching activities or the interests of the Programs. The first MCU mentioned is covered by several Programs of the Clinical Psychology Institute, and the second by the Psychological Diagnosis and Evaluation Program of the same Institute, composed of ten faculty members.

This Program addresses the field of diagnostic and assessment instruments used within the psychological discipline in the clinical setting, conceived as a broad spectrum with a high level of complexity. It ranges from aspects related to the purely statistical perspective, a level not without complexity, to the creation of new instruments and the analysis of the theoretical and epistemological foundations of this approach, among other issues (Martínez, 2012). It is responsible for teaching in both undergraduate and postgraduate levels, through its participation in the Specialization in Psychological Assessment and in the Continuing Education courses for graduates.

The description of these aspects of university training for the Bachelor's degree in Psychology in Uruguay is relevant because it affects the practice of this professional modality. Several cohorts of professionals are already graduating with limited or barely minimal training in the subdiscipline of psychological assessment. As mentioned earlier, the mandatory specific training is limited to two semesters, and the elective training only reaches a small percentage of students, with two or three seminars offered per year for up to 40 students, as well as pre-professional practicums and/or research or extension projects that do not cover a hundred students. The MCU Clinical Psychology Tools course can only provide a merely introductory overview of the concept of psychological testing, covering its ethical, theoretical, methodological, and epistemological dimensions, and introduce a few paradigmatic techniques almost informatively (Wechsler Scales, Bender test, a few projective tests, and some inventories), contextualized in psychological diagnosis and/or assessment in the clinical field.

In this context, Cristóforo (2019) states, "Rorschach training has disappeared, at least in Uruguay. What has happened with Rorschach training is not unrelated to the 'mandates' of the Bologna model" (p.1), though not exclusively, as it also responds to other changes related to transformations in the academic structure, as well as to programmatic content that has disappeared or been reduced in the curriculum, and in the disintegration and formation of new working groups, among other factors.

In parallel, within the framework of the university reform, with the strengthening of postgraduate training and its articulation with undergraduate studies, the Specialization in Psychological Assessment was created in 2012. It offers a common training cycle and another oriented toward the clinical, occupational, judicial, and forensic fields, allowing the awarding of diplomas in: Specialist in Clinical Assessment, Specialist in Psycholaboral Assessment Techniques, or Specialist in Assessment Techniques in Judicial and Forensic Psychology. This Specialization, as a program for deepening and professional development, was designed in a different academic context since it began while the 1988 curriculum was still in effect. It relied on the existing undergraduate training, so the configuration of psychologists who graduated after the first cohort was different, as the 2013 curriculum was implemented. This has led to the current situation where the Specialization cannot fully meet the objectives initially proposed with psychologists graduated under the 2013 curriculum.

This postgraduate training aims to respond to the current demands of psychological practice, which require knowledge and management of a broader range of techniques, whether for neuropsychological diagnosis, intellectual or projective assessment, as well as objective techniques (questionnaires, inventories) used as assessment and research instruments (Muniz & Moll, n.d.). The training logic, then, aims for the student who wishes to do so, to build a pathway in psychological diagnosis and assessment that begins at the undergraduate level, continues in the professional Specialization with differentiated profiles, and may even culminate in a more academic level with master's and doctoral programs. Of course, there is a bottleneck, whereby only a very limited number of professionals can access this complete training cycle. Admission to the specializations only opens its registration every 2 years for a quota of 40 applicants.

Regarding the state of research in and with projective techniques at the Faculty of Psychology, Cristóforo (2015, p. 7) notes that there has been a boost in this activity, including research in the undergraduate curricula and through the creation of postgraduate programs. This has enabled an increase in researches involving Projective Techniques, elevating them "not only as tools for professional practice in clinical settings, but as valid instruments for the production of knowledge in Clinical Psychology" (Cristóforo, 2015, p. 7), addressing current clinical issues such as "violence and abuse against children, medicalization and pathologization, adolescence and its current problems, among others" (Cristóforo, 2015, p. 7). However, she points out that postgraduate theses focus on individual research production, highlighting the need to form group research teams.

Although the Faculty of Psychology at the University of the Republic, with its 15,000 active students in 2022, represents the university space that contributes the most Psychology professionals to Uruguayan society, the two other private universities that also grant degrees in the discipline recognized by the Ministry of Education and Culture should not be overlooked. These are the Faculty of Psychology at the Catholic University of Uruguay (UCU) and the Bachelor's degree in Psychology at the Francisco de Asís University Institute (UNIFA).

Regarding private education, the curriculum at UCU includes several courses labeled as psychological assessment, although they are primarily focused on development and cognitive processes, as well as psychometrics. At UNIFA, courses include Introduction to Psychometrics and Statistics in the first year, Theory and Technique of the Interview in the second year, Techniques for Exploring Intellectual Aspects and Projective Techniques in the third year, Projective Techniques II in the fourth year, and Psychodiagnosis in the fifth year.

Another aspect to mention is the limited number of techniques with national norms available, which becomes problematic when using them. In terms of intellectual evaluation, the WISC-III norms for the Montevideo population, published in 2010 (Martínez & Álvarez, 2010), are available. This research was carried out by faculty members that later founded the Psychological Diagnosis and Evaluation Program at the Clinical Psychology Institute of the Faculty of Psychology at the University of the Republic (UdelaR). Currently, the validation of the Chilean version of the WISC-V is underway, a study that, like the WISC-III research, received competitive funding from the Sectorial Commission for Scientific Research (CSIC). In order for Uruguayan psychologists to become familiar with this latest version of the intelligence scale, a publication was produced that mainly addresses aspects related to the administration and interpretation of results with national case studies (Kahan & Salvo, 2022).

In summary, in Uruguayan services, the WISC-III is predominantly used for diagnosing intellectual functioning in the public sector, while the WISC-IV is used in the private sector. Regarding personality evaluation, Selma (2017) has done research about personality and psychopathology, evaluating Uruguayan population with the SCL-90-R and adaptations of the short versions of the TCI-R, ZKPQ, and NEO-PI. This author has also worked on the Rorschach test from a cognitive and neuropsychological perspective (Selma, 2016, 2015). The study and research involving projective techniques within a psychoanalytic dynamic reference framework has a long tradition in Uruguay, as evidenced by several publications (Carrau et al., 1990; Muniz, 2000; Martínez, 2018).

In recent years, regarding professional practice, Andrade (2007) suggests that Psychodiagnosis in our country "once had a solid foundation in theory and technique" (p.20), but it has lost value at both the professional and social levels, as there is less interest in furthering knowledge among many students, who are dedicating fewer hours to study and practice. However, clinical practice remains the most attractive option and the one that offers the most opportunities for employment, within a framework of job insecurity and flexibility, with significant professional competition due to the high number of graduates entering the labor market.

Furthermore, these graduates show difficulties in appropriating the university training they have received and face challenges in accessing personal therapy for various reasons. A paradox, indeed, as, in many cases, job opportunities are linked to institutional settings (health, education, staff selection, judicial), where they must demonstrate expertise in the use of various psychological assessment techniques. On the other hand, new practices within Psychology have had to keep pace with changing times. The importance of openness in using techniques across different areas is recognized, whether clinical, labor, judicial, sports, educational, or psychogerontology, as these are connected to the specific field of work of psychologists. In a hypermodern context that witnesses new productions of subjectivity, the practice of Psychology has undergone transformations, and thus, psychological assessment has had to adapt to these changes, to which psychological techniques are not immune.

The shift toward the paradigm of Complexity has generated significant transformations, advancements, and challenges in various areas of society. Lipovetsky (2006) expresses that today, the culture of instant gratification prevails, where immediate pleasure reigns with little awareness of the future. Life is lived at an accelerated pace, searching for immediate satisfaction, where individualism predominates, along with hyperconsumerism and significant advances linked to Information and Communication Technologies. This has impacted the clinical field, which has had to respond to new pathological configurations, referred to as "pathologies of emptiness," with repercussions at both intra- and intersubjective levels. Cristóforo (2006) refers to diagnosis from the complexity paradigm as chance and uncertainty, emphasizing the encounter with another's knowledge rather than the search for a truth.

This epochal metamorphosis is further compounded by the COVID-19 pandemic, which has forced a reevaluation of clinical practices, both in terms of psychological evaluation processes and psychotherapeutic approaches, leading to the adoption of online care modalities (WhatsApp, Zoom, Skype, video calls, Discord) (Capnikas & Kahan, 2022).

In this context, it is necessary to rethink diagnosis and evaluation, as their tools should adapt to the demands of the current era. Globalization, hypermodernity, and the post-pandemic society, as well as new information and communication technologies, imprint particularities on the processes of subjectivities. These new paradigms force the reformulation and revaluation of technical instruments, which are linked to a specific and exclusive activity of the professional profile, and challenge the field of clinical practice in the present. As Muniz says, "projective techniques have not expired nor will they, as long as they can penetrate human suffering to grasp it, to predict, to seek forms of relief" (Muniz, 2002, p. 77).

In Summary

Throughout this chapter, aspects related to the history of psychological assessment have been discussed, which, as observed, existed and evolved in parallel with the evolution of the discipline and its practice in Uruguay, strongly shaping the professional identity.

The space devoted to this subject in the curriculum framework of official university training centers, as well as the terminology used, allows us to infer underlying theoretical models and epistemological perspectives.

The current curriculum of the undergraduate Psychology degree at the Faculty of Psychology, University of the Republic (UdelaR), shows that graduates, with a generalist profile, receive a minimum mandatory training in the Psychological Interview technique. It is placed at the beginning of the program (second semester) and lasts one semester. Contents directly related to tests are provided later in the program under the title Tools of Clinical Psychology (fourth semester). Both courses, due to their duration and placement in the training cycle, can only cover very basic and limited content. Further exploration of the subject of psychological assessment and diagnosis is offered in elective seminars, which only a small number of students can access during their undergraduate training.

This curricular reality could lead to the mistaken conclusion that psychological assessment has lost relevance in professional practice. However, it still occupies an important place in various areas of practice, even expanding into new fields such as neuropsychological assessment and determining psychological suitability for carrying firearms, among others.

In Uruguay, a difficulty in using these techniques is the lack of normative studies for the country. For this reason, it is necessary to rely on norms from other countries, which goes against the guidelines of international codes regarding the use of tests.

Currently, there is a certain disconnection between the demands of the labor market and the basic curricular training of psychologists. While, for the first time, there is now a specialization in Psychological Evaluation with three distinct profiles (clinical, work-related, and forensic), it is available to only a small number of graduates.

The creation of the National Integrated Health System and the intention to implement the Mental Health Plan have multiplied the creation of Psychology positions in both state-run mental health services and private collective medical care institutions. One highly positive consequence has been the increase in job opportunities for young psychologists. However, they do not always have the necessary training to, for example, conduct high-quality psychological evaluations.

These transformations within universities pose significant challenges and raise questions about the development of a highly specialized area of psychological knowledge that must address new demands and new spaces, with the goal of understanding human subjectivity to prevent, intervene, and research.

References

Andrade Eiroa, J. (2007). La diversidad de la Psicología en el ayer y hoy del Uruguay. *Boletín Sociedad de Psicología del Uruguay, 45*, 15–22. http://pepsic.bvsalud.org/scielo.php?script=sci_arttext&pid=S1688-43372007000300004&lng=pt&tlng=es

APUU. (1973). *Boletín informativo*, 3(3).

Artecona, E. (1969). Validez y confiabilidad de los tests verbales y no verbales en niños de nivel sociocultural elevado. En *XII Congreso Interamericano de Psicología: Memorias* (pp. 435–439).

Artigas, S. (2014). *La Reforma Universitaria (2007–2010): Ejes temáticos, actores e influencias* [Tesis de maestría, Universidad de la República]. Universidad de la República. https://www.cse.udelar.edu.uy/wp-content/uploads/2014/10/tesis_selva_artigas_2017.pf

Capnikas, E., & Kahan, E. (2022, 29–30 setiembre-1o. Octubre). *Intervenciones virtuales en la Clínica Infantil en tiempos de pandemia* [Ponencia]. 4tas Jornadas del Instituto de Psicología Clínica, "Transformaciones de la clínica en y más allá de la pandemia". Universidad de la República, Facultad de Psicología, Montevideo.

Carrasco, J. C. (2005). *Relato reflexivo y crítico de una historia de la psicología en el Uruguay*. www.latinoamericano.edu.uy

Carrau, P., Cristóforo, A., Culshaw, F., Garcia Firpo, A., Kachinovsky, A., Martínez, S., Montiel, S., Muniz, A., & Toucedo, N. (1990). *Análisis dinámico del Rorschach: una integración teórico-clínica*. Roca Viva.

Cristóforo, A. (2005). Enseñar diagnóstico en contextos de masividad. En A. Muniz (Comp.), *Diagnósticos e intervenciones: Enfoques teóricos, técnicos y clínicos en la práctica Psicológica* (Vol. 3, pp. 29–34). Psicolibros.

Cristóforo, A. (2006, agosto). *El paradigma hace el método: Diagnóstico o evaluación. Análisis crítico de una práctica* [Conferencia]. XIII Jornadas de Investigación en Facultad de Psicología y 2o. Encuentro de Investigadores en Psicología del Mercosur. Universidad de Buenos Aires, Facultad de Psicología.

Cristóforo, A. (2015, julio). *Estado de la investigación en y con técnicas proyectivas en la Facultad de Psicología—UdelaR* [Conferencia]. Congreso Asociación Latinoamericana de Rorschach (ALAR), Santiago de Chile.

Cristóforo, A. (2019, agosto 22–24). *La ausencia de Rorschach en el currículo: El Plan Bolonia en Uruguay* [Conferencia]. XVII Congreso Latinoamericano de Rorschach y otras técnicas proyectivas, XII Congreso Argentino de Rorschach en la Universidad, UMSA, Buenos Aires.

Desideri de Castiglioni, B., & Migliarino de Motta, E. (1969). Estudio psicológico de 5.000 alumnos del ciclo Primario en el Distrito de Maroñas, Montevideo. In *En XII Congreso Interamericano de Psicología: Memorias* (pp. 445–449). Montevideo.

Domínguez, M. E. (1948). Interpretación funcional de los tests. *Hoja de Psicología, 5*, 10–12.

Domínguez, M. E., Paysée, C., & Faílde Nogués, E. (1948/1949). Estudios Psicotécnicos. *Hoja de Psicología, 3–4*, 39.

Flores Cabral, E. (1950). Necessidade do Psico-diagnóstico do candidato ao Magistério. En *I Congreso Latinoamericano de Psicología* (pp. 308–314). Cepur.

Giorgi, V. (2002). Prólogo. En A. Muniz (Comp.), *Diagnósticos e intervenciones: Enfoques teóricos, técnicos y clínicos en la práctica psicológica* (Vol. 1, pp. 7–9). Psicolibros.

Harris, D. (1991). *El test de Goodenough: Revisión, ampliación y actualización*. Paidós.

Kahan, E., & Salvo, L. (2022). *Evaluación de la inteligencia en niños: Actualización en WISC-V*. Universidad de la República, Facultad de Psicología, Comisión Sectorial de Educación Permanente. https://udelar.edu.uy/eduper/?p=7712

Lipovetsky, G. (2006). *Los tiempos hipermodernos*. Anagrama.

Martínez, P. (2016). *Movimientos hacia la reglamentación de la Psicología durante la época de la dictadura: entre documentos y memorias* [Trabajo final de grado, Universidad de la República]. Colibrí. http://hdl.handle.net/20.500.12008/8632

Martínez, S. (2012). *Desarrollo e investigación en y con técnicas de diagnóstico y evaluación psicológica*. https://clinica.psico.edu.uy/desarrollo-e-investigacion-en-y-con-tecnicas-de-diagnostico-y-evaluacion-psicologica

Martínez, S. (2018). Algunas consideraciones acerca de las técnicas proyectivas. En A. Muniz (Comp.), *Manual de intervenciones en Psicología Clínica y herramientas para la evaluación y el diagnóstico*. Universidad de la República, Comisión Sectorial de Enseñanza.

Martínez, S., & Álvarez, R. (2010). *El WISC-III en los escolares: Baremo Montevideo*. Psicolibros.

Meneses, J. (Coord.). (2013). *Psicometría*. Universita Oberta de Catalunya.

Mundel, Tabarez, M. (2022). *El perfil del psicólogo en el Uruguay: inscripciones discursivas del psicoanálisis entre 1950 y 1970*. [Tesis de grado] Universidad de la República, Colibrí, Uruguay. https://hdl.handle.net/20.500.12008/33021

Muniz, A. (2000). *Análisis dinámico del Rorschach: una integración teórico-clínica*. Psicolibros.

Muniz, A. (2002). Los métodos proyectivos en los países latinoamericanos: Formación, perfeccionamiento y ejercicio profesional. En A. Muniz, *Diagnósticos e intervenciones: Enfoques teóricos, técnicos y clínicos en la práctica psicológica* (Vol. 1, pp. 71–79). Psicolibros.

Muniz, A. (2005). Conceptualizaciones acerca del diagnóstico y la intervención psicológica. En A. Muniz (Comp.), *Diagnósticos e intervenciones: Enfoques teóricos, técnicos y clínicos en la práctica psicológica* (Vol. 3, pp. 11–28). Psicolibros.

Muniz, A., & Moll, C. (n.d.). *Carrera de Especialización en Técnicas de Evaluación Psicológica*. Universidad de la República, Facultad de Psicología. https://psico.edu.uy/ensenanza/posgrado/especializaciones

Oiberman, A. (2001). Pioneros de la Psicología: Historias de vida ... cuando la vida es historia. Entrevista a la Prof. Élida Tuana y al Prof. Juan Carlos Carrasco. En *Psicodebate 3: Psicología, cultura y sociedad* (pp. 29–44). Universidad de Palermo, Facultad de Humanidades y Ciencias Sociales.

Pascual del Roncal, F. (1950). Contribución al estudio de la esquizofrenia con el método de Rorschach. In E. W. Radecki, C. A. Tuboras, & M. D. Nieto (Eds.), *Relatoría del Primer Congreso Latinoamericano de Psicología* (pp. 292–307).

Passalacqua, A., Alessandro de Colombo, M., Alonso, H. L., Codarini, M. S., Gravenhors, M. C., & Herrera, M. T. (Col.). (1994). *Psicodiagnóstico de Rorschach: Sistematización y nuevos aportes* (3a. ed.). Klex.

Radecki, W. (1944). Vida y obra de Waclaw Radecki (1887-1953). *Revista Latinoamericana de Psicología, 9*(2), 343–346. https://www.redalyc.org/pdf/805/80590222.pdf

Radecki, W. (1950a). Actividades del Centro de Estudios Psicológicos de Montevideo en el año 1950. *Hoja de Psicología, 7*, 29.

Radecki, W. (1950b). Programa de los cursos para el año lectivo 1951. *Hoja de Psicología, 7*, 30–32.

Radecki, W. et al. (1950). *Relatorio del Primer Congreso Latinoamericano de Psicología*. Cefur.

Real Academia Española. (2022). Psicagogia. En *Diccionario de la lengua española* (Edición del Tricentenario). https://dle.rae.es/psicagogia

Selma, H. (2016). Rorschach y psicobiología de la personalidad. *Universitas Psychologica, 15*(1), 39–64.

Selma, H., Benedetti, M., Luzardo, M., Boggio, K., Bagnato, M. J., Martín, A., Vázquez, A., & Premuda, P. (2017). Adaptación a población adulta montevideana de la Escala de Temperamento y Carácter Revisada (TCI-R): resultados preliminares. *Psicología, Conocimiento y Sociedad, 7*(1), 169–198. http://www.scielo.edu.uy/scielo.php?script=sci_arttext&pid=S1688-70262017000100169&lng=es&tlng=es

Sobrado, E. (1993). *Rol de Psicólogo*. Imago.

Terman, L., & Merrill, A. (1937). *Medición de inteligencia: una guía para la administración de las nuevas pruebas de inteligencia de Stanford-Binet revisadas*. Houghton Mifflin company.

Universidad de la República, Facultad de Psicología. (2013). *Plan de Estudio de la Licenciatura en Psicología*. https://psico.edu.uy/ensenanza/grado/licenciatura/plan

Universidad de la República, Facultad de Psicología. (n.d.). *Historia: más de 20 años desde su creación*. https://psico.edu.uy/institucional/facultad/historia

Universidad de la República, Instituto de Psicología del Uruguay. (1988). *Reglamento General de Estudios: Plan 1988*. https://psico.edu.uy/ensenanza/grado/licenciatura/plan-de-estudio-1988

Weigle, M. C. (1999). *Cómo interpretar el Rorschach: Su articulación con el psicoanálisis*. Guadalupe.

Chapter 15
Psychological Assessment in Venezuela: Origins, Expansion, Restriction/ Reinvention, and Challenges

Carmen Chilina-León, Eleonora Vivas Peñalver, Luisa T. Angelucci Bastidas, Janet Guerra Rendón, Aysbel González Álvarez, and María Carolina Berrios

Introduction

Psychological assessment, fundamental to both the training and practice of psychology, is present in all areas, both basic and applied. In Venezuela, the conceptualization of Fernández-Ballesteros (1994, 1999), confirmed by Muñiz (2021), has been adopted, emphasizing its crucial importance in the decision-making process to meet

C. Chilina-León (✉)
Universidad Católica Andrés Bello, Caracas, Venezuela

Asesores de Desarrollo Integral S.C, Caracas, Venezuela
e-mail: chilinaleon@adinsc.org

E. V. Peñalver
Universidad Simón Bolívar, Caracas, Venezuela
e-mail: vivas@usb.ve

L. T. Angelucci Bastidas
Universidad Católica Andrés Bello, Caracas, Venezuela

Universidad Simón Bolívar, Caracas, Venezuela
e-mail: langeluc@ucab.edu.ve

J. Guerra Rendón
Universidad Católica Andrés Bello, Caracas, Venezuela
e-mail: jguerra@ucab.edu.ve

A. G. Álvarez
Universidad Central de Venezuela, Caracas, Venezuela
e-mail: aysbel.gonzalez@ucv.ve

M. C. Berrios
Asesores de Desarrollo Integral S.C, Caracas, Venezuela
e-mail: mariaberrios@adinsc.org

S. V. Pugliese et al. (eds.), *Origins and Challenges of Psychological Assessment in Ibero-American Countries*, https://doi.org/10.1007/978-3-032-21380-8_15

the needs of the patient/client—a general notion further developed by Casullo (2009), Sendín (2000), Weiner (1992), and Sattler (2010). According to these authors, psychological assessment can be defined as a branch of psychology that studies human behavior in various contexts for descriptive, predictive, control, and intervention purposes, considering the abilities and potential of the individual or group to ensure high psychological significance. These authors note that psychological assessment has traditionally emphasized the use of psychometric or standardized tests; however, they assert that it should be approached from a multimethod perspective and include other forms and procedures for gathering information, such as interviews, observation, rating scales, among others (Fernández-Ballesteros, 1994; Fernández-Ballesteros et al., 2003; Leibovich de Figueroa & Schmidt, 2008; Sattler, 2010; Muñiz, 2021).

Conducting high-quality psychological assessment requires the acquisition, during undergraduate training, of competencies in the management of basic psychological and methodological knowledge to underpin the operationalization of constructs and to master the scientific process, by putting into practice the triad of theory/practice/research to meet these demands. This requires the creation and adaptation of techniques and instruments for recording information and systematizing experiences across different areas of psychological application, stages of human development, and relevant contexts (Fernández-Ballesteros et al., 2003; Nunes Baptista et al., 2006).

Within Venezuelan academia, broad models of psychological assessment have been proposed, which have contributed to the strengthening of applied areas of psychology in the country (León, 1994, 2007; Vivas, 2000). Assessment has been approached from a comprehensive, contextual, cumulative, diverse, and flexible perspective, which has been adapted in response to social demands (Arana et al., 2006).

Against this background, this chapter provides an overview of the origins, development, current state, the contributions and challenges of psychological assessment in Venezuela, based on: a) a review of publications on the subject (Rodríguez & Sánchez, 1999; Vivas, 1996; Vivas, 2000; Vivas et al., 2011; León, 1994; León, 2003; León, 2007; León, 2018a and 2018b; Sánchez & Dembo, 2015: Canga & Yáber, 2015; León et al., 2021; Canga, 2021); b) the perspective of the heads of psychology schools, postgraduate and research centers, c) the analysis of undergraduate curricula, and d) the status of professional psychological practice (León et al., 2021; Vivas et al., 2011).

Development of Psychological Assessment in Venezuela

Psychology as a science and profession is grounded in the historical advances of psychological assessment. This section describes the evolution of Psychological Assessment in Venezuela across three major periods: beginnings (1936–1970), expansion (1971–2001), and restriction/reinvention (2002–2022).

Beginnings (1936–1970)

In Venezuela, psychological assessment emerged to address needs within institutional settings. The literature identifies two sources: on the one hand, "there was a certain interest in psychology among other professionals who trusted the contribution this discipline could make to the assessment and resolution of psychiatric, educational, and occupational problems" (Sánchez & Dembo, 2015, p. 197), and on the other, the "training of educators and improvements in teaching techniques" (Straka, 2017, p. 22).

Sánchez and Dembo (2015) identify the origins of assessment in institutions such as the Venezuelan Child Council, the Mental Hygiene League, and the Mental Hygiene Division of the Ministry of Health and Social Welfare. These institutions began to use psychological tests for diagnostic purposes. This period was also characterized by the absence of psychologists in the country and the need for personnel assessment. Hence North American oil companies sent Venezuelans abroad to study psychology, particularly in the United States and France.

At the same time, professionals from other countries were present in Venezuela, such as Francisco Del Olmo, Guillermo Pérez Enciso, José Ortega Durán, among other academics, whose training contributed to the establishment of psychology courses in educational and governmental institutions, with a focus on psychometrics. Straka (2017) notes that in 1936 the first Chair of Psychology was created at the Pedagogical Institute of Caracas, which a year later became the Chair of Psychology and Psychometrics.

In this regard, Ramirez (2021) presents a second account, mentioning that the founder of the Chair of Psychology and Psychometrics was Dr. Eugenio González, philosopher, former minister, and former Rector of the University of Chile, who, together with Prof. Francisco Del Olmo, launched a Psychotechnics Course aimed at training teachers at the Pedagogical Institute in the proper use of psychological tests. In 1943, José Ortega Durán, a Spanish psychiatrist, founded the Psychometrics Section in the School Hygiene Directorate of the Ministry of Health, and in the same year, the "Paidological Office" was established by Father Carlos Guillermo Plaza at the San Ignacio School in Caracas (Straka, 2017).

Although psychological assessment began with courses offered in training programs at various institutions, it made its formal academic debut with the creation of the Institute of Psychology and Psychotechnics in 1949 at the Central University of Venezuela, dedicated to vocational guidance for new students (Sánchez & Dembo, 2012).

Formal studies in psychology as a discipline began in 1956, when the Faculty of Humanities at the Central University of Venezuela (UCV) established the Psychology Section, which later became the School of Psychology. A year later, the second School of Psychology was founded at the Andrés Bello Catholic University (UCAB). Graduates from the first cohorts, supported by immigrant professionals from Europe and Latin America, strengthened professionalism within academia in a prosperous country, laying solid foundations for the expansion of psychology.

During this period, psychological assessment focused on clinical and educational settings, gradually extending its utility to organizational and social contexts. Its reputation was thus consolidated as a tool for strengthening the nation's human capital.

Expansion (1971–2001)

The development of psychological assessment during this period was characterized by the expansion of undergraduate provision, the creation and growth of postgraduate courses and research centers, the formalization of psychology as a professional association, as well as the establishment of consultancies dedicated to the field.

At the national level, demand for psychology professionals increased, leading to the creation of the first two schools outside the capital region: one in the area with the highest oil exploitation (Rafael Urdaneta University), and another in the country's industrial hub (Bicentenaria de Aragua University), laying the groundwork for the gradual expansion of academic provision (see Table 15.1).

During training in psychological assessment in this period, students had access to the knowledge and use of the most widely used instruments in the United States, Europe, and Latin America, thanks to the efforts of professionals and certain universities that acquired and provided access to up-to-date, high-quality assessment materials. Undergraduate and postgraduate students have not only been consumers of foreign tests but have also developed, validated, and applied local tests.

Parallel to the expansion of Psychology Schools, professional organization was consolidated. In 1978 the Psychologists' Law was enacted in Venezuela and in 1981 the Code of Ethics of the Federation of Psychologists was approved, which remains in force to date, thereby regulating the management and use of "Resources and Instruments of Psychological Work" in its Chapter III (Federation of Psychologists of Venezuela [FPV], 1981). These professional milestones demonstrate the consolidation and expansion of psychologist training in Venezuela and their organization for professional practice.

In the year 2000, a sociopolitical situation began that slowed the pace of scientific and technical progress achieved in previous decades, mainly due to budgetary problems in the university sector, the elimination of government agencies that supported academic and scientific research, the decline in purchasing power, and the onset of a brain drain to other countries, a situation that marks the third period of psychological assessment in the country.

Table 15.1 Universities that created Schools of Psychology in Venezuela from 1971 to 2001

Name	Year founded	Region	Type of organization
Central University of Venezuela (UCV)	1956	Capital	Public
Andrés Bello Catholic University (UCAB)	1957	Capital	Private
Rafael Urdaneta University (URU)	1977	Zulian	Private
Bicentenaria de Aragua University UBA)	2000	Central	Private

Restriction/Reinvention (2002–2023)

This period began with a transformation of public administration to align with the ideological and political model of those governing the country since 1999, characterized by the systematic dismantling of initiatives that had been operating within the government sector. This adjustment and its collective impact significantly affected the quality of training, employment opportunities, and the professional practice of psychologists and psychological assessment.

In this context, psychology training has been affected as a consequence of the country's socioeconomic crisis. As a result, public universities, even today, face budget cuts, and private universities experience financial difficulties in maintaining subscriptions to specialist journal databases, acquiring psychological tests, and coping with the threat of low salaries and the constant loss of qualified staff to teach courses, including those related to assessment (Scholars at Risk, 2020). Added to this are the challenges posed by the deterioration of educational quality at all levels, as evidenced by the recent introduction of remedial courses in undergraduate and postgraduate programs.

Regarding the provision of professional services, the national situation has led to the elimination of psychologist posts in most free public services, both in health and educational centers, affecting access to psychological assessments and interventions in disadvantaged sectors. Similarly, in both public and private organizations, there are limitations in assessment practices in the area of human resources, exacerbated by the migration of multinational companies and graduates trained in the country.

Practicing professionals have seen their purchasing power eroded, making it difficult to access and purchase psychological techniques and tests, as well as to participate in up-to-date continuing education programs (León et al., 2021). According to a report by PH9 Medio Digital (2021), in 2012 the minimum wage in Venezuela was 476 US dollars according to the official exchange rate of the Central Bank of Venezuela. From 2014 onward its value began to fall rapidly as the economic crisis deepened. For example, by 2021 the minimum wage was $2.4 and although there was a slight increase by February 2023, the minimum wage remained at $5.32. This national decline is also reflected among professionals, whose incomes do not correspond to their experience and professional qualifications (PH9 Medio Digital, 2021).

This period has also been marked by a reduction in employment opportunities, due to the elimination of jobs for psychologists in governmental and nongovernmental organizations and the replacement of posts with unqualified personnel. This has led to a restriction in the employment and development of assessment psychologists.

Despite the restrictions this period has seen a significant increase in the demand for psychology training, with 8 out of the 12 existing Schools of Psychology nationwide being established (see Table 15.2), featuring a variety of systems, credit units, and percentages of courses dedicated to psychological assessment.

Table 15.2 Universities that created Schools of Psychology in Venezuela from 2002 to the present

Name	Year founded	Region	Type of organization
Arturo Michelena University(UAM)	2003	Central	Private
Metropolitan University (UNIMET)	2004	Capital	Private
Yacambú University (UNY)	2005	Western	Private
Centroccidental Lisandro Alvarado University (UCLA)	2006	Western	Public
Nacional Experimental del Táchira University (UNET)	2014	Andean	Public
Bolivarian University of Venezuela (UBV)	2015	Capital	Public
Andean University (ULA)	2017	Andean	Public
Margarita University (UNIMAR)	2021	Insular	Private

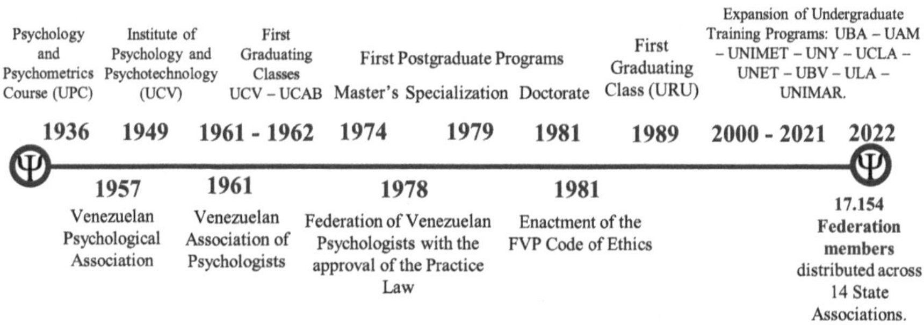

Fig. 15.1 The development of Psychology in Venezuela: Training institutions and professional organizations. *Note:* Psychology training (upper timeline) and the professional association (lower timeline). Author's own work

In parallel there has been a greater presence of the professional association, in two respects: on the one hand, the unification of efforts led by the Board of the Venezuelan Federation of Psychologists against "unqualified practice" in the field of Psychology (Yáber, 2020), and on the other, an increase in professional commitment in the face of structural, social, and professional challenges, as evidenced by its website. Currently, this Federation brings together 17,154 psychologists with 14 active regional branches (personal communication, October 2022) and is working toward nationwide coverage. Figure 15.1 summarizes, in parallel, the development of psychology training and the professional association.

Figure 15.2 shows the geographical location of the 12 universities that currently offer undergraduate degrees in Psychology in the country, highlighting the inequitable distribution of opportunities for psychology training and the shortage of professionals to meet the needs of a current population of 33,360,238 inhabitants (National Institute of Statistics, 2022).

This academic and professional development is taking place at a historic moment of restriction and socioeconomic hardship impacted by the consequences

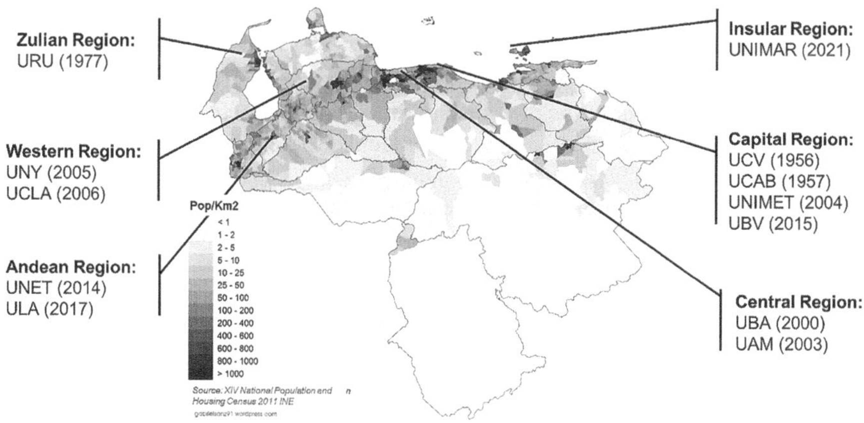

Fig. 15.2 Location of universities offering psychology programs on the population map

of the COVID-19 pandemic (lockdown, preventive measures, closure of educational institutions and private health services). Nevertheless, there is a collective effort to strengthen Psychology in response to the needs of the population, which has led to reinvention. Although this situation limited training and the management of professional practice, the use of the internet has made it possible not only to maintain undergraduate and postgraduate training programs, but also to expand the reach of academia and the professional association as key players in social responsibility during times of crisis, despite the fact that access is limited to 42.8% of the population and is of low quality (Venezuelan Observatory of Public Services, 2022).

In this context of limitations, reinvention and heterogeneity in training alternatives, it is necessary to examine in greater depth what academia and professionals in the country are doing in the field of psychological assessment. The following section reports data collected in 2021 and 2022 from the Schools of Psychology, focusing on psychological assessment and psychometrics.

The Role of Psychological Assessment in Training and Professional Practice

Academic Training

Undergraduate

The information in this section was obtained through a general review of the curricula of the 12 universities authorized by the National Council of Universities and of the syllabuses for courses in psychological assessment and psychometrics, based on credit units (CU), as well as from the findings of an online survey completed by 8 of the 12 School Directors.

The data summarized in Table 3 demonstrates the heterogeneity of undergraduate training provision in terms of course duration and structure. Three universities offer a 4-year curriculum (38%) and the remainder, 5 years (62%); 67% follow a semester system and 33% a trimester system.

With regard to curriculum organization, three universities initially offer a set of core subjects for all students, followed by specialized courses, which may include specializations such as clinical psychology, educational psychology, organizational psychology, psychological counseling, or social psychology. In the other universities, where the degree does not include specializations, the Directors indicated that courses are organized by area, starting with core subjects and progressing to courses in organizational, educational, social, or clinical/health psychology.

To obtain a Bachelor's degree in Psychology, students must complete between 139 and 317 credit units, with an average of 186 CUs. On average, 12% of the credit units are associated with courses in psychological assessment, ranging from 5% to 30%, enabling students to acquire a diverse set of skills for the administration, management, and interpretation of psychological tests.

This information demonstrates that psychological assessment is present in all Venezuelan universities, with variations regarding its fundamental principles, procedures, and training for the administration of techniques and tests. According to the Directors, psychological assessment accounts for between 4% and 60% of the curriculum, with an average predominance of 19% (SD = 18.75). In fact, a review of the analyzed curricula revealed that between 2 and 5 courses are directly related to assessment and between 0 and 7 courses refer to psychological assessment indirectly, representing between 2% and 22% of the total credits for the degree across different universities. Up to 21% of the courses in the curriculum focus on the application and interpretation of psychological tests to reach conclusions, support, and monitor the effectiveness and efficiency of intervention plans.

Additionally, they reported differences in the importance given to psychological assessment in their schools depending on the area of application. In some universities, assessment is taught extensively in educational psychology, social psychology, and health psychology, while in others, it is emphasized in the clinical (behavioral and dynamic), counseling, and educational tracks, since in organizational and social psychology greater emphasis is placed on intervention.

The formative heterogeneity revealed by the analysis of 12 curricula is confirmed by the Directors of the Schools of Psychology, with whom their theoretical and applied positions were explored. While there are points of convergence, differences were observed in their views of psychology and, consequently, in their approaches to teaching it. Regarding the prevailing theoretical conception or approach to psychological assessment in their school, 50% report a cognitive-dynamic or cognitive-behavioral orientation; 38% report an integrative approach, noting the predominance of a humanistic or constructivist conception and, at the methodological level, a mixed (quantitative–qualitative) stance. One school is framed within positive psychology. Another Director indicates that the approach is varied, especially in the basic cycle, but depending on the specializations, it may be more behavioral, humanistic, psychodynamic, or constructivist.

A review of the content of the psychological assessment course programs shows that they are linked to both basic and applied training, being fundamental for internships and of elective courses in university programs. Most psychology schools have psychological assessment as a cross-cutting theme, alongside intervention and research, training students in the use of psychological assessment as a basis for decision-making, data collection, integration and interpretation of information that supports and monitors psychological interventions in order to enhance their quality and thus improve professional standards.

A review of Psychometrics programs found that 11 out of 12 universities include it as a course. Differences were found in the weighting assigned, with credit units ranging from 1% to 4.5%. Most offer psychometrics training in two courses, which are delivered on a semester basis in 58% of schools and on a trimester basis in 33% (see Table 15.3).

Regarding content in Psychometrics, it is notable that all universities cover topics related to psychometric properties, such as reliability, validity, and normative data, and in some cases, this is the main focus of their training. There is greater variation in the teaching of basic elements of psychometrics, such as the conceptualization of measurement, types of instruments, criterion-referenced tests, and stages in the construction or design of instructions, each school places different emphasis on these topics. It is noteworthy that few universities include ethics in psychometrics as part of the curriculum. Training in data processing also varies across schools, but it was observed that most of them tend to teach programs such as SPSS, Excel, or R. Those schools with more credits tend to provide broader and more robust psychometric training to students.

With regard to the methods of assessment in courses related to psychological assessment, all universities include theoretical and practical activities with varying degrees of supervision, which involve the use of techniques and tests in case studies and for the evaluation and monitoring of intervention plans. In courses related to psychometrics, most universities implement practical activities, ranging from simple analytical reports on psychometric properties to the construction of psychological assessment instruments following international guidelines, which are formalized when used in dissertations or published in peer-reviewed journals. Academic experience has shown that as students gain experience in creating their own instruments, they approach psychometrics and psychological assessment with greater readiness and are better prepared to fulfill their professional roles.

The % of the (CU) of the other specializations are: Counseling 11 (53%), Social Psychology 3(14%), Clinical Psychology 11(35%), Industrial Psychology 7(32%), Educational Psychology 8(38%).

A review of the content relating to the methods, techniques, and tests included in courses associated with assessment and psychometrics reveals a focus on the characterization of psychological assessment, its foundations, the characteristics and administration of psychometric and non-psychometric tests, scales, projective and graphic tests. Among the techniques and tests taught and contributing to the

Table 15.3 Percentage of subjects and credit units for Psychological Assessment and Psychometrics in Venezuelan Schools of Psychology

University	Regime	Specialization	Total career CU	Subjects	% of the total of subjects	% of CU of subjects of the total CU
1. UCV**	Semester	Counseling, social, clinical, educational, organizational, and clinical (dynamic)	180	PA*	39.39	23.88
				Psychometrics	3.03	1.11
2. UCAB	Semester		305	PA	19.4	24.92
				Psychometrics	1.49	2.52
3. URU	Semester		177	PA	26	29.38
				Psychometrics	4	4.51
4. UBA	Trimester	Clinical, educational, and organizational	175	PA	13.89	20
				Psychometrics	2.78	3.42
5. UAM	Semester	Clinical, educational, and organizational	160	PA	18.2	15
				Psychometrics	3.63	3.75
6. UNIMET	Trimester		180	PA	26.67	26.67
				Psychometrics	3.33	3.33
7. UNY	Trimester		195	PA	8.47	10.26
				Psychometrics	3.36	4.1
8. UCLA	Semester		152	PA	12.5	28
				Psychometrics	3.57	3.94
9. UNET	Semester		139	PA	28	30.93
				Psychometrics	2	2.15
10.UBV	Semester		NA	PA	9.61	0
				Psychometrics	0	0
11. ULA	Semester		174	PA	14	17.2
				Psychometrics	4	3.44
12. UNIMAR	Trimester	Social intervention	199	PA	9.52	10.55
				Psychometrics	3.17	3.01

Note. Credit Units (CU)
*Subjects in Psychological Assessment (PA)
**% of the CU corresponding to the Clinical Dynamic Psychology specialization

integration of the case study, in the cognitive and visuomotor domain, the following are included: Raven, Wechsler Scales, and Bender; in the affective, family, occupational, and socio-adaptive domains, the Human Figure Drawing Test (Koppitz and Machover corrections) and Corman's Family Test are prominent, as well as the projective tests CAT, TAT, or WARTEGG (see Table 15.4).

This analysis of psychological assessment techniques and tests highlights the importance and emphasis placed on the subject within the curricula of universities offering a specialization, as the clinical psychology specialization is focused on

Table 15.4 Techniques and tests reported in the subject programs of five universities

	UNIVERSITY				
Techniques or tests	UCV	UCAB	URU	UAM	ULA
Observations	✓	✓	✓	✓	✓
Interviews	✓	✓	✓	✓	✓
RAVEN	✓	✓	✓	✓	
WAIS	✓	✓	✓		
WISC	✓	✓	✓		
K-ABC	✓	✓			
K-bit	✓	✓			
DAT	✓	✓			
IPP	✓	✓			
Mini-mental Test	✓			✓	
Bender Koppitz	✓	✓	✓	✓	
Bender Hutt	✓	✓	✓	✓	✓
Human Figure	✓	✓	✓	✓	
Machover Human Figure	✓	✓	✓	✓	
Corman Family	✓	✓	✓	✓	
Kinetic Family	✓	✓			
CAT	✓	✓	✓	✓	
TAT	✓	✓	✓	✓	
House-Tree-Person	✓	✓		✓	
Duss Fables		✓		✓	
Desiderative		✓		✓	
16 PF	✓				
Rorschach	✓	✓	✓		
Wartegg	✓	✓	✓		
MMPI	✓	✓	✓	✓	
Rotter Incomplete Phrases				✓	
Eysenck Personality				✓	
Kinetic School		✓			
Educational Couple		✓			
Vineland		✓			
Diagnostic Play Time	✓	✓		✓	

individual psychological assessment, whereas the educational psychology specialization maintains a balance between assessment and intervention components. The social and organizational specializations have few modules related to psychological assessment, with research predominating in the social specialization and assessment in human resource management processes and the monitoring of action plans aimed at improving organizational workflow.

Finally, the Heads of the Schools of Psychology were asked about the pedagogical and didactic activities used for training in techniques and tests for data collection, based on three dimensions: theoretical, supervised application, and construction, as detailed in Fig. 15.3. These data reveal the heterogeneity of training in psychological assessment in Venezuela.

Interview and observation techniques are taught across all three dimensions. Psychometric tests and scales are taught in the theoretical and supervised application dimensions, during practical training, whereas elements of design and construction are covered in fewer Schools.

In the case of projective tests, all School Directors reported that their students are trained in both theoretical aspects and supervised application, but only a small proportion reported training in test construction. Behavioral records are predominantly taught at the theoretical level, with less emphasis on supervised application or construction. Finally, physiological records are mainly taught in the theoretical dimension.

The overall analysis of the curricula, together with the data reported by the Heads, allows us to conclude that there is no uniform standard for training in psychology and psychological assessment in the country. Notably, 91.67% of universities require students to demonstrate the acquisition of methodological, quantitative, qualitative, or mixed-methods competencies, with standardization of techniques and tests that have validity and reliability indicators, through the completion of a dissertation, which is a requirement for obtaining the degree of Bachelor of Psychology. In one university, a socio-integrative project is required.

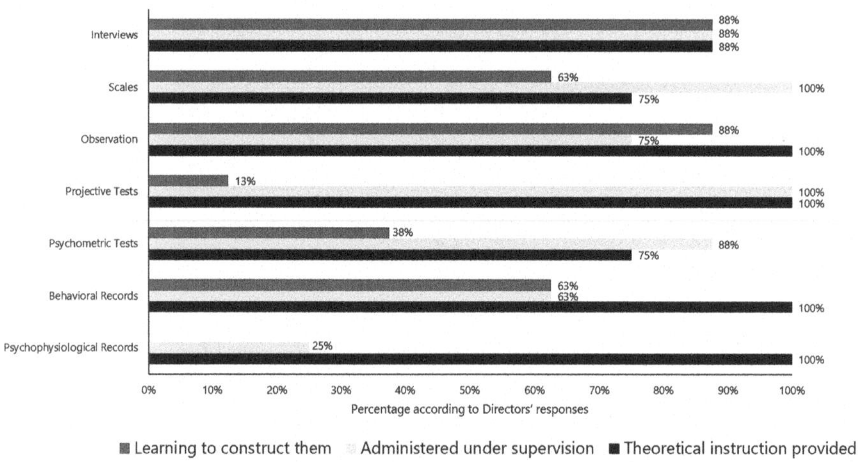

Fig. 15.3 Training in psychological assessment techniques and tests

Postgraduate

Information was obtained from six coordinators or directors of postgraduate psychology programs, as well as from an online review of curricula. Data obtained shows that training in psychological assessment at the postgraduate level, and the role it plays, differs from that at the undergraduate level.

In specialist programs, psychological assessment is included as one of the courses. However, in master's and doctoral programs it is considered as procedures and techniques for data collection, both from a quantitative and qualitative perspective, since the emphasis at these two levels is on research. Assessment topics include the development of tests, questionnaires, or other procedures, as well as the translation or adaptation of instruments with their corresponding validation processes, highlighting both psychometric and methodological rigor.

It should be noted that there are no postgraduate courses dedicated solely to psychological assessment or to the psychometric field.

Research Centers

Active Research Centers are linked to the academic sphere. With the creation of the Institute of Psychology and Psychotechnics at the Central University of Venezuela, the foundations were laid for what, from 1963 onward, would be known as the Institute of Psychology at UCV. It currently comprises three departments: Applied Research, Fundamental Research and Neuropsychology, and supports master's and doctoral programs in Psychology (Roca et al., 2020; UCV, 2022). In addition, it offers the Psiconexo psychological care service, providing psychological care and conducting psychological assessments for the community.

In 1978 the Psychology Laboratory was established at the University of the Andes, attached to the Faculty of Medicine, with the aim of conducting research and teaching in Social Health Psychology. Ten years later, it became the Centre for Psychological Research. As part of its research and thesis advisory work, it produced many assessment instruments that were later included in various outreach publications shared with other educational institutions (University of the Andes, 2022).

The Centre for Psychological Research (CINVEPSI) at Rafael Urdaneta University was founded on 23 November 1988, for the purpose of investigating and centralizing the studies conducted up to that point within the School of Psychology.

At UCAB, there is the Centre for Institutional Research and Evaluation (CIEI), which was established "as a unit dedicated to carrying out evaluative research processes in the academic field, planning institutional academic projects, maintaining relations with university planning bodies, and processing the academic information required to meet the demands of these bodies and other UCAB units" (UCAB,

2022a). The main role of the CIEI is to conduct institutional evaluations, primarily using surveys, interviews, questionnaires, and scales, which are specific techniques of psychological assessment.

The Centre for Humanistic Research and Training (CIFH also at UCAB) is organized on an interdisciplinary basis and comprises researchers from education, philosophy, literature, psychology, social communication, theology, and history. Among its objectives is to "carry out research, preferably inter- and transdisciplinary, that contributes to scientific endeavor and to the understanding and proposal of solutions to issues of national interest" (UCAB, 2022b).

The centers reviewed so far, although they encompass psychological research and use data collection techniques, they are not focused on psychological assessment, except for Psiconexo and CIEI, where part of their work involves conducting psychological and educational assessment.

In conclusion to the section on academic training, research in psychological assessment is carried out within academia through students' dissertations and faculty promotion work, which generate knowledge through the inclusion of standardized techniques and tests, whether local or not, that possess indicators of validity and reliability and promote psychometric studies. This is limited by the time required to complete the construction of an instrument and the validation process for both normative (Muñiz, 2021) and criterion-referenced tests (Lezama, 2013), which is only feasible within the timeframe required for doctoral theses.

Graduates in Professional Practice

This section reports relevant data from the survey "Realities and Perspectives of Psychological Assessment in Venezuela" completed by 565 psychologists (León et al., 2021). The average age of participants was 42 years, ranging from 22 to 80 years; 15.6% were men and 84.4% women. The majority graduated from the Capital Region of Venezuela, as summarized in Fig. 15.4.

Regarding professional experience, graduates reported an average of 15.4 years (SD = 12.9), ranging from 0 to 54 years. Forty six percent of Venezuelan psychologists surveyed indicated they had attained a postgraduate academic level, reflecting their interest in furthering their undergraduate education. The hierarchy of psychology fields in which this group practices, as shown in Fig. 15.5, is: clinical (74%), health and well-being (42%), industrial or organizational (16%), educational or school (12%), and counseling (5%). This coincides with the classic specializations reported by the directors and demonstrates that professionals predominantly practice in the applied areas for which they were trained.

Figure 15.6 shows that 56% of the professionals surveyed reside and practice in Venezuela, while 44% are living abroad in various countries, reflecting the high level of professional migration from the country.

The graduates report that they mainly work with adults (41%), followed by adolescents (25%) and children (23%), and to a lesser extent with older adults (8%).

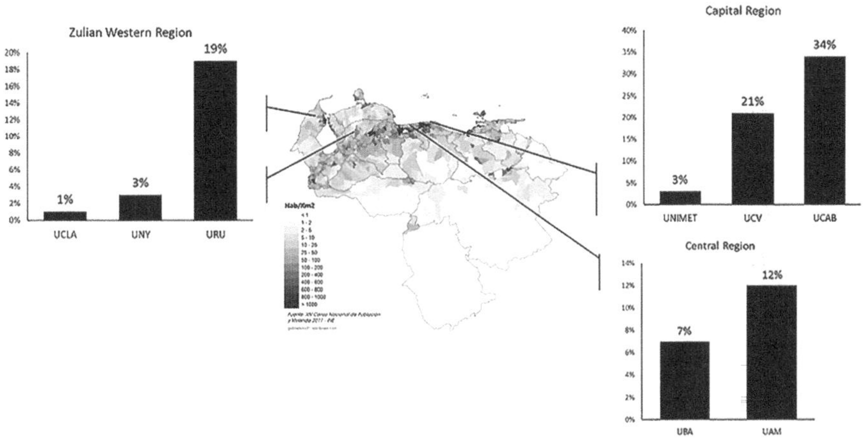

Fig. 15.4 Universities attended by surveyed professionals

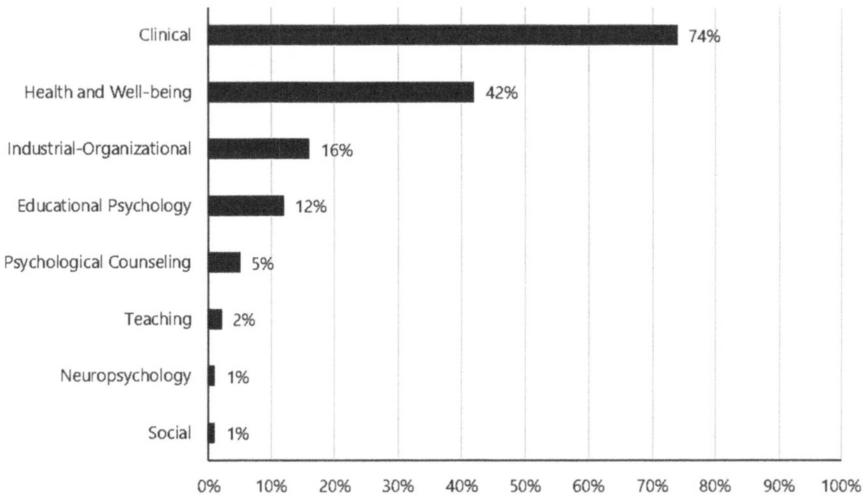

Fig. 15.5 Area of practice in psychology and years of experience

Ninety percent of the psychologists surveyed report conducting psychological assessment directly, while the remainder consult or contract third parties. Regarding the assessment techniques most frequently used, it was found that the majority employ interviews, observations, and psychological tests (see Fig. 15.7). Most respondents (66%) combine different assessment techniques in their professional practice, using between four and six techniques.

There is currently a notable need to incorporate the administration of psychological assessment techniques and tests into virtual environments, a process that accelerated as a contingency measure during the COVID-19 pandemic, when

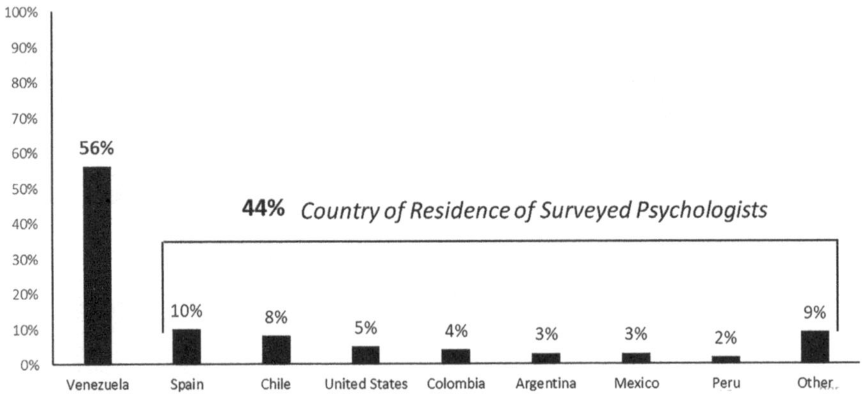

Fig. 15.6 Country of residence of surveyed psychologists

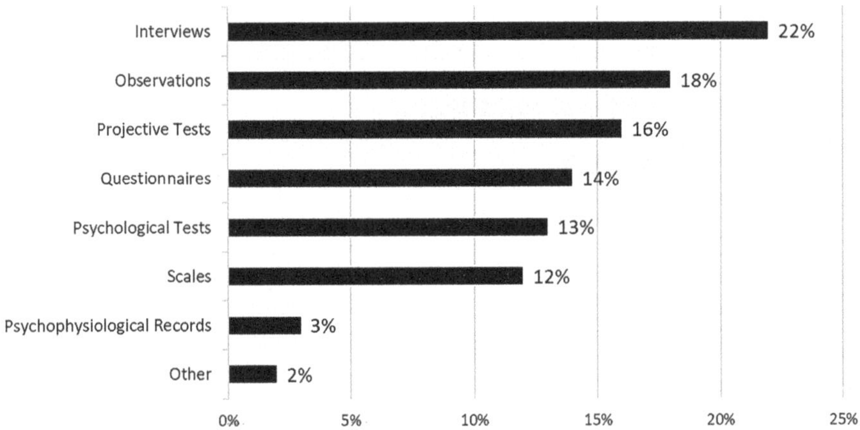

Fig. 15.7 Psychological assessment techniques used by Venezuelan psychologists

assessment activities intensified through the use of technology (Farmer et al., 2021; Pérez et al., 2021; Vijayanand & Raman, 2022; Wright et al., 2020). Initially, assessment activities were suspended until the challenges of face-to-face contact could be overcome; however, as the pandemic persisted, it became necessary to adapt and adjust procedures in order to fulfill the mission of assessment and to inform appropriate intervention decisions regarding mental health, learning, and the well-being of the individual being assessed, while upholding safety principles: ensuring that the respondent is the patient or client (Pérez et al., 2021; Vijayanand & Raman, 2022; Wright et al., 2020); guaranteeing the ethical standards of in-person psychological assessment services, such as informed consent, systematization, and disclosure of any modifications made to the tests (Farmer et al., 2021; Pérez et al., 2021), among others.

To address this crucial issue of psychological assessment, the survey administered to professionals explored the mode of administration used (see Fig. 15.8), which demonstrates the progressive adoption of virtual modalities by Venezuelan psychologists, with a predominance of the mixed mode. For those residing in Venezuela, this considers the difficulties in accessing the internet due to the digital divide and the instability of the service.

Regarding the changes implemented by psychologists during the pandemic, it was found that most of them adjusted instructions, the administration process, and language adaptation. To a lesser extent, they modified or eliminated subscales or certain items; this reflects the initial efforts to align with global guidelines to maintain the quality of psychological assessment in virtual settings. In response to this global challenge, graduates were asked for their recommendations to improve psychological assessment in the country (see Table 15.5).

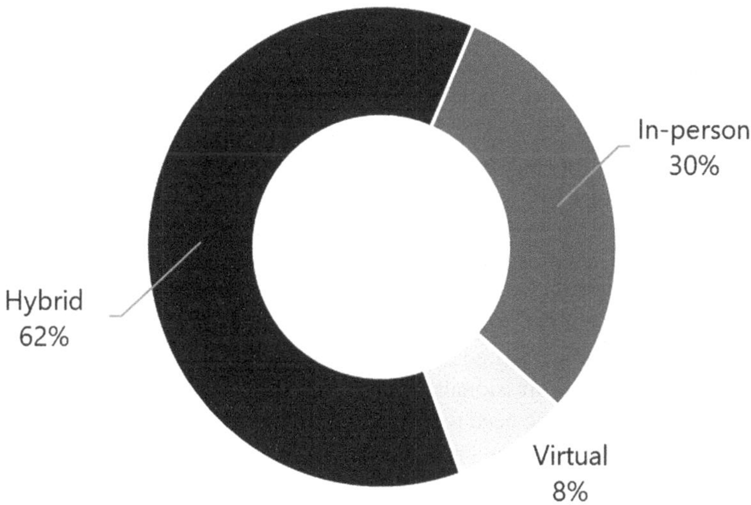

Fig. 15.8 Mode of administration

Table 15.5 Recommendations to improve Psychological Assessment in Venezuela

Recommendation	*Percentage*
More access to training and education	32%
Improve access to tests and its adaptations	27%
More research, development, and updates in psychological testing, in-person and virtual, of the process and conceptualizations of psychological assessment	27%
Changes in legislation to regulate and control assessment	7%
Improve quality of psychological services	3%
Adjust assessment practices to reconcile in-person and virtual mode: in person, virtual, and mixed	2%
Greater activity in associations	1%
Internationalization	1%

Consultancy Firms

The development of psychological assessment techniques and tests is an activity undertaken by psychologists who have founded consultancy firms to meet the needs for measurement and data recording related to initial or follow-up assessments of intervention plans, with the aim of obtaining weighted indicators that address their needs, effectiveness, efficiency, and impact evaluation of their initiatives. These organizations emerged and expanded during the golden age of Venezuelan psychology, among which PROINVESCA stood out, active until 2007, with a portfolio focused on educational organizations, including tests for admission to private universities, recording academic performance in primary education, and selecting young people for government talent development programs.

Currently, PSICOCONSULT remains active, a Venezuelan organization with an international presence, focused on the design, development, and distribution of psychometric tests. They are the creators of the PsicoMet 1 software and the PsicoEnline@ platform for online personnel selection, developed in parallel with measurement systems for organizational climate and other topics related to Human Resources consultancy. SOFTMETRICS, which specializes in the organizational field, is dedicated to developing tools to support selection, promotion, and career development processes within organizations. ADINs.c., a psychoeducational consultancy offers consultancy services, training, and product design incorporating initial and follow-up assessment instruments, as well as impact studies of initiatives in clinical, educational, and community contexts.

From the review of consultancy firms identified to date, it is notable that their focus is on organizational and educational applications, areas in which only 16% and 12% of practicing professionals surveyed in 2011 and 2021, respectively, are engaged. This highlights the need to broaden the scope of consultancy firms' contributions to strengthen psychological assessment in the country.

Contributions of Venezuelan Psychological Assessment

The assessment of human behavior has been and will continue to be the cornerstone of the development of psychology as a science and profession, as it is the mechanism that ensures the quality of professional services, not only for initial assessments but also for monitoring intervention plans and evaluating service quality. Therefore, both in academia and in professional practice, the goal remains to conduct valid and reliable assessments, as far as circumstances allow, within an increasingly complex and diverse social and cultural reality.

This chapter focuses on the overall contribution of psychology, and specifically psychological assessment, to the strengthening of the discipline and Venezuelan society. A detailed record of the many specific contributions on this topic falls outside the scope and space of this chapter and they can be consulted in university libraries and internationally recognized databases.

Contributions come from complementary sectors:

1. *Academia,* as universities, not only train professionals at undergraduate and postgraduate levels, but also maintain research centers and, to varying degrees, generate knowledge and have a social outreach component.
2. *Students and lecturers,* who personally, through their undergraduate and promotion theses, contribute to psychological assessment, the presentation and review of assessment techniques, the validation of international assessment instruments within the Venezuelan context, and the development of tests within the scope permitted by these academic activities, highlighting the importance of doctoral research.
3. *Graduates,* who, during their professional practice, incorporate psychological assessment into their respective specialties and have taken on the challenge of systematizing their local experiences to adapt them to the populations they serve.
4. *Authors of publications,* who, to varying degrees, emphasize the role of psychological assessment in their books, chapters in international volumes, and articles in peer-reviewed specialist journals, both national and international.
5. *Speakers* at national and international conferences, who share research topics related to human behavior and include psychological assessment.
6. *Consultants,* who conduct assessments to meet the needs of governmental, non-governmental, and private organizations, in order to design intervention plans that contribute to the contextualization of psychological assessment.

Contributions, Challenges, and Opportunities

At present, humanity is developing in times of crisis, which imposes political, economic, social, legal, and ethical challenges that impact training, professional practice, and the necessary research to adapt techniques and tests to new demands, the impact of which varies by country, region, and locality. In Venezuela, although there are circumstances beyond professional control, it is possible to reorganize in order to minimize the impact of threats to the discipline and its tool, psychological assessment. Below, some of the challenges are summarized, alongside the opportunities presented by this historical moment.

1. *Political.* The political situation has been characterized by a systematic devaluation of education and professionalism, which has led to the disintegration of universities and the migration of staff, impacting the quality of educational and care organizations, as well as the promotion of research, resulting in a crisis in the higher education sector that threatens psychological assessment. Fortunately, the crisis has strengthened the links between universities and the professional association, as evidenced by the III Venezuelan Congress of Psychology, held in 2021, which brought together academia and the profession.

2. *Economic*. Venezuelans face a situation of socioeconomic decline (National Survey of Living Conditions [ENCOVI], 2021), which poses challenges for psychological assessment, among which the following stand out:

   a. Professionally, psychologists face, on the one hand, low salaries, and few well-paid job opportunities, which has led to an unprecedented migration of qualified personnel, and on the other, the high cost of tests makes it difficult to acquire those needed to practice their specialty.
   b. Academically, funding options have been reduced, resulting in budget cuts for maintaining postgraduate programs and research centers. There is a lack of opportunities for training specialists in psychological assessment; in fact, there are no postgraduate programs in assessment. Nevertheless, the flame of academia has remained alight thanks to the commitment of university authorities, lecturers, and students, who take advantage of access to academic publications online; engage in collaborative work both nationally and internationally; and strengthen their social outreach in partnership with local organizations, a structure aimed at supporting the development of psychological assessment by making use of technological alternatives.

3. *Social*. Social and technological gaps require greater contextualization of professional practice, techniques, and tests, both for initial assessment and for monitoring psychological interventions in vulnerable populations, in order to contribute to the implementation of the Sustainable Development Goals (United Nations, 2023). This drives networked collaboration among psychology professionals and related sciences who provide services at local, regional, and national levels, with the support of academia, regional associations, and the Venezuelan Federation of Psychologists, aimed at agreeing plans to strengthen psychological assessment, give greater sociocultural meaning to the assessment and intervention process, and measure the growing diversity at both individual and collective levels. Cumulative and idiographic tools should be incorporated, enabling progress toward the systematization of local norms to prioritize needs based on a robust assessment process that underpins high-quality interventions, the final goal of assessment.
4. *Legal*. In Venezuela, the Psychologists' Act has been in force since 1978 and the Code of Ethics since 1981, documents that regulate the practice of the profession and psychological assessment, but there is still a lack of a legal framework requiring the validation of tests at the national population; the presence of psychologists in both public and private organizations; regulations to ensure the quality of psychological assessment services, both in-person and online, as well as measures to prevent unqualified practice. These issues are being addressed by the Federation of Psychologists of Venezuela and the Regional Associations, with the collaboration of academia and graduates.
5. *Ethical*. Given the obligation to comply with the Code of Ethics of the Venezuelan Federation of Psychologists, it is necessary to move toward a consensus on the parameters and quality criteria for psychological assessment, with adaptations for the various specialties within the ethical framework of psychology in the

country (Canga, 2021). This consensus should be shared with the universities that train psychologists and with the Regional Associations that bring together practicing professionals, as all are called upon to contribute to the profession by controlling the unrestricted dissemination of psychological instruments on social media, as well as unqualified practice, supporting the work of the Federation of Psychologists of Venezuela and compliance with the Code of Ethics for Psychology in Venezuela.

In conclusion, Venezuelan psychologists are committed to reviewing and renewing psychological assessment to adapt to new demands, making use of technological advances with the following goals:

1. To share, in national and international journals, the assessment procedures and instruments developed in research projects involving psychological assessment, including undergraduate and postgraduate theses, research centers, and consultancy firms, as well as to encourage the systematization of local experiences of good practice.
2. To promote the importance of high-quality psychological assessment by providing parameters and criteria for evaluating assessment quality.
3. To disseminate opportunities for continuing professional development in psychological assessment, whether in-person, blended, or online.
4. To advance toward the digitalization of procedures and instruments, while promoting their standardization and psychometric validation.
5. To join efforts to offer a postgraduate program in psychological and psychometric assessment, encompassing all current and cutting-edge approaches.

These collective goals require the collaboration of academia, the professional association, and practitioners, for which it is necessary to improve communication channels in order to strengthen the profession and professional activity. Today's psychologists face the challenge of reviewing and renewing their practice in times of crisis, as demonstrated by academia in overcoming obstacles during the pandemic to continue operating, and as Venezuelan psychologists do, both within and outside Venezuela, practicing their respective specialties with high professionalism across the diverse organizations, locations, and countries in which they provide services.

References

Arana, J. M., Meilán, J. J. G., & Pérez, E. (2006). El concepto de psicología. Entre la diversidad conceptual y la conveniencia de unificación. Apreciaciones desde la epistemología. *Revista Intercontinental de Psicología y Educación, 8*(1), 111–142. https://www.redalyc.org/articulo.oa?id=80280107

Canga, J. (2021). Psychological ethics in Venezuela. In K. L. Parsonson (Ed.), *Handbook of international psychology ethics* (pp. 226–239). Routledge.

Canga, J., & Yáber, G. (2015). Psicología en Venezuela: Ciencia, disciplina, profesión y sus retos. *Información Psicológica, 109*, 129–136. https://doi.org/10.14635/IPSIC.2015.109.6

Casullo, M. M. (2009). La evaluación psicológica: Modelos, técnicas y contextos. *Revista Iberoamericana de Diagnóstico y Evaluación—e Avaliação Psicológica, 1*(27), 9–28. https://www.redalyc.org/articulo.oa?id=459645443002

Encuesta Nacional de Condiciones de Vida. (2021). *Documento Técnico ENCOVI.* UCAB. https://www.proyectoencovi.com/encovi-2021

Farmer, R., McGill, R., Dombrowski, S., Benson, N., Smith-Kellen, S., Lockwood, A., Powell, S., Pynn, C., & Stinnett, T. (2021). Conducting psychoeducational assessments during the COVID-19 crisis: The danger of good intentions. *Contemporary School Psychology, 25*(1), 27–32. https://doi.org/10.1007/s40688-020-00293-x

Federación de Psicólogos de Venezuela. (1981). *Código de Ética profesional de la Psicología.* http://www.fpv.org.ve/

Fernández-Ballesteros, R. (1994). *Evaluación Conductual Hoy*. Pirámide.

Fernández-Ballesteros, R. (1999). Psychological assessment: Future challenges and progresses. *European Psychologist, 4*(4), 248–262. https://doi.org/10.1027/1016-9040.4.4.248

Fernández-Ballesteros, R., De Bruyn, E. E. J., Godoy, A., Hornke, L. F., Ter Laak, J., Vizcarro, C., Westhoff, K., Westmeyer, H., & Zaccagnini, J. L. (2003). Guías para el proceso de evaluación (GAP): una propuesta a discusión. *Papeles del Psicólogo, 23*(84), 58–70. https://www.redalyc.org/articulo.oa?id=77808407

Instituto Nacional de Estadística. (2022 de 29 de septiembre). *Población Proyectada al 30/06/2022—Base Censo 2011.* http://www.ine.gov.ve/

Leibovich de Figueroa, N., & Schmidt, V. (2008). Reflexiones acerca de la Evaluación Psicológica y Neuropsicológica. *Revista Argentina de Neuropsicología, 12*, 21–28.

León, C. (1994). El Modelo Octogonal Integrador del Desarrollo Infantil y sus implicaciones para la evaluación e intervención a nivel de prevención primaria y secundaria. *Analogías del Comportamiento, 1*, 97–112.

León, C. (2003). *Proceso de Validación del Modelo Octogonal Integrador del Desarrollo Infantil* [Tesis Doctoral]. Universidad Católica Andrés Bello.

León, C. (2007). Estudio descriptivo, comparativo y relacional del desarrollo infantil integral en una muestra de niños y niñas de diferentes edades, niveles socioeconómicos y regiones de Venezuela. *ORBIS. Revista Científica Ciencias Humanas, 3*(7), 64–124.

León, C. (2018a). *Manual MOIDI Kit* (5th ed.). Asesores de Desarrollo Integral s.c.

León, C. (2018b). *Secuencias del Desarrollo Infantil Integral* (5th ed.). Abediciones.

León, C., Vivas, E., Berrios, M., Angelucci, L., & Guerra, J. (2021, 9 de Julio). *Realidades y perspectivas de la Evaluación Psicológica en Venezuela* [Ponencia]. I Congreso Iberoamericano de Evaluación Psicológica, Lima, Perú.

Lezama, L. (2013). Construcción de pruebas criteriales: Aspectos teóricos y metodológicos. *Revista Psicología, tercera época, 32*(1), 75–105. http://saber.ucv.ve/ojs/index.php/rev_ps/article/view/7811/7726

Muñiz, J. (2021, de 2 de julio). *Evaluación psicológica en la era digital: Perspectiva actual y retos futuros* [Conferencia]. I Congreso Iberoamericano de Evaluación Psicológica, Lima, Perú.

Nunes Baptista, M., García Capitão, C., & Alba Scortegagna, S. (2006). Evaluación psicológica en la salud: Contextos actuales. Estudios Sociales. *Revista de Alimentación Contemporánea y Desarrollo Regional, 15*(28), 138–161. https://www.redalyc.org/articulo.oa?id=41702805

Observatorio Venezolano de Servicios Públicos. (2022, Agosto). OVSP: *Calidad del Internet fijo continúa con deficiencias a pesar de buenas valoraciones en algunas ciudades.* https://www.observatoriovsp.org/ovsp-calidad-del-internet-fijo-continua-con-deficiencias-a-pesar-de-buenas-valoraciones-en-algunas-ciudades/

Organización de las Naciones Unidas. (2023, Febrero). *Objetivos de Desarrollo Sostenible.* https://www.un.org/sustainabledevelopment/es/objetivos-de-desarrollo-sostenible/

Pérez, P., Ramos, D., & Arango, J. (2021). Teleneuropsicología en países de habla hispana: Una mirada crítica al uso de tecnologías de información y comunicación en la evaluación neuropsicológica. *Revista Iberoamericana de Neuropsicología, 4*(1), 1–27. https://neuropsychologylearning.com/portfolio-item/teleneuropsicologia-paises-habla-hispana-mirada-critica-uso-tecnologias-comunicacion-evaluacion-neuropsicologica/

PH9 Medio Digital. (2021, Junio). *La realidad del salario en Venezuela*. https://latinoamerica21.com/es/la-realidad-del-salario-en-venezuela/

Ramirez, H. (2021, noviembre). *La psicología en Venezuela*. https://maspsicologia.com/la-psicologia-en-venezuela/

Roca, M. J., Rondón, J. E., Cardozo, I., Ramjam, N., & Rangel, A. L. (2020). *Instituto de Psicología: 70 años venciendo las sombras*. Ediciones Especiales, Universidad Central de Venezuela. http://www.ucv.ve/institutopsicologia

Rodríguez, P., & Sánchez, L. (1999). La psicología en Venezuela. In A. Modesto & A. Eagly (Eds.), *Psicología en las Américas* (pp. 307–316). Sociedad Interamericana de Psicología.

Sánchez, L., & Dembo, M. (2012). Venezuela. In D. Baker (Ed.), *Oxford handbook of the history of psychology: International perspective* (pp. 595–615). Oxford University Press.

Sánchez, L., & Dembo, M. (2015). Historia de la Psicología Venezuela. *Revista Psicología, Tercera Época, 34*, 195–212. http://saber.ucv.ve/ojs/index.php/rev_ps/article/view/14878/144814481536

Sattler, J. (2010). *Evaluación Infantil fundamentos cognitivos* (Vol. 1, 5th ed.). Manual Moderno.

Scholars at Risk (SAR). (2020, Noviembre). *Free to think. Report of the scholars at risk academic freedom monitoring project. The decline of the Venezuelan university*. https://www.scholarsatrisk.org/resources/free-to-think-2020/

Sendín, M. (2000). *Diagnóstico Psicológico. Bases conceptuales y guía práctica en los contextos clínico y educativo*. Psimática.

Straka, T. (2017). Contexto para el nacimiento de una ciencia: Psicología y modernidad en Venezuela (1936–1957). *Analogía del Comportamiento, 15*, 18–24.

Universidad Católica Andrés Bello. (2022a, Octubre). *Centro de Investigación y Evaluación Institucional*. https://www.ucab.edu.ve/investigacion/centros-e-institutos-de-investigacion/ciei/historia/

Universidad Católica Andrés Bello. (2022b, Octubre). *Centro de Investigación y Formación Humanística*. https://www.ucab.edu.ve/investigacion/centros-e-institutos-de-investigacion/cifh/

Universidad Central de Venezuela. (2022, Octubre). *Instituto de Psicología*. http://www.ucv.ve/institutopsicologia

Universidad de Los Andes. (2022, Octubre). *Centro de Investigaciones Psicológicas*. http://www.medic.ula.ve/cip/index.php

Vijayanand, M., & Raman, V. (2022). Online psychological assessment for children and adolescents with neurodevelopmental disorders: Exploring new avenues in times of social distancing. *Indian Journal of Psychological Medicine, 44*(2), 181–184.

Vivas, E. (1996). Evaluación conductual: Una experiencia de integración. En L. Pascuali (Ed.), Teoría e Métodos de Medida em Ciencias do Comportamento (pp. 405–417). Instituto de Estudios Pedagógicos, .

Vivas, E. (2000, Agosto). *Assessment trends in Venezuela and Latin America. 108 Annual Conference of the American Psychological Society*" [Ponencia]. Washington, EE.UU.

Vivas, E., León, C., & Berrios, M. C. (2011, Julio). *Estado actual y perspectivas de la evaluación psicológica en Venezuela*. [Ponencia]. VIII Congresso Iberoamericano de Avaliação/Evaluación Psicológica, XV Conferéncia Internacional Avaliação Psicológica: Formas e contextos, Lisboa, Portugal.

Weiner, I. (1992). *Métodos en psicología clínica*. Limusa.

Wright, A. J., Mihura, J., Pade, H., & McCord, D. (2020, Mayo). *Guidance on psychological tele-assessment during the COVID-19 crisis*. https://www.apaservices.org/practice/reimbursement/health-codes/testing/tele-assessment-covid-19

Yáber, G. (2020). Cooperación y Competencia "Si", Intrusismo "No". *In Coaching, 8*, 15–19. https://saber.ucab.edu.ve/xmlui/handle/123456789/20304

Index

A

Academic institutions, 117, 119

Academic training, 11, 24, 41, 67, 117, 123, 165, 167, 173, 237–244

Advances, 8, 15, 43, 54, 88, 93, 111, 118–121, 130, 161–176, 183, 197, 225, 232, 251

Assessment, 1, 18, 34, 47, 61, 77, 101, 116, 123, 139, 162, 179, 194, 211, 232

Assessment instruments, 3, 30, 36, 39, 42, 71, 83, 85, 93, 105, 109, 128, 147, 156, 164, 167, 171, 173, 174, 176, 184, 189, 190, 222, 239, 243, 248, 249

B

Bolivia, 10, 11, 33–43, 65, 200

C

Challenges, 1, 11, 30, 33–43, 47–57, 61–73, 77, 80, 93, 99–112, 115–121, 134–135, 140, 145, 151, 153, 156, 161–176, 179–191, 193, 221, 225–227, 231–251

Costa Rica, 4–7, 77–94

Current reality, 179–191

D

Development, 1, 13, 33, 47, 62, 77, 99, 115, 123, 139, 163, 179, 193, 211, 232

E

Ecuador, 2, 5, 7–11, 99–112, 200

Education, 2, 3, 6, 8, 10, 14–18, 21, 28, 33, 37, 41–43, 48, 54, 55, 61, 65, 67, 71, 77–80, 82, 89, 90, 92, 93, 100–103, 106, 108, 111, 115–121, 125, 146, 148, 152, 154, 164, 166, 174, 180–183, 185, 186, 189, 211–213, 215, 221–225, 235, 244, 247–249

F

Forensic Psychology, 82, 216, 223

G

Guatemala, 5, 6, 10, 65, 139–157, 200

H

Histories, 13, 34, 41, 49, 55, 57, 78, 99, 100, 102, 106, 107, 111, 112, 121, 123, 125, 134, 141, 143, 145, 155–157, 169, 179, 180, 183, 193–202, 213, 226, 244

I

Interamerican psychology, 65, 116

Interamerican society of psychology (SIP), 5, 65, 115, 141, 161

S. V. Pugliese et al. (eds.), *Origins and Challenges of Psychological Assessment in Ibero-American Countries*, https://doi.org/10.1007/978-3-032-21380-8

L
Latin America, 1–3, 5, 6, 9, 13, 14, 33, 41, 42, 49, 54, 61, 139–140, 153, 163, 190, 200, 221, 233, 234

M
Measurements, 10, 13, 17, 24, 35, 53, 61, 62, 64, 65, 70, 77, 80, 87, 88, 90, 93, 94, 103, 119, 125–129, 131–135, 139, 141, 151, 152, 162, 163, 165, 166, 168, 170, 175, 179, 184, 190, 197, 199, 213, 216, 239, 248

P
Paradigms, 22, 29, 135, 139–157, 168, 173, 182, 225, 226
Paraguayan Psychology, 188
Peru, 2, 3, 7, 9–11, 41, 65, 193–202
Professional identity, 22, 115, 164, 170, 173, 213, 219, 226
Professional legislation, 70, 183, 190
Professional practices, 1, 4, 5, 8, 20, 25, 26, 38, 39, 42, 43, 48, 52, 54, 55, 57, 62–64, 66–68, 70, 77, 79–83, 87, 93, 94, 116, 119, 121, 123, 129, 143, 145, 149–150, 161, 165, 167, 171, 176, 181–183, 189, 190, 193, 211, 216–218, 221, 224–226, 234, 235, 237–250
Professional training, 19, 48, 56, 63, 79, 83, 116, 120, 130, 147, 155, 167–175, 180, 182, 184, 185, 187, 190, 212, 215
Projective tests, 19, 21, 22, 29, 35, 36, 39, 41, 51, 62, 68, 72, 107, 109, 111, 151, 168, 187, 223, 240, 242
Psychiatry, 16, 19, 91, 100, 106, 150, 164, 165, 167, 196, 217
Psychodiagnosis, 3, 5, 6, 8, 10, 16, 18–26, 29, 35, 52, 81, 82, 118, 126, 139, 211, 213, 215–220, 224, 225
Psychological assessment, 1, 20, 33, 48, 62, 99, 120, 123, 140, 161, 179, 193, 211, 231
Psychological evaluations, 27, 84, 196, 211–227
Psychology, 1, 13, 33, 47, 61, 77, 99, 115, 123, 161, 179, 193, 211, 231
Psychology in latin america, 14
Psychometric tests, 19, 22, 26, 29, 35, 38, 40, 41, 43, 68, 69, 120, 121, 140, 143, 148, 187, 199, 201, 242, 248
Psychometrics, 2, 15, 35, 51, 62, 77, 105, 115, 123, 139, 162, 179, 193, 212, 232

R
Research, 2, 14, 36, 48, 62, 79, 103, 117, 130, 140, 165, 180, 193, 212, 232
Research groups, 37, 112, 142, 143, 197

S
Scientific associations, 53
Scientific criteria, 52
Spain, 1–3, 7–10, 15, 19, 49, 65, 66, 70, 73, 118, 119, 123–135, 143, 197, 201, 202

T
Test assessment, 5, 71
Test development, 15, 92, 130
Tests, 1, 14, 36, 47, 62, 77, 101, 118, 123, 139, 161, 184, 193, 211, 232
Test use, 10, 65–73, 127, 130
Training, 1, 14, 37, 48, 61, 77, 99, 116, 124, 140, 163, 179, 195, 211, 231

U
Uruguay, 2–5, 7–9, 200, 211–227

V
Venezuela, 2–4, 6, 11, 65, 200, 231–251

The manufacturer's authorised representative in the EU is Springer Nature Customer Service Centre GmbH, Europaplatz 3, 69115 Heidelberg, Germany. If you have any concerns regarding our products, please contact ProductSafety@springernature.com

Printed and bound by CPI Group (UK) Ltd, Croydon, CR0 4YY
17/09/2026
02218430-0008